The National Debt
of the United States, 1941 to 2008

SECOND EDITION

The National Debt of the United States, 1941 to 2008

Second Edition

ROBERT E. KELLY

Foreword by NELSON K. BENTON

McFarland & Company, Inc., Publishers

Jefferson, North Carolina, and London

LIBRARY OF CONGRESS CATALOGUING-IN-PUBLICATION DATA

Kelly, Robert E., 1926–
    The national debt of the United States, 1941 to 2008 / Robert E.
Kelly ; foreword by Nelson Benton.— 2nd ed.
        p.   cm.
Rev. ed. of: The national debt. 2000.
    Includes bibliographical references and index.

    ISBN 978-0-7864-3233-2
    softcover : 50# alkaline paper ∞

    1. Debts, Public — United States.   2. Budget deficits —
United States.   3. Goverment spending policy — United States.
I. Kelly, Robert E., 1926– National debt.   II. Title.
HJ8119.K45   2008
336.3'4097309045 — dc22   2007049741

British Library cataloguing data are available

Cover images ©2008 Shutterstock

Manufactured in the United States of America

*McFarland & Company, Inc., Publishers
    Box 611, Jefferson, North Carolina 28640
    www.mcfarlandpub.com*

To Margaret
the love of my life
and to the memory of
Jim and Mil
who gave me life
and
Jim Jr.
protector and brother

Acknowledgments

This book could not have been produced without the editing assistance and the moral support of my wife, Margaret Rodden Kelly, or without the expert guidance of the editing staff of the publisher.

The patience, assistance and support of friends and colleagues made perseverance possible. It was and is deeply appreciated.

Table of Contents

Foreword

by Nelson K. Benton

For years now, columnist Robert Kelly has endeavored to help readers of the Eagle-Tribune newspapers navigate the very complex issues of the day. His subjects have ranged from the crisis in the Catholic Church to the vagaries of the Red Sox batting order.

Working from his home, and taking time each March for a Florida sojourn in search of sun and a few Grapefruit League games, Kelly has made his column a must-read for both the average citizen and public officials in our North of Boston communities.

His management experience and analytical gifts come to the fore when he takes on matters of government spending, the subject of this book as well as numerous essays that have appeared in our papers and elsewhere.

In his columns, subjects of his cost-benefit analysis have ranged from the test scores achieved by students in the local school systems to the federal spending priorities which are examined in great detail in the pages that follow.

Many of his columns, as is also the case with this book, end with a list of "conclusions" that sum up the important points and allow Kelly to offer his take on the facts presented in the preceding narrative.

And Kelly doesn't pull any punches in describing the problems that confront the country at this very early stage of the 21st century.

After summarizing the history of debt under earlier presidents, Kelly begins his analysis with the administration of Franklin Delano Roosevelt, and he is especially critical of Texan Lyndon Johnson's Great Society idea, which he describes as "nothing more or less than the most recent failed attempt to enslave people in a bureaucratic quagmire which ... reduces them to the status of dependent cogs in a well-oiled centralized machine."

Nothing ambiguous about that statement.

Well dispersed informational charts in the body of the book, and many exhibits at the end of it, put government spending practices and the rising tide of debt in perspective. And the section in each chapter that reviews U.S. Supreme Court activity provides insight into the relationship between law and behavior that makes interesting and — as usual — controversial reading.

Many numbers cited in this book are in the billions of dollars which brought to this writer's mind an analogy making the rounds of the Internet: The next time you hear a politician use the word "billion" in a casual manner, think about whether you want the "politicians" spending your tax money.

A billion is a difficult number to comprehend, but one advertising agency's release did a good job of putting that figure into some perspective.

- A billion seconds ago it was 1959.
- A billion minutes ago Jesus was alive.
- A billion hours ago our ancestors were living in the Stone Age.
- A billion days ago no-one walked on the earth on two feet.
- A billion dollars ago was only 8 hours and 20 minutes at the rate our government is spending it.

Good to keep in mind while reading this book, for the figures are indeed startling. But Kelly's exposition of them is always informative and entertaining.

Kelly's opinions are seldom unclear. Indeed, our newspapers have been accused of using his columns as a means of generating more letters to the editor, some of which express outrage over the author's take on current affairs.

But Kelly has plenty of fans as well, ranging from the Bay State's anti-tax activist Barbara Anderson to the 50-year subscriber who's quick to reach for the phone if Kelly's column doesn't appear in its normal space in Wednesday's *Salem News*.

The relationship between Kelly and this editor has had its share of contentious debate, which has been more than countered by a healthy measure of respect on both sides. And always there's an appreciation on this side of the telephone line for the columnist's knowledge, prodigious research, and strongly-held convictions.

Writers like Kelly give life to a community newspaper and keep readers coming back for more whether they're seeking confirmation of a previously-held opinion or another dose of the medicine they dislike but can't resist taking.

These are uncertain times for the newspaper industry as a whole. Kelly gives people a reason to read.

Nichols Leman, dean of the Columbia School of Journalism, pointed out in a 2004 New Yorker piece that "it's hard to imagine a healthy public life ... without the aid of good journalism, because people can't participate civically if they don't know anything."

Through his weekly columns, Kelly has become an important element in the civic life of North of Boston communities. Like this book, they provide enlightenment and a definite point of view that's well worth the time spent reading them.

This is a surprisingly readable book — given the core subject matter — because it also provides a unique look at the life and times, including the legal, social and financial challenges, facing our presidents from FDR through George W. Bush.

You'll come away from it enlightened, if also a little discouraged about what faces the United States as we embark on a new century.

Nelson K. Benton
Editorial Page Director
Eagle-Tribune Newspapers
March 2008

Introduction

"National debt" as a descriptive term means different things to different people. So it is important to define the "debt" that one is talking about.

The number that flashes on some billboards or appears in most newspapers is total federal debt — the total value of all U.S. securities issued and outstanding to government and to private owners. In 2008 (estimated), for example, it amounted to $9.9 trillion, divided as follows:

National Debt — 2008 (in trillions of dollars)[1]

Owner	Amount
U.S. Govt. bodies	$4.3
Held by the public	5.6
Total	$9.9

Federal trust funds, mostly Social Security, are required by law to invest in U.S. securities, which explains the size of the government's holdings in the above table.

This study focuses on public holdings only and in this book they will be consistently referred to as "public debt" or "debt."

Why did it to grow so big? Who made it grow? Is it dangerous? How do we measure it? This book responds to such questions, and it will probe others that relate to America's most underreported domestic nightmare — runaway debt.

But before doing so it is useful to make a brief comment about the nature of the "trust fund" securities that are issued by and to the government.

This is important because of the commotion caused by Al Gore during the election campaign of 2000 about the "raid" on the so-called lock box that, by inference, he said contained the Social Security cash that was held by the government in order to meet its obligations to retired citizens.

In fact, *there is no lock box*, and there never has been such a thing. From the beginning, the Social Security system has been based upon a promise to pay whatever is due out of current funds.

There is nothing special about Social Security taxes, or how they are handled. Like all tax revenue, they are collected and spent on current expenses, including Social Security payments, as needed. And a piece of paper is issued by the United States Treasury to the Social Security Administration that promises to pay at some future date the amount of Social Security funds that were "borrowed."

And how strong is that piece of paper?

It can be ripped up by the U.S. Congress whenever a majority of its members decide to do so.[2]

The Cause of the Problem

Many believe that the persistent growth of public debt is a legacy of war, economic recession and inflation. That description is incomplete and misleading to an astonishing, almost wicked, degree.

Politicians, not external events, are responsible for most of the increase in public debt. Political decisions have made budget deficits and climbing debt inevitable.

And politicians have allowed these ruinous circumstances to continue even when the evidence became incontrovertible that structural change in entitlement programs was an imperative that no responsible person could ignore.

A small group of political leaders, who will be specifically identified in this book, took the free America of Dwight D. Eisenhower and, without firing a shot, surreptitiously led it into the Second American Revolution (under the cover of war, inflation and recession) and into their preferred world of socialism. And in less than four decades they transformed the great American experiment into the great American Welfare State, with the budget and debt consequences that one normally associates with intrusive government.

The Media

Contemporary press coverage hovers over the story of the annual budget and its associated deficit. Not much emphasis is focused by the media on additions to debt, or on the impact that total debt has on the yearly budget, in terms of interest expense, foreign policy or, say, the invaluable ability of the nation to borrow in times of war or emergency.

This is unbelievable.

Concentrating on annual deficits is like worrying about the five dollars borrowed last week and ignoring the size of the mortgage that is beyond one's ability to carry.

To be sure, current expenses must be paid or lowered to a painless level, as one prepares to deal with a debt crisis. But procedure must not be confused with substance. When current deficits are gone, long-term debt remains. Deficits are simply the hurdles that precede debt reduction.

Until federal budgets are once again balanced, debt will continue to grow bringing with it the interest expense that will increasingly draw funds away from more useful expenditures. For example, *Interest* in 1960, Dwight Eisenhower's last year in office, was 14 percent of *Defense*; in 2008 (estimated), it was 55 percent of Defense.[3]

How can so large a cost be ignored? Better yet, why is it ignored? Could it be because the discussion of it would necessarily place the size of the debt before the public and raise embarrassing questions about how and why it was allowed to grow to such a dangerous level?

Consider, for example, the meaning of high debt versus such apparently unrelated issues like national security.

The early pages of this book amply illustrate the standard policy of all American presidents, collectively, through Dwight Eisenhower. They borrowed to cover emergencies and paid back when normalcy returned so that successors in office could do the same.

How important is this flexibility to a president? A glance at President Franklin D. Roosevelt's behavior during World War II is sufficient to make the point.

Percent of Public Debt to Gross Domestic Product

Time	Year	Debt (billions)	GDP[4] (billions)	%
Prior to the war	1940	$ 50.7	$ 96.8	52
End of war	1946	271.0	222.7	122

President Roosevelt did not have enough federal revenue to pay for *Defense* in the federal budget for five years (1942–46).[5] Absent the ability to borrow, which had been protected by his predecessors, he would have been unable to protect America as he did during World War II. The ability of America to borrow during that critical period was as important to the allied cause as the ships and planes that were sent overseas.

The lessons of the past have meaning in the present. America has not had a major shooting war since Vietnam. In spite of this, debt has zoomed upward.

We are now in World War III, a truth that is not diminished because many have so far refused to face it. And President George W. Bush does not have the borrowing power he needs to face this enemy from the East.

As a consequence, America is not as well protected as he would like it to be, and as Americans want it to be, because he does not have the borrowing power that more fortunate presidents once enjoyed.

This book will demonstrate that the priceless power to borrow has been squandered over the past four decades in a reckless orgy of social spending on social problems that do not bend to the ministrations of a paternal government, as other socialist nations have painfully learned.

Politicians' avoidance of such topics is understandable. But how can journalists bemoan with a straight face the size of various line items in a federal budget and at the same time ignore the deeper meaning of high debt in terms of budget and foreign policy consequences? Indeed, if they became more vigorous in their pursuit of this question the solution to the consequential problems that attach to high debt would be easier to solve.

This does not mean that the media should take their eyes away from federal deficits, but their concentration on them should not be so exclusive that they overlook dangers and penalties associated with a debt level that has been too large, for too long, for the wrong reason.

The Political Muddle

Ronald Reagan's assumption of the presidency in 1981 marked the first effective shift of political power away from Lyndon Johnson's acolytes and toward a more conservative view of the role of government. To be sure, Republicans Richard Nixon and Gerald Ford occupied the White House for eight of the twelve years between Johnson and Reagan, but neither had control of the House or the Senate,[6] nor did either have the conservative credentials of Reagan.

The election of Reagan was not an overwhelming political victory as much as it was a rejection of President Jimmy Carter and the Congress that supported him. The Democratic majority in the House decreased to 242 seats from 277; Republicans assumed control of the Senate for the first time since President Eisenhower's first term (1953–56).

Conservative fires burned brightly under Reagan and they continued to do so into the 1990s as is evidenced by the election of 1994 when, after four decades of unwavering Democratic control, Republicans captured the House of Representatives and joined the Republican-led Senate in a united attempt to put an end to the Second American Revolution and to return the nation to fiscal sanity. The result was the first budget surplus in decades, a happening that is reported in detail in an upcoming chapter.

The fervor to downsize the role of government and to restructure its worthwhile projects seemed to dissipate after the Republicans lost the Senate in the election of 2000, and when the fiery Newt Gingrich (R–GA) was replaced by the low-key Dennis Hastert (R–IL) as the Speaker of the House.

Today, confused by war and comfortable with power, too many Republican politicians appear to be as intoxicated by the spending virus as the liberals they once chastised, and President Bush has been discouragingly reluctant to use his veto power that, when used wisely, can lead troublesome colleagues to more wholesome spending decisions.

The result? The Reagan dynamic that could have led Congress to address its self-caused fiscal problems is almost dead. The political process in the first decade of a new century is locked in a partisan power struggle that will not permit prudent budget decisions. And the conservative politicians from both political parties, while in power, failed to deliver fiscal sanity and, justifiably, they lost control of the Congress in 2006.

Who Will Solve the Problem?

The people and the media will solve the problem, or it will not be solved at all.

Political leaders may worsen it but they will not fix it, or even lessen it unless driven to do so. The appetite for power and prestige motivates behavior in most of them. And active proponents of ever-expanding federal power are popular in today's culture, more so than thoughtful, restrained types who argue for a smaller federal role.

These facts of life castrate politicians as problem solvers: Spending equals victory at the polls, economizing equals defeat, and winning equals power, the aphrodisiac of the politician.

Citizens must solve the problem of paralyzing public debt by:

- Getting beyond generalizations (recessions did it) to the truth (people did it).
- Learning that they are threatened by the problem (high taxes, job loss, less security).
- Making realistic solutions of problems a popular cause for politicians to adopt.
- Voting the spenders out of office.

And the media must cooperate by keeping a hot focus on the issue until a path to solution has been found.

Education

Those with the background, talent and time should improve upon the simple offerings in this book and broadcast their knowledge about the dangers of extended debt and the need for political action to the widest possible audience in the most understandable terms of which they are capable.

Average Americans do not learn about the economy from charts or from self-serving political speeches on economics. They turn instead to favored columnists, books, commentators, professors, executives, periodicals, and conversations with family, friends, and associates, sources that express ideas in ways that, to them, are truthful and understandable.

But whatever the resource, citizens owe it to themselves to seek out and study the views of their most objective sources of information on current affairs. It would be a tragedy of history if the great American culture were destroyed by the deadly marriage of tampering do-gooders and an indifferent public.

The Objective

This book hopes to meet the test of acceptability enunciated above in being truthful and understandable. In it, the trail of public debt from George Washington through Franklin D. Roosevelt (1940) is cursorily traced. From Roosevelt (1941) through George W. Bush, analysis is presented in detail.

The source and condition of public debt is outlined and examined through the prism of one with no political past, present or future, each chapter aspiring to be a link in the thin chain of understanding forged by thoughtful columnists and authors, part of an effort that may someday motivate citizens to accept the thesis that the level of public debt is an important problem that endangers them and all Americans.

Why Begin with FDR?

Succeeding Herbert Hoover, FDR was elected in 1932. Government assumed many new duties under his leadership, presumably to help a citizenry reeling under the unrelenting attack of an economic crisis that began in 1929.

FDR introduced a blitz of programs managed by new federal agencies[7]— AAA (Agricultural Adjustment Administration), CCC (Civilian Conservation Corps), WPA (Works Progress Administration), TVA (Tennessee Valley Authority), NRA (National Recovery Administration), FSA (Farm Security Administration)— that were directed against the immediate pains of the Great Depression.

FDR's programs did not work, but new relationships forged during those years between the people and Washington remained, and they paved the way for the social service activities that now make up the *Human Resources* cost center.

So it is fitting that FDR, the president who sank the footings for a socially active federal government, serves as the touchstone of this study. For good or ill, the Great Depression and FDR's reaction to it changed the fundamental idea of what a federal government should be in the United States of America.

Why 1941?

FDR's social programs were minor budget items in 1941 and the buildup of *Defense* for World War II was in its infancy.

The level and makeup of public debt at the start of FDR's third term is also important because it demonstrates how the united practices of all thirty-one preceding presidents, who saw the nation through six wars (Revolution, 1812, Mexican, Civil, Spanish-American, World War I), and through the expansion of a handful of colonies located in the East to a coast-to-coast nation of 48 nationwide states, manipulated the power to borrow in such a way that debt rose when extraordinary funds were needed, and it declined when the uncontrollable need for extra funds passed.

For example, public debt at the end of 1940 was $42.8 billion, allocated as follows:

Billions of dollars

Budget Deficits— Great Depression	
1931–40	$24.6
Deficits — World War I	
1917	$ .9
1918	9.0
1919	13.4
Total	23.3
Repaid	5.1
Net	18.2
Public debt 1940	$42.8

Source: Historical Tables 1.1, 7.1.

The decks were clear. Except for deficits caused by the Great Depression, and some of those caused by World War I, the problems related to all previous wars, recessions and emergencies had been dealt with. The nation's credit reputation was deservedly great. Borrowing power was intact. FDR was in a position to fight the war that had to be fought.

Analytical Technique

Apart from pure administrative functions and their related costs, federal spending represents projects and programs approved by federal politicians. *The focus in this book is not on what was approved but, rather, on what was financed.* The analytical period used is a four-year presidential term.

When a deficit exists, expenditures are too high because they were planned that way (as in a time of war) or because spending controls are inadequate or ignored. Whatever the reason, the deficit will be herein allocated to *Defense, Interest, Government,* or *Human Resources,* which will be referred to as cost centers.

A deficit may be caused in any period by underfunding one or more of the cost centers, which raises the question of priorities: Should any cost center be considered more important than another? The short answer is yes.

The first responsibility of government is to protect the nation; the second, to protect its currency. Why? Because a weak America with an out-of-favor dollar is a nothing.

From this principle of priorities there arises an axiom that is followed throughout this book: *Defense* and *Interest* get first bite of the revenue apple. Other analytical principles followed are:

- To contribute to a deficit is to add to public debt, a statement of the obvious to many but not to all. Interviews reveal that to some citizens, public debt equals the sum total of private debt.
- If a deficit exists, and *Defense* increases over the previous period at a faster rate than revenue, then *Defense* is held responsible for the deficit to the extent of that excessive increase. For example, if revenue increases 15 percent, *Defense* is allowed a 15 percent increase. Under techniques being employed, growth beyond that rate contributes to a deficit. The same procedure is applied to growth in *Interest.*
- If *Defense/Interest* do not grow as fast as revenue, all federal receipts above the needs of those primary cost centers are deemed to be available for *Government/Human Resources* cost centers.
- Funds available for *Government/Human Resources* versus spending by those cost centers in the previous period represents the rate of allowable growth beyond which one or both of the cost centers will add to the deficit.
- In the allocation of responsibility for deficits, there are nuances that are handled and explained within each presidential period. Except to correct errors or to take advantage of superior information, the allocation procedure in this book is the same as it was in my previous book on the subject, *The National Debt from FDR (1941) to Clinton (1996)* (McFarland, 2000).

Perspectives

A section labeled "Perspectives" is found in each chapter. In my original book on National Debt, comments under this heading were essentially limited to a description of world events that put all other comments in the chapter into an understandable context.

In this book, two other sections have been added so as to make plain that the Second American Revolution did not deal with fiscal matters alone — it had as well judicial and social components, just as radical and just as consequential, that had a budgetary impact.

Numbers without context have little meaning. For that reason, the buildup to budget analysis in this book is extensive. For example, facing war or avoiding it has budget consequences; space, diplomatic, and social policy do the same. Judicial decisions can cause more or less law enforcement expense; the growth or decline of religious beliefs above behavior that is related to legal decisions can have an impact on state and federal budgets.

True, such subjects cannot be treated comprehensively in a book that primarily seeks answers to a fiscal crisis, but a brief acknowledgment of them can be, and has been, provided to the reader.

Conclusion

Holding politicians accountable for spending beyond the limits of the revenue stream is not a harsh standard to apply when measured against fiscal restraints that are commonplace in the home and in industry. If anything, the federal government should be the most niggardly of all of our institutions.

From the early 1960s until the end of President Clinton's second term in 2000, federal revenue has never increased less than 24.8 percent in a four-year period.[8] In the high inflation years of Jimmy Carter, it increased more than 60 percent.

Until George W. Bush assumed the presidency in 2001, spending — not a lack of revenues — had been the fundamental problem since the mid–1950s. When and where the spending aberrations occurred will be presented in the remaining chapters, as will the travails of the Bush administration as it struggled with revenue loss and other cataclysmic events in the 2001–08 period.[9]

Society, according to conservative thought, is the marriage of what was, what is, and what is to be. Ancestors teach us, reason guides us, children make us responsible. In the handling of America's resources, have political leaders since Roosevelt acted prudently? We shall see.

Notes

This book contains many tables expressing dollar amounts. These amounts are reported *in the unadjusted dollars of the period indicated.*

Public debt amounts prior to 1940 were taken from a listing of "Historical Information" published by the Bureau of Public Debt. Thereafter amounts were taken from Table 7.1, "Federal Debt at the End of the Year," included in the publication *Historical Tables; Budget of the United States Government,* U.S. Government Printing Office.

The numbers in this book dealing with the years 2007 and 2008 are estimates taken from the above-mentioned *Historical Tables.*

The primary source for federal budget statistics is the publication of the Office of Management and Budget, *Historical Tables.* An earlier addition of the same source was used in writing my previous book on the public debt. In each edition of that book the numbers for, say, the last decade are apt to be slightly adjusted. The same was done in the edition used for this book. But for purposes of continuity, most of the previously published figures were not changed, because the minor changes noted did not change the thrust of the published information.

Commentary on world and political events is based upon known information through 2006 as it was published by February 2007 in various publications. Comments made about events after 2006 are based upon speculation and the estimates provided by the federal government.

1

Background, 1789–1940

A Look at the Presidents

GEORGE WASHINGTON (1789–1796)—NO POLITICAL PARTY AFFILIATION

Thumbnail: Life span, 1732–1799; six feet, two inches, 175–200 pounds; fashionable dresser, false teeth (not wood, as some believe); a temper usually, but not always, under control; a poor public speaker; a direct and candid private speaker; billiard player; exercised regularly; a natural born leader; no natural children — two adopted children; local education that did not include college; Episcopalian; wife, Mary Custis; surveyor, officer in British army, commander of American Army, politician, landowner; refused a third term and the possibility of becoming King George 1 of the newly formed and still fragile country; died peacefully at 69—"first in war, first in peace, and first in the hearts of his countrymen."[1]

Major events: Washington's overriding contribution was to provide leadership and stability to the new government, and to turn it over intact to his successor, John Adams.

Washington was burdened with a war debt of $75–$80 million[2] during his two terms in office. Despite this, by 1794 the United States "had the highest credit rating in Europe"[3] thanks to wise presidential leadership and the skillful management of the first secretary of the treasury, Alexander Hamilton.

JOHN ADAMS (1797–1800)—FEDERALIST

Thumbnail: Life span, 1735–1826; five feet, six inches and portly; a brilliant logician and a persuasive speaker, but a social misfit; a voracious reader and a long-distance walker; four children, one of whom (John) became the sixth president; Harvard degree, law school in Massachusetts; Unitarian; wife, Abigail Smith; lawyer, diplomat, politician; died at home on Independence Day within hours of his lifetime rival and friend, Thomas Jefferson.

Major events: A pivotal figure prior to and during the Revolution, Adams was not an impressive president. The Adams administration has been mostly remembered for the Alien and Seditions Acts (1798) that, among other things, attacked the freedom of the press. By 1802, these acts had been repealed.

Adams took on an $83.7 million public debt and a growing economy. America moved into the nineteenth century with a debt of about $83 million.

THOMAS JEFFERSON (1801–1808)—DEMOCRATIC-REPUBLICAN

Thumbnail: Life span, 1743–1826; six feet, two inches and thin; relaxed dresser—almost sloppy; easy temperament; reserved and somewhat aloof; sensitive to criticism; poor speaker—great writer (generally credited with the composition of the Declaration of Independence); a genius with skills in many disciplines, Jefferson's avocations ranged from architecture to meteorology; horseback riding and music engaged him; a Deist; two children; wife of ten years, Martha Skelton; College of William and Mary; lawyer, diplomat, politician, landowner; died on Independence Day within hours of John Adams's demise.

Major events: Jefferson's election signaled the beginning of modern political parties that competed for power. The westward expansion of the United States was symbolized by the Louisiana Purchase from France, a deal organized by Jefferson that doubled the size of the United States and was followed by the extensive explorations of Lewis and Clark; pirates of the Mediterranean were tamed during the Tripolitan War (1801–05); the slave trade was abolished in 1807; Jefferson established the precedent of executive privilege, an action that was dramatically tested during the administration of Richard Nixon (*U.S. v. Nixon*) in 1974.

Public debt was reduced to $65 million under Jefferson.

JAMES MADISON (1809–1816)—DEMOCRATIC-REPUBLICAN

Thumbnail: Life span, 1751–1836 (the last of the Founding Fathers); five feet, four inches, 100 pounds; conservative dresser; poor speaker; shy; nonargumentative but firm decision maker; a walker, horseback rider and reader; no children; College of New Jersey (now Princeton); not a lawyer; Episcopalian; wife Dolley Todd; spent a lifetime in politics.

Major events: The Father of the Constitution was no less steadfast during the War of 1812 (1812–14) which can be correctly thought of as the second war for independence from the still acquisitive British. The British impressed American seamen, interfered with U.S. vessels in international waters and incited Indian uprisings in the West. The War of 1812 resulted, perhaps the most underpublicized crisis in U.S. history during which the British, among other things, destroyed the White House.

Public debt rose to $127 million.

James Monroe (1817–1824) — Democratic-Republican

Thumbnail: Life span, 1758–1831 (like Adams and Jefferson, he too died on Independence Day); six feet tall and powerful; well groomed; warm personality but reserved; horseback rider and hunter; disturbed by critics; two children; College of William and Mary (left school to serve in the army); wife, Elizabeth Kortright; military officer (highly valued by Washington), politician. He was penniless when he died.

Major events: Chronic unrest in Spanish-owned Florida resulted in the First Seminole War (1817–18), which was followed by the acquisition of Florida (1819) and the Monroe Doctrine (1823), which warned foreign powers to refrain from involvement in the Western Hemisphere — a document from the past that could again have special relevance in the 21st century; Monroe suffered the first major economic recession in 1819; the Missouri Compromise (1820) indicated that no president was yet ready to face the slavery issue headon.

Debt dropped to $90 million.

John Quincy Adams (1825–1828) — Democratic-Republican

Thumbnail: Life span, 1767–1848; five feet, seven inches, 175 pounds; son of John Adams, the second president; plain dresser; poor speaker; given to depression; a billiard player, horseback rider and reader; a successful diplomat despite his cold personality; three children; Harvard College, law school in Massachusetts; Unitarian; wife, Louisa Johnson; law, diplomacy, politics. Adams returned to Washington as a Congressman after his presidency and he died in the Speaker's office in 1848.

Major events: A tremendously effective diplomat and secretary of state, Adams was not an effective president. He sponsored the development of infrastructure (Chesapeake and Ohio Canal).

Debt dropped to $67.5 million.

Andrew Jackson (1829–1836) — Democrat

Thumbnail: Life span, 1767–1845; six feet, one inch, 140 pounds; a fashionable dresser; charismatic and tough; a good friend and a fearful enemy; intimidating; earthy language in private; bred and raced horses; no natural children — one adopted son; indifferent education, including law school; Presbyterian; wife, Rachel Robards; law, veteran of the War of 1812 and the First Seminole War (1817–18), politician; died naturally, influential to the end — the dominant political figure from Jefferson to Lincoln.

Major events: "Disunion by armed force is treason," Jackson thundered when South Carolina balked against a federal law, a threat that Jackson didn't have to implement, but one that must have been remembered by Abraham Lincoln decades later when faced with the secession of southern states. Jackson's Indian policy was harsh but it accelerated the settlement of the western frontier. He survived an assassination attempt in 1835; he refused to renew the charter for the Bank of the United States , land speculation, inflation and a banking crisis followed.

Public debt was almost eliminated under Jackson, having dropped to $38 thousand.

MARTIN VAN BUREN (1837–1840)—DEMOCRAT

Thumbnail: Life span, 1782–1862; five feet, six inches and sturdy; a fashionable dresser; open, friendly personality; a difficult speaker to listen to because of his rapid, sometimes accented speech; a careful and unpredictable decision maker; theater, opera and fishing filled his idle hours; four children; unimpressive formal education followed by legal studies; Dutch Reformed church; wife for ten years, Hannah Hoes; lawyer, politician. He died of natural causes, the only president whose life touched both the Revolutionary and Civil Wars.

Major events: Economic recession in 1837 — 900 banks closed; border clashes with Canada were resolved; Jackson's harsh Indian policy was continued and the final rebellion of the Seminoles in Florida was quelled.

Debt increased to $4 million.

WILLIAM HENRY HARRISON (1841)—WHIG

Thumbnail: Life span, 1773–1841; average height and slim; good-humored, accessible and unpretentious; a walker, rider of horses and a Bible student; nine children; University of Pennsylvania Medical School (until he ran out of money); Episcopalian; wife, Anna Symmes; soldier, politician.

Caught a cold while delivering his inaugural address and died April 4, 1841.

JOHN TYLER (1841–1844)—WHIG

Thumbnail: Life span, 1790–1862; a lean six-footer; generally unhealthy; well-bred, charming snob; a violinist and a hunter; 14 children; College of William and Mary; law clerk; Episcopalian; first wife, Letitia Christian (died 1842); second wife Julia Gardiner; soldier, politician; died a natural death.

Major events: Tyler continued to oppose a federal bank; his succession to the presidency in April 1841 established the right of succession; he was the first president to face the threat of impeachment, and the only president to switch parties while in office; a treaty was signed with Great Britain settling the boundaries of Maine and Canada, a sore spot to both countries that had caused skirmishes. Texas became a state.

Public debt increased to $33 million.

James Polk (1845–1848) — Democrat

Thumbnail: Life span, 1795–1849; short, sturdy build; generally unhealthy; introvert with few friends; top orator; hyperactive; no hobbies.

Major events: Oregon Treaty with Britain (1846) settled the northwest border questions; after the Mexican War (1846–48), the Rio Grande was established as the border, and the territory now forming the states or part of the states of California, Nevada, Utah, Wyoming, Colorado, Texas and Arizona was relinquished by Mexico (Mexico still resents this deal, a sentiment especially relevant during the immigration crisis that plagues the United States in the first decade of the 21st century).

Debt went up to $47 million.

Zachary Taylor (1849–1850) — Whig

Thumbnail: Life span, 1784–1850; five feet, eight inches, 170–200 pounds; sloppy appearance; a warm, plain-spoken gentleman; simple pleasures; four children; basic education; professional soldier and a bona fide war hero (War of 1812, Black Hawk War [1832], Second Seminole War [1837–40], Mexican War [1846–48]); no political experience prior to the presidency.

Died of food poisoning on July 9, 1850.

Millard Fillmore (1850–1852) — Whig

Thumbnail: Life span, 1800–1874 — the first president born in the 19th century; handsome six footer and a fashionable dresser; likable and capable mixer; poor speaker but a well-reasoned thinker; books were his passion; two children; routine education, law clerk; Unitarian; first wife Abigail Powers (died 1853); second wife Caroline McIntosh; lawyer, politician; a fierce critic of Abraham Lincoln. He died a natural death.

Major events: Fillmore, vice president to Taylor, was the second man to succeed a deceased president (1850). He signed the Compromise of 1850 dealing with slavery in western states that again failed to address that gnawing question headon — California was admitted to the Union as part of the compromise — and a looming civil war over the question of slavery was postponed. The (hot potato) slavery problem was passed on to the next president.

Public debt rose to $66 million.

Franklin Pierce (1853–1856) — Democrat

Thumbnail: Life span, 1804–1869; five feet, ten inches, sturdy and handsome; a congenial man who sought approval; drinking problem; bouts of depression; avid fisherman; one child; Bowdoin College; Episcopalian; wife, Jane Appleton; lawyer, politician.

Major events: The United States bought land from Mexico that completed the boundaries of Arizona and New Mexico; the Kansas-Nebraska Act repealed the Missouri Compromise and permitted these two states to decide the slavery issue for themselves; the slavery problem continued to simmer.

The public debt dropped to $32 million.

JAMES BUCHANAN (1857–1860)—DEMOCRAT

Thumbnail: Life span, 1791–1868; a handsome six footer with a weight problem; a conservative dresser; a gifted speaker; affable, generous and meticulously honest; reading and card playing amused him; no children—a lifelong bachelor; lawyer, politician. He died a natural death.

Major events: A large insurance company went bankrupt in 1857, an event followed by bank failures and a deep depression; the Dred Scott decision, which declared the Missouri Compromise (that tried to regulate slavery) unconstitutional muddied the political waters; the defeat of Buchanan and the election of Abraham Lincoln disheartened the South—before Lincoln was sworn in, Alabama, Florida, Georgia, Louisiana, Mississippi, South Carolina and Texas seceded from the Union.

Public debt rose to $64.8 million.

ABRAHAM LINCOLN (1861–1865)—REPUBLICAN

Thumbnail: Life span, 1809–1865; six feet, four inches, 170 pounds; muscular; homely; careless dresser; possible undetected weak heart; disarming and unpretentious; a good listener; a storyteller; wrestled with depression; poor speaker; effective writer; enjoyed classical literature, poetry, the theater and the company of his friends; three children; little formal education; perhaps a Deist; wife Mary Todd (a difficult wife); essentially a lifetime politician. Lincoln was assassinated while attending Ford's Theater in Washington with his wife about a month after he was sworn in for his second term.

Major events: The Civil War was the predominant issue. Four more states seceded from the Union: Virginia, North Carolina, Arkansas and Tennessee. The first shot of the war was fired on April 12, 1861; Lee surrendered on April 9, 1865. Lincoln was assassinated on April 14, 1865.

Public debt skyrocketed to $2.7 billion. Absent the ability to expand debt in this way, Lincoln might have been unable to preserve the Union.

ANDREW JOHNSON (1865–1868)—REPUBLICAN

Thumbnail: Life span, 1808–1875; five feet, ten inches and stocky; healthy, neat dresser; simple, direct, polite; a gifted speaker; five children; no church; enjoyed checkers and gardening; wife, Eliza McCardle; lifelong politician.

Impeached by the House in a political war but acquitted in the Senate; elected to the Senate in 1874 but died a few months later.

Major events: Survived impeachment after a squabble over the limits of presidential authority; bitter clashes on how to handle the postwar South and ex-slaves; the Thirteenth and Fourteenth Amendments of the U.S. Constitution were the result (slavery was outlawed and citizenship was guaranteed to anyone born or naturalized in the United States); Alaska was purchased.

Three years after the war public debt was $2.6 billion.

Ulysses S. Grant (1869–1876)—Republican

Thumbnail: Life span, 1822–1885; five feet, seven inches, sturdy build; suffered from migraine headaches; modest, mild-mannered; somewhat prudish—almost the opposite of what one would expect a hard-hitting general to be; four children; West Point graduate (a lackluster student); Methodist; enjoyed art and fast horses (a gifted horseman); smoked cigars incessantly (developed mouth cancer when he was older); wife, Julia Boggs; professional soldier. He died peacefully four days after completing his autobiography.

Major events: Scandals stained Grant's first term to an extent that they reached his personal secretary and his war secretary—he was personally honest and poorly served by others; Europe went into recession and negative national events, including the great Chicago fire (1871), drew the American economy into a five-year depression—millions were unemployed; stitching up the slavery question took another step forward with the passage of the Fifteenth Amendment of the U.S. Constitution (protecting the right to vote).

Debt dropped to $2.2 billion, despite the hard times—an admirable demonstration of the respect that the president and the Congress had for the need to protect borrowing power whenever possible.

Rutherford B. Hayes (1877–1880)—Republican

Thumbnail: Life span, 1822–1893; five feet, nine inches, 170–180 pounds; handsome with a thick beard; healthy, dressed casually; extrovert, good mixer, an adequate speaker; five children; Kenyon College and Harvard Law School; perhaps a Deist; hunting, fishing and chess attracted him; wife, Lucy Ware; lawyer, politician. Died peacefully.

Major events: Federal troops were removed from the South; Panama Canal policy—"The United States cannot consent the surrender of this control to any European power or to any combination of European powers." All American presidents who followed Hayes adopted this position until President Carter in 1977 signed a treaty that transferred ownership to Panama in 1979, a decision that America may one day live to regret.

Public debt was $2.1 billion in 1880.

JAMES GARFIELD (1881)—REPUBLICAN

Assassinated July 2, 1881, by Charles Guiteau, a former political supporter. Guiteau was hanged in 1882.

CHESTER ARTHUR (1881–1884)—REPUBLICAN

Thumbnail: Life span, 1831–1881; six feet, two inches, 175–225 pounds; a fashionable dresser; handsome; amiable, polished, emotional; two children; Union College, law clerk; Episcopalian; enjoyed conversation and fishing; wife, Ellen Herndon (she died from pneumonia; he was never the same after her death); teacher, lawyer, bureaucrat, politician. After failing to win a second term, Arthur ran for the Senate and lost—he died two years later at his home of Bright's disease.

Major events: Chinese Exclusion Act (1882) suspended Chinese immigration for ten years; Pendleton Act (1883) created the modern civil service system.

Debt dropped to $1.8 billion.

GROVER CLEVELAND (1885–1888)—DEMOCRAT

Thumbnail: Life span, 1837–1908; five feet, 11 inches, 250 pounds; powerful speaker; carefree socially but a stern, dedicated worker with a high sense of duty; quick tempered and blunt; four children; incomplete formal education due to his father's death; law clerk; fishing, food and drink attracted him; teacher, lawyer, law enforcement, politician. Cleveland was the only president to serve two nonconsecutive terms. He died peacefully.

Major events: The first Presidential Succession Act (1886) was passed that clarified a process that had been murky; the Interstate Commerce Act (1887) established the first federal regulatory agency, the Interstate Commerce Commission.

Public debt, $1.7 billion.

BENJAMIN HARRISON (1889–1892)—DEMOCRAT

Thumbnail: Life span, 1833–1901; five feet, six inches and portly; poor speaker; fashionable dresser; healthy; stiff, formal; a poor speaking voice but an effective extemporaneous speaker; a poor mixer; honest, intelligent and hard working; a legal expert; two children; Miami University; law clerk; Presbyterian; first wife, Caroline Scott (died 1892); second wife after his presidency, Mary Dimmick (his children disapproved); soldier (Civil War), lawyer, bureaucrat, politician. He died peacefully.

Major events: Harrison's loyalty to veterans yielded the Dependent and

Disability Pensions Act (1890); the McKinley Tariff Act (1890) probably cost him his reelection because some of the tariffs were too high and too unpopular.

Public debt, $1.6 billion.

GROVER CLEVELAND (1893–1896) — DEMOCRAT

The second time around.

Major events: Business failures in 1893 brought financial panic and a four-year depression; the Wilson-Gorman Act (1894) provided for, among other things, a federal income tax for the first time — the Supreme Court struck it down as unconstitutional (1895).

Public debt at the end of Cleveland's term was $1.8 billion — a minor increase considering the economic climate of the times, and a tribute to the sense of personal responsibility that was exercised by federal politicians during that troublesome period.

WILLIAM McKINLEY (1897–1901) — REPUBLICAN

Thumbnail: Life span, 1843–1901; five feet, seven inches, 200 pounds; handsome; good speaker; conservative dresser but quite vain; healthy; friendly and well liked; disliked earthy humor; two children; Allegheny College (dropped out due to illness); law clerk; Methodist; wife, Ida Saxton; soldier (Civil War), lawyer, politician. McKinley was assassinated in 1901 by Leon F. Czolgosz, an unemployed millworker who was electrocuted a month later.

Major events: The Hawaiian Islands were annexed (1898). Spain's attempts to maintain its rule in Cuba kept tensions between Spain and the United States acute. To settle the issue, America declared war in April 1898. By August 1898, Spain's Atlantic and Pacific fleets were destroyed — a treaty was signed in December and Cuba became independent. Puerto Rico and Guam were ceded to the United States. The Philippine Islands were sold to America for $20 million.

Public debt, $2.1 billion.

THEODORE ROOSEVELT (1901–1908) — REPUBLICAN

Thumbnail: Life span, 1858–1919; five feet, eight inches, 200 pounds of brawn; a fashionable dresser; almost blind in his left eye; energetic and loved being president; a poor voice but a powerful speaker; proud, decisive; intolerant of earthy humor; a photographic memory; six children from two wives; Harvard College, Columbia Law School (dropped out to enter politics); Dutch Reformed church; virulently supported the separation of church and state — opposed to "In God We Trust" on U.S. coins and tried to have it removed;

athletic and engaged in strenuous physical activity, including boxing; first wife of four years, Alice Lee; second wife, Edith Carow; lifetime politician. Roosevelt died suddenly of a cardiac embolism.

Major events: A vice president under McKinley, Theodore Roosevelt succeeded to the presidency in 1901 and then in 1904 he won the election to continue in service; land needed to construct the Panama Canal was bought from Panama (open for traffic in 1920); Roosevelt's reputation for "big stick" diplomacy came from his insistence on enforcing the Monroe Doctrine to the extent that he would intervene if American nations by their behavior threatened the peace of the continent; laws were passed (Roosevelt's Square Deal) that strengthened the supervisory powers of the Interstate Commerce Commission over corporate practices that some regarded as abusive; the current system of food inspection by the federal government was started; Roosevelt, the Great Conservationist, created the national park system and funded irrigation projects in the West; a brief financial panic took place in 1907–08.

Public debt rose to $2.6 billion.

WILLIAM TAFT (1909–1912)—REPUBLICAN

Thumbnail: Life span, 1857–1930; six feet, two inches and, when he was president, over 300 pounds (once got stuck in a White House bathtub); cheerful, friendly but, at the same time, reserved; his rift with Roosevelt disturbed him — didn't enjoy being president; fought depression; three children; Yale University, University of Cincinnati Law School; a brilliant student; Unitarian; the first presidential golfer; a baseball fan; enjoyed theater; wife, Helen Herron; lawyer, state judge, U.S. Solicitor General, U.S. Circuit Court of Appeals judge; law professor, dean of a law school, politician. After his presidency Taft returned to his first love, the law. And in 1921 he was made Chief Justice of the U.S. Supreme Court. Taft retired from the Court in February 1930 — he died a month later.

Major events: Taft perpetuated the Republican policy of protectionism through tariffs that mobilized Democrats and others against him; he expanded the power of the Interstate Commerce Commission to embrace the supervision of the telephone and telegraph industries; "The Congress shall have the power to lay and collect taxes on incomes." Taft was still president when these words first appeared in the U.S. Constitution (Sixteenth Amendment). Prior to that point the fundamental revenue stream to the U.S. government was provided by tariffs on incoming goods, which in turn provoked endless partisan arguments about what and how much to tax. With the Sixteenth Amendment in place, presumably the tariff argument would diminish as federal politicians looked ahead to the juicy promise of being able to tax the growing incomes of all Americans; New Mexico and Arizona joined the Union under Taft, making him the first president of the 48 contiguous states.

Debt went up to $2.9 billion.

Woodrow Wilson (1913–1920)—Democrat

Thumbnail: Life span, 1856–1924; five feet, 11 inches, 175–185 pounds; poor health; neat, but not attractive; few close friends; women more than men were close to him; apparently confident in public; didn't mix well in smaller gatherings; three children; College of New Jersey (now Princeton); a good student, a good writer and a good speaker; Presbyterian; many hobbies—golf, music, horseback riding, theater, reading; first wife, Ellen Axson (died 1914); second wife, Edith Galt—after Wilson's stroke in 1919, some say she became the de facto president. Wilson died in his sleep.

Major events: Democrats lost no time in lowering tariffs and establishing a new income tax now permitted under the Sixteenth Amendment—1 percent on incomes over $3,000; a graduated surtax of 1 to 6 percent on incomes above $20,000; by the end of World War I marginal rates were over 70 percent; the Federal Reserve Act (1913) established the Federal Reserve system that remains in existence today; the Federal Trade Commission was established to seek out and eliminate unfair practices in the marketplace; the Clayton Anti-Trust Act (1914) set the foundation for the powerful labor movement that followed; the Adamson Act (1914) set the stage for the general acceptance of an eight-hour workday; troubles with Mexico, dramatized by the chase of Pancho Villa by General Pershing, also revealed attempts by the Germans to ally with Mexico in the event that the United States entered World War I, dangling as bait Germany's promise to support Mexico's bid to reacquire territory lost in the Mexican War; The Seventeenth Amendment (senators are to be elected by the people not by, as before, state legislatures), the Eighteenth (prohibition) and the Nineteenth (women gained the right to vote) were passed; the United States entered World War I, which ended under Wilson, who put all his energy into the establishment of the League of Nations; he regarded his inability to persuade Congress to share his vision as his greatest disappointment.

The cost of World War I lifted the public debt almost ten times to a height of $27.4 billion.

After the war, obedient to history, debt dropped. It was down to $26.0 billion at the end of Wilson's term. Absent the ability to expand debt so enormously during this era, America might have stayed out of the war and Germany might have prevailed.

Warren Harding (1921–1923)—Republican

Thumbnail: Life span, 1865–1923; six feet, well built; handsome; neat and fashionable dresser; poor health; nervous; friendly; avoided confrontation; wishy-washy; not grounded in principle; one illegitimate child; Ohio Central College; very verbal, written or spoken; Baptist; a golfer; enjoyed fishing; read little; wife, Florence DeWolfe—a poor marriage that led Harding to dalliances;

teacher, salesman, reporter, publisher, politician. Harding died suddenly of an embolism in August of his final year as president. His presidency was not highly regarded.

Major events: The League of Nations idea finally died under Harding, World War I was formally closed and the great powers came to agreement on arms limitation and other matters that helped to keep the peace. But the Harding administration will always be best known for the Teapot Dome scandal that uncovered bribery at a level that shocked even the most cynical observers of the Washington scene.

The public debt was $22.3 billion.

CALVIN COOLIDGE (1923–1928)—REPUBLICAN

Thumbnail: Life span, 1872–1933; five feet, nine inches, small build; not healthy, tired easily; good dresser; general neat appearance; shy, cautious, self-reliant and exclusive; a man of few words and a sharp wit; two children; Amherst College, law clerk; Congregationalist; a walker, horseback rider and prankster; wife, Grace Goodhue; lawyer, politician. Coolidge was popular and could have run for a second term, but he refused. He died peacefully five years after leaving office.

Major events: Coolidge lowered immigration quotas and dropped taxes (including the elimination of inheritance taxes); in 1928, 15 countries (United States, France, Germany, Belgium, Great Britain, Ireland, Canada, Australia, New Zealand, India, South Africa, Italy, Japan, Poland and Czechoslovakia) agreed to renounce war as a method for resolving disputes. Five years later Hitler came to power and in three years (1936) Nazi Germany was on the march. Soon after most of the nations that had voted to renounce war were fighting each other.

Public debt fell to $17.6 billion.

HERBERT HOOVER (1929–1932)—REPUBLICAN

Thumbnail: Life span, 1874–1964; five feet, 11 inches, husky; hardworking, honest, aloof; uncomfortable with crowds, the press and with Congress; a logician who was demanding of subordinates; a poor speaker with a brilliant mind; two children; Stanford University; a geologist; strenuous exercise; fisherman; Quaker; wife, Lou Henry; engineer, leader of the American Relief Committee that provided assistance to 120,000 Americans who were stranded in Europe at the start of the war; bureaucrat, politician. Hoover had a long and productive post-presidency career and he died a natural death.

Major events: All other events paled compared with the impact of the stock market crash in 1929 and the Great Depression that followed. The conditions that brought the negative economic circumstances into being preceded Hoover, but the consequences of them were laid at his feet. Perhaps the unluckiest man to ever hold the presidency, Hoover was also the wrong man at the wrong time to address the problems of a nation that, at the time, needed a fearless, exuberant leader — fearless he was; exuberant he wasn't. His dour features were not the anecdote that was needed to rebuild national morale.

Debt had fallen to as low as $16 billion in the 1920s but it increased to $19 billion by the time Hoover left Washington.

From that time until the present, no president has left office with a smaller debt than the one that greeted him, except for Harry Truman (1949–52).

Franklin D. Roosevelt (1933–1940)

Thumbnail: Life span, 1882–1945; six feet, one inch, 180 pounds, handsome; paralyzed legs from poliomyelitis; otherwise healthy and strong; a charmer whose views were never completely clear; decisive and handled pressure well; supremely self-confident; five children; Harvard, Columbia Law School (dropped out because he passed the bar before graduation); not a great student; Episcopalian; swimming, poker, a stamp collection and motion pictures held his attention; wife, Eleanor Roosevelt (who had a formidable career of her own); law, politics. Roosevelt died before World War II ended — he was 63 and looked twenty years older.

Major events: When Franklin D. Roosevelt (FDR) took office, the pains of the Great Depression were visible on the countenance of Herbert Hoover and in the numbers of the budget.

At the end of FDR's first term (1936), debt was $33.8 billion; in 1940, the end of his second term, it was $42.8 billion.

Conclusion

In 1940, with nothing but personality and a message of hope going for him, FDR ran for a third term (legal at the time). He beat Wendell Wilkie by five million votes.

Taxes and debt per capita hit an all-time high on his watch, but voters loved him. The entertainment business had Houdini; politics had FDR.

Franklin D. Roosevelt was the thirty-second president of the United States; George W. Bush is the forty-third. Prior to FDR, federal government was a minor presence in the average American's life, confining itself to defense, infrastructure, foreign policy, remote economic guidance, tax collection, and modest assistance to citizens in times of stress. Taxes were low, debt increased only when emergencies or expansion opportunities arose, and it declined thereafter.

FDR broke with the past. He expanded the role of the federal government to a degree that must have had the Founding Fathers spinning in their graves.

His vision, perhaps appropriate for that time, emboldened liberal disciples of later years to break similarly with tradition — to ignore long-established principles of debt management.

The vision of planned deficits and an expanded role for government in domestic matters that was followed by FDR during the Great Depression and during the war, legitimized in the minds of modern social engineers, who faced no such stresses, the subsequent *unfunded* growth in federal domestic spending. As a result over the decades budgets have spun out of control. Debt and interest, for the wrong reasons, have skyrocketed.

Whether true to FDR's inner beliefs or to distortions of them, the fiscal legacy of FDR's early years in office, especially as it was later interpreted by President Lyndon Baines Johnson, serves as the primal cause of the unacceptable level of national debt that faces us today.

2

Franklin D. Roosevelt, 1941–1944

Lawyer, Governor, President

Charles J. Guiteau, an active supporter of James A. Garfield in the presidential election of 1880, traveled to Washington after the contest in search of a diplomatic post he thought he deserved. Turned away as unqualified, Guiteau sought revenge against the man upon whom he had spent his loyalty, James A. Garfield. On July 2, 1881, he shot Garfield twice. After three operations, the president died on September 9, 1881, and he was succeeded by Vice President Chester A. Arthur. By June 1882, Guiteau was tried, found guilty, and hanged.

In the same year, in Hyde Park, New York, Franklin D. Roosevelt (FDR) was born. In another time it might have been said that the blood of kings poured through FDR's veins. He was a fourth cousin of presidents Ulysses S. Grant and Zachary Taylor, a fifth cousin of President Theodore Roosevelt, and a seventh cousin of Prime Minister Winston Churchill, with whom he shared some of the headiest moments in the history of international relationships.

FDR's bloodline, as blue as it gets, was also political. Nicholas Roosevelt was involved in New York politics in the late 1600s. Isaac Roosevelt, a wealthy sugar refiner, served in the New York state senate; FDR's great-grandfather, James, in the state assembly.

By the time Franklin's father James arrived on the scene, the family fortune was intact, requiring only prudence to assure a high lifestyle. Father James managed his estate efficiently, served on the proper boards of directors, invested wisely, and lived well as a country squire, traveling to and fro in his private railroad car.

Father James's second wife, Sara Delano, was 26 years younger than he, and Franklin was their only son. At her death in 1941, she left $920,000 to Franklin (equivalent to $9 million in 2000 dollars). But during her lifetime, Sara ruled her son's financial well-being.

FDR was the privileged child of parents who, as a measure of their snobbery, looked down on the Vanderbilts. Educationally, he learned the basics from tutors and at age 14 he entered Groton.

Governor Theodore Roosevelt (soon to be vice president) spoke at Franklin's graduation from Groton in 1900, and he was president of the United States when Franklin, in 1904, graduated from Harvard. Roosevelt was a mediocre student. Following Harvard, he spent three years at Columbia Law School. When he prematurely passed the bar examination in 1907, he dropped out and never graduated.

Roosevelt moved to New York with his wife, Eleanor, whom he married in 1905. There he joined the prestigious law firm of Carter, Ledyard and Milburn and he disappeared from public life until his election as a state senator in 1911.

Roosevelt's political career was on the move, over mother Sara's objections. While serving in the New York senate, Roosevelt supported Woodrow Wilson in the 1912 presidential race; in 1913, he was rewarded with an appointment as assistant secretary of the navy. He resigned to become the vice presidential nominee of the Democratic ticket in 1920, which was headed by James M. Cox. They were swamped almost two to one in the popular vote by the Republican pair, Warren G. Harding and Calvin Coolidge.

The defeat in 1920 moved Roosevelt temporarily out of the public spotlight. And an attack of poliomyelitis that paralyzed his legs in 1921 could have made his absence permanent, but it did not. Something in Roosevelt's blood, something in that "spoiled brat" background gave him the admirable strength and gumption to persevere.

In 1924, at the Democratic convention, Roosevelt made the nominating speech for Alfred E. Smith for president, to no avail. John W. Davis was nominated and he was beaten badly by Calvin Coolidge — Smith tried again in 1928 and he won the nomination, but he was trounced by Herbert Hoover in the presidential election.

Roosevelt returned to the practice of law in 1924, working on the fringes of the political system until his breakthrough in 1929 as governor of New York. From this mighty perch, he lambasted Hoover's regime and he won his party's nomination as the Democrat's presidential candidate. In 1932, about a decade after he was stricken with polio, Roosevelt whipped Hoover by more than seven million votes to become the thirty-second president of the United States.

It may have been, as some claim, that the 1932 election stood more as a rejection of Hoover than it did the election of Roosevelt. But the margins of victory FDR garnered in later elections made it clear that the man now known as FDR had a claim on the voters' affections that was almost visceral.

In came FDR and out went Prohibition, a wildly popular decision. Out went the sense of defeat that was (fairly or unfairly) associated with Hoover and up went the hope ("The only thing we have to fear is fear itself") that FDR sold with the fervor of a medicine man. Out went the idea that government should not unduly intrude into the affairs of the private sector and in went a large assortment of New Deal programs that were supposed to attack and defeat the Great Depression.[1]

And, in the background, the world began to watch with growing trepidation the antics of Germany's new leader, Adolf Hitler, who in 1934 withdrew Germany from the League of Nations and proceeded to build a mighty war machine that should have concerned anyone who had read *Mein Kamf*, the book written in 1923 by the then-imprisoned Hitler that detailed his sick ideas and his plans for the future.[2]

In 1941–44, FDR controlled the Congress through House Speaker Sam Rayburn (D–TX) and Senate leader Alben Barkley (D–KY).[3] Together they faced a $42.8[4] billion public debt, summarized as follows:

Table 2.1
Unrecovered Cost (In Billions of Dollars)

World War I			
1919		$18.3	
Great Depression:			
1931 — deficit	$.5		
1932 — "	2.7		
1933 — "	2.6		
1934 — "	3.6		
1935 — "	2.8		
1936 — "	4.3		
1937 — "	2.2		
1938 — "	.1		
1939 — "	2.8		
1940 — "	2.9	24.5	
Total	$42.8		

Source: Historical Tables 2006, 1.1

Several comments regarding this table are in order.

The previous chapter noted that it was the Civil War that drove public debt from $65 million under President Buchanan to almost $3 billion under Lincoln. Thereafter, through various recessions and despite costs associated with the continued expansion to the West that did not terminate until New Mexico and Arizona joined the Union under President Taft (1909–12), public debt held steady until World War I lifted it again to a degree even greater than that which was experienced by Lincoln.[5]

There are lessons to be learned here, and in the years that followed prior to FDR's second term:

- Wars are expensive; borrowing is inevitable; the ability to do so is an indispensable asset to a president.
- After the Civil War, and despite other cost challenges associated with growth and hard times, debt levels stabilized (in a growing economy

this means that the relationship of debt to Gross Domestic Product progressively decreased).

• American presidents and politicians prior to the FDR era valued the ability to borrow; they protected it for those who followed them in office, permitting large increases only when confronted by significant and uncontrollable forces.

The following table demonstrates the flow of debt from Lincoln to FDR:

Table 2.2
Public Debt, Lincoln to FDR
(in billions of dollars)

Abraham Lincoln	1865	$2.7
Andrew Johnson	1868	2.6
U.S. Grant	1876	2.2
Rutherford B. Hayes	1880	2.1
James Garfield/Chester Arthur	1884	1.8
Grover Cleveland	1888	1.7
Benjamin Harrison	1892	1.6
Grover Cleveland	1896	1.8
William McKinley	1900	2.1
Theodore Roosevelt	1908	2.6
William Taft	1912	2.9
Woodrow Wilson	1920	26.0
Warren Harding	1923	22.3
Calvin Coolidge	1928	17.6
Herbert Hoover	1932	19.0
Franklin D. Roosevelt	1940	42.8

Source: Bureau of Public Debt, Historical Information, 17911939, Internet, 1998

Pre–World War II debt ($42.8 billion) makes up a small part of current debt ($5.3 trillion).[6] Reasons for the buildup of additional public debt will be found in the upcoming analyses of presidencies, from FDR to Bush.

Perspectives

GENERAL

In FDR's unprecedented third term (that he won with 55 percent of the vote[7]), America was drawn into a war on two fronts against Germany and Japan. The unemployed gratefully poured into defense-associated jobs as the economy raced to supply goods needed by the Allies and by the rapidly expanding armed forces of the United States.

FDR's declaration of war in December 1941 took minutes to make but, in the ensuing four years, it did what the policies of Hoover and FDR had failed to do over a period of 12 years—it buried the Great Depression.

The war was more than two years old by the time America joined the Allied forces. Hitler was on the march. Poland, the Netherlands, Belgium, Luxembourg, Yugoslavia, and France had fallen. The Balkans, Greece, the Soviet Union, and other countries were under attack. Britain turned to Winston Churchill for leadership and Nazi bombs rained down on London.

Japan was equally on the offensive in the Pacific. For the Allies, 1942 was a year best forgotten.

Then the worm turned in 1943. The Nazi attack on Russia fizzled, the first major setback for Hitler. German dominance in North Africa was ended. Mussolini was deposed and Italy was invaded. By the end of the year, plans were set in motion to invade Europe from Britain as a major first step in an all-out offensive against Germany. General Douglas MacArthur, director of the Pacific effort, was also making plans for a comeback.

The war didn't end in 1944, but the going was all downhill that year in both theaters. The Normandy invasion took place in June, paving the way for the ultimate destruction of the German war machine. MacArthur landed in the Philippines and planned an onslaught against Japan. It was a good time for America and a good time for FDR. Whatever his deficiencies as a leader of the economy, he stood tall as a war chief, a proud figure dealing eye to eye with great leaders of the world.

As American troops were busy in both eastern and western theaters of war, so were American scientists busy at home. The super-secret Manhattan Project, first organized in 1942, frantically carried out research into construction of the atomic bomb, a venture that would resonate through the ages. Use of the bomb would eventually end the Japanese conflict.

THE HOME FRONT

American citizens became an integral part of the war effort in 1943 when FDR imposed controls on prices and wages. Also in 1943, the seductive pill that would soon desensitize the public to tax increases slid into the picture — the federal withholding tax, a mechanism that scooped up earnings before they were ever seen.

FDR did not cure the Great Depression with his grand schemes, but the depression numbers did improve on his watch, before the needs of World War II became an economic factor. For example, the unemployment rate was 24.9 percent, 16.9 percent and 14.6 percent in 1933, 1936, and 1940, respectively.[8] Thereafter, war-related production demand gradually pulled the United States out of the economic doldrums and produced in 1944 a 1.2 percent rate of unemployment.

The costs of maintaining a large military force were huge and deficits increased sharply as the war progressed — $20 billion in 1942, $55 billion in 1943 and $48 billion in 1944.[9]

The magnificent American economy responded to the wartime challenge, making the fourfold increase in debt doable and tolerable. For example, in 1940, GDP (Gross Domestic Product) was $97 billion and public debt was 44 percent of that amount; in 1944, GDP was $209 billion and public debt was 88 percent of it.

If America had continued its borrowing rate of 44 percent, debt in 1944 would have amounted to $92 billion instead of the actual amount of $185 billion. America was able to borrow the additional billions because at least half of its borrowing capacity was available at the outbreak of the war and because its economy was booming at an unprecedented rate.

The meaning of this is clear: America's reserve strength for military or economic emergencies is determined in part by the prudent management of its debt during normal times and by the wisdom of its domestic policies that have an impact on economic growth.

Expenditures increased ten times from 1940 to 1944.[10] Everything was moving up, up and up again.

Could America meet a similar emergency to the same degree today? Could it increase spending and debt as it once did, and survive?

FDR, always the master politician, oversaw adoption of the GI Bill of Rights in 1944 — before victory in Europe became final — a federal program that everybody applauded, even those who cynically noted that it was passed in an election year.

Domestically, FDR had all the power that a president could desire. Speaker Sam Rayburn (D–TX) controlled the House, and Alben Barkley (D–KY) served as leader of the Senate — a Democratic administration from top to bottom.

SUPREME COURT[11]

> The Congress shall have the power ... to provide for the ... general Welfare of the United States ... To regulate Commerce ... among the several States.... To make all laws which shall be necessary ... for carrying into Execution the foregoing Powers....— U.S. Constitution, Section 8.
>
> The powers not delegated to the United States by the Constitution ... are reserved to the States respectively, or to the people.— U.S. Constitution, Amendment X

The Tenth Amendment of the Constitution supports the philosophy of limited government, which was the intent of the Founding Fathers. By and large it is a restriction that was accepted by presidents prior to FDR with little complaint.

But for an activist like FDR, faced with a problem such as the Great Depression, it was a legal inhibitor that stood in the way of his grand designs. As a consequence, he waged a running battle with the Supreme Court throughout his first term. The Court, as FDR saw it, attacked his beloved alphabet agencies

(AAA, CCC, FTC, FDIC, FERA, NRA, PWA, TVA, etc.), agencies that he regarded as necessary tools in the fight against the Great Depression.

In 1935, for example, the National Recovery Administration (NRA) was declared unconstitutional; the National Labor Relations Board (NLRB) met the same fate in 1935.

FDR was furious, as only a would-be emperor can be. And in 1937 he tried to expand the size of the Supreme Court, filling it with allies (something he could do because Democrats controlled the Senate.) But that high-handed notion was too much even for some of his supporters. And he backed off—a rare action for him.

Fortunately for FDR, the Constitution also contains Section 8 that serves to challenge the clarity of Amendment X. FDR took full advantage of this for reasons that, arguably, were justified during a Great Depression and a world war. But in so doing he showed the less beleaguered presidents who followed him how to manipulate the Constitution to their advantage.

The issues upon which the Supreme Court ruled are as meaningful today as they were in 1941–44. And the justices who made the rulings were a mixture of men, some of whom supported FDR's leadership style and some who did not. They included Chief Justice Harlan Stone and the nine associates who served with him: Wiley Rutledge, Robert Jackson, James Byrnes, Owen J. Roberts, Frank Murphy, William Douglas, Felix Frankfurter, Stanley Reed and Hugo Black.[12]

Thumbnail sketches of each man appear below:

- Harlan Stone, Chief—Dean of Columbia Law School when appointed by Calvin Coolidge to the bench in 1925; elevated to the role of Chief Justice by FDR in 1941; judicial self-restraint was his credo, one that put him in opposition to his more liberal colleagues and his liberal president; he died suddenly in 1946 and was succeeded by Fred Vinson. Chief Stone handled 11 cases in 1941–44.
- Robert Jackson — IRS legal council, Assistant Attorney General, Solicitor General and Attorney General before being appointed by Roosevelt in 1941 to the bench; served as chief U.S. prosecutor during the Nuremberg Trials; surprisingly conservative for an FDR appointment; died in office, 1954.
- James Byrnes— Byrnes was a lawyer/politician; served in the House and the Senate; FDR considered him (but never chose him) twice as a running mate; reluctantly accepted an appointment to the Court in 1941 but resigned after 16 months; preferred a more active life and later served as Harry Truman's secretary of state.
- Wiley Rutledge — Former dean of the University of Iowa Law School; supported FDR's attempt to stack the Supreme Court; rewarded with an appointment to the U.S. Court of Appeals in 1939 where he con-

tinued to exhibit strong liberal leanings; made a Supreme Court judge by FDR in 1943 (replaced Byrnes); died in office, 1949.
- Owen Roberts— Phi Beta Kappa graduate from the University of Pennsylvania (1895) and law school graduate of the same school in 1898; prestigious private practice before being selected by President Herbert Hoover in 1930; retired in 1945 to become dean of the law school of his alma mater.
- Frank Murphy — Mayor of Detroit, governor general of the Philippines, governor of Michigan and U.S. Attorney General before being appointed by FDR in 1940; he died in office in 1949.
- William Douglas— Served on Securities and Exchange Commission before being appointed to the Court. FDR almost chose him over Truman as his running mate. An unconventional liberal (four marriages) who influenced Court opinions and the nation for almost 37 years, he retired in 1975.
- Felix Frankfurter— Born in Vienna; private practice and U.S. attorney experience before he became secretary of war under President Taft; appointed to the Court in 1938 while a member of the Harvard faculty; an adviser to FDR; a highly articulate liberal; retired in 1962.
- Stanley Reed — Private law practice, bureaucrat, solicitor general before being appointed by FDR in 1938 — a New Deal liberal but disapproved of an overly strict interpretation of the church/state issue; retired in 1957.
- Hugo Black— A lawyer/politician, a New Deal liberal and a dedicated supporter of FDR before moving to the Court in 1937 (FDR's first appointment); retired in 1971, an active liberal to the end.

A few selected cases indicate some of the concerns of the day:

United States v. Darby, 1941. Congress passed a law that was designed to regulate many aspects of employment (minimum wages, maximum hours, child labor, etc.) in companies engaged in interstate commerce. Darby argued that Congress had overstepped its authority to regulate under the Commerce Clause. The unanimous Supreme Court decision affirmed the right of Congress to exercise "to its utmost extent" its powers under the Commerce Clause.

Chaplinsky v. State of New Hampshire, 1942. Chaplinsky called a city marshal "a God-damned racketeer" and "a damned fascist." He was arrested and convicted for violating a breach of the peace. His defense was to claim that his words were protected under the First Amendment —"Congress shall make no law ... abridging the freedom of speech." The Supreme Court ruled that some forms of expression do not have First Amendment protection, among them obscenities and fighting words. Such a ruling today would be considered quaint — a sign of the changed times.

Skinner v. Oklahoma, 1942. Oklahoma law permitted the sterilization of individuals convicted more than three times for "felonies amounting to moral turpitude." The issue: Did the law violate due process and equal protection clauses of the Fourteenth Amendment? The Supreme Court ruled that it did and, further, that any attempt to limit such a fundamental right as the ability to procreate would receive strict scrutiny by the Court. This issue is as pertinent today as it was in 1942.

West Virginia State Board of Ed. v. Barnette, 1943. Saluting the flag was compulsory in West Virginia schools; refusal to obey was treated as "insubordination" punishable by expulsion and charges of delinquency. The rule was challenged. The issue: Does the rule violate the First Amendment? The Court ruled that it did, saying, in effect, that while external signs of patriotism are welcome, they are not compulsory.

These decisions, made over a half-century ago, are as controversial today as they were then.

Prior to 1937, FDR (first elected in 1933) had to contend with the judicial mentality of judges appointed by others, mostly Republicans. But from 1937 on, he gradually replaced those who opposed his vigorous leadership style as being constitutionally invasive with men whose worldview was in accord with his own.

Democrats were supreme in 1944. The presidency, the House, the Senate, and the Supreme Court were headed in the same direction, a formula destined to change the face of America.

Change in Public Debt

During Roosevelt's third term, public debt increased from $42.8 billion to $184.8 billion. From the beginning, American presidents financed wars and great disasters with debt. It was entirely appropriate for FDR to do the same in 1941–44.

Transactions during the period reveal the anatomy of a deficit which grew in four years to more than twice the size of all public debt accumulated during the previous years of American history.

TAXES

The most striking thing about tax income in 1941–44 was its inadequacy relative to the needs of national defense.

The United States entered World War II late in 1941 (Pearl Harbor, Dec. 7, 1941). In 1942, *Defense* increased by $19 billion — tax income increased $6 billion; in 1943, *Defense* went up $42 billion — tax income, $10 billion — and it wasn't until 1947 that total federal income was large enough to cover *Defense*.[14]

The unfunded spending related to war costs, plus funds needed to cover

Table 2.3
Transactions (in billions of dollars)

		1941–44		Base*
Taxes		$ 91.0		$ 26.0
Less:				
Defense	$177.9		$ 6.8	
Interest	5.7		3.6	
Total		183.6		10.4
Net		$-92.6		$ 15.6
Less:				
Government	$ 22.8		$ 11.2	
Human Resources	12.4		16.4	
Total		35.2		27.6
Surplus/deficit		$-127.8		$-12.0
Adjustment[13]		-14.2		
Total		$-142.0		
Debt				
Beginning		-42.8		
Ending		$-184.8		

*1940 figures times four were used to create the base.

Source: Historical Tables 2006, 1.1, 3.1

other budget costs (*Interest, Government, Human Resources*) had to come from an expansion of public debt that, from the end of 1940 to the end of 1944, increased by $142 billion.

This significant expansion of debt was made possible by the fiscal prudence of FDR's predecessors. Had they spent beyond their needs on postponable, discretionary projects, — no matter how noble or worthy they might theoretically be — FDR's ability to borrow would have been less, and America's role in the war may have been less decisive and robust than it was.

FDR's strategy during World War II was to finance the conflict with a mixture of debt, taxes and cost control. Part of his problem was solved when the gross domestic product grew by 115 percent from 1940 to 1944.

The cure for the Great Depression had finally been found, not in the myriad of programs and agencies created by FDR for that purpose, but because of the need to make and send guns, bullets, planes and ships to two theaters of war.

The mighty American economy was on the march and it was the ultimate weapon of war that destroyed the ambitions of Germany's demented political genius, Adolf Hitler.

Taxes did not play a large part in the life of Americans in 1940. Three years later about one-third of their earnings departed untouched and unseen with a one-way ticket to Washington, thanks to the Current Tax Payment Act of 1943[15] that inaugurated the withholding tax system that has been in force ever since.

The passage of that act brought to light a human characteristic that is not edifying: Many people do not pay their share of the tax burden when nobody is looking. The proof: Federal revenue in 1944, which was governed by the same rates in effect in 1943, under the withholding system increased by 82 percent.

GOVERNMENT

The size of *Government* doubled in the same period, a rate of growth permitted by the rate of revenue growth (3.5).[16]

Table 2.4
Government (in billions of dollars)

	1941–44	1937–40	% Change
Energy	$ .4	$ .4	0.0%
Natural Resources/Environment	3.0	4.0	- .3
Commerce & housing credit*	4.8	2.3	108.7
Transportation	8.9	1.6	456.3
Community/regional development	.7	1.1	- .4
International affairs	3.8	.2	190.0
Science/space/technology	.0	.0	0.0
Agriculture	2.3	1.5	53.3
Justice	.6	.3	100.0
General	2.3	1.1	109.1
Total	26.8	12.5	114.4
Offsetting receipts	4.0	1.3	207.7
Net	$22.8	$ 11.1	106.4%

*Made up of earnings from various Federal Housing and other programs— subject to major changes from year to year relative to market conditions. (Historical Tables 2007, 3.2)

Source: Historical Tables 2007, 3.1

Since revenues increased at a faster rate than *Government*, no allocation of deficit to that cost center is appropriate. Further, the major cost increases (e.g., Transportation, International) appear to be war related and not unexpected. There are no signs of promiscuous spending here.

HUMAN RESOURCES

Human Resources actually decreased in 1941–44 and it was in no way involved in the deficit problem for the period. Nevertheless, it is useful to briefly visit the spending ingredients of this cost center in order to deepen one's insight into the spending attitudes of the time.

The following schedule illustrates wartime, tighten-the-belt attitudes about spending. The willingness to allow the maximum amount of current revenue to primary cost centers was commendable, and it minimized the need to borrow.

Table 2.5
Human Resources (in billions of dollars)

	1941–44	1937–40	% Change
Education, training, services	$ 3.4	$ 7.9	-.6%
Health	.4	.2	100.0
Income Security	6.9	6.0	15.0
Social Security	.4	.1	300.0
Veterans	1.3	2.2	-.4
Total	$ 12.4	$ 16.4	-.2

Note: Social Security (started in 1935) was still an infant program and there were few other social programs.

INTEREST

Interest increased substantially during the 1941–44 period, but the rate of increase was less than the rate of revenue increase and no portion of the deficit can be assigned to this cost center.

The increase in *Interest* was solely caused by the increase of 332 percent in the size of the public debt during the period.[17] Fortunately, interest rates remained stable[18] and they did not add a new dimension to the budget pressures.

DEFENSE

Since all cost centers except *Defense* did not add to the deficit, the entire 1941–44 deficit of $127.8 billion is assigned to that cost center. And the indications were that that would primarily be the case for the near future.

Conclusion

The United States was at peace in 1940 with a public debt of about $43 billion and it had a small military force (about 500,000[19]). A year later, FDR took the nation from the Great Depression to World War II, began creation of a national debt of $185 billion and started the buildup of a massive military force of 11 million, all of this in a blink of the historical eye.

America's public debt was about 44 percent of GDP when it entered World War II. In four years, GDP doubled and the debt was almost its equal in size.

The America that FDR led in 1933 was one of many large players on the international scene. But the angry, after being attacked, and newly energized United States, that grew on his watch in 1941–44 charged into World War II as the only nation with the capacity to deliver victory to the Allies—the United States of 1944 was a powerhouse, economically and militarily, ready to take on major global obligations during and after the war.

A lesser man would have paled before the need to plunge the nation so deeply into debt. But FDR charged on with the assurance of one who knew that his mission was a just one. He was a presidential force in terms of popularity and charisma, not seen since Washington, which is why, unlike Washington, he could and he did indulge in a third term and, then, a fourth.

Wars change everything, including how the government spends the tax-payers' money. As the following table shows, the distribution of federal tax spending at the beginning of FDR's third term was nothing like it was at the end.

Table 2.6
Spending Priorities

	1940	1944
Primary costs		
Defense	17.5%	86.7&
Interest	9.5	2.4
Total	27.0%	89.1%
Government	29.3	8.8
Education/services	20.8	0.0
Health/Medicaid	0.6	0.2
Medicare	0.0	0.0
Income Security	16.0	1.6
Social Security	0.3	0.3
Veterans	6.0	0.0
Total	100.0%	100.0%

Source: Historical Tables 2007, 3.1

This table demonstrates better than any collection of words could how much the nation changed in four years, from a crippled, depression-ridden state to a powerful international force, which the Allies looked to for leadership and power.

It took a war to do it, but the Great Depression that started in 1929 was finally over, and the nation that had made a religion out of its isolation from world affairs had become the generally acknowledged leader of the free world.

Many argue that the passage of time and the increasing stability of the world economy were more responsible for lessening the pain of the Great Depression than were FDR's programs. But there is no argument about one thing: FDR made a very public and dramatic attempt to fix the problem and, as he bent his shoulders to the task, he lifted the nation's spirit. He made himself, in the public eye, the happy warrior who would, and did, lead the country into a justifiable war that, as a badly needed side effect, also provided a cure for America's economic ills.

Roosevelt's favorite child, the Social Security Act of 1935 — with its component, Aid to Families with Dependent Children — marked the first major foray of the federal government into the field of social welfare. Together with the inspirational GI Bill of Rights, they present a heroic legacy for historians to ponder, and for liberals to admire.

But there is a dark side to the FDR legacy that conservatives have no difficulty finding. Tax policies introduced during the depression changed the face of America by establishing as a matter of law a society of classes, known as tax brackets, within which the income and wealth of one class (tax bracket) can be taxed differently from those in the other classes (brackets).

The progressive rate tax system is an FDR invention, plus the inheritance, estate, gift and dividend taxes. Those creations, arguably needed during the depression, have been resented ever since by many because of their disruptive social impact and because of, in some cases (for example, the inheritance tax), the intrinsic unfairness of the tax.

Without those taxes, and the withholding system (1943) that mutes the impact of tax increases on wages, it is highly probable that the politicians who followed FDR would have been unable to raid the federal pantry as they have.

Social Security, arguably the most beloved of federal programs, also has a dark side. Its financing mechanism (the payroll tax) is flawed to a degree that will become increasingly recognizable in subsequent chapters of this book.

Social Security, disability pensions, helping veterans and students and soothing the pains of unemployment have, over time, been accepted, even by conservatives, as proper roles for Washington. But the ideas that supported such worthy programs were later seized upon by others, and they were expanded to embrace any hardship suffered by American citizens, an evolutionary result of which FDR might or might not have approved.

FDR left behind a debt of $184.8 billion in 1944, a problem that he had managed during the early stages of the war, and one that would remain with him until the end.

Table 2.7
Public Debt, 1944
(billions)

Event	Inherited	Added 1941–44	Total 1944	%
World War I	$ 18.3	$	$ 18.3	9.9%
Great Depression	24.5		24.5	13.3
World War II		127.8	127.8	69.2
Defense				
Interest				
Government				
Human Resources				
Treasury, net		14.2	14.2	7.6
Total	$ 42.8	$142.0	$184.8	100.0%

Source: Exhibits 1, 11, 12, 16

Can FDR be held responsible for the extrapolations of his students that have led to the debt crisis? On that question debate will never end.

Like Winston Churchill in Great Britain, Roosevelt's reputation as a war leader tends to bolster the value of his efforts in other matters. He was America's greatest cheerleader at home and abroad at a time when the nation needed such a man. If he didn't defeat the Great Depression — and he didn't — he did defeat other dragons of equal size.

3

Franklin D. Roosevelt and Harry S Truman, 1945–1948

The Last Days of FDR

In 1944, Franklin D. Roosevelt was reelected to a fourth term, a circumstance that led to the Twenty-second Amendment (1951), which prohibits more than two consecutive terms.

FDR was sick, a shadow of the man with the exuberant personality who had charmed the American public for so many years. His intimates, perhaps he himself, knew his days were numbered when on January 20, 1945, he took the familiar oath of office. "We have learned to be citizens of the world," he said in his inaugural address, referring to lessons learned during World War II. "The only way to have a friend is to be one," he said in a simple comment that laid the foundation for the Marshall Plan, the brilliant idea that under Harry Truman made possible the recovery of war-ravaged Europe.

FDR cast a large shadow and attained an international reputation that few before or after him have enjoyed. He was the only president most American soldiers had ever known. He died in April 1945. Vice President Harry Truman succeeded him.

Sam Rayburn, a Democrat from Texas, was the House Speaker; Joseph Martin, a Republican from Massachusetts, replaced him in 1947–48. Alben Barkley, a Democrat from Kentucky, was majority leader in the Senate, and Wallace White, a Republican from Minnesota, held that position in 1947–48.[1]

Public debt stood at $184.8 billion at the beginning of FDR's last term, as follows in Table 3.1.

In 1944 it was accurate to explain America's debt in terms of external events. Soon, however, internal attitudes were shaped by the British economist John Maynard Keynes (1883–1946), and his aggressive theories concerning the role of a central government.[2] Generally speaking, Keynes favored an activist government, a creed that appealed to FDR. This point of view was the opposite

Table 3.1
Public Debt, 1944
(in billions of dollars)

Event	Total	%
World War I	$ 18.3	9.9%
Great Depression	24.5	13.2
World War II	127.8	69.2
Treasury	14.2	7.7
Total	$184.8	100.0%

Source: Exhibits 1, 11, Chapter 2, Table 2.1

of that preached by Adam Smith (1723–90), the Scottish guru whose more conservative ideas had guided earlier presidents.

Given the fascination that politicians have for spending and the loose controls over it that existed, it was deeply troubling to see an economic philosophy appear that gave intellectual support to their greatest weakness; it was frightening to consider that the advice to presidents and congressmen of the future would inspire the spenders, and increasingly invite them to indulge in even more economic engineering in the private sector.

Here began the separation of modern America from its roots; here began the establishment of the thought process that would separate FDR and his later followers from the Founding Fathers; here began the collision of FDR with his ancestors, whose attitudes toward government intervention were perhaps best summed up by Thomas Paine, who said that government is best which governs least. FDR, and the flotilla of big spenders who followed him for the next half century disagreed, with, as you will see, disastrous consequences.

Perspectives

GENERAL

War in Europe was in its mop-up stage. And in the Pacific theater, General Douglas MacArthur, like an inspired running back, whirled and weaved his way through Japan's Pacific strongholds to the heart of his enemy — Tokyo.

Events moved swiftly. FDR died in April and, in the same month, Hitler committed suicide. In May, Germany surrendered; Japan did the same in September. War ended and reconstruction began.[3]

In 1946, war in both theaters moved into history as signs of "getting on with it" appeared all over the globe. The United Nations General Assembly held its first meeting in London. The Nuremberg war crimes trials began and ended. In 1947 the Marshall Plan, an American idea to get Europe back on its feet, came into being.

Relations with Russia, tenuous throughout the war, fell apart afterward when the Soviets blocked the flow of supplies to Berlin. America responded with an airlift program that lasted for almost a year.

THE HOME FRONT

Defense spending peaked in 1945 ($83 billion); two years later it was 85 percent lower.[4] Wartime price and wage controls were dropped. Pent-up demand and other factors gave President Truman an inflation problem. These and other events of significance substantially changed the financial profile of the United States.

GDP grew by 32 percent from 1944 to 1948, but the growth was an illusion because of inflation — in adjusted dollars, GDP actually decreased during that period.[5]

By 1948, the Misery Index had increased from 4 percent to 14 percent,[6] a sign that, during this cooling-down period, America was experiencing bumps in the road as its wartime production muscle slowly turned toward butter and away from guns.

A livable unemployment rate of 4 percent in 1948 heartened those who wondered if America could be economically healthy in peacetime. And the relationship of revenue to expenditures in 1948 (a surplus of $12 billion)[7] gave hope that public debt could be reduced to even lower levels that would allow future presidents maximum flexible spending options when confronted by another economic or physical war.

Average income per capita in 1948 was 21 percent higher than it was four years earlier,[8] but the benefits of the increase to the worker were sharply reduced by the inflation rate during the period.

SUPREME COURT[9]

A total of 11 justices participated in Supreme Court rulings during the 1945–48 period[10]: Chief Justice Harlan Stone, who was succeeded by Fred Vinson, plus associate justices from the previous Court, Wiley Rutledge, Robert Jackson, Frank Murphy, William Douglas, Felix Frankfurter, Stanley Reed, Hugo Black and Owen Roberts, who was succeeded by Harold Burton.

The two new faces were Fred Vinson, the new Chief Justice, and Harold Burton, who succeeded Owen Roberts.

A thumbnail sketch of both men appears below:

- Fred Vinson, Chief — Congressman, bureaucrat, U.S. Court of Appeals, and secretary of the treasury when appointed to the bench in 1946 by President Harry Truman; a New Deal loyalist who succeeded the conservative Harlan Stone, thus adding a leftward tilt to the Court; died in office in 1953 of a heart attack. Chief Justices Stone and Vinson heard eight cases in 1945–48.

• Harold Burton — Harvard Law School, a lawyer and the mayor of Cleveland when appointed to the bench in 1945 by President Truman; a liberal who replaced the more conservative Owen Roberts, which moved the Court even farther to the left.

A few cases from the period appear below that provide a sampling of the judicial mind-set on issues so relevant today that they could appear on tomorrow's docket.

Everson v. Board of Education, 1946. State law permitted all parents, including Catholic parents, to be reimbursed for the cost of public busing to school. The issue: Did the reimbursement to Catholic parents violate the First Amendment? In a 5–4 decision the state law was validated. This issue in different forms continues to haunt the halls of U.S. courts.

McCollum v. Board of Education, 1947. A Council made up of Jews, Catholics and Protestants offered voluntary religious classes that were conducted in regular public school classrooms. The issue: Did this practice violate the First Amendment? In an 8–1 decision the Court ruled that the voluntary practice was unconstitutional. This is the Court, dominated by Roosevelt and Truman judges, that put into place the interpretation of the First Amendment that outlawed God in the public school system.

Shelley v. Kraemer, 1948. A black couple moved into a neighborhood governed by a restrictive covenant that prevented blacks from moving in. The state enforced the covenant. The issue: Was the state's action constitutional? In a 6–0 decision the Court ruled that the state violated the Fourteenth Amendment.

Lincoln Union v. NW Metal, 1949. State law prohibited employment discrimination relative to union membership. Unions objected. The issue? Is the state law constitutional? In a unanimous decision the Court supported the state.

At the end of 1948, after the replacement of Harlan Stone and Owen Roberts with Fred Vinson and Harold Burton, the Court was clearly dominated by justices who shared the worldview of FDR and Truman.

Change in Public Debt

Officially, FDR began his fourth term in 1945, but he died in the April of his inauguration year and, for the most part, the presidential seat was occupied by his vice president and successor, Harry S Truman. Public debt, under Truman's supervision, grew from $185 billion to $216 billion.[11] War costs were the root cause of the debt increase.[12]

By the end of 1948, budget surpluses suggested that the upward trend of public debt was coming to a close.[13] World War II was over; normalcy was around the corner.

Transactions shown below indicate that while the times were still difficult, change was in the wind and responsible fiscal management could result in dramatic debt reductions over the near term.

Table 3.2
Transactions (in billions of dollars)

		1945–48		1941–44*
Taxes		$ 164.6		$ 91.0
Less:				
Defense	$147.6		$177.9	
Interest	15.7		5.7	
Total		$ 163.3		$ 183.6
Net		$ 1.3		$ -92.6
Less:				
Government	$ 21.7		$ 22.8	
Human Resources	27.1		12.4	
Total		48.8		35.2
Surplus/deficit		$ -47.6		$-127.8
Debt, beginning		-184.8		-42.8
Total		$-232.4		$-170.6
Adjustment†		16.1		-14.2
Debt, Ending		$-216.3		$-184.8

*1940 figures times four were used to create the base.
†Treasury cannot be exact when it finances a budget deficit and the difference between what is needed and the value of securities traded inevitably produces a relatively small variance.

Source: Historical Tables 2006, 1.1, 3.1

When the war ended in 1945, it became the lot of Harry Truman to assist the Allies in their rehabilitation attempts while, at the same time, he attempted to guide America from a wartime to a peacetime economy and, as shall be seen, to further the FDR agenda while wartime tax receipts were still pouring into federal coffers.

Reducing the military, dealing with returning veterans, and loosening wartime controls all fed into spending plans of the federal government — a difficult process to control.

The numbers in the above table clearly demonstrate that the needs, challenges and attitudes of the time were as radically different from the previous four years as were the postwar political leaders who handled them. Transactions for the period represent an early snapshot of the new world in which Harry Truman operated and they hint at the fiscal world to come.

TAXES

Revenue continued to increase in 1945. But it dropped by about 15 percent in 1946, and remained relatively stable for the next two years, reflecting the stabilization of an economy that was feeling its way toward peacetime production.

The overall effect was to increase revenue in 1945–48 (a period of high to low income) by 80.9 percent[14] over 1941–44 (a period of low to high revenue).

The top personal income tax rate dropped from 94 percent to 82 percent in 1945–48, and the top corporate rate dropped from 40 percent to 38 percent.[15]

Federal revenue in 1947, for the first time since 1941,[16] was greater than the cost of *Defense*, which was still a major cost, and was trending down, for the whole period. Lowering *Defense* costs lessened the fiscal pressures during 1945–48, but total tax revenue was still less than the inherited cost structure.

It is not surprising, therefore, that a sizable deficit was reported. The good news is that the deficit was 63 percent lower, and trending down, a sign that debt reduction was on the horizon.

Taxes collected from individuals and from corporations in 1948 were lower than in 1944, an indication that a new tax policy for peacetime was moving into place.[17]

The reduction in federal revenue due to rate reductions appears modest because inflation during the period bloated wages and the taxes withheld therefrom.

Taxes are paid by people. Even corporate taxes (which some pundits sell as a tax on the "rich") find their way into the cost stream and reappear to taxpayers in the form of higher prices or lower wages.

In 1948, taxpayers got a break. The part of a week's pay sent to Washington dropped from $319 in 1944 to $286 in 1948, a drop of about 10 percent. In 1944 the average worker sent more than 14 weekly paychecks to Uncle Sam, in 1948, less than 11 weeks.[18] Times were improving.

GOVERNMENT

The cost of *Government* actually dropped in 1945–48 and was, therefore, not a contributor to the deficit for the period. It is nevertheless useful to look behind the overall numbers to gain insight into the thinking of the contemporary politicians. How were they handling this transition from war to peace? What were they doing with the excess revenues?

These are questions that needed answers, and the net result of the deliberations of congressmen, namely, spending, is one way to get them.

The drop in spending would have been more substantial had it not been for the cost of rebuilding Europe, a venture in which America participated via the Marshall Plan (1947). Except for the line item of International Affairs, the cost performance in this cost center was not troubling during the subject period.

The rate of cost increase in Agriculture and Justice merits attention, but it is too early to levy a charge of promiscuous spending. This cost center was not a major problem in 1945–48.

Table 3.4
Government (in billions of dollars)

	1945–48	1941–44	% Change
Energy	$ .4	$ .4	0.0%
Natural Resources/Environment	2.4	3.0	-20.0
Transportation	7.6	8.9	-14.6
Community/regional development	.8	.7	14.3
International affairs	14.2	3.8	273.7%
Science/space/technology	.2	.0	
Agriculture	3.1	2.3	34.8
Justice	.8	.6	33.3
General	3.5	2.3	52.2
Total	$33.0	$22.0	50.0%
Commerce & housing credit*	- 5.1	4.8	106.3
Total	$27.9	$26.8	4.1
Offsetting receipts	6.1	4.0	52.5
Net	$21.8	$22.8	- 4.4%

*Made up of earnings from various federal housing and other programs—subject to major changes from year to year relative to market conditions. (Historical Tables 2007, 3.2)

Source: Historical Tables 2007, 3.1

HUMAN RESOURCES

Human Resources was not a cost center of unusual importance during this time frame. The Social Security program was still in its infancy and the range of other social services emanating from Washington was, compared to what it would later become, limited.

The cost of operating this center in 1945–48 increased by 118.5 percent, well above the rate of revenue increase (80.9 percent). This means that some spending in this cost center was not funded by revenue — to the extent of $4.8 billion.[19]

Table 3.5
Human Resources (in billions of dollars)

	1945–48	1941–44	% Change
Education, training, services	$ .4	$ 3.4	-11.8%
Health	.8	.4	100.0
Income Security	8.9	6.9	29.0
Social Security	1.6	.4	300.0
Veterans	15.4	1.3	1084.6
Total	$27.1	$ 12.4	118.5%

Note: Social Security (started in 1935) was still an infant program and there were few other social programs.

Source: Historical Tables 2007, 3.1

One cannot quibble over spending for Veterans during and after a war. Over 16 million men/women served in World War II, over 400,000 were killed, almost 700,000 were wounded, and about 15 million returned whole, many of whom would be welcomed into the arms of FDR's GI Bill of Rights (1944)[20] which, among other things, made available college educations to many who otherwise would never have embarked on such a career-building journey.

The other changes were either inconspicuous or they were less than the rate of change in revenue with one very large exception: Social Security went up 300 percent. At this time the program should have been reevaluated, not for worthiness, but from the standpoint of stability. The question should have been asked: Can it be financed some other way? But it wasn't — and it never has been.

INTEREST

The cost of World War II borrowings hit the federal budget hard in 1945–48, one of many possible examples of how the policies of a predecessor president — justified or not — can have great impact on the fiscal fortunes of the current one.

Public debt was relatively low until 1943. Over the 1945–1948 period, however, debt climbed from $128 billion in 1943 to $216 billion in 1948; interest rates went up and the combination produced a total cost of *Interest* that was 175 percent higher than the previous period, as opposed to a revenue increase of 80.9 percent. This means that the growth in this cost center was greater than the growth in revenue and contributed to the deficit — to the extent of $5.7 billion.

DEFENSE

Military spending decreased from $83 billion in 1945 to $9 billion in 1948, an institution-breaking level of cutbacks that did not seem to fit the times (the Soviet Union was a looming threat), and one that Truman would soon regret.

The allocation of a deficit amount to *Defense* is more easily handled as a matter of logic than as a calculation that would do no more than prove the obvious, which is this:

- A deficit of $47.6 billion was the result of the 1945–48 government operation.
- To the extent that the deficit was not caused by unfunded spending in the *Government, Human Resources and Interest* cost centers, it must be assigned to the only remaining cost center, *Defense*.
- There was unfunded spending of $4.8 billion in *Human Resources*, and $5.4 billion in *Interest* — a total of $10.2 billion
- Therefore, the remaining deficit of $37.4 billion is assigned to *Defense*.

The war was over and in 1948 *Defense* spending approached prewar levels. The budget numbers seemed to say that America had disarmed into a peaceful world. But this attitude was unrealistic, given the troublesome noises emanating from the Soviet Union. The United States should have kept its guard up to confront developments that were not difficult to see in 1948.

Conclusion

FDR lived for four months into his fourth term, time enough to leave behind a "thank you" to war veterans that in one form or another is with us today: the GI Bill of Rights, legislation that voiced the approval of American citizens to their fighters in the form of housing, education, employment and health assistance.

The major fear and the greatest surprise of the 1945–48 period related to Harry Truman. To some extent, modern-day Americans can relate to the notion of a beloved president because they remember Ronald Reagan, who in 1984 won 59 percent of the popular vote and 98 percent of the electoral vote.

FDR was even more popular in the 1936 election when he secured 61 percent of the popular vote and 98 percent of the electoral vote. And FDR's hold on the public had endurance. In his fourth presidential race in 1944, the rapidly aging chief executive gained 53 percent of the popular vote and 81 percent of the electoral vote — the nation still supported him just before his death.[21]

When he died so abruptly just a few months after his inauguration, "shock" is the only way to describe the impact on the nation, most especially on the nation's troops. To many, he was the president, the only president to have made an impact on their lives. So it was with a worried eye that they looked at his successor, Vice President Harry S Truman.

Who was he? Could he step into FDR's huge shoes? Could he direct the war and meet with world leaders with comparable, even acceptable dignity? These were the questions in people's minds as Truman took the oath of office. And what did they see?— An inconspicuous politician from Missouri who had not been among FDR's close advisers.

But Truman fooled the world (and perhaps himself) when he took the helm and managed the affairs of government with skill, decisiveness and class both during and after the war.

Ordering the use of the atomic bomb was the wartime action that will forever be attached to his name, just as will the Marshall Plan (1947) in the postwar period, an exercise in American support for a ravaged Europe that made possible the recovery of badly damaged but highly valued economies and cultures.

The Misery Index (the total of interest, inflation and unemployment rates) took a dive to 4.4 percent in 1944 (during the war) and grew to 13.9 percent in 1948, as all three elements surged during the changeover years.

But there was also a sign of better times ahead. Instead of a horrendous decline in GDP that many expected when wartime production was discontinued, it stood at 22 percent higher in 1948 than in 1944 in current dollars, and only 8 percent down in inflation adjusted dollars. This meant that the enormously elastic U.S. economy was rapidly and successfully adjusting to the new economic realities.

Once again the spending habits of the U.S. government experienced a sea change as the nation lurched from a fighting stance to a peacetime mode. The 1945–48 period had some of both, which masks the drift of the budget numbers, but the comparison between what the United States had been and what it had become continues to fascinate.

Table 3.6
Spending Priorities

	1940	1944	1948
Primary costs			
Defense	17.5%	86.7%	30.5%
Interest	9.5	2.4	14.4
Total	27.0%	89.1%	44.9%
Government	29.3	8.8	21.9
Education/services	20.8	0.0	.6
Health/Medicaid	0.6	0.2	.5
Medicare	0.0	0.0	0.0
Income Security	16.0	1.6	8.4
Social Security	0.3	0.3	12.6
Veterans	6.0	0.0	5.9
Total	100.0%	100.0%	100.0%

Source: Historical Tables 2007, 3.1

At the height of its military power in 1945, *Defense* and *Interest* costs comprised 93 percent of the federal budget,[22] but by 1948 their combined cost was halved as the country wrenched itself back into a peacetime posture, never again to be what it had been and resembling little what it was to become.

Priorities at the conclusion of the FDR/Truman era were remarkably different as the United States reassessed its new role at home (a more intrusive government) and abroad (a world leader).

The change in all cost centers was dramatic. *Defense* was lower for obvious reasons. Higher *Interest* was no surprise, given more debt and rising inflation.

Changes in the relative size of *Government* and *Human Resources* produced confusion at this stage and time would be needed to provide clarity. Much would depend upon the attitudes of the governing politicians as they confronted the options of either reducing spending, debt and taxes or spending more on social problems, Rooseveltian style.

And so ended the World War II era and, with it, the passing of its leading players—FDR, Hitler, Mussolini, dead in 1945; Churchill, replaced in 1945; Tojo, dead in 1946. Of the war leaders, only Stalin remained.

The huge presence of FDR was gone, the man with the grand ideas of an activist government, moved to the pages of history. He had dominated the American stage for 13 years and he left behind a political philosophy that, through his apostles, led to the expansion of the size and the duties of federal government until the 1980s and the ascendancy of Ronald Reagan.

For so long as stories are told about the Great Depression or World War II and for so long as Social Security checks are issued each month, the memory of FDR will be kept alive.

Harry Truman replaced FDR and surprised everybody with his courage and the ability he showed during his shared presidency. He earned the respect of Americans; he was a proven leader when he took to the hustings in 1948 in search of his own administration for the next four years. Few gave Truman a chance to win that election because the economy was not performing well, and because his opponent, Governor Thomas E. Dewey from New York, was a highly regarded politician and was far more polished than was the president. But give-'em-hell Truman had a few more surprises up his sleeve. He won the election and assumed a public debt, which can be summarized as follows:

Table 3.7
Public Debt, 1948
(in billions of dollars)

Event	Inherited 1944	Added 1945–1948	Total	%
World War I	$ 18.3	$	$ 18.3	8.5%
Great Depression	24.5		24.5	11.3
World War II	127.8	37.4	165.2	76.4
Interest		5.4	5.4	2.5
Human Resources		4.8	4.8	2.2
Treasury	14.2	-16.1	-1.9	-.9
Total	$184.8	$ 31.5	$216.3	100.0%

Source: Exhibits 1, 11.1

The war was over. It was expected that debt would be reduced over the next four years.

4

Harry S Truman, 1949–1952

Businessman, Judge, Senator, President

Chester Arthur was president in 1884 when Harry S Truman was born in Lamar, Missouri, at the family home.

Truman's father, John (1851–1914), was a farmer. After his marriage to Martha Ellen Young (1852–1947), John Truman left the family farm in Jackson County, Missouri, and he established his own place in Lamar with his bride.

The parents survived lean days and they provided a secure home life for their three children, the oldest of whom was Harry S. The "S" in his name was not the first letter of his middle name, as is the normal custom. The single letter was his full middle name.

John Truman, given to speculating on commodities, took a financial bath in 1901. After working at odd jobs, he established a second farm in 1904, but that did not work out either, and in 1906 he moved himself and his family into his mother-in-law's farm near Grandview, Missouri.

Harry Truman went to grade school and high school in Independence, Missouri. Known as a hardworking student, he was considering college and a possible career as a musician (he was an accomplished pianist) after leaving high school in 1901. But his father's financial troubles put an end to those dreams. He went to work as a timekeeper.

Theodore Roosevelt was president at the time, and the public debt was $2.1 billion.

For the next five years, Truman held nondescript jobs in Kansas City until, in 1906, family troubles pulled him in a different direction.

His father could not run the Grandview farm alone, so Truman returned home only to be faced with another stroke of bad luck that seemed to pull him even closer to an unselected career as a farmer — his father injured himself in 1914 while working and he died soon after, never suspecting that his 30-year-old son would one day become the thirty-third president of the United States. Truman's mother, Martha, lived long enough to see her son succeed Franklin Roosevelt.

Harry Truman had one prestigious relative: John Tyler was his great-uncle.

Managing the farm became Truman's problem after his father's death, and there he remained until World War I beckoned. He joined the army in 1917, but not before demonstrating that he was his father's son. In 1915 and 1916 he absorbed sizable losses from speculative ventures involving lead, zinc and oil.

Truman was 33 years old in 1917. Woodrow Wilson was president, and the public debt was $5.7 billion.

Truman served with the Missouri National Guard in 1905–11, and when he joined the army in 1917, it was with the rank of lieutenant. He had an honorable military career and at the end of the war he commanded his own artillery unit. He was discharged as a major in 1919 and he returned home to establish a haberdashery in Kansas City. He was 35 years old.

Woodrow Wilson was still president. Public debt, reflecting the costs of war, had risen to $27.4 billion, the highest in American history to that point — about five times the 1917 level.

Marriage to his childhood sweetheart, Elizabeth Virginia Wallace (1885–1982) was the main event in 1919 for Truman. A product of finishing schools, Elizabeth never fully approved of Truman's later political career, not even when he won the presidency. He probably spent more nights alone in the White House than any married president in history.

Truman's political career began when in 1922 his haberdashery business failed. His road to success was slow but consistent. In 1922 he was elected as a county judge. This put him in the political loop controlled by Thomas Pendergast, a controversial political operator who was to become an influential backer of Truman's career.

To equip himself for his new work, Truman attended Kansas City Law School (1923–25). He continued to grow in influence in local politics until, in 1934, he ran against and defeated incumbent senator Roscoe Patterson — he was 50 years old. Franklin Roosevelt was president. The public debt was $27.1 billion, about the same as it was when Truman had left the army in 1919.

In 1944, after a decade of solid service in the U.S. Senate that had made him a national figure, Truman reluctantly agreed to share the Democratic ticket with FDR in his successful campaign for a fourth term.

In April 1945, Roosevelt died and was replaced by Harry S Truman, who served as a surprisingly valiant and capable leader who will forever be remembered as the man who ended World War II by unleashing the atomic bomb against Japan (the enemy that would not surrender) and as the president who authorized the Marshall Plan under which Europe was rebuilt.

Truman ran under his own banner in 1948 and, contrary to the predictions of the pundits, he defeated the heavy favorite, Thomas Dewey, by two million votes.

Harry S Truman, the man who fired Douglas MacArthur (1951) (the

national hero who opposed Truman's war policies) retired in 1952 to Independence, Missouri, where in 1972 he died after several years of illness.

Public debt was $216.3 billion in 1948, summarized as follows:

Table 4.1
Public Debt, 1948

Event	Total 1948	%
World War I	$ 18.3	8.4%
Great Depression	24.5	11.3
World War II	165.2	76.4
Interest	5.4	2.5
Human Resources	4.8	2.2
Treasury	-1.9	-.8
Total	$216.3	100.0%

Source: Exhibit 1, 11, 12, 16

Truman avoided a budget deficit in 1949–52. The pay-as-you-go policies
originally imposed by the Republican-led Congress of 1947–48 continued (with
a blip in 1950) under Democrats until, in 1952, the costs of the Korean War
brought deficits back.

The Korean War (1950–53) returned America to a wartime footing and
thwarted whatever plans Truman had to substantially add to the social programs of FDR. He and the Congress supported both the war and the government with current tax revenues, and to that extent they deserve credit.

But did the war-conscious public realize that domestic spending was bur-
geoning during the conflict? Would Americans have tolerated the high taxes
needed to fund social programs absent the camouflage of a war?

No president acts alone. What he does greatly depends upon those with
whom he must deal in Congress. Those who appraise the results of a president's
term must give weight to the influence of congressional leaders as well. Sam
Rayburn (D–TX) had firm control in the House; Scott Lucas (D–IL) and Ernest
McFarland (D–AZ) acted as Senate leaders.

Democrats enjoyed full control of the government under Truman, but he
did not get full support for his Fair Deal programs. For example, his proposal
for national health insurance failed, an elusive cause that liberals have continued to pursue into the twenty-first century.

Congress in those days contained within it men with strong conservative
impulses in both parties whose memories reached back to a time when fiscal
integrity was deemed a virtue. Their careers were nearing an end when Truman retired and the Democrats of the future would prove to be more attentive
to their own career objectives, and less admiring of the ideas that moved the
Founding Fathers and the presidents who followed them — the men who had
made America great.

Perspectives

GENERAL

Truman began his second term in peace and he left it in war. Tension in Korea exploded in his second year. *Defense*, down (unwisely) to $9.1 billion in 1948, increased fivefold during the Korean War to $46.1 billion in 1952.[1]

The Soviet Union was considered to be dangerous enough by the Allies for them to form in 1949 the North Atlantic Treaty Organization (NATO),[2] a formidable defensive tool composed of 12 nations.

This seemed justified when the Soviet Union demonstrated its own atomic weapon in late 1949, thus electing itself to the exclusive atomic club despite the attempts of America to contain atomic weapons (and thanks to an assist from American traitors).

Truman replied in 1950 with a program designed to build the hydrogen bomb. In the same year, North Korean Communists invaded South Korea. America, with United Nations assistance, responded. And the ongoing war was a part of Truman's legacy that was handed to his successor, Dwight D. Eisenhower.

THE HOME FRONT

After a slow start in 1949, the GDP bounced back in 1950, and by 1952 it was 36 percent higher than it was four years before.[3] The American economic engine was on the move again and it was reflected in federal revenues, which in 1952 were 59 percent higher than in 1948.[4]

Truman increased taxes across the board, personal, corporate and Social Security.[5] But:

- Were the increased taxes used for war or for social programs?
- Were the people aware of how their government was expanding behind the cloud of war?
- Was the possibility of shrinking government considered as an alternative to higher taxes?

Questions such as these will be probed in the upcoming analysis.

Working with a Democratic majority, Truman reduced the size of public debt in relation to GDP from 84 percent to 62 percent.[6] That is commendable. But the question is: Could it have been more? Upcoming analysis will also seek an answer to that question.

The Korean War was financed with current revenues. This too appears commendable, but not so surprising when one remembers that federal revenues from World War II taxes were still pouring in, that tax rates were climbing and that the war in Korea did not require the level of financial support that World War II did.

Nevertheless, this at the least must be said for the Truman administration: It recognized that some level of debt was too high. It is important to remember that this was the mental cast of the politicians of that age, a frame of mind that would not last too much longer.

The "misery" index in 1948 was 13.9 percent; in 1952 it was 7.6 percent — a major improvement. Unemployment and inflation were down, but the cost of money was continuing on its upward path.[7]

Average income per capita in 1952 was 19 percent higher than it was in 1948,[8] but inflation, higher interest and higher taxes reduced the apparently healthy increase.

Supreme Court[9]

The days of all-out conflict with the Supreme Court typical of FDR's early years were a thing of the past to Harry Truman. Court membership had evolved into an entity that was more cordial toward initiatives of the federal government, and there was not the need to test the boundaries of the Constitution in 1949–52 that had existed during the era of the Great Depression.

Fred Vinson was the Chief Justice for the entire 1949–52 period during which he participated in 11 cases[10] (the reason for tracking Chief Justice case activity will become clear to readers as they progress through this book).

Vinson was joined by former members, Justices Burton, Rutledge, Jackson, Murphy, Douglas, Frankfurter, Reed and Black. And two new men appeared: Sherman Minton, who replaced Rutledge (nominated by FDR), and Tom Clark, who replaced Murphy (nominated by FDR).

A thumbnail portrait of the new men appears below.

- Sherman Minton — A strong supporter of FDR and a personal friend of Harry Truman who was appointed by FDR to the U.S. Court of Appeals, Seventh Circuit, before Truman in 1949 made him a Supreme Court judge; ill health forced Minton's retirement in 1956; while serving he was not the activist that his supporters expected him to be.
- Tom Clark — A Texas politician who joined the Justice Department in 1937 before Truman in 1945 made him Attorney General, and in 1949 a Supreme Court justice. Truman regretted his choice and once referred to Justice Clark as "the dumbest sonofabitch I ever met." Clark resigned in 1967 when President Lyndon B. Johnson, a fellow Texan, made his son, Ramsey, his Attorney General. Ramsey Clark (still alive in 2007) turned out to be one of the most radical anti–American activists of modern times — one of Saddam Hussein's defense attorneys (2006–07).

The Truman administration was blighted by the anticommunist attitudes that swept the nation, a reaction to the activity of the Soviets in international affairs and in the arms race. By this time it was the increasingly accepted wisdom that the Soviet Union was the enemy that America would one day have to face.[11]

The activities of Senator Joe McCarthy (R–WI, 1947–57) helped to leave the impression that the Truman administration was soft on communism, and that it was riddled with spies. And Truman's defense wasn't helped when Julius Rosenberg (a government employee) and his wife Ethel were arrested in 1950 by the FBI as spies (executed in 1953).

Given this background one would expect to find cases concerning communism on the Supreme Court docket, but the other issues of the day were very much like they are today. A few cases are summarized below that give a feel for the concerns of the time.

Terminiello v. Chicago, 1949. A priest delivered a vitriolic political speech that angered the crowd and resulted in several disturbances. The police arrested the priest and charged him with "a breach of the peace." The issue: Was the priest's right of free expression under the First Amendment violated? In a 5–4 decision, the Court ruled in favor of the priest. Chief Vinson and Associate Justices Frankfurter, Jackson and Burton dissented.

Sweatt v. Painter, 1950. A black man applied for admission to a law school that was available to whites only. The university made the attempt to provide him with separate but equal facilities. The issue: Did the separate but equal proposal resolve the black man's rights under the Fourteenth Amendment? The Court ruled unanimously in favor of the black man — the university had to admit him.

Dennis v. U.S., 1950. Leaders of the Communist Party were arrested for violation of the Smith Act, which made it unlawful to knowingly teach, conspire or advocate the destruction of the U.S. government. State courts found them guilty. The issue: Do the restrictions enumerated in the Smith Act violate the First Amendment right to free speech? In a 6–2 decision the Court upheld the conviction and noted that "advocacy" was the key charge because it presented a "clear and present danger" to the nation. Justices Black and Douglas dissented.

Zorach v. Clauson, 1952. A state program permitted public school students to be excused from school so that they could attend religious classes elsewhere. The issue: Does this practice violate the establishment clause of the First Amendment? In a 6–2 decision the Court upheld the school program. Justice Douglas argued: Government should not be hostile to religion or oppose efforts designed to widen the influence of religious instruction. Justices Black and Frankfurter dissented.

Terminiello and *Dennis* present cases that bring out the important difference between pure speech and speech with an anti–American agenda. These issues continue to appear in the Court.

Sweatt and *Zorach* present two different issues that are also with us today:

the right of a black man (a minority) to an equal education, and the right of the religious community to pray in a manner that is not coercive.

All cases at the Supreme Court level deal with issues that touch America's heartbeat and, for that reason alone, are worth reviewing.

Change in Public Debt

The possibility of debt reduction appeared to be good when Harry Truman began his first solo term as an elected president. *Defense* spending was over $70 billion less than it was at the height of the war and in 1947 and 1948 the federal budget yielded surpluses.

But external events would demonstrate that the precipitous stripping of the U.S. military machine had been a mistake and that a costly job of rebuilding it was necessary.

Trouble loomed in Korea and the spending on *Defense* in the United States increased in 1950 by about 50 percent to meet it.[12] And out the window went the drive to reduce debt. The remainder of Truman's term was dominated by the Korean War (1950–53).[13]

Under remarkably different circumstances, Truman managed an overall budget surplus in 1949–52 — a deficit in the first two years of $2.5 billion and a surplus over the final two years of $4.5 billion.

Federal transactions for the period are summarized below.

Table 4.2
Transactions (in billions of dollars)

		1949–52		1945–48
Taxes		$ 196.6		$ 164.6
Less:				
Defense	$ 96.6		$147.6	
Interest	18.7		15.7	
Total		115.3		163.3
Net		$ 81.3		$ 1.3
Less:				
Government	$ 31.6		$ 21.7	
Human Resources	47.7		27.1	
Total		79.3		48.8
Surplus/deficit		$ 2.0		$ -47.5
Debt, beginning		-216.3		-184.8
Total		$-214.3		$-232.3
Adjustment*		-.5		16.0
Debt, Ending		$-214.8		$-216.3

*Treasury cannot be exact when it finances a budget deficit and the difference between what is needed and the value of securities traded inevitably produces a relatively small variance.

Source: Historical Tables 2007, 1.1, 3.1

A few surface observations about the numbers in Table 4.2 can be usefully made at this point:

- The 1945–48 period contained the high and the low end of *Defense* spending, the net effect being a much lower deficit.
- The remaining federal revenue in 1945–48 after primary costs are deducted ($1.3 billion) dramatically demonstrates the impact of war on the budget, and illustrates the absolute need to cut all other costs to the bone during wartime.
- The 1949–52 transactions demonstrate the comeback capability of the federal budget when the demands of primary costs are reduced to a peacetime basis. The remaining tax revenue after primary costs were deducted ($81.3 billion) were 67 percent higher than the cost of operating the other two cost centers in 1944–48 ($48.8 billion), which means that in 1949–52 impressive cost growth was possible and, if cost control was exercised, debt reduction was also possible.

Public debt reduction was realized in 1949–52. The inherited amount was $216.3 billion in 1948; the debt passed on to President Eisenhower was $214.8 billion.[14]

But was the reduction as much as it could have been? Continuing analysis will attempt to uncover the answer to that question.

TAXES

Overall, revenue in the subject period went up 19 percent,[15] a healthy indication that the inherited cost base had room to grow without, at the same time, causing an increase in debt.

One reason for the short-term jolt to tax income was the across-the-board increases in tax rates, personal, corporate and Social Security.

And an even more important reason was the improved economy.

GDP in 1952 was 36 percent higher that it was four years before[16] and tax receipts were pouring in — tax receipts in 1952 were 59 percent higher than they were in 1948.

On the surface one would assume that the tax increases were a response to the demands of the Korean War. But were they? Or were the higher taxes a smoke screen behind which Truman could indulge himself with a guns-and-butter-too policy that, in later years, would be emulated by another dedicated Rooseveltonian, President Lyndon B. Johnson?

Harry Truman's reputation as a friend of the average guy might not be as solid as advertised, depending upon how one measures the proper role of government. For example, even while he was cutting military costs to the bone, Truman vetoed a tax reduction bill in 1947 and did so again in 1948, but Congress overrode his veto.

GOVERNMENT

The cost of government increased by 46 percent in 1949–52, well above the rate of revenue increase (19 percent). This means that the subject cost center contributed to the deficit by the amount of unfunded spending, or $5.6 billion.[17]

Table 4.3
Government (in billions of dollars)

	1949–52	1945–48	% Change
Energy	$ 1.5	$ .4	275.0%
Natural Resources/Environment	4.9	2.4	104.2
Transportation	4.0	7.6	-47.4
Community/regional development	.1	.8	-87.5
International affairs	17.1	14.2	20.4
Science/space/technology	.2	.2	0.0
Agriculture	3.8	3.1	22.6
Justice	.9	.8	12.5
General	4.1	3.5	17.1
Total	$36.6	$33.0	10.9%
Commerce & housing credit*	4.3	- 5.1	184.2
Total	$40.9	$27.9	46.6%
Offsetting receipts	-9.3	6.1	152.5
Net	$31.6	$21.7	45.6%

*Made up of earnings from various Federal Housing and other programs— subject to major changes from year to year relative to market conditions. (Historical Tables 2007, 3.2)

Source: Historical Tables 2007, 3.1

Energy, Natural Resources and (again) Agriculture draw the eye, but in budget terms they were not unusually troubling. But it should be noted that lawmakers must learn to control domestic spending especially during wartime, and it is a matter of some concern that they failed to do so with these three line items.

HUMAN RESOURCES

This cost center grew by an outlandish 77 percent during the subject period, and it was higher in 1952 than it was in 1951, which suggests that it was a deliberate and planned level of spending that was unwisely and imprudently authorized during a period of war.

This tendency of some politicians to place social engineering on a par with the needs of national security was clearly demonstrated during the subject period, and would later serve as the underlying philosophy of government that eventually resulted in back breaking deficits and debt.

Table 4.4
Human Resources (in billions of dollars)

	1949–52	1945–48	% Change
Education, training, services	$ 1.0	$ .4	150.0%
Health	1.1	.8	37.5
Income Security	14.4	8.9	61.8
Social Security	5.1	1.6	218.8
Medicare	0.0	0.0	
Veterans	26.1	15.4	69.6
Other			
Total	$47.7	$27.1	76.6%

Note: Social Security (started in 1935) was still an infant program and there were few other social programs.

Source: Historical Tables 2007, 3.1

This orgy of spending took place in the following context:

• The decision makers were aware that federal revenues in 1949–50 were below those of 1948 — a rare occurrence.
• The North Korean problem was looming in 1948 and it broke loose in 1950.
• Presumably the tax increase was supposed to fund the increase in military spending as the services tried to quickly reverse the cuts of 1947.
• Common sense, and historical precedent, demanded that in a time of war discretionary spending should be tightly controlled.

Truman and his congressional allies refused to deny themselves the opportunity to build upon the previous initiatives of FDR, and war provided them with the excuse to increase taxes across the board thereby making it possible to fund the war *and* their pet programs.

Truman, for example, expanded the jobs covered by Social Security, he increased the benefits and he approved the first Cost-of-Living Adjustment (COLA). The consequence? Payments to retirees in 1952 were almost four times higher than they were in 1948.

Apart from the merits of these changes to Social Security, they should not have been made during a time of war; they should have been proposed during a time of peace when people were looking and learning.

The unemployment rate was 6.6 percent in 1949 and it gradually dipped to 2.7 percent by the end of 1952.[18] But payments made during this business cycle to the unemployed were the major reason for the large increase in Income Security that is reflected in Table 4.4. Truman cannot be faulted for this increase because it took place as a matter of law, with no assist from him.

Similarly, the cost of Veterans was comparatively high and didn't begin to level off until 1951, a welcome and justifiable cost that Truman did nothing to accelerate.

Justifiable or not, the unfunded growth in this cost center amounted to

$15.2 billion.[19] Arguably, except for the excess growth in Social Security, it represents costs that were legitimate and unavoidable.

Questions were raised earlier about the size of the cost increase in *Human Resources*. Were they justified? Were they self-serving? Except for the poorly timed expansion of the Social Security program, the cost increases were largely justified and unavoidable.

INTEREST

Interest expense increased by the same amount as revenue in 1949–52 and it presented no fiscal problems. The prime rate was higher in 1952 than it was in 1948 and, although it had not yet generated a budget problem, it was a warning that it could be if debt were not brought under tighter control.

DEFENSE

Compared with 1945–48, Defense went down by $51.0 billion. In terms of budget impact, this was a positive turn of events that promised some level of debt or tax reduction.

But the previous analysis identified $5.6 billion of unfunded spending in Government, and $15.2 billion in Human Resources—a total of $20.8 billion in unfunded growth. All but $2.0 billion of the peace dividend was eaten up by a desie to spend that overwhelmed the desire to control the budget.

Conclusion

There are many memorable chapters in the presidential life of the man from Missouri, Harry Truman, and they extended beyond the reach of World War II into his 1948–52 term. They included the Marshall Plan (1947–51); the Korean War (1950–53); the firing of the American military icon, Douglas MacArthur; the scandal related to communism and, finally and importantly, the establishment of the road to the Welfare State that was started by FDR, and was continued by Harry Truman.

There has been nothing in history to compare with the Marshall Plan. Europe was ravaged and badly in need of help — as much as France, Britain, the Soviet Union and others needed help during World War I, they needed it more after the war. The Marshall Plan provided that help.

The United States, over four fiscal years beginning in July 1948, poured over $13 billion into the reconstruction plan (equivalent to $130 billion in 2006). Forgotten by many, the Marshall Plan was Europe's lifeline back to civilization.

The Korean War was important because of the Soviet Union's support of the North Koreans and the fear that the entire region would fall under its control. Eventually, America committed almost four million troops to the conflict, the cost of which, together with new social programs, made budget deficit control difficult, and substantial debt reduction impossible. The war was ongoing when in 1953 Dwight Eisenhower took his oath of office.

General Douglas MacArthur, an imperious man, never quite accepted Harry Truman as his president, and it showed in his behavior. Finally, Truman had had enough of his impertinence and he fired him. Neither man's reputation was overly soiled by the event — but history was changed by it.

The Communist scandal that surrounded the Truman years was a real and a nasty one. The Rosenberg incident was a big embarrassment to the president and it seemed to confirm the charge persistently made by Senator Joe McCarthy (R–WI) that the Truman administration had been infiltrated by Russian spies.

McCarthy finally reached too far with his charges and he eventually lost credibility. But during his most active years, he gave Truman headaches.

Relative to modern-day budget problems, including high debt, the administration of Harry Truman in 1948–52 was a perfect example of the temptations that can confront a wartime president and his congressional allies. Why?

- It is considered to be politically dangerous to raise tax rates.
- But in a time of war, the danger diminishes. Increases can be couched in terms of military needs, and loyal Americans support them.
- Once higher tax revenues begin to flow, programs can slip though the cracks and before one realizes what has happened.... Presto! The expected post-war tax or debt reduction doesn't occur because the new programs need the money.

This is the cycle that Truman took the nation through in 1948–52. The impact at that time was not huge, but the idea, the method and the procedure lived to contaminate future budget decisions.

Given the fluctuations between peace and war it was still difficult to see the shift that was taking place in Washington, but the Table 4.5 makes the effort a bit easier.

The year 1952, Truman's last in office, was one dominated by war, and the budget showed it. Three-quarters of the spending was going to the primary cost centers, and the numbers seem to suggest that the other cost centers were under control.

But previous analysis demonstrated that the cost of Social Security was booming, and that the reaction to this by the Truman administration was to broaden and increase benefits and to increase the payroll tax rate, and the amount of payroll subject to tax. That was an irresponsible reaction during a time of war.

Mark it well — in 1949–52 there was a budget surplus of $2.0 billion. Harry Truman was the only president during the period 1941 to 2008 to pass forward

Table 4.5
Spending Priorities

	1940	1944	1948	1952
Primary costs				
Defense	17.5%	86.7%	30.5%	68.1%
Interest	9.5	2.4	14.4	6.9
Total	27.0%	89.1%	44.9%	75.0
Government	29.3	8.8	21.9	7.6
Education/services	20.8	0.0	.6	.4
Health/Medicaid	0.6	0.2	.5	.4
Medicare	0.0	0.0	0.0	.0
Income Security	16.0	1.6	8.4	5.5
Social Security	0.3	0.3	12.6	3.1
Veterans	6.0	0.0	5.9	8.0
Total	100.0%	100.0%	100.0%	100.0%

Source: Historical Tables 2007, 3.1

a public debt lower than the one he inherited — a drop from $216.3 billion to $214.8 billion.

Table 4.6
Public Debt, 1948 (billions)

Event	Inherited 1948	Added 1949–52	Total 1952	%
World War I	$ 18.3	$	$ 18.3	8.5%
Great Depression	24.5		24.5	11.4
World War II	165.3	-22.8	142.5	66.3
Interest	5.4		5.4	2.5
Government		5.6	5.6	2.6
Human Resources	4.7	15.2	19.9	9.3
Treasury	-1.9	.5	-1.4	-.6
Total	$216.3	$ -1.5	$214.8	100.0%

Source: Exhibit 1, 11, 12, 16

In the context of this work, Truman gets good short-term grades because he held the line on debt, but he did so kicking and screaming. Fate, not philosophy, made him a successful fiscal president. Given his way, the Welfare State would have assaulted America sooner than it did.

Love him or hate him, it was difficult not to admire Harry S Truman. Few men could walk into the shoes of an immortal man like FDR and not look silly trying. But Truman put his head down and pushed against the tasks of the day until they yielded to his own problem-solving style.

Truman never tried to copy FDR. He was his own man from beginning to end. He was 61 when he succeeded FDR and 68 when he left the White House. He enjoyed a healthy retirement for 14 years; then he fell ill to a variety of conditions that finally overcame him six years later. When give-'em-hell-Harry died in 1972 he was 88 years old.

5

Dwight D. Eisenhower, 1953–1956

Soldier, President

Benjamin Harrison was president when Dwight D. Eisenhower (Ike) was born in Denison, Texas, in 1890. Ike, the third of six surviving children of David and Ida Eisenhower, grew up in a warm and stable household.

Father David (1863–1942), a Pennsylvanian, moved to Abilene, Kansas, when he was 15 years old. After his marriage to Ida Stover (1885), David dropped engineering courses he had been taking and, with a partner, he opened a store in Hope, Kansas.

David's partner later absconded with the company's cash and left him to face the creditors alone. He closed the store and, over time, he paid them all. Thereafter he worked as a mechanic and as a manager of a gas company. Ike was on overseas assignment to General George Marshall when his father died.

Mother Ida (1862–1946), a religious pacifist, had trouble dealing with Ike's occupation. She saw his greatest days as a soldier before she died.

Ike attended grade school and high school in Abilene, Kansas, an indifferent student and an enthusiastic athlete in baseball and football. He did nothing consequential after graduation from high school in 1909 until he entered West Point in 1911. He had no urgent political or military ambitions but he wanted an affordable education. At West Point it was free and through effort and influence he qualified for admittance. Ike's grades at the academy were unimpressive — in his first year 74 percent of his class got higher marks; in his last, 64 percent. And he was not a model of good behavior; 42 percent of his classmates were better behaved.

Football was Ike's best subject. He was a competent halfback until in 1912 he hurt his knee. He graduated in 1915 and he was commissioned a second lieutenant.

Woodrow Wilson was president; public debt was $3.1 billion.

Ike was assigned to training and organizational duties in the United States during World War I, and he rose to the permanent rank of captain. A few years later, it was Major Eisenhower, tank commander, at Camp Dix, Fort Benning, and at Camp Meade.

Following a stint in the Panama Canal Zone, Ike was selected to attend the Command and General Staff School in Kansas, the first educational institution to offer him a learning program that wasn't also attached to football or baseball. Absent the diversion of sports, Ike blossomed intellectually — he finished first in a class of 275 hand-picked officers, a result that must have amazed his West Point professors — Ike was 36 years old when he left the school in 1926 and his military career was in full gear.

Calvin Coolidge was president; public debt was $19.6 billion.

Ike circulated in the higher circles of military life for the next decade. He received more education at the Army War College (1928–29) after which he was assigned to the War Department (1929–32).

In 1932 he joined General Douglas MacArthur's staff and, in 1935, Lieutenant Colonel Eisenhower followed MacArthur to the Philippines as his aide. He served in that capacity until 1939, when he was 49.

Franklin Roosevelt was president. Public debt, after dropping from $27 billion under Woodrow Wilson (World War I) and to $16 billion under Herbert Hoover, had increased again to $40 billion, thanks to the Great Depression.

Ike returned to stateside duty in 1940. He was a brigadier general at the time of Pearl Harbor serving on the staff of General Walter Krueger. His advancement was swift. In March 1942, he was made a major general. A few months later, Lt. General Eisenhower commanded America's forces in Europe; later, he was Allied commander for the invasion of North Africa. He became a full general in February 1943, and in December of that year he was made Supreme Allied Commander.

After the war, Ike served as chief of staff for Harry Truman as a five-star general (1945). He resigned from the army in 1948.

In 1950–52, at the behest of Truman, Ike came out of retirement to serve as commander of the North Atlantic Treaty Organization forces. He was the first to command NATO's multinational troops.

Ike kept his attitudes toward civilian issues to himself until he was ready to enter the political arena. Headhunters dispatched from both political parties sought the hand of the individual who, arguably, was the most popular man in the world.

Truman apparently thought he had a lock on Ike's loyalties, and he was livid when he learned that his hand-picked successor would run for president in 1952 as a Republican.

The war hero of heroes easily defeated Adlai E. Stevenson in the race for the presidency.[1]

Ike assumed office in January 1953. The Korean War was ongoing; public debt, summarized below, was $214.8 billion.[2]

Table 5.1
Public Debt 1952 (in billions of dollars)

	Total	%
World War I	$ 18.3	8.5%
Great Depression:	24.5	11.4
World War II	142.1	66.2
Interest	5.4	2.6
Government	5.6	2.6
Human Resources	19.9	9.3
Treasury, net	-1.4	-.6
Total	$214.8	100.0%

Source: Historical Tables 2006, 1.1

World War II, the cost of which had driven debt to new ceilings was over and, normally, one would have expected Ike's first term to feature debt reduction, tax reduction, or both. But, apart from the issue of congressional support, two powerful forces were working against those possibilities: The cost of the Social Security program was booming and the Korean War was ongoing.

Ike's control of Congress was short lived. For the first two years, he had Republican leadership in the House and Senate, Joe Martin and Robert A. Taft of Ohio, respectively — when Taft resigned, he was succeeded by William F. Knowland of California.[3]

Democrats returned to power in the 84th Congress (1955–56), Rayburn in the House, and Lyndon B. Johnson in the Senate. Both were Texans, and both worshipped at the political shrine of FDR.

The Truman regime had two defining characteristics:

- Nonmilitary spending during wartime was not cut; instead, it increased, on the surface a break with past procedure.
- Truman's tax increase, allegedly to support the Korean War, was also used to fund expansion of the Social Security program.

These two factors established the budget atmosphere within which Ike had to work. He inherited a war, accelerating domestic spending, and high taxes.

A president's power is increased when he controls Congress and limited when he doesn't. In this, his first term, Ike was fortunate. His control of the 83d Congress set the fiscal tone of his first four years that, for all practical purposes, featured a balanced budget.

The modest deficit during his first term ($6.6 billion) mostly took place in his first year, during which he operated under the last budget of the Truman administration.[4]

Perspectives

GENERAL

Ike matured in the weak military institution that existed after World War I. He dutifully accepted that weakness, happily directed its renewed strength in Europe, sorrowfully saw it diminish again under Truman, and energetically helped it back to its feet to meet the challenge of Korea.

As well as any man in the world, Ike respected the Soviet threat, and by his actions he prepared America to face it. When Stalin died (1953), Malenkov became the Soviet premier. Winston Churchill, who returned to power in 1951,[5] and Ike were the greatest World War II personalities still operating on the world stage.

A hero in the Soviet Union and Europe, as well as in the United States, Ike by his mere presence acted as a deterrent against adventurous foes. He reeked of credibility.

As promised during his election campaign, he brought the Korean War to a close (1953),[6] thus ending one Communist threat. But the explosion of a hydrogen bomb by the Soviet Union in the same year[7] made it clear that the days of trouble were not entirely gone.

Vietnam reached the consciousness of Americans in 1954 when the French military post in Dien Bien Phu was overrun, signaling the end of French influence in that country.

As far back as 1950, America had been quietly and modestly involved in France's attempt to maintain a colonial presence in Vietnam. Ike continued that practice but consistently opposed a deeper involvement (a wise posture, from one well-trained in the logistics of warfare that lesser-trained leaders later ignored, much to their regret and to the regret of the United States).

America's deadly dance with the Soviet Union moved in a different direction in 1955 when Nikolai Bulganin succeeded Malenkov as Soviet premier. And direction shifted again when the "Lion of London," Winston Churchill, resigned, thus removing from the international arena one of communism's staunchest and most able antagonists and America's most trusted ally.

International nerves grew unsettled when America's own lion, Dwight Eisenhower, suffered an attack of coronary thrombosis that temporarily felled the highly respected and feared American president.

Perhaps sensing weakness, perhaps driven by events, the Soviet Union became bolder in 1956 — Nikita Khrushchev, who followed in the footsteps of Bulganin, crushed the revolts against Soviet rule in Poland and Hungary.

In another part of the world, disputes over the Suez Canal involving Egypt, Israel, France, and Britain resulted in a short war, which, with the assistance of the United States, was settled.

Ike recovered his health during this frenzy and ran again for president on a record of peace and prosperity. He won easily. Ike was amazingly popular with voters. His image as a man who would and could stand up to Communists was a large part of this attraction.

THE HOME FRONT

The rights of America's African-American citizens drew long-needed attention in Ike's first term, perhaps triggered by the Supreme Court decision (*Brown v. Board of Education,* Topeka) that banned racial segregation in public schools.

Separate but equal was a dogma in disrepair. Protests followed. Martin Luther King, Jr., became a prominent voice urging the elimination of segregation in schools, buses, restaurants, and wherever else the hated practice prevailed.

America was at peace, it was prosperous, and it turned its eyes inward, desiring to cleanse aspects of its national character that had been stained for too long by race issues. The wheels of confrontation were in motion, and soon the position of blacks in American society would be a preoccupying issue.

This racial tension and the national mood to resolve it in 1953–56 were major considerations when arguments emerged at a later time in support of a more active role for the federal government.

After World War II, *Defense* dropped from a high in 1945 of $83.0 billion to a low in 1948 of $9.1 billion. In 1950, the first year of Korea, Truman increased *Defense* to $13.7 billion. In 1953, the last year of the war and the first of Ike's administration, *Defense* was $52.8 billion.[8]

Few comparative numbers more dramatically demonstrate the difference between a president who prepares for the trouble he sees on the horizon and one who "hopes for the best." This is a lesson learned under Ike and that has been forgotten by the Americans of the current age.

Unlike Truman, the first Cold War president, who abruptly dismantled America's arsenal after World War II, Ike maintained a strong military when its immediate justification, the Korean War, ended. He was the first president to face the Soviet threat with actions as well as words—the second Cold War president, but the first to pay the piper. Over the next three years, *Defense* ranged from $42 billion to $49 billion.

Ike attempted through more conservative policies to slow the rate of growth in federal spending (181 vetoes) and to otherwise impress his personal stamp on the financial profile of America. But his success was minimal due to a lagging economy that, among other things, was struggling to deal with the continuation of confiscatory tax rates that were first imposed during World War II.

GDP in 1956 was only 22 percent higher than it was in 1952, as compared with a four-year growth of 36 percent under Truman.[9] This desultory performance reflected everywhere, including federal revenues which were essentially flat for three years until finally, in 1956, they showed signs of strength (14 percent above 1955).

The all-important Misery Index reflected the same bad economic news— up from 7.6 percent to 9.5 percent. Interest and unemployment rates were rising; the inflation rate was lower.[10]

For those who were working, the personal income index[11] was positive and more valuable than before because inflation was lower. The down side of this was the increased slice of earnings that was being scooped by the federal government—a worker in 1956 gave 11.9 weeks of work to the government as opposed to 10.3 weeks in 1952.[12] And when the same worker borrowed a few dollars to buy his secondhand car he discovered that the interest rate was almost a third higher than it was four years before.

In short, the years from 1953 to 1956 were not a great time for the government or for the worker because both fed from the same trough — the American economy — and it was not as full as expected.

SUPREME COURT[13]

When an unusually energetic and innovative president is in office during difficult times, as was the case during the Great Depression, the chief executive may be tempted into activities that sooner or later come under the scrutiny of the Court.

But ordinarily, the judicial branch of the U.S. government does not unduly interfere with the plans and programs of the other two branches and it concentrates instead on the daily problems that beset society at large. Its rulings, in the most general sense, affect people more than they affect presidents.

But presidents are also people, and they harbor a worldview that is important to them and to the political party that they represent — they prefer to have judges on the bench who share their vision of society and of government. So, for that reason, the makeup of the bench is important to every president, and he tries to influence it through the Supreme Court nominations that he sends to the Senate Judiciary Committee.

Ike inherited a Supreme Court that was largely stacked with FDR and Truman appointments.

During his first term, 12 men served on the bench, nine holdovers and three new appointments. Ike had his chance during his first term to change the shape of the Court.[14]

The three new men were Earl Warren, John Harlan and William Brennan. A thumbnail sketch of each appears below.

- Earl Warren — Warren was a graduate of the University of Berkeley and its law school. After graduation, he worked with law firms for five years before beginning his political career as a three-term district attorney. He became attorney general of California in 1939 and governor in 1941. He ran as vice president on the Thomas Dewey ticket in 1948 that lost a close election to Harry Truman. In 1953, Ike appointed him to the bench as chief justice to succeed the retiring Fred Vinson. Ike expected Warren to be a conservative judge but, from that standpoint, he was mistaken. Warren embraced and enthusiastically led the liberal justices below him.

- John Harlan — Harlan was educated at Princeton and Oxford (law) before he went to New York University Law School and earned in 1925 his American law degree. He spent his early years after graduation working for a prestigious Wall Street law firm, with occasional forays into the public sector on assignment to Governor Thomas Dewey. Ike appointed him to the U.S. Court of Appeals, Second Circuit, and then later in 1955 he appointed him to the Supreme Court to replace Robert Jackson (appointed by FDR). Harlan, unlike Warren, was true to his credentials — he was the intellectual leader of the conservative point of view (the Scalia of his day).
- William Brennan — After completing his Harvard education, Brennan entered private practice before becoming a trial judge and finally, in 1952, a member of the New Jersey Supreme Court. Four years later, Ike made him a member of the U.S. Supreme Court to replace Sherman Minton (appointed by Truman). It was his second judicial mistake — Brennan was in fact a leading liberal who influentially served for decades.

To his supporters, Ike's batting average as a selector of judges was terrible. He had a chance to shift three seats from the liberal (activist) to the conservative (strict constructionist) point of view and he failed. Two of his appointments, Warren and Brennan, would haunt conservatives, and they would change the face of America long into the future.

The usual array of cases dealing with speech, religion, etc. was presented to this Court as they have been to most. But this was a time of growing racial unrest and fear of communism, subjects that also found their way to the Court.

A few examples of the concerns of the day appear below.

Bolling v. Sharpe, 1952. Public schools in Washington, D.C., were racially segregated and black children could not attend white schools. The issue: Does the segregated school system violate the due process clause of the Fifth Amendment? In a unanimous decision the Court ruled that the Fifth Amendment did not have a due process clause, but it did have a guarantee of "liberty" under which the segregation system could be ruled unconstitutional.

Brown v. Board of Education, 1954. State law established separate but equal schools for public school students. Blacks could not attend schools with white children. The issue: Does the separate but equal school system violate the due process clause of the Fourteenth Amendment? In a unanimous decision, the Court ruled that separate but equal was an unconstitutional doctrine. In so doing, the Supreme Court outlawed, in this key case, public school segregation in America. The implementation of the law would take time, and it caused trouble. But the law held firm and changed the face of America — to the good.

Brown II, 1955. The *Brown v. Board of Education* ruling left unclear the problems of how to do what by whom. The Court requested further argument on those questions. The issue: How should the original *Brown* decision be implemented? The Court held local school authorities and local courts responsible for implementation in the broadest of language. Out of this ruling came such things as forced busing.

Hernandez v. Texas, 1954. A Mexican agricultural worker was found guilty of murder by a jury that contained, as a matter of practice, no Mexicans. The decision was appealed on the grounds that the practice of ignoring Mexicans was discriminatory. The issue: Does the exclusion of Mexicans because of their race violate the equal protection clause of the Fourteenth Amendment? In a unanimous decision, the Court agreed that discrimination in jury selection on the basis of race alone is unconstitutional.

It is clear from these cases that Court members may have differed on many subjects, but racial discrimination wasn't one of them. America was on a march to firmly establish minority rights, and the Court was leading the way.

Change in Pubic Debt

Optimism that the debt could be reduced in 1953–56 was low mostly because the war in Korea was ongoing, but for other reasons as well:

- The economy was sluggish.
- The surge in Social Security costs was headed for unpredictable heights.
- The Republican hold on the Congress was a tenuous one that could easily disappear in the midterm elections.

All things considered, it was commendable that Ike's first term ended with a relatively small $6.6 billion deficit. See Table 5.2.

The economy was slow when Ike took office, but his startup level of federal revenue was much higher than it was in 1949–52, and it resulted in a four-year comparative increase of 42 percent,[15] a rate of growth that, in peacetime, would have made serious tax or debt reduction possible.

But this wasn't peacetime and Ike was determined to build a war machine that would make the North Koreans tremble and would, at the same time, get the *attention* of the increasingly adventurous Soviet Union. *Defense* increased

Table 5.2
Transactions (in billions of dollars)

		1953–56		1949–52
Taxes		$ 279.4		$ 196.6
Less:				
Defense	$187.3		$96.6	
Interest	20.0		18.7	
Total		207.3		115.3
Net		$ 72.1		$ 81.3
Less:				
Government	$ 22.9		$31.6	
Human Resources	55.0		47.7	
Total		78.7		79.3
Surplus/deficit		$ -6.6		$ 2.0
Debt, beginning		-214.8		-216.3
Total		$-221.4		$-214.3
Adjustment*		-.8		-.5
Debt, Ending		$-222.2		$-214.8

*Treasury cannot be exact when it finances a budget deficit and the difference between what is needed and the value of securities traded inevitably produces a relatively small variance.

Source: Historical Tables 2007, 1.1, 3.1

by 94 percent, a whopping increase that won the intended international results but at the expense of tax and debt relief at home.

Other than *Defense,* it appeared that the other cost centers exercised admirable control, something that is expected during wartime, and something that made the small deficit possible.

TAXES

Republicans controlled Congress in 1953–56 and tax rates remained steady. But Democrats resumed control over the final two years of Ike's first term the tax and spending environment changed: Despite the needs of war, the Social Security program was expanded again, the payroll tax rate was increased from 3 to 4 percent, and the level of taxable payroll increased from $3,600 to $4,200.[16]

GOVERNMENT

The cost of *Government* actually decreased in 1953–56 and it therefore was in no way responsible for the deficit. Nevertheless it is useful to examine the details of this phenomenon so as to better understand the fiscal dynamics of the time.

The overall performance of the *Government* cost center was commendable but, not surprisingly, there was a hitch — spending on Agriculture went through the roof.

Table 5.3
Government (in billions of dollars)

	1953–56	1949–52	% Change
Energy	$ 1.3	$ 1.5	-13.3%
Natural Resources/Environment	4.1	4.9	-16.3
Transportation	5.2	4.0	30.0
Community/regional development	.4	.1	300.0
International affairs	8.3	17.1	-51.5
Science/space/technology	.3	.2	50.0
Agriculture	11.0	3.8	189.5
Justice	1.1	.9	22.2
General	3.9	4.1	- 4.9
Total	$ 35.6	$ 36.6	- 2.7%
Commerce & housing credit*	1.4	4.3	-67.0
Total	$ 37.0	$ 40.9	- 9.5
Offsetting receipts	-14.1	-9.3	51.6
Net	$ 22.9	$ 31.6	-27.5%

*Made up of earnings from various federal housing and other programs—
subject to major changes from year to year relative to market conditions.
(Historical Tables 2007, 3.2)

Source: Historical Tables 2007, 3.1

In the first two years of Ike's administration, while Congress was controlled by Republicans, total spending for Agriculture was $4.1 billion; in the final two years under Democratic control, it was $6.9 billion, an increase of 68 percent.[17]

It appears that spending on this line item was going to increase substantially under either party, but with Democrats the rate of increase was even higher.

It is the aim of this book not to question the what-or-why of spending, but rather to focus on the financing and the timing of spending increases.

In this case, the increase in Agriculture was unfunded in the amount of $5.6 billion and the timing of the spending splurge could not have been worse. Had spending been limited to the 42 percent increase that modeled the rate of revenue increase, the deficit for the period would have been, for all practical purposes, eliminated.

HUMAN RESOURCES

The overall increase in *Human Resources* of 17 percent was also fully funded. But it is usually the case that a more detailed analysis of a cost center reveals bones in the closet that need to be uncovered if one is to make sense out of budget trends.

Table 5.4
Human Resources (in billions of dollars)

	1953–56	1949–52	% Change
Education, training, services	$ 1.8	$ 1.0	80.0%
Health/Medicaid	1.4	1.1	27.2
Income Security	18.0	14.4	25.0
Social Security	16.0	5.1	213.7
Medicare	0.0	0.0	0.0
Veterans	18.6	26.1	-28.7
Other			
Total	$55.8	$47.7	17.0%

Note: Social Security (started in 1935), which included unemployment compensation, and the GI Bill were the only major social programs in this time.

Source: Historical Tables 2007, 3.1

The most liberal test of whether spending is funded in *Human Resources* is the rate of revenue increase. One would tend to believe that the 42 percent increase in spending that was allowable under this formula would have been more than adequate to satisfy a normal appetite to provide services. But it wasn't.

Two line items went astray, one of which (Education, etc.) had significance more in what it revealed about attitude than it did in immediate fiscal impact, and the other of which (Social Security) was of major significance both for the subject period and for the future.

The cost of Social Security was out of control in 1953–56, as it had been from the beginning. In 1956, for example it was 162 percent more expensive than it was four years earlier. This budget line item was now beyond presidential control and, as an entitlement program, its cost could be changed only by new legislation designed to restructure it — Congress could have changed the program, but it didn't.

A sacred cow had been created; Social Security was regarded by politicians as untouchable; they voluntarily made it the third rail of politics — touch it and you die at the voting booth was the common wisdom.

INTEREST

The increase in *Interest* in 1953–56 was fully funded by the rate of revenue increase. This cost center had no impact on the ultimate budget deficit for the period.

DEFENSE

The Korean War ended in 1953 when defense spending reached its peak of $52.8 billion. Ike trimmed this a bit to $42.5 billion by 1956. Unlike Truman before him, he kept a robust military establishment in place out of respect for the potential danger posed by the expansive ambitions of the Soviet Union.

The previous analysis of the other cost centers revealed that current revenues had fully funded the cost increases in each of them. By deduction, therefore, the full deficit of $6.6 billion for the period is charged to the remaining cost center, *Defense*.

Conclusion

"Cold War." It was a new term and a new world that featured a relatively high *Defense* during a time of curious peace that featured a nonshooting enemy who could, in minutes, destroy America or impair its national interests throughout the world. In such a climate, the priorities of America remained essentially stable.

Table 5.5
Spending Priorities

	1940	1944	1948	1952	1956
Primary costs					
Defense	17.5%	86.7%	30.5%	68.1%	60.2%
Interest	9.5	2.4	14.4	6.9	7.2
Total	27.0%	89.1%	44.9%	75.0	67.4%
Government	29.3	8.8	21.9	7.6	9.9
Education/services	20.8	0.0	.6	.4	.8
Health/Medicaid	0.6	0.2	.5	.4	.5
Medicare	0.0	0.0	0.0	.0	0.0
Income Security	16.0	1.6	8.4	5.5	6.7
Social Security	0.3	0.3	12.6	3.1	7.8
Veterans	6.0	0.0	5.9	8.0	6.9
Total	100.0%	100.0%	100.0%	100.0%	100.0%

Source: Historical Tables 2007, 3.1

Defense in 1956 was the cost center that commanded most of the dollars, as it should have given the unstable character of international affairs.

But hidden in the bowels of *Human Resources* was a time bomb that was getting larger and more dangerous by the day — Social Security. Ike had seen enough of the program to realize that, as structured, it could become a budget killer. But his warnings to the public about this were unheeded and ineffective.

FDR faced mounting involvement in the European war and increasing tensions with Japan in 1940, yet he did little to improve America's military machine until war was declared in 1941.

Truman disarmed the military after World War II, despite the Soviet Union's antagonistic international stance, and he didn't rebuild it until 1950, when the shooting started in Korea.

Ike, in contrast, kept a strong military in place after the Korean War was finished, because of continuing Soviet pressures against America and its allies.

Ike wanted a smaller federal government, not a larger one — fewer federal programs, not more. And few presidents could claim the international admiration that was bestowed upon Ike, even in unlikely places like Moscow. Having him in the White House, with his reputation as a keen-eyed military man, was, by itself, a priceless weapon that made potential enemies slow to test U.S. interests.

Given the resistance of Congress to lower spending and the needs of *Defense* in a troubled world, Ike was probably lucky to restrict the budget deficit to $6.6 billion.

In 1953–56, public debt went from $214.8 billion to $222.2 billion, as follows:

Table 5.6
Public Debt, 1956 (billions)

Event	Inherited 1952	Added 1953–1956	Total 1956	%
World War I	$ 18.3	$	$ 18.3	8.2%
Great Depression	24.5		24.5	11.0
World War II	142.5		142.5	64.1
Korean War		6.6	6.6	3.0
Interest	5.4		5.4	2.4
Government	5.6		5.6	2.5
Human Resources	19.9		19.9	9.0
Treasury	-1.4	.8	-.6	-.2
Total	$214.8	$7.4	$222.2	100.0%

Source: Exhibits 1, 11, 12, 16

The makeup of debt in 1956 showed that war and bad times accounted for most of the public debt — the budget was in good shape except for one item, Social Security.

Obviously, correcting that problem would bring substantial benefits to an American public that had built the most formidable economy that the world had ever seen. And it could be done if the Washingtonocrats managed federal revenues wisely, something they had yet to prove.

Because of a heart attack in 1955 and an ileitis operation in 1956, many wondered if Ike would retire. But the old soldier, looking fit, fooled them all and gave it another try.

Would things be better the "second time around"?

6

Dwight D. Eisenhower, 1957–1960

Second-Term President

Dwight D. Eisenhower ran for reelection in 1956 and he defeated Adlai Stevenson with a 58 percent vote, a majority greater than he had enjoyed in their first contest,[1] and a two-election popularity record that places him among the most popular presidents in American history.

Ike's popularity was especially irksome to the media that delighted in ridiculing his un–Harvard-like demeanor which, to them, translated into dimwittedness, a common characterization of Republican presidents that included Lincoln, about whom Senator William Saulsbury (D–DE) said: "I never did see or converse with such a weak and imbecile a man."[2]

Now 67, Ike not only faced, in his second term, a violent world and a growing public debt, but he did so after suffering a stroke in 1957, his third collision with a major medical problem in as many years.

America was at peace, a peace in the middle of a Cold War with the Soviets. Nobody was shooting at the United States, but bullets, so to speak, were whizzing over its head from all parts of the world.

Korea had settled down but required onsite American firepower as a stabilizer. The American presence in Europe also served as a deterrent against Soviet aggression.

Soviet technologists were adept competitors in the space race. The Middle East was in its usual bedlam, with Israel fighting for its life. Off the Florida coast, Castro succeeded Batista in 1959, and by the close of 1960, Cuba's alliance with the USSR was obvious and ominous.

In such a climate, Ike maintained a healthy *Defense*, and he began his second term with a public debt of $222.2 billion,[3] summarized in Table 6.1.

Ike's contribution to public debt was the $6.6 billion charged to the Korean War, the result of his buildup of military spending during that conflict. As was

Table 6.1
Public Debt 1956 (in billions of dollars)

	Total	%
World War I	$ 18.3	8.3%
Great Depression:	24.5	11.0
World War II	142.1	64.0
Korea	6.6	3.0
Interest	5.4	2.4
Government	5.6	2.5
Human Resources	19.9	9.0
Treasury, net	-.6	-.2
Total	$222.2	100.0%

Source: Tables 5.6, Chapter 5

the case with Wilson, FDR and Truman, who were responsible for world war and depression debt, Ike's unfunded spending to meet the needs of Korea was an acceptable and time-honored use of the ability of the government to borrow in a time of stress.

The remaining public debt, some of it related to necessity and some to whimsy, represented a challenge to future presidents and congresses. Planned surpluses designed to eliminate that portion of the debt should have been a priority of the times because financing operating expenses with debt, over an extended period of time and to a substantial degree, is self-defeating fiscal policy that should never be allowed to sink roots.

Presidents and members of Congress develop and approve the ideas that result in budget surpluses or deficits. Working in harness with congressional leaders from his own party, a president can be a dynamic force. But if Congress is controlled by the opposition, a president can be impotent, capable of little more than slowing down the programs of others.

For the first two years of his two-term presidency, Ike had a chance to plant his own ideas for a smaller government. But ideological roots do not sink deeply in such a short period of time.

In his second term, Ike operated under the thumb of Democrats Sam Rayburn and Lyndon Johnson,[4] two of the most powerful congressional leaders in modern American political history. In terms of presidential power, Ike was in the weakest possible position.

His fiscal objective in his second term had to be a reduction in public debt and, perhaps, a tax decrease. Working for him in that respect was the absence of a shooting war, which should have meant that military spending could stabilize; working against him was the arms race with the Soviets and, of equal importance, a Congress controlled by Democrats.

Given the balance of power in Washington at the time, few bet heavy money on the ability of Ike to implement his conservative policies.

Perspectives

GENERAL

Ike was the second president to preside over the Cold War, a term denoting the tension-filled era when a Soviet-dominated group of nations held the capacity to destroy America. The doctrine of Mutually Assured Destruction (MAD) ruled the day — the reply of each to an attack by the other would result in the destruction of both. For that reason alone, Ike was justified in keeping his forces on a quasi-wartime footing.

Congress was controlled by Democrats in 1957–60, as it had been in 1955–56, but there was a very important difference. The hard-driving FDR apostle, Lyndon B. Johnson, had solidified his position as the Senate Majority Leader and, with the aging of the formidable Sam Rayburn, he emerged as America's most powerful politician.

With Johnson's rise, the congressional bloc that had resisted New Deal/Fair Deal programs gradually retired or collapsed. And over the next three decades, Johnson and his followers steered the government toward an ocean of debt.

The civil rights debate grew in intensity during Ike's second term, epitomized by his decision in 1957 to send federal troops to Little Rock, Arkansas, in support of attempts to integrate its schools. His well-publicized decision to put the weight of the federal government behind the Supreme Court decision (that made separate-but-equal education illegal) was probably more important than the actual event because it served clear notice to those who were reluctant to abandon that racist doctrine that their cause was hopeless.

Khrushchev, the Soviet leader, fresh from brutal victories in Poland and Hungary, solidified his power base in 1957–60 and, generally, it was a good time for the USSR.

Sputnik was launched in 1957, the first earth-orbiting satellite, and in so doing the Soviets began the so-called space race with the United States. In that regard, *Sputnik* gave the Soviets a public relations advantage that was little diminished when in 1958 America countered with *Explorer I*.[5]

Internationally, the space triumph over America lifted the Soviet image as a power broker to a level equal to that of America's, and it provided all nations that harbored an animus toward the United States (Cuba, for example) with a supportive Big Brother.

In a technological era that also featured a brutal quest for expanded power by the Soviets, the loss of superiority in technology was a national security issue in America with budget ramifications that American presidents had to face for more than three decades.

American presidents had confronted the specter of the Soviets at every turn since the end of World War II. Throughout the era the persistent question was: What are they up to now? And it was an intelligent focus because lurking behind a regional disturbance (like Korea) could often be found Soviet influence, urging and support.

In Cuba, for example, Fidel Castro's revolutionary forces deposed President Batista in 1959. Castro was hailed as the great liberator. But by the end of 1960, he was confiscating U.S. property. Diplomatic relations with Cuba were terminated in 1961. The USSR had a new friend off the Florida coast, an unpleasant development for the United States.

THE HOME FRONT

Race issues increasingly dominated the news during Ike's second term, especially after his decision to send federal troops in support of the Supreme Court ruling that theoretically ended racial segregation in the nation's schools.

Old wounds were opened, wounds so serious that they had kept all presidents prior to Lincoln from seriously attacking the problem of equal rights for blacks.

But a new day had arrived. Amendments Thirteen (no more slavery, 1865), Fourteen (equal status to all U.S. citizens, 1868) and Fifteen (voting rights, 1870) were on the constitutional books. And the *Brown v. Board* decision (1954) brought the issue of race to the public with an emphasis that couldn't be denied.

These things, taken together, along with a national and judicial mood that finally said *Enough*, made it perfectly clear that racial segregation was on its last legs, that a new and inclusive America was on the horizon.

But habits and attitudes are difficult to change, even among the willing. And full implementation of the new rules of behavior was difficult to enforce in 1957–60, as to some extent they still are today.

World War II had left in its wake an America that was different. No longer an isolationist nation beset by the Great Depression and removed by two oceans from wars in Europe and Asia, America had become an international power supported by economic prosperity and ready for free-world leadership.

This metamorphosis, occurring in less than 20 years, shocked the United States into a maturity that was reflected in the fiscal/economic numbers of the time, which silently reported mixed blessings.

Over the four-year period, for example, military spending ranged from $45 billion to $49 billion[6]—a stable era for *Defense*, which was a plus when compared with recent administrations.

But the growth in GDP was still modest (21 percent)[7] a fact that correlates with federal receipts, which were flat for three years. Thereafter, in 1960, they grew by almost 17 percent.[8]

The Misery Index told the same news—up from 9.5 percent to 13.1 percent.[9] Inflation was still under control, but interest and unemployment rates were up.

Personal income per capita increased by a weak 14 percent, made weaker by the fact that taxes per capita increased again. In 1960, a worker sent 12.1 weeks of work to Washington, as opposed to 11.9 weeks four years before.[10]

The economy was still growing in 1960, as were personal incomes, but robust was not the correct word to describe either.

SUPREME COURT[11]

Ike had three chances during his first term to man the Court with more conservative justices who, presumably, would be less playful with constitutional language. But he failed to do so because two of his selections proved to be as liberal as those who retired, including his new Chief Justice, Earl Warren, who some conservatives considered an ideological traitor.

Ike had two more chances to redeem himself in 1957–60, and he selected Potter Stewart and Charles Whittaker. A thumbnail sketch of these men appears below.

- Potter Stewart — Stewart graduated from Yale and Yale Law School. After his war service with the U.S. Navy, Stewart was active in private practice until, at 39, he was, in 1954, appointed by Ike to the U.S. Appellate Court, Sixth Circuit. Four years later Ike chose him for the U.S. Supreme Court to replace the retiring Harold Burton (appointed by Truman). While on the Court, Stewart was labeled by some as a moderate, but his later aggressive support of *Roe v. Wade* (1973) indicated that once again Ike had picked the wrong man, from a conservative point of view.
- Charles Whittaker — Whittaker was a 1924 graduate of the Kansas City School of Law, which he attended with Harry Truman. He built a practice in corporate law before his appointment in 1954 to the District Court in western Missouri. This was followed soon after by an appointment by Ike to the Appellate Court, Eighth District, and finally his appointment in 1957 to the U.S. Supreme Court, replacing Stanley Reed (appointed by FDR). As a judge, Whittaker was inconsistent and it is said that he agonized so much over decisions that in 1961 he resigned.

This brought to five the number of justices selected by Ike during his eight years in office, enough to form a majority on any issue. But, from a conservative point of view, except for John Harlan, his choices were disastrous.

Racial issues did not deluge the Court during the subject period as they were destined to do, but they did importantly appear, as did other issues that had come before the Court for decades. A few examples of the issues of the day appear below.

Roth v. US, 1957. Roth, a bookseller, was convicted under state law for mailing obscene material. The issue: Did state law deprive Roth of his free speech rights under the First Amendment? In a 6–3 decision, the Court ruled that obscene speech was not protected speech under the Constitution — Justices Douglas, Black and Harlan dissented. Justice Brennan, who wrote the opinion, went on to define obscene material as being "utterly without redeeming social importance." And he supplied a test: "whether to the average person, applying contemporary standards, the dominant theme of the material, taken as a whole appeals to prurient interest." The Court's refusal to restrict itself to the specific issue at hand (the constitutionality of the state law) is an example of the judicial activism that disturbs many Americans.

Mallory v. U.S., 1957. Federal officers arrested Mallory on a charge of rape and questioned him for seven hours before he confessed. The issue: Did the questioning of the defendant prior to his appearance before a commissioner violate his due process rights under the Federal rules of criminal procedure? In a unanimous decision, the Court ruled in favor of the defendant.

Cooper v. Aaron, 1958. The governor and legislature of Arkansas refused to obey the desegregation ruling of the Court in *Brown v. Board of Education* (1954). The issue: Were Arkansas officials acting within the law? The Court affirmed that desegregation was the supreme law of the land that applied to all states, and Arkansas officials were duty-bound to obey.

Flemming v. Nestor, 1960. Nestor was deported and demanded his Social Security checks as a matter of contract right. The issue: When Nestor became eligible to receive Social Security did a contract to provide benefits exist under which they must be paid? With Justice Black dissenting, the Court ruled that no contract exists to pay benefits— that Congress can change the Social Security program when it so chooses. Second, the Court ruled that the section of the law that terminated benefits to deported aliens is constitutional. To this day, most people do not realize that the Social Security program is not a right — it is a benefit that can be removed, lowered or increased by the Congress.

As these cases illustrate, people and their concerns do not change much over the years.

Change in Public Debt

When the Soviets launched *Sputnik* and began the space competition, which was in part a smokescreen for an arms race dealing with long-range missiles, thoughts of tax or debt reduction during Ike's second term grew dim, and the possibility of war with such a superpower became a troubling reality.

In such a climate, one would have expected an air of caution to descend over the Congress, a mood that would lead it to conserving dollars for the perils in view.

Was that the case?

The summary of transactions below is the first step toward finding an answer to that question, not by listening to the words of politicians, which rarely reveal what they intend to do, but rather by examining decisions actually made that, inevitably, find their way into the budget numbers.

Table 6.2
Transactions (in billions of dollars)

		1957–60		1953–56
Taxes		$ 331.3		$ 279.4
Less:				
Defense	$189.3		$187.3	
Interest	23.7		20.0	
Total		213.0		207.3
Net		$ 118.3		$ 72.1
Less:				
Government	$ 38.8		$22.9	
Human Resources	91.6		55.8	
Total		130.4		78.7
Surplus/deficit		$ -12.1		$ -6.6
Debt, beginning		-222.2		-214.8
Total		$-234.3		$-221.4
Adjustment*		-2.5		-.8
Debt, Ending		$-236.8		$-222.2

*Treasury cannot be exact when it finances a budget deficit and the difference between what is needed and the value of securities traded inevitably produces a relatively small variance.

Source: Historical Tables 2007, 1.1, 3.1

Ike's deficit in 1953–1956 was relatively small because of several major factors:

- Revenue was up a healthy 42 percent.
- Except for *Defense,* spending was fully funded.
- The opposite was the case in 1957–60.
- Revenue was up a modest 18.6 percent.
- Primary costs (*Defense* and *Interest*) were fully funded.
- Spending in other cost centers increased by 65.7 percent, a rate of growth far beyond the ability of normal revenues to fund,[12] and one that prevented the use of the peace dividend on tax or debt reduction.

TAXES

In 1956, the last year of Ike's first term, the Social Security program was expanded again, this time to embrace disabled children. And it was expanded again in 1960 by dropping the retirement age from 65 to 62. Wartime personal and corporate tax rates were still in force.[13]

In an act of apparent responsibility, Congress moved to finance the changes in Social Security by increasing the payroll tax from 4 percent of $4,200 to 6 percent of $4,800.

In fact, these increases were another step in the wrong direction — the cost growth of Social Security was out of control and should have drawn the Congress toward a search for a restructuring of the entire program, including an investigation of how best to finance it. The payroll tax as a method was not the way to go because:

- The number of workers per retired person was steadily declining.
- It was the cruelest tax of all to low income groups.

Also, additional benefits should not have been considered until the restructuring questions were answered.

Congress ignored the warnings: It expanded already unaffordable benefits and increased the tax on the average worker.

When taxes on people and companies are too high, there is less money in the market to invest; when business investment declines so does job creation. Sooner or later, in other words, confiscatory tax policy has a negative impact on the ability of the economic cow to deliver the milk that supports everything else —cash.

Warning signs were there to read, when Ike was in office, to suggest that high taxes were becoming counterproductive to a healthy revenue stream. In 1955, for example, federal revenue dropped; in 1957–59, revenue was relatively flat.

When compared with spending tendencies of the Congress, this was not a formula that was likely to reduce debt or taxes.

DEFENSE

Military spending peaked at $53 billion in 1953, the final year of the Korean War. It declined steadily to $43 billion by 1956, and then went up again to $48 billion in 1960.

Total military spending in 1957–60 compared to the previous four years was flat and in no way contributed to the increase in public debt during the period.

Apart from budget impact, *Defense* spending in the subject period was consistent with the atmosphere of the times. Ike, experienced in world affairs, had been personally affected by Soviet capabilities. And he brought that experience to bear when he approved defense budgets. With Korea behind him, he did not purge the military establishment as Harry Truman had done after World War II. Instead, he maintained a strong defense and projected a powerful presence to the Soviets.

America was at peace but Ike kept his powder dry, a decision that benefited the nation and the next presidents who had to deal with the Vietnam War.

Interest

Debt levels are seldom reported to the public in any meaningful way — out of sight, out of mind.

One is left with the impression that many politicians prefer it that way, and many economists seem to accept increased debt to fund federal programs as examples of progressive leadership within sound economic theory.

This attitude, born during the FDR years, was completely at odds with the sum total of presidential behavior before he arrived on the scene.

Interest is a tattletale that by its mere presence silently draws attention to public debt. The inevitable question is: *Interest* on what? Arrogantly, brusquely or politely, depending on his disposition, the bureaucrat when questioned may reluctantly admit that debt gives birth to *Interest* every day of every year, and that less debt reduces the cost of *Interest*.

In 1957–60, *Interest* was 7 percent of federal revenue, not enough in the hurly-burly days of the Cold War to get anyone but insiders excited.

But as a budget item, it was larger than Energy, Natural Resources, Commerce, or Transportation, or all of them put together; about the same as International and Agriculture; about 20 times larger than Justice — more costly than many line items about which "cost-savers" argue vociferously each year.

Interest went up 18.5 percent, less than the rate of revenue increase (18.6 percent). The increase was fully funded and did not add to the deficit for the period.[14]

Government

Government grew by 69.4 percent during the subject period. Under the allocation system in play, when primary costs do not use growth funds available to them, the excess is made available to the other cost centers — spending growth available to Government and to Human Resources increased from 1.19 to 1.50 times.

This adjusted formulation permitted funded spending in *Government* of $34.4 billion — $4.4 billion less than actual. To that extent, Government contributed to the 1957–60 deficit, largely because of two line items that expanded immoderately.

The contribution to the deficit of *Government* was calculated using the growth factor explained above, but in measuring cost trends it is more informative to use the current revenue growth rate of 18.6 percent as the benchmark beyond which dangerous cost trends can be found.

With that as the focus, concentration is most productively placed on the comparison of all costs before "Commerce" (highly volatile) and "Offsetting Receipts" are considered.

At that level of comparison, cost growth was 42.3 percent, and all line items except Energy, Agriculture and General were well above the spending limits imposed by the revenue curve.

Table 6.3
Government (in billions of dollars)

	1957–60	1953–56	% Change
Energy	$ 1.4	$ 1.3	7.7%
Natural Resources/Environment	5.7	4.1	39.0
Transportation	11.8	5.2	126.9
Community/regional development	.7	.4	75.0
International affairs	12.6	8.3	51.8
Science/space/technology	1.1	.3	266.7
Agriculture	11.9	11.1	7.2
Justice	1.4	1.1	27.3
General	4.2	3.9	7.7
Total	$50.8	$35.7	42.3%
Commerce & housing credit*	5.8	1.3	346.2
Total	$56.6	$37.0	53.0%
Offsetting receipts	-17.8	-14.1	26.2
Net	$38.8	$22.9	69.4%

*Made up of earnings from various federal housing and other programs—
subject to major changes from year to year relative to market conditions.
(Historical Tables 2007, 3.2)

Source: Historical Tables 2007, 3.1

Given the events of the era, there is no apparent reason for the high spending on Environment and Community Development except the desire to do so.

Ike's valuable national highway project boosted Transportation costs temporarily, a recoverable cost overage as the project matured.

The European Economic Community Treaty was signed; the Eisenhower Doctrine calling for aid to Middle Eastern countries that resisted communism was announced; U.S. Marines were sent to Lebanon at the request of its besieged president; Egypt seized, then later released, the Suez Canal; Fidel Castro assumed power in Cuba. This sampling of events establishes the busy tone of 1957–60 during which the cost of International grew by 52 percent.

The increasing cost of the arms race with the Soviets is reflected in the Science/space costs, which figured to get bigger sooner than they'd get smaller.

And the implementation costs in support of the desegregation ruling of the Supreme Court were reflected in the increased cost of Justice.

Overall, no sign of significant and foolish spending in *Government* appeared during the subject period.

The overage was essentially the regrettable cost of supporting a maturing government in a troubled world.

HUMAN RESOURCES

Human Resources went up 64.1 percent in 1957–60. But, as with *Government*, allowable growth in the subject period became 1.50 times because primary cost centers passed along their unused growth funds to the other cost centers.

As a consequence, the funded spending level was lifted to $83.9 billion or $7.7 billion less than actual. To that extent, *Human Resources* contributed to the federal deficit for the period.

Table 6.4
Human Resources (in billions of dollars)

	1957–60	1953–56	% Change
Education, training, services	$ 3.0	$ 1.8	66.6%
Health	2.5	1.3	92.3
Income Security	28.5	18.0	58.3
Social Security	36.3	16.0	126.8
Medicare	0.0	0.0	0.0
Veterans	21.3	18.7	13.9
Total	$91.6	$55.8	64.1%

Note: There were few social program of consequence prior to the 1960s except for Social Security (started in 1935) and the GI Bill.

Source: Historical Tables 2007, 3.1

Although the contribution of *Human Resources* to the deficit was calculated on the basis of an allowable growth rate, it is more informative to appraise spending within this cost center using as a benchmark the rate of revenue increase, 18.6 percent. On that basis, only the line item Veterans was fully funded.

With an unemployment rate of 6.6 percent in 1960,[15] weekly payments to the unemployed continued to be reflected in the spending increases of Income Security and in Education/Training Services.

The rate of cost increase in Health was something to watch, but in the context of a total budget, it was not in 1957–60 a consequential line item.

Not so, however, with Social Security. Costs were out of control, as were the politicians who pressed them into the budget at ever-increasing levels. With any responsible degree of control over this line item, the deficit for the period could have been avoided.

SUMMARY OF DEFICIT ALLOCATION

The years from 1941 to 1956 were heavily influenced by war, and a separate method was used to allocate deficits. Beginning with 1957, the same method was employed for the remaining presidential periods.

Under both methods, primary cost centers stand alone in the sense that their growth allowance, in the context of a balanced budget, is limited by the growth in revenue. The allowable growth in the other cost centers, in the context of a balanced budget, is expanded or contracted depending upon the need of the primary cost centers for the funds allocated to them.

For the subject period the deficit amounted to $12.1 billion, all of it allocated to *Government* and *Human Resources*, as follows:

Table 6.5
Summary of Deficit, 1957–60 (in billions of dollars)

Cost Center	Amount
Defense	$ 0.0
Interest	0.0
Government	-4.4
Human Resources	-7.7
Total	$-12.1

The factor that saved 1957–60 from having a huge deficit was the stabilization of military spending. The peace dividend that could have come from that went instead to the reasonable increase in *Government* spending and to the unreasonable increase in Social Security. And the trend was bad. *Human Resources*, home of the Welfare State, was still out of control.

Conclusion

Ike came into office in 1953 with the Korean War and the Cold War in process, and with a Republican Congress to help him. Eight years later, the Korean War was over; the Cold War was more dangerous than ever; Castro was snarling in Cuba, backed by the Soviets; and Congress was firmly in the hands of Democrats.

Public debt in 1960 was a bit higher but, considering the lagging economy and the spending habits of the controlling liberals, budget performance during Ike's watch was commendable. And he left behind a set of spending priorities that could serve as a base of comparison for future Cold War presidents.

Table 6.6
Spending Priorities

	1940	1944	1952	1960
Primary costs				
Defense	17.5%	86.7%	68.1%	52.2%
Interest	9.5	2.4	6.9	7.5
Total	27.0%	89.1%	75.0	59.7%
Government	29.3	8.8	7.6	11.9
Education/services	20.8	0.0	.4	1.0
Health	0.6	0.2	.4	.9
Medicare	0.0	0.0	.0	
Income Security	16.0	1.6	5.5	8.0
Social Security	0.3	0.3	3.1	12.6
Veterans	6.0	0.0	8.0	5.9
Total	100.0%	100.0%	100.0%	100.0%
	(1)	(2)	(2)	(3)

1=peace; 2=war; 3=cold war

Source: Historical Tables 2007, 3.1

Ike's America was about as close to the Founder's dream as circumstances would permit. His profile of the nation said to the outside world: We are prepared to defend ourselves (primary costs 59.7 percent), and we can expand our size to meet new international demands, and to meet the reasonable needs of our citizens on a planned basis that, at the present time, is in need of adjustment.

Public debt in 1957–60 increased from $222.2 billion to $236.8[16] billion because of the expansion of government to meet modern needs and to finance the unwise expansion of an already overextended and poorly organized Social Security program.

Table 6.7
Public Debt, 1960 (billions)

Event	Inherited 1956	Added 1957–1960	Total 1960	%
World War I	$ 18.3	$	$ 18.3	7.7%
Great Depression	24.5		24.5	10.3
World War II	142.5		142.5	60.2
Korean War	6.6		6.6	2.8
Interest	5.4		5.4	2.2
Government	5.6	4.4	10.0	4.3
Human Resources	19.9	7.7	27.6	11.8
Treasury	-.6	2.5	1.9	.7
Total	$222.2	$14.6	$236.8	100.0%

Source: Exhibits 1, 11, 12, 16

Ike's greatest contribution as president was, arguably, just being Ike. The international reputation he gained on the battlefields of Europe was one of America's greatest assets during the early years of the Cold War. Once he left office, Soviet experiments with America's resolve increased, as they never had before, a happenstance that may or may not have been related to his retirement from public service.

Concerning expanded government services, Ike was not inclined to add to the Welfare State. But he was active in building infrastructure — extensive highways in the United States — and he joined with Canada in the development of the St. Lawrence Seaway.

Ike was also the first president to authorize federal muscle in support of the Supreme Court's decision to desegregate schools, a dramatic action by a conservative Republican that is seldom mentioned.

Perhaps Ike's greatest failure was his inability to pick judges for the Supreme Court who were not activists determined to rebuild America in a way that met some personal standard.

This failure resonated through the next decades and played a huge role in the development of the social chaos that gradually evolved.

Overall, Eisenhower produced a commendable record in his eight years.

His expansion of government (HEW) was for organizational, not programmatic, purposes; his deficits were small, and they largely represented legitimate additions to public debt. The debt problem that plagues modern-day America cannot be laid at the feet of Dwight Eisenhower.

Ike left behind a few advisers who had been assigned to Vietnam, a military capability that the next two presidents gratefully utilized, and his advice, which they ignored, to remain unentangled in Asian affairs.

7

John F. Kennedy and Lyndon B. Johnson, 1961–1964

Representative, Senator, President

Woodrow Wilson was president when John F. Kennedy was born in 1917 in his Brookline, Massachusetts, home in the midst of World War I. The second son of wealthy parents, Joseph and Rose, he had a political heritage long and deep that came from both sides of the family.

Paternal grandfather Patrick served in the Massachusetts House and Senate in the 1800s; maternal grandfather "Honey Fitz" Fitzgerald participated in local and national politics until a few years before John's birth. And most important of all, John's father Joseph became an intimate of Franklin Roosevelt.

A career in politics for John Kennedy was almost a certainty from the day of his birth. His father, Joseph Kennedy (1888–1969), Harvard graduate at 24, was the youngest bank president in Massachusetts at 25; he married Rose Fitzgerald at 26, and he became a millionaire at 35.

Kennedy amassed a huge fortune in banking, investing, liquor, real estate and movies. He became, in the process, a colorful character and a ladies' man. His support of Roosevelt in 1932 led him into the public sector as chairman of the Securities and Exchange Commission (1934–35) and the U.S. Maritime Commission (1937), and, finally, as ambassador to Great Britain (1937–40).

In the latter post, Kennedy's relationship with FDR disintegrated because of Kennedy's resistance to involvement of America in World War II.

Young John Kennedy led the privileged life of a rich boy. Private schools in Massachusetts, New York and Connecticut groomed him until, at 14, he entered Choate School in Wallingford, Connecticut. He was graduated in 1935, 64th in a class of 112, apparently more a prankster than a student.

Kennedy lost most of the next year due to illness (jaundice), but in 1936 he entered Harvard. He graduated cum laude in 1940.

FDR was president. Public debt was $42.8 billion[1]; the Depression was 11 years old.

Kennedy took courses at Stanford Business School in 1940–41, and he toured South America before joining the navy as an ensign. He was Lieutenant Kennedy in 1942, captain of a PT boat. Kennedy's boat was rammed in 1943 and several of his crew were lost, but days later, he and other survivors were rescued partly due to his leadership. He received several decorations for this incident, the strains of which aggravated his bad back. Kennedy returned stateside and in 1945 he returned to civilian life.

Harry Truman was president; public debt was $235.2 billion; John Kennedy was 28 years old.

Kennedy dabbled in journalism for a short time after his discharge, but with the death of his brother Joe (his navy plane exploded in flight in August 1944) he knew that he was destined for a political career under the energetic sponsorship and direction of his father. The development of his future in politics was his father's final occupation and, in this effort, he was typically effective.

Kennedy in 1947 began his political career in the House of Representatives (1947–52); in 1952, he ran for the Senate seat occupied by the aristocratic Henry Cabot Lodge. The Kennedy political machine (it is still a powerful, expensive and effective organization) went into high gear in that race against one of the best-known names in Massachusetts politics.

Kennedy won impressively, and celebrated by marrying Jacqueline Bouvier (1953), who had a background of privilege to match his own.

The ambitions of Joseph Kennedy for his son did not end with the Senate, nor did those of the son himself, a willing and able puppet in the hands of his father, the master manipulator.

There was, for example, the vice presidential nomination that John Kennedy lost in 1956. But it gained him national recognition that he put to good use in 1960 when he wrested from Senator Hubert Humphrey (D–MN) the nomination of the Democratic Party and went on to beat Vice President Richard Nixon in one of the most controversial contests in presidential history (49.72 percent vs. 49.55 percent, popular vote).[2] Nixon's reaction to this defeat was roundly admired.

Throughout his term in office, JFK had the support of Democratic leaders in Congress, Sam Rayburn (D–TX) and John McCormack (D–MA) in the House; Mike Mansfield (D–MT) in the Senate.[3] And his vice president, Lyndon B. Johnson, had been one of the most powerful lawmakers in the history of the Senate.

JFK was assassinated on a street in Dallas, Texas, in November 1963. Lyndon B. Johnson succeeded him.

The Eisenhower administration passed forward to Kennedy a public debt of $236.8 billion, summarized as follows:

Table 7.1
Public Debt 1960 (in billions of dollars)

	Total	%
World War I	$ 18.3	7.7%
Great Depression:	24.5	10.3
World War II	142.5	60.2
Korean War	6.6	2.8
Interest	5.4	2.2
Government	10.0	4.3
Human Resources	27.6	11.8
Treasury, net	1.9	.7
Total	$236.8	100.0%

Source: Table 5.6, Chapter 6

President Kennedy approached the debt problem with justifiable confidence. To be sure, there was unrest in Cuba and in Vietnam, and the Soviets were as dangerous as ever, but there was no Korean War to deal with and the need for expensive military spending was lower than that which faced Eisenhower when he took office eight years before.

There was good reason to hope that a planned budget surplus could at least wipe out the increased debt that had been caused by previous overspending in the overhead cost centers, *Government and Human Resources.*

In order to do this, four things had to happen:

- No important and expensive international incidents.
- An improved economy.
- Control of spending in Human Resources, especially Social Security.
- No additions to the Welfare State until current programs were restructured to become affordable.

President Kennedy (JFK) was in firm control of the government. Congress was controlled by Democrats; the Supreme Court was packed with supporters of Democratic causes. What happened next, good or bad, would be nailed to his name.

Perspectives

GENERAL

Fidel Castro was a major bee in the JFK bonnet. The Cuban leader fostered revolutionary movements in Central America and took every opportunity to besmirch the reputation of the United States. His power base was a stone's throw from Florida; his patron was the USSR.

JFK was determined to do something about Cuba. He failed when the Bay of Pigs invasion of Cuba in April 1961, which was designed to overthrow Castro's government through the use of American-trained Cuban exiles, didn't work as planned, partly due to his own indecisiveness.[4]

This huge blow to his reputation was somewhat repaired in the next year when he confronted the Soviets over the installation of missiles in Cuba. His blockade of Cuba and the U.S-Soviet confrontation on the high seas made Khrushchev blink, and it led to the dismantlement of the missiles. But Castro continued to be a major pest in the region for years thereafter and the Cuban problem had a direct budget impact.

First of all, there was the military cost of dealing with the issue (Bay of Pigs, naval blockade, etc.). But, more importantly, JFK's failure in Cuba may have been one of the reasons for his willingness to become more engaged in Vietnam than his predecessor, Dwight Eisenhower, had advised.

Had there not been the embarrassment of the Bay of Pigs and all that followed, would there have been a felt need to prove America's strength in Vietnam, an event that dominated foreign affairs beginning in 1961.

Under Ike, the United States only supplied arms and a few military advisers to the South Vietnamese. It was his stated policy that America should not get more deeply involved. But in May 1961, JFK changed the role of the United States from that of a supplier of services to that of a co-combatant.

By the end of that year he had 16,000 troops in Vietnam. And by the time he died in 1963, the U.S. footprint amounted to more than 20,000 men.

Lyndon B. Johnson (LBJ), commander in chief in 1964, was determined to win the war that JFK had started. By July, U.S. troops were up to 25,000. In August, all but two congressmen supported LBJ's war policy in the Gulf of Tonkin resolution. America was poised to commit substantial military resources to the ongoing war.

Space and who controlled it was an issue of importance. The Soviets were embarrassingly efficient in this competition; JFK pledged to get America up to speed. Yuri Gagarin, a Russian, was the first prominent international astronaut. And in April 1961 the Russians sent another man into orbit, Gherman Stepanovich. America's riposte with space flights by Alan Shepard and Virgil Grissom was not competitive. Nor was the short around-the-world orbit of John Glenn in 1962 (3 orbits vs. 17 for the Russians).

The Berlin Wall was erected in 1961.[5] It was a monument to strained relations—an institutionalization of the Cold War presented in solid stone. The two giants, the USSR and America, stared at each other over the wall, each having little to offer the other except the power of mutual destruction that so far had kept the peace — and had kept the cost of *Defense* high.

THE HOME FRONT

The civil rights pot was put on the burner under Dwight Eisenhower; it reached simmer temperature under JFK, and it moved to a boil with Lyndon Johnson, Kennedy's successor in office.

The integration of southern colleges continued. Huge rallies were held in Washington. Supreme Court rulings and legislation begun in the Eisenhower/Kennedy/Johnson era would establish equal rights under law that would make segregation a bad memory.

The rush to solve racial problems had a direct impact on the climbing costs of *Human Resources* as politicians tried to accomplish with programs what should have been done out of principle.

The business cycle had dealt Ike a weak hand in 1957–60, and it showed in the limp flow of tax revenue that was available to him. But Kennedy and Johnson had an easier time.

In current dollars, GDP was 24 percent higher in 1964 than in 1960; in adjusted dollars, it grew by 18 percent, both numbers considerably higher than Ike experienced during his last term.[6]

This good news from the private sector, of course, expressed itself in the federal budget in the form of robust tax receipts—$113 billion in 1964 versus $92 billion in 1960, an increase of 23 percent,[7] a good indicator that better days were ahead.

The administration was blessed economically with a healthy business cycle buttressed by the stimulation of wartime spending that was provoked by the increased involvement of the United States in Vietnam.

At this stage in the analysis, it would appear that budget problems, if any, would come from the spending side of the equation, not the revenue side.

America counted 133 million people in 1941 and 192 million in 1964—1.4 times larger. In a quarter of a century, the nation had changed significantly. There were now high taxes, an activist government, less reliance on individuals, more security, and less liberty.

The Misery Index showed some improvement in 1961–1964—a drop from 13.1 percent to 10.8 percent.[8] All three indicators were down, but unemployment at 5 percent was still too high.

The taxpayer got a break in 1964 due to revised tax policy that lowered personal and corporate tax rates.[9] The increase in average income per capita was good news—up 20 percent.[10]

Combined with controlled inflation and lower taxes, it was a comparatively good time for workers. A worker sent 11.5 weeks of work to Washington as opposed to 12.1 weeks four years before.

The low end of the wage earners, however, didn't fare as well—the payroll tax assessment increased from 6.0 percent of $4,800 to 7.25 percent of the same maximum amount.

SUPREME COURT[11]

Ike had replaced five judges over the eight years of his presidency so it didn't seem likely that either JFK or LBJ would have much of a chance to make selections of their own, but the Court was already tilted to the left.

One new judge did appear — Arthur Goldberg. A thumbnail sketch of his background appears below.

- Arthur J. Goldberg — Goldberg in 1930 was graduated from the Northwestern University School of Law. Eight years later he was a highly successful practitioner in the field of labor law. During World War II he served as the U.S. contact with Europe's underground labor movement, after which he served in several high executive posts with the CIO, an organization of labor unions. Unsurprisingly, JFK made him his secretary of labor (1961–62) after which he appointed him to the U.S. Supreme Court to replace the ailing Felix Frankfurter (appointed by FDR). Goldberg's stay on the Court was a short one because in 1965 LBJ persuaded him to replace Adlai Stevenson as the U.S. ambassador to the United Nations. Goldberg resigned from that position, hoping once again, at a later time, to be re-appointed to the Court. But LBJ passed him by and chose instead a close friend, Abe Fortas. Disappointed, Goldberg unsuccessfully ran for governor of New York, after which he essentially returned to private practice until his death in 1990. President Carter in 1978 awarded him the Presidential Medal of Freedom. While on the bench Goldberg was true to his liberal credentials; for example, he supported the *Griswold* decision (the discovery of the right to privacy that led to legalized abortion) and he opposed the death penalty as being "cruel and unusual punishment" (Eighth Amendment).

Court ideological balance remained about the same in the swap of Goldberg for Frankfurter.

The number of cases heard by Chief Justice Warren zoomed from 13 in 1957–60 to 31 in 1961–64.[12]

Why?

Perhaps liberal groups were intimidated by the mere presence of Ike in the White House and were slow to bring forward their concerns, or it could be they were energized by the election of one of their own.

Whatever the reason, this was the beginning of a fundamental change in the view of what the Court should or should not hear — a decision that is entirely left to the Court (unless restricted by congressional action).

Where does local jurisdiction end and Supreme Court jurisdiction begin? That underlying question was increasingly answered by the Court in favor of itself. As a consequence it got heavily involved with local issues, which in turn created more and more cases for the Court to adjudicate.

A review of a few cases of the time provides a sense of the concerns of the immediate era.

Braunfeld v. Brown, 1961. Braunfeld, a Jewish merchant, wanted to keep his store open on Sunday, in violation of local law, because his faith did not permit him to work on the Sabbath (Saturday). The issue: Did the local Sunday law violate the merchant's right to practice his faith without penalty? In a 6–3 decision, the Court upheld the blue law. Justices Douglas, Brennan and Frankfurter dissented.

Engel v. Vitale, 1962. The state of New York, in an attempt to defuse a hot local issue approved the blandest voluntary prayer it could think of to be recited in public schools each morning — "Almighty God, we acknowledge our dependence upon Thee, and beg Thy blessings on us, our teachers and our country." The issue: Was the state law concerning voluntary prayer a violation of First Amendment rights? In a 4–1 decision, the Court ruled that any prayer in school, voluntary or not, constituted the approval of religion by the state and, as such, was unconstitutional. Justice Potter Stewart was the lone dissenter.

Edwards v. South Carolina, 1963. About 200 black petitioners organized a peaceful demonstration that took place on the grounds of the South Carolina State House. When police ordered the marchers to disperse, they held fast, sang songs and were arrested. The issue: Did the arrest of these marchers violate their rights under the First and the Fourteenth Amendments? In an 8–1 decision, the Court ruled that the demonstration was constitutional. Justice Tom Clark dissented. This decision paved the way for public demonstrations that were fairly common in some parts of Europe, but had been seldom seen in the United States. The key was to keep them nonviolent, a lesson that the Reverend Martin Luther King, Jr., carefully noted.

Gideon v. Wainwright, 1963. Gideon was a robber. He asked that an attorney be appointed to defend him. The judge refused on the grounds that the law required him to oblige a defendant's request for an attorney only in murder cases. Gideon defended himself and was found guilty. The issue: Did the judge err by denying Gideon his rights to a fair trial and due process (Sixth and Fourteenth Amendments)? In a unanimous decision, the Court ruled that the defendant had a right to an attorney. In so ruling, the Court overruled its 1942 decision on the same subject (*Betts v. Brady*). *This, and other cases, puts to rest the fiction that Court decisions become constitutional law and so they can't be reversed. They can be and, when circumstances justify, they are.*

Two factors in 1961–64 tended to increase the Supreme Court's caseload:

- The desire of activist judges to make new law.
- The civil rights movement itself that preferred legal and centralized decisions as opposed to slow-moving, local and democratic processes.

These two factors overlapped and in combination created a caseload at the Court that grew exponentially.

Whether one agrees or disagrees with the decisions of the Supreme Court during this era, there can be no disagreement over one fact: For better or for worse they were changing the face of America from one that had been created by the Founding Fathers to something as yet undefined.

SOCIETY[13]

This section is introduced at this point because a Second American Revolution in the United States began with the JFK/LBJ administration, and selected social statistics from that period establish a baseline for comments in upcoming chapters as the impact of fiscal and legal decisions weaves its way into the fabric of American society.

Marriage, still relatively strong in the 1960 world of President Eisenhower, showed signs of deterioration for reasons that are left for others to discover.

Relative to modern-day attitudes between men and women, the pre–1960 America was an innocent time, from a formal standpoint. Hell-raising had its time and place but in the world of society, for example, living together outside of marriage was referred to as shacking up, and it was not looked upon favorably. Women were highly regarded protectors of public morality, and the great majority of them did not easily bend before the blandishments of less-than-serious suitors. The U.S. profile began to change as politicians and judges of the era abandoned their social heritage.

Life expectancy in Ike's time was in the mid sixties.[14] With a persistently growing population,[15] including a strong mix of immigrants,[16] one would normally expect as well an increase in the number of violent crimes.

There are two schools of thought afloat about how to appraise crime statistics. Some, for example, do not get concerned until the crime per capita increases. Others recognize that just a handful of bad guys can create havoc in a society and, with that in mind, they are disturbed when the number of them significantly increases.

In this book, the latter viewpoint is held and the changes in the absolute numbers in subsequent chapters will be examined with interest.

Change in Public Debt

The JFK administration must have begun on a note of optimism. There were no shooting wars, the Cuban situation didn't appear to be unduly troubling, Vietnam was a contained situation, the Soviets posed no observable immediate dangers and Congress was controlled by fellow Democrats who could be supervised by one of the most competent ex-congressmen who ever served in that body, Vice President Lyndon B. Johnson.

Then the wheels came off the bus.

In 1961, the Bay of Pigs fiasco made the United States appear arrogant and incompetent. JFK lost face and the reputation of the United States in the Americas— not too good to begin with — deteriorated even more.

Then the Soviets sneaked missiles into Cuba. If their installation had been completed the United States would have faced a Soviet satellite that was more than eager to further intimidate its foremost international rival.

JFK's stern reaction to this threat made the public forget about how the United States permitted it to develop in the first place, and his reputation for competence was at least partly restored.

Then came JFK's decision to change tactics in Vietnam, to join South Vietnam as a fighting partner instead of maintaining the relationship Ike had established, namely, as a remote supplier and supporter of their cause.

Most sources date the beginning of the Vietnam War to 1964, but that is incorrect. It began on JFK's watch, when, before he was killed, he committed over 20,000 men to the cause of South Vietnam.[17] To be sure, LBJ greatly expanded the effort, but the trigger that put the United States into the conflict in the first place was pulled by JFK.

These events took the rosy glow off of expectations. They demanded funds; so did the appetite of those who wanted to expand the Welfare State. Would they contain themselves or would they persist in their strategy to build it at any cost?

The analysis of the transactions for the period will assist in finding answers to these questions.

Table 7.2
Transactions (in billions of dollars)

		1960–64		1957–60
Taxes		$ 413.3		$ 331.3
Less:				
Defense	$210.1		$189.3	
Interest	29.5		23.7	
Total		239.6		213.0
Net		$ 173.7		$ 118.3
Less:				
Government	$ 64.5		$ 38.8	
Human Resources	130.2		91.6	
Total		194.7		130.4
Surplus/deficit		$ -21.0		$ -12.1
Debt, beginning		-236.8		-222.2
Total		$-257.8		$-234.3
Adjustment*		1.0		-2.5
Debt, Ending		$-256.8		$-236.8

*Treasury cannot be exact when it finances a budget deficit and the difference between what is needed and the value of securities traded inevitably produces a relatively small variance.

Source: Historical Tables 2007, 1.1, 3.1

A cursory glance at the above numbers indicates that the deficit was not apparently related to major external events.

Primary cost centers, *Defense* and *Interest*, for example, did not grow disproportionately, but other cost centers, where one would expect controls to be firm, grew at a much higher rate than revenue.

But experience has demonstrated that cursory opinions need the clarification that analysis provides. And the step-by-step appraisal of the major components of the problem will continue.

TAXES

Federal revenue in 1961–64 was 24.8 percent more than the revenue for the previous four years.[18]

Federal revenues increased every year of the JFK/LBJ administration.[19] America's economic system, its most precious material asset, poured dollars into Washington almost (but not quite) as fast as politicians could find ways to spend it.

The economy was more productive than it had been,[20] but JFK (uncharacteristically for a Democrat) believed it needed a federal stimulant to improve productivity and he approved a reduction in personal and corporate tax rates.[21]

Oddly, JFK also increased the payroll tax rate, an act that disproportionately attacked low wage earners.

Apparently this was an attempt to maintain the illusion of a trust fund for Social Security that gave comfort to taxpayers. In fact, this was but another example of the refusal of Washingtonocrats to face the central issue — the payroll tax was not the way to fund this prized program. And until it was restructured to endure, no additions to Social Security should have been made.

In a period of relatively stable *Defense* cost, the revenue increase of 24.8 percent during the subject period should have been enough to avoid a deficit budget. But it wasn't.

The question: What happened?

DEFENSE

The increase in *Defense* of 11 percent was fully funded by the 24.8 percent increase in revenue.[22]

JFK inherited a military force of 2.5 million.[23] The Cold War with the Soviets was ongoing, the Cuban tension erupted in 1961 and a year later JFK changed America's hands-off Vietnam policy and sent troops to that troubled nation, a decision that LBJ vigorously copied when he succeeded to the presidency.[24]

The existing number of troops reflected the force of a nation at peace. And since America was at war, a buildup in the size of the military loomed.

INTEREST

The increase in *Interest* was fully funded by the revenue increase, and it played no part in the development of the deficit.

The prime interest rate stubbornly remained in the 4.5 percent area[25] reflecting, in part, the federal level of borrowing that, in the marketplace, competed with the private sector in the search for investment dollars.

Interest was ignored by the public despite long-term implications because its short-term penalties were not too painful. But by itself it was a symptom of larger problems:

- The size of the public debt.
- The abandonment of fiscal disciplines (pay bills and tax only when necessary).
- The adoption of a code that regarded a certain percentage of GDP as the federal property of liberal politicians owed by taxpayers.

Social needs as perceived by politicians, not the government's ability to pay, determined spending levels in the world of Kennedy and Johnson. That policy (promoted vigorously for the first time by Lyndon Johnson in 1965–68) could be captured in a catchy phrase: Charge it.

Public debt versus GDP was on a downward glide path under Ike, and that positive trend continued under JFK/LBJ.[26]

Others would pay the price for the Welfare State that was born in the 1960s.

GOVERNMENT

Primary costs did not increase as much as revenue in 1961–64 and the amount of overfunding to those cost centers flowed to the other centers under the allocation system that is in play in this book. As a consequence, *Government* and *Human Resources*, could grow by 1.33 times before their spending would contribute to a deficit.[27]

Had *Government* expanded 1.33 times as provided by the flow-through formula, its cost would have been $51.7 billion, or $12.8 billion less than actual. To that extent, it contributed to the deficit for the period.

Although the flow-through system permits growth without penalty of 1.33 times, it is more productive and informative to appraise spending increases by using the revenue indicator — 1.25 times — as the yardstick of cost control.

Agriculture, Justice and General operated within guidelines. The other line items overspent during a time of stress and war.

Was this overspending justified on some other basis?

The space race that JFK vowed to win is the justification for the enormous increase in Space, etc. costs.

Energy, Transportation and International line items increased as the sit-

Table 7.3
Government (in billions of dollars)

	1961–64	1957–60	% Change
Energy	$ 2.2	$ 1.4	57.1%
Natural Resources/Environment	8.5	5.7	49.1
Transportation	18.1	11.8	53.3
Community/regional development	2.3	.7	228.5
International affairs	19.0	12.6	50.8
Science/space/technology	10.6	1.1	863.6
Agriculture	15.1	11.9	25.9
Justice	1.8	1.4	28.6
General	5.1	4.2	21.4
Total	$82.7	$50.8	62.8%
Commerce & housing credit*	3.1	5.8	-46.5
Total	$85.8	$56.6	51.6%
Offsetting receipts	-21.3	-17.8	19.7
Net	$64.5	$38.8	66.2%

*Made up of earnings from various federal housing and other programs—subject to major changes from year to year relative to market conditions. (Historical Tables 2007, 3.2)

Source: Historical Tables 2007, 3.1

uation in Vietnam heated up. On those grounds, they can be given a nod of acceptance as being an indirect cost of war.

But the increases in Natural Resources and Community Development appear to be based on nothing more than the desire to spend.

HUMAN RESOURCES

This cost center increased by 42.1 percent, well above the rate of revenue increase.

Under the flow-through method of allocation, spending growth of 1.33 times is allowed, and the addition to the deficit amounted to $8.2 billion.

Table 7.4
Human Resources (in billions of dollars)

	1961–64	1957–60	% Change
Education, training, services	$ 5.3	$ 3.0	76.7%
Health/Medicaid	5.4	2.5	116.0
Income Security	37.8	28.5	32.7
Social Security	59.2	36.3	63.1
Veterans	22.5	21.3	5.6
Total	$130.2	$91.6	42.1%

Note: There were few social programs of consequence prior to the 1960s except for Social Security (started in 1935) and the GI Bill.

Note: Major federal programs since the 1960s include Food Stamps 1961 (pilot) and Food Stamps 1964.

Source: Historical Tables 2007, 3.1

There is no sign of restraint in these numbers, nor is there any indication of an acceptance of the wisdom of the past, based upon which the ability to borrow was carefully protected to cover nonrecurring costs of emergencies.

During a time of expanding military activity, spending in this cost center should have been tightly controlled so that the full borrowing power of the United States could be used for the imminent dangers ahead.

But the opposite was the case. The Welfare State expanded under the cover of war while high tax rates still prevailed. Programs that could not be funded out of current revenues were introduced and budget deficits became a characteristic of the federal government.

"Guns and butter too" was the saying of the times, meaning that social programs could expand vigorously even during wartime.

And they did.

New Frontier and Great Society programs, on top of the FDR/Truman legacy, flexed their muscles under the combined leadership of JFK and LBJ. Absolute amounts of overspending were not yet troubling, but the signs of unstoppable growth were clear.

And debt grew again.

Summary of Deficit Allocation

Ironically, during a time of war, the overspending was not in *Defense*. JFK and LBJ either figured that victory in Vietnam would be quick and cheap, or they planned to draw down on the war machine created by Ike.

Whatever the reason, the overspending that took place during the period did not make America stronger — it just made the American government bigger.

Interest growth was no problem because the increase in debt was in absolute terms nominal, and interest rates were relatively stable.

Government overspent hugely, but about two-thirds of the overage related to unavoidable international events. Where unexplained spending did appear, it was troubling, because it suggested that Congress was off in a direction of its own that had little to do with fiscal discipline and debt control.

That suspicion was confirmed in the analysis of *Human Resources*. Spending in that cost center was out of control.

Table 7.5
Summary of Deficit, 1961–1964 (in billions of dollars)

Cost Center	Amount
Defense	$ 0.0
Interest	0.0
Government	-12.8
Human Resources	-8.2
Total	$-21.0

In some periods, with some presidents, deficits are unavoidable. This was not such a period.

Conclusion

Into World War II under Roosevelt, out of it under Harry Truman, into Korea under Truman, out of it under Dwight Eisenhower, and back into war in Vietnam under Kennedy.

It was a nasty quarter of a century, one bound to change the priorities of the United States had nothing been changed except its emergence as an international power, but one bound to change even more when its governing philosophy switched from that of the freedom-seeking Founding Fathers to that of well-meaning politicians who installed, as a substitute, a Welfare State.

Table 7.6
Spending Priorities

	1940	1952	1960	1964
Primary costs				
Defense	17.5%	68.1%	52.2%	46.2%
Interest	9.5	6.9	7.5	6.9
Total	27.0%	75.0	59.7%	53.1%
Government	29.3	7.6	11.9	17.0
Education/services	20.8	.4	1.0	1.4%
Health/Medicaid	0.6	.4	.9	1.5
Medicare	0.0	.0	0.0	0.0
Income Security	16.0	5.5	8.0	8.2
Social Security	0.3	3.1	12.6	14.0
Veterans	6.0	8.0	5.9	4.8
Total	100.0%	100.0%	100.0%	100.0%
	(1)	(2)	(3)	(2)(3)

1 = peace; 2 = war; 3 = cold war
Source: Historical Tables 2007, 3.1

The 1940 profile shows the picture that prewar America showed to the outside world, a self-sufficient, inward-looking nation at peace, one that devoted about 40 percent of its resources to citizen services—a picture that in the 1960s was no longer relevant because World War II changed the U.S. into an outward-looking, heavily involved world power with all of the expanded governmental services that are attached to such a role.

The 1960 profile is one of a nation also at peace, but a different kind of peace in a different kind of world. It was the peace of the Cold War period, meaning that bullets weren't flying but danger was high. And it was a world in which America was the leader of the free world—the only nation capable of deterring the expansionistic ambitions of the Soviet Union.

In that world, under those conditions, the most capable man in the nation to determine its proper military stance was Dwight Eisenhower, former leader of Allied Forces during World War II. Ike devoted 52 percent of the federal budget to *Defense.*

In subsequent chapters, the 1940 profile will be dropped, and the 1960 profile will be substituted as the yardstick that measures the America established by the Founding Fathers against the America that was born in the 1960s— one that has evolved over time, and one that still attempts to dominate, unchastened by the fiscal and judicial consequences of what it has already done.

In the 1964 profile, the first to reflect the new ideas of the Great Society, signs of defection from past wisdom are easy to find.

A hot war had begun in Vietnam, and the Cold War continued as usual. Under these circumstances one would have expected that Eisenhower's allowance of 52 percent for *Defense* would be exceeded.

It wasn't!

Under worse comparative conditions, JFK/LBJ lowered the *Defense* allowance to 46 percent of all spending.

Under these more dangerous conditions one would also have expected that discretionary spending would drop — that the movement to install a Welfare State would at least be postponed.

Not so.

The cost center *Human Resources* grew disproportionately and gobbled tax dollars that the public thought were going to the defense of the nation.

How could politicians face such spending growth and remain complacent? What information demonstrated that revenues to cover such expansion would be forthcoming? What economic theory defended ever-increasing debt caused not by heavy *Defense,* but by the unrecovered costs of federal social programs?

If those expenditures were valid, why didn't politicians argue for the taxes needed to support them? Did they find it easier to blame deficits on Vietnam than to explain the need to restrain spending?

What made political leaders decide that the cost of new federal welfare programs should be borne by *future* taxpayers? Where were the conservative, responsible politicians in 1961–64? Where was the press? Had America forgotten how to count?

Federal revenues are reductions in the people's income. Funds sent to Washington represent a slice of freedom given up by the taxpayer. Except for the wealthy who, whatever the tax policy, always have enough, citizens with less money, because of higher taxes, curtail activities that require money — vacations, movies and a cold beer.

They sent a big slice of themselves to Washington in 1961–64, the slice that eases the burdens of life, not to defend America or to help a neighbor, but to make the world conform to some image of perfection imagined by imperfect federal politicians.

Did the people know what they were paying for? Would they have paid it had they known?

In 1964 the Vietnam War, the civil rights movement, protest marches, and the power chess game with the USSR lulled Americans to sleep as the federal government moved deeper into their private lives, establishing in the process a structure of social programs that would strap average-income taxpayers to the plow with or without war, with or without the USSR.

Public debt increased $20.0 billion in 1961–64, as follows:

Table 7.7
Public Debt, 1964 (billions)

Event	Inherited 1960	Added 1961–64	Total 1964	%
World War 1	$ 18.3	$	$ 18.3	7.1%
Great Depression	24.5		24.5	9.5
World War 2	142.5		142.5	55.5
Korean War	6.6		6.6	2.6
Interest	5.4		5.4	2.1
Government	10.0	12.8	22.8	8.9
Human Resources	27.6	8.2	35.8	13.9
Treasury	1.9	-1.0	.9	.4
Total	$236.8	$20.0	$256.8	100.0%

Source: Exhibits 1, 11, 12, 16

Government and *Human Resources* at the end of 1964 represented almost 23 percent of the total debt.

A relatively small amount of overspending in these overhead cost centers is not unusual, and should not be surprising — a well-motivated Congress can overcome them in future years.

But a steady increase in debt caused by such unfunded spending signals a fundamental change in government policy, which until JFK/LBJ was a pay-as-you-go system, except in a time of emergency.

The subject period qualified as such a period, and no complaint would be raised if the overspending had been concentrated on homeland security or on those things (like international spending) that are closely linked to a war effort. But building a Welfare State during a time of war was hardly a national emergency, and the leaders of that period are to be chastised for irresponsible spending.

Mostly, the period carries the name of John Kennedy, but its legislative successes bear the unmistakable mark of Lyndon B. Johnson, the father of the public debt we experience today. Had he lived, JFK may or may not have approved of LBJ's initiatives.

LBJ labeled Barry Goldwater, his 1964 opponent in the presidential race, a warmonger, one not to be trusted with war-making power. LBJ was the peace candidate. While he was president, the Vietnam War matured into the most expensive military embarrassment in the history of the United States.

8

Lyndon B. Johnson, 1965–1968

Teacher, Local Politics, House of Representative, Senate, Vice President, President

Theodore Roosevelt was president when Lyndon B. Johnson was born in 1908 in a farmhouse near Stonewall, Texas, his origins as humble and unpromising as John Kennedy's were posh and auspicious. Johnson was the oldest of five children, three girls and two boys.

Lyndon Johnson had political blood in his veins. His father, Sam Johnson (1877–1937), a teacher, farmer and trader, was an on-and-off-again member of the House of Representatives in Texas for two decades (1905–25).

Sam lost significant assets during a 1906 earthquake. He resurfaced in middle-management positions with the state railroad commission. He had a natural wit and a high school education; his wife, Rebekah Baines Johnson (1881–1958), was a graduate of Baylor University where she worked as a teacher and as a journalist before and after her marriage to Sam in 1907.

Sam lived to see his son serve in the House, and Rebekah saw her son become the Senate Majority Leader.

Lyndon, a precocious child partly because of his mother's tutoring, could read at age four. But he was also somewhat of a hellion.

After attending local grammar schools, he went to Johnson City High School. Never prominent in sports, he became known instead as a debater and the youngest member of his 1924 graduating class.

Calvin Coolidge was president; public debt was $21 billion.[1]

The presidency and public debt were far from Lyndon B. Johnson's untamed mind. He ignored college, despite his mother's urgings, until in 1927 ambition finally reared its head and steered him to Texas State College (1927–30). He worked his way through, and he did well in subjects like political science, and poorly in others like mathematics. On campus the tall young man drew attention as a debater, writer, and politician.

After graduation, Johnson taught debate and public speaking in Pearsall and Houston, Texas. But his eyes were on the political ring. He became secretary to Representative Richard Kleberg (1931–34); he saw Washington and smelled the power and he loved it.

After his stint with Kleberg, Johnson waited for an opportunity to get into politics as an active player, patiently serving as director of a Texas youth program until in 1937 his chance arrived. He ran for and won a House seat. Johnson at 29 was a firm supporter of the New Deal.

Roosevelt was president; public debt was $36 billion, and the Great Depression was in full swing.

Johnson represented Austin, Texas, except for a short stint in the navy (1941–42); at age 41, he won a Senate seat (1949). There he built an impressive record (1949–60) that made him one of the most powerful majority leaders in the history of that legislative body.

Johnson joined John Kennedy in 1960 in the run for the presidency against Richard M. Nixon. In a controversial result (that Nixon with good reason could have contested), Kennedy won by 119,000 votes, and less than 1 percent.

Lyndon Baines Johnson (LBJ) assumed the presidency after JFK was assassinated in November 1963.

LBJ won the presidency on his own in 1964 and he faced one of the busiest agendas in history—Vietnam, civil rights, protest marches, college riots, an exploding drug culture, the implementation of an enormously expensive social agenda, a world full of tension and the Cold War with the Soviet Union.

Problems of this magnitude amplify the need for a president to have congressional support. LBJ had no problems—John McCormack (D–MA) in the House and Mike Mansfield (D–MT) in the Senate were solid supporters of his agenda.[2] In the 89th Congress the majority controlled with an anything-goes 68 percent in the House and Senate; in the 90th Congress it slipped to 57 percent and 64 percent, respectively.[3]

LBJ took office in 1965 with a public debt of $256.8 billion,[4] summarized as follows:

Table 8.1
Public Debt 1964 (in billions of dollars)

	Total	%
World War I	$ 18.3	7.1%
Great Depression:	24.5	9.5
World War II	142.5	55.5
Korean War	6.6	2.6
Interest	5.4	2.1
Government	22.8	8.9
Human Resources	35.8	13.9
Treasury, net	.9	.4
Total	$256.8	100.0%

Source: Table 7.7, Chapter 7

Alert readers will remember that 100 percent of new debt from the Kennedy/Johnson administration had nothing to do with external events; it is especially interesting that, in a time of war, there was no new debt related to *Defense.*

Given that background, one could not predict the budget outcome of a new presidential term that featured even more international tension. If the LBJ administration were rooted in tradition, one would expect a surge in military spending and a cutback or holding action in other cost centers so as to get maximum security value out of each tax dollar.

One thing was sure: If the costs of the Vietnam War, on top of the costs of the Cold War, did not act as a spending deterrent to the liberals who controlled the government, nothing would — and America would be headed for a future filled with deficits and debt until the bubble finally burst.

LBJ had the tools he needed to lead the country in those troubled times — a Democratic Congress, a liberal Supreme Court and a public (still mourning the death of JFK) that was staunchly supportive.

No president had more power, psychological and actual, than did Lyndon B. Johnson, and few knew how to use it better than he.

Whatever happened in 1965–68 was the direct responsibility of Johnson, McCormack, Mansfield and the acolytes who followed them, the leaders of round two of the Second American Revolution.

In 1968 the tall Texan, broken by disappointments in Vietnam and embarrassed by the lack of support for his war policies, announced he would not again run for office. LBJ died five years later after a heart attack.

Perspectives

GENERAL

Johnson had the usual trouble with Communist nations in 1965–68. China, for example, joined the hydrogen bomb club, which was especially notable because of China's ideological split in 1960 with the Soviet Union.[5]

On the other side of the world, the USSR followed its rape of Poland and Hungary (1956) with in 1968 an invasion of Czechoslovakia — the Cold War was omnipresent.

But LBJ's administration will be remembered more for domestic decisions than for direct confrontations with the Soviets, and for its policies in Vietnam — for the marches and mayhem that tore at the fabric of American society, and for its social and civil rights legislation.

America's involvement with Vietnam began with a trickle of advisers under Harry Truman. Dwight Eisenhower handled the situation the same way — in 1960, about 2,000 advisers were in Vietnam.

John Kennedy was more aggressive; he put over 20,000 men in Vietnam. And under JFK/LBJ, the civil war in Vietnam became America's war.

The Vietnam War never drew the public support that existed during World War II. The press became negative, and the conflict had two unusual characteristics that didn't sit well with Americans: (1) The United States fought to contain, not to win, the war, and (2) College students who, in the midst of the war, became exempt from the draft.

The first aspect made American troops look ineffective; the second resulted in two undesirable things: (1) a military force unfairly made up of less-advantaged young men and (2), a self-conscious student body ripe for mischief.

The country seethed with discontent.

Civil rights leaders (especially active during the administrations of liberal presidents) were joined by students who, apart from sincere idealists, were frightened or guilt-ridden because others were fighting the war of their generation.

It was a dark hour for LBJ. By 1968 he had sent over a half-million men to Vietnam, and the problem was as bad as ever. In the face of a raging populace, LBJ in effect resigned from politics at the end of his term, refusing to seek the nomination of his party.

THE HOME FRONT

Johnson's social legislation stands today partly as a reaction to the civil rights conflicts of the 1960s and partly as a collection of grandiose ideas that nobody yet has shaped into affordable form.

The most charismatic and effective civil rights leader, Martin Luther King, Jr., born in 1929 during the Great Depression, was assassinated in 1968, the final year of LBJ's presidency.

Growing up as a black man in those years meant exposure to all of the inequities that would one day serve as the subject matter of civil rights legislation, and that exposure was made even more dramatic by the miserable economic conditions that plagued the nation until King was about 12 years old.

Such a background explained in part the passion that King brought to the protest marches he led during the JFK/LBJ years, protests that enjoyed LBJ's support while they, at the same time, brought intense pressure on the White House.

LBJ's reaction to the civil rights movement set the tone for all subsequent responses to complaints from minority groups—throw money at the problem.

The legislative activity that followed was, in terms of quantity and substance, without precedent in the United States. Included, for example: Medicaid, Medicare and Head Start Programs in 1965 and the Child Nutrition Act in 1966.

Nobody disputed the objectives of these ideas—helping the ill, the young and the defenseless—but debate raged over how best to reach them.

The answer from the LBJ administration was inevitably the same, namely, that it is the responsibility of the federal government. States, persons and charitable organizations were let off the hook. Poverty, illness and hard times became officially the province of the federal government.

Rev. King's speeches were inspiring. But it could be that his most important legacy (not intended by him) will be that he scared the pants off of Democrats, which resulted in a new strategy that continues to rule the actions of politicians: Throwing money at problems, effective or not, wins votes.

The last year of Johnson's administration was approximately four decades away from the Great Depression, and the ending year of this study, the midpoint between an America that was essentially uninvolved in world affairs and an America that led the free world.

Such a dramatic journey was bound to change the financial profile of the United States. And it did.

The Misery Index in 1968 was 13.9 percent, up from 10.8 percent in 1964.[6] This was caused by the increased cost of money and the surge in the inflation rate. In the short term, this wasn't painful to either the government or the worker — federal revenue was up 32.9 percent,[7] earnings per capita increased by 29.4 percent[8] and the unemployment rate was down.

But these negative signs in two of the three indicators were warnings that the economy was unstable and could worsen if, among other things, federal fiscal policy didn't become more responsible.

LBJ in 1968 increased tax rates across the board, presumably to finance the increased costs of war.[9] Again, the increase was especially difficult for low wage earners because both the rate and the taxable level of payroll income were raised from 7.25 percent to 7.6 percent, from $4,800 in earnings to $7,800.

A worker, on an income per capita basis, sent 11.5 weeks of work to Washington before he/she could pay the rent.

Johnson had four straight years of income growth,[10] and a healthy rate of GDP growth.[11] As under Kennedy, these were good times.

Federal income in 1965–68 was no problem. The deficit was strictly cost related.

SUPREME COURT[12]

The dominant message of the LBJ administration was: We can do everything.

The sky was the limit. America was so rich and so powerful and so unique that it could fight a hot war, contain the Soviets in a Cold War and, at the same time and with no particular difficulty, build a new society in which people would be free from worry and concern because the benevolent arms of government would protect them from life's burdens.

This unrealistic Utopian vision conquered the political mind of the day and infected as well the judgments of the Supreme Court's judges.

In their decision making, they led the legal side of the second American Revolution while LBJ concentrated on hammering into the federal budget a smorgasbord of welfare programs that would progressively eat away at the fiscal integrity of the wealthiest nation on earth.

Ironically, Chief Justice Earl Warren led the legal assault against American values, and he was appointed by the most conservative previous postwar president, Dwight Eisenhower.

Warren heard 33 cases during the subject period,[13] a relatively light load when measured against contemporary standards, but he presided over decisions so controversial that they added to the caseload of future justices to a degree never before imagined.

Warren was joined on the Court by ten associate justices, all but three carryovers from the previous administration — Thurgood Marshall, Abe Fortas and Byron White. A thumbnail sketch of each new judge appears below:

- Thurgood Marshall — Marshall was the product of Lincoln University and Howard University Law School. Racial injustice dominated his legal ambitions and he immediately joined forces with the National Association for the Advancement of Colored People (NAACP), eventually rising to become the head of that organization's Legal and Defense Fund. He was a key strategist in the dismantlement of racial segregation throughout society in which role, for example, he served as chief counsel in the ground-breaking case, Brown v. Board of Education. LBJ appointed Marshall, 59, to the Court in 1967 to replace Tom Clark (appointed by Truman), four years after JFK had appointed him to the U.S. Court of Appeals, Second Circuit. Marshall was a dependable liberal vote on the Court until his retirement in 1991. He died two years later of a heart attack.
- Abe Fortas — Fortas graduated from Southwestern University, Memphis, and he attended Yale Law School, where he remained as a teacher until Washington and its insiders lured him into the private practice world of New Deal lawyers. As such, he became an adviser to Democratic politicians, whom he defended in the Texas election scandal of 1948. LBJ appointed him to the bench in 1965 to replace Arthur Goldberg (appointed by JFK). Fortas was accused of unethical financial deals in 1969 and he resigned from the bench. He denied any wrongdoing.
- Byron White — White attended the University of Colorado on a scholarship and was a man of distinction on campus, athletically and intellectually. He won a Rhodes scholarship to Oxford after which he returned to Yale to complete his law school education. In between he played professional football for Pittsburgh and Detroit. While engaged in his private law practice in Colorado, White met JFK and organized the Colorado campaign for the president-to-be. In gratitude, JFK

made him at 45 years old the U.S. Attorney General in 1961, and, a year later, he appointed him to the Court to replace Charles Whittaker (appointed by Eisenhower). During his years on the Court, White became known as a moderate. He retired in 1993 and he died nine years later.

This exchange of judges resulted in a net gain of one for the liberals.

Activist Supreme Court judges were in full stride during the JFK/LBJ years, and issued rulings that, in many cases, rendered the common meaning of words useless. For example, "free speech" was once understood by everybody, and is now understood by nobody.

The cases sampled below present, in concrete form, some of the concerns of the day.

Griswold v. Connecticut, 1965. Griswold, executive director of the Planned Parenthood League in Connecticut, gave birth-control advice to married couples. State law criminalized instruction for the purpose of preventing conception. The issue: Does the Constitution protect the right to marital privacy against state laws that forbid birth control instruction? In a 7–2 decision (Stewart and Black dissented), the Court ruled the state law to be unconstitutional. In so doing it acknowledged that the Constitution does not explicitly protect the right to marital privacy but, together, the First, Third, Fourth and Ninth Amendments *create a new constitutional right in matters of marital relations.* With this imaginative decision the Court opened the door to the numerous abortion cases that would appear before future courts.

Brown v. Louisiana, 1965. Brown and four other black men entered a branch library and requested a book. The book was not available but the librarian said she would order it and notify them of its availability. Their business apparently finished, the men sat down and refused to leave — they were making no disturbance. They were arrested for not leaving a public building when it was requested by an officer. The issue: Did the arrest infringe on the defendants' rights of free speech, assembly etc. as protected by the First and Fourteenth Amendments? In a 5–4 decision (Clark, Black, Stewart and Harlan dissented), the Court ruled that the actions of the black men constituted a peaceful demonstration and that the practice of the state to maintain separate facilities for blacks and whites was discriminatory — the arrest was therefore unconstitutional.

Memoirs v. Massachusetts, 1965. The state outlawed the sale of *Fanny Hill* as an obscene book. The issue: Was the state correct? In a 6–3 decision (Harlan, Clark and White dissented), the Court ruled that the book was not obscene because it did not meet the standard for obscenity established in *Roth v. United States* (1957). In so doing, the Court again made it clear that local control of such matters was a thing of the past.

Miranda v. Arizona, 1966. A number of cases presented to the Court involved the questioning of suspects who had little knowledge of their constitutional rights, and no lawyer to advise them. The issue: Is the practice of questioning individuals before reminding them of their right to an attorney and their protection against self-incrimination under the Fifth Amendment constitutional? In a 5–4 decision (Clark, White, Stewart and Harlan dissenting) the Court ruled that such a practice was unconstitutional. *This decision led to the now famous Miranda warning that is given to arrested suspects.* In the minds of many the interpretation of this decision by some justices has often resulted in the rejection of persuasive evidence that, if presented in court, would have convicted an obvious criminal.

These decisions, and others during the period, were momentous. And they were made by judges who couldn't even agree among themselves. The face of America was being changed by the plurality vote of nine men.

In a spirit of sublime activism, the Court discovered a new constitutional right to privacy (7–2); states lost their right to prohibit ad hoc protests on anybody's property (5–4); states lost their right to define obscenity for their citizens (6–3) and the police were tied to new procedural restrictions that, though well-intended, often allowed known criminals to walk free (5–4).

It would have been bad enough if these informed legal minds had recognized the importance of their subject matter, and had arrived at unanimous decisions. But to see the moral and ethical landscape of America decided by the plurality vote of nine judges was insulting.

Local officials can handle many frictions that now go to the Supreme Court; state legislators can handle many others. But such democratic solutions did not appeal to Johnsonians on the bench. They can, and they do, find reasons to inject themselves into everything, and the more they do, the higher the caseload, and the higher the caseload, the more they do, and the more....

Society[14]

There are two sets of laws that govern social behavior:

- Moral law — This usually comes from a religion or from religious readings. It deals mostly with observance rules and guidelines for personal behavior.
- Civil law — This comes from government. Its scope is broader than religious law, dealing as it does with business affairs and international agreements. But it also deals with personal behavior directly (criminal law) and indirectly through its perceived attitudes toward social behavior.

Civil law is useful, and no civilized society can live without it. But it is, ultimately, the silent consensus among the people of what is right and what is wrong that sets the moral/ethical tone of a society. No amount of civil law will bring peace to a society that can't agree on what peace is. And a country is headed for the danger zone when the values it proposes or supports are not the values shared by most citizens.

America's values have changed radically over the past half century, and some of that change can be traced to the modernists who in the 1960s ruled the nation.

Appendix 4 displays a variety of social statistics, a few of which are readily available back to the 1940s. At this stage, 1968, they reveal little to support comment, except that the stability of marriage appeared to slip after World War II, and has never recovered.

Seeing the drift of the numbers suggests that the moral/ethical forces at work in 1968 were beginning to change radically.

Change in Public Debt

The war in Vietnam heated up in 1965 when LBJ began the first year of his own presidency. Two things appear to have motivated him the most:

- Determination to fight and win the war in Vietnam.
- Determination to create a Rooseveltian legend for himself by moving American society ever closer to being a Welfare State. To him, kindness was action by the federal government; the more government, the more kindness.

Initially, the people supported him. Why not? He was giving; they were taking. And if the taxes went up a bit, so what? It was for the war.

LBJ was selling a free lunch and patriotism. And the public bought it.

The fact that debt was climbing was not unduly disturbing to most because they expected that it would as war continued. And no blame would have attached to LBJ if, when the smoke of war cleared, higher military costs had caused the increase.

Did they?

The analysis of transactions for the period will reveal the answer to that question (see Table 8.2).

These numbers do not reveal what one would have expected in a time of war, namely, heavy defense and controlled spending elsewhere. But they do reveal what have come to be the expected results under the leadership of LBJ.

He fought the war by depleting the Eisenhower war machine, an action that future presidents would have to mend, and it appears that he spent the taxes that citizens assumed were pouring into national defense on the broadening of his social programs.

The typical analysis of major revenue and cost elements on Table 8.2 will reveal how the tax revenues flowed through the 1965–1968 budget.

Table 8.2
Transactions (in billions of dollars)

		1965–68		1961–64
Taxes		$ 549.4		$ 413.3
Less:				
Defense	$262.0		$210.1	
Interest	39.4		29.5	
Total		301.4		239.6
Net		$ 248.0		$ 173.7
Less:				
Government	$ 96.3		$ 64.5	
Human Resources	190.6		130.2	
Total		286.9		194.7
Surplus/deficit		$ -38.9		$ -21.0
Debt, beginning		-256.8		-236.8
Total		$-295.7		$-257.8
Adjustment*		6.2		1.0
Debt, Ending		$-289.5		$-256.8

*Treasury cannot be exact when it finances a budget deficit and the difference between what is needed and the value of securities traded inevitably produces a relatively small variance.

Source: Historical Tables 2007, 1.1, 3.1

TAXES

LBJ started with revenue of $112.6 billion in 1964 and ended with $153.0 billion in 1968, an increase of 35.9 percent.[15] And his four-year revenue was 32.9 percent higher[16] than the revenue of the previous presidential period.

Income was high; the trend was up.

Politicians love to make citizens believe that they create jobs and income through their mysterious legislative maneuvers, but in truth, economic goodies come from private sector activity.

And the economy was good to the LBJ administration.

With such luck, one might expect debt reduction even with the war; with such luck, LBJ delivered a deficit of $38.9 billion.[17]

LBJ reversed the tax decreases of JFK.[18] An odd result of this maneuver appeared for the first time in 1968 — payroll taxes yielded more revenue than corporate income taxes.[19] This, the most punishing tax of all on the low-income earner, was the gift of those who were in the process of creating the Welfare State — liberty was in effect shifting to the central government in exchange for government programs.

Taxes in relation to average earnings per capita were about the same,[20] but this was illusory because spending per capita was on a steep upward path, meaning that America had officially abandoned the pay-as-you-go approach to governance in favor of LBJ's "charge it" school of economics.

Washington was not paying for what it was spending. Someone, sometime, would.

DEFENSE

In 1965–68, LBJ spent $262.0 billion, 24.8 percent above the *Defense* levels of 1961–64 (Table 8.2), and well below the rate of revenue increase. But in 1964, America had 20,000 advisers in Vietnam; in 1968 it had 525,000 troops there.[21]

Increased dollars are not compatible with the degree of new effort. Why didn't *Defense* increase more? The main reason is that LBJ did not seriously spend on *Defense* until 1968, at which time the cost was $81.9 billion, 49 percent more than it was four years earlier.[22]

Defense was fully financed by the revenue increase and in no way added to the deficit for the period. Thus is the notion eliminated that LBJ financed war with debt.

INTEREST

Interest was 35 percent higher in 1968 than in 1964 and prime interest rates had climbed to 6.3 percent,[23] a sure signal that the child of debt (*Interest*) would soon become a primary budget problem in its own right.

Interest in the federal budget has two determining components: the level of debt and the interest rate. Since 1948, interest rates were on a steady upward course.

In 1968, the prime interest rate was 51 percent higher than it was in 1964. And the debt in 1968 was over $30 billion higher.[24]

This combination spells trouble for the budget.

Had *Interest* grown at the same rate as revenue (32.9 percent),[25] it would have cost $39.2 billion, $.2 billion less than it actually did. To that extent, *Interest* was not financed by the revenue increase and was responsible for the budget deficit.

This addition to the deficit was trivial in terms of immediate impact. But in terms of meaning for the future, it was a momentous happening. Interest was now a consequential budget item; government was spending more and more on a cost center that delivered nothing.

GOVERNMENT

The 1.329 times increase in revenue during the subject period established the upper level of spending for the primary cost centers and to the extent that it was not needed (spent), the excess flowed to the remaining cost centers, *Government* and *Human Resources,* to be measured against the combined cost of those centers during the previous period. This exercise produced a growth factor of 1.275 times, beyond which those centers would contribute to the deficit for the period.

Under this formulation, the unfunded spending in *Government* during the subject period was $14.1 billion.

Table 8.3
Government (in billions of dollars)

	1965–68	1961–64	% Change
Energy	$ 3.1	$ 2.2	40.9%
Natural Resources/Environment	11.1	8.5	30.6
Transportation	23.6	18.1	30.9
Community/regional development	4.7	2.3	104.3
International affairs	21.8	19.0	14.7
Science/space/technology	24.1	10.6	128.3
Agriculture	13.9	15.1	- 7.9
Justice	2.4	1.8	33.3
General	6.6	5.1	29.4
Total	$111.3	$82.7	34.6
Commerce & housing credit*	12.7	3.1	309.6
Total	$124.0	$85.8	44.8%
Offsetting receipts	- 27.7	-21.3	30.0
Net	$ 96.3	$64.5	49.3%

*Made up of earnings from various federal housing and other programs— subject to major changes from year to year relative to market conditions. (Historical Tables 2007, 3.2)

Source: Historical Tables 2007, 3.1

Congress doesn't have a crystal ball to use that reports on command the amount of future revenues, and undoubtedly many who were active at the time would claim innocent ignorance when accused of overspending. But that excuse doesn't wash because Congress has more access to budget numbers than any other citizen, and a cursory examination of them would have yielded this simple and valid proposition in 1965: If you want to avoid adding to the deficit in 1965–68, do not plan on a revenue increase of more than 28.5 percent, the average four-year revenue increase during recent presidencies.[26]

This is slightly higher than the multiplier used to calculate the deficit, but it is also a fair indicator when the focus switches to cost efficiency management, and it is the yardstick in use when the line items in Table 8.3 are analyzed.

Every line item except International and Agriculture overspent in 1965–68. But the *amount* of overspending, except for the Commerce and housing credit (wildly unpredictable and of little critical interest to this study) was not obscene.

Two line items, Commerce etc., and Space etc., deserve special comment.

- The amount of spending on Space was effectively approved by the public when JFK and LBJ were elected. Both vowed to overtake the Soviets in the space race; both financed their promises. This was, however, a level of overspending that one would expect to recover in future budgets when stress is lower than it was in the subject period.

• The spending in Commerce, never predictable, has not been unduly probed in this study except to say that its level is determined by uncontrollable external events.

The level of unfunded spending in Government was largely caused by the violent cost fluctuations in Commerce and in Space.

The other overages were inconspicuous in amount, but disturbing in meaning, and they leave the overwhelming impression that spending was not a concern of this Congress.

HUMAN RESOURCES

Table 8.2 demonstrates that this cost center grew 1.46 times in 1965–68, well above the growth factor for revenue (1.33), or the one developed for *Government* and *Human Resources* (see above), 1.275.

Because the cost center did not limit its spending according to the above formula, its unfunded spending for the period amounted to $24.6 billion.

Table 8.4
Human Resources (in billions of dollars)

	1965–68	1961–64	% Change
Education, training, services	$ 20.5	$ 5.3	286.8%
Health/Medicaid	12.1	5.4	124.1
Income Security	41.3	37.8	9.3
Social Security	83.8	59.2	41.6
Medicare	7.5	0.0	
Veterans	25.3	22.5	12.4
Total	$190.6	$130.2	46.4%

Note: There were few social program of consequence prior to the 1960s except for Social Security (started in 1935) and the GI Bill.

Note: Major federal programs since the 1960s— Food Stamps 1961 (pilot), Food Stamps 1964, Medicaid 1965, Student Aid 1966, Medicare 1967

Source: Historical Tables 2007, 3.1

Spending for Income Security and Veterans was fully funded. Other increases reflect the expansion of government services to a degree and in a manner that reflected the grand social designs of the LBJ–led government.

The spending increase in Education and Health can only be described by one word. Ridiculous! How could anyone approve of such a thing?

And the increase in Social Security was yet one more example of how badly that program needed to be restructured into affordable form.

Cost growth in this cost center as demonstrated in Table 8.4 tells only part of the story. The true headlines are these:

- The cost of LBJ's plans and programs hit the federal budget in a meaningful way for the first time in 1967.
- No new plans to reform Social Security were even attempted before a deluge of other programs hit the budget over the last two years of LBJ's presidency.
- The rate of cost growth that LBJ passed forward to his successor was unconscionable — there was insufficient revenue to pay for it, *and he knew it.*

This analysis makes plain that the next president, Richard M. Nixon, would have huge fiscal problems.

SUMMARY OF DEFICIT ALLOCATION

It was a time of war. Taxes were increased presumably to pay for growing military costs. For that reason, complaints about higher taxes were easily drowned out by calls to patriotism.

If there was to be a deficit in 1965–68 it should have been caused by higher *Defense* spending.

It wasn't.

Increased revenues easily supported increased military needs.

The deficit, therefore, for the most part represents the cost of discretionary spending that could have been postponed, or legislated out of existence. It represents funds that could have been used to reduce taxes or debt.

Table 8.5
Summary of Deficit, 1965–1968 (in billions of dollars)

Cost Center	Amount
Defense	$ 0.0
Interest	.2
Government	14.1
Human Resources	24.6
Total	$38.9

Sources: Exhibits 1, 11–1, 16

The deficit was mostly avoidable. LBJ and his supporters created a fiscal monster that would haunt future presidents and diminish the ability of the United States to afford the military establishment needed to meet global challenges.

Conclusion

The Vietnam War was a major, prolonged (1963–75), expensive event that involved over 200,000 casualties.[27]

In World War II, the resources of the United States were primarily devoted to the war, domestic spending being curtailed. In 1942, for example, 73 percent of expenditures went to *Defense*; in 1944, 87 percent.[28]

One would have expected similar emphasis in 1965–68, but it didn't happen.

Table 8.6
Spending Priorities

Primary costs	1960	1964	1968
Defense	52.2%	46.2%	46.0%
Interest	7.5	6.9	6.2
Total	59.7%	53.1%	52.2%
Government	11.9	17.0	14.5
Education/services	1.9	1.4%	4.3
Health/Medicaid	.9	1.5	2.5
Medicare		0.0	2.6
Income Security	8.0	8.2	6.6
Social Security	12.6	14.0	13.4
Veterans	5.9	4.8	3.9
Total	100.0%	100.0%	100.0%
	(3)	(2)(3)	(2)(3)

1 = peace; 2 = war; 3 = cold war

Note: 1940 as a base year for comparison purposes was eliminated in favor of 1960, a more up-to-date profile of a leading power, at peace and in a dangerous world.

Source: Historical Tables 2007, 3.1

Despite the increased intensity of the Vietnam War, *Defense* received a smaller slice of resources in 1968 than it did in 1964. And the relative slice of domestic spending continued to rise as the absolute amounts of higher revenue poured into Washington. Priorities were the reverse of what one might have reasonably expected.

The public debt increased by $32.7 billion to $289.5[29] billion, as follows:

Table 8.7
Public Debt, 1968 (billions)

Event	Inherited 1964	Added 1965–68	Total 1968	%
World War I	$ 18.3	$	$ 18.3	6.3%
Great Depression	24.5		24.5	8.5
World War II	142.5		142.5	49.2
Korean War	6.6		6.6	2.3
Interest	5.4	.2	5.6	1.9
Government	22.8	14.1	36.9	12.7
Human Resources	35.8	24.6	60.4	20.9
Treasury	.9	-6.2	-5.3	- 1.8

| Total | $256.8 | $ 32.7 | $289.5 | 100.0% |

Source: Exhibits 1, 11, 12, 16

LBJ changed America from a defense-minded, independent nation into a Welfare State. He changed economic thinking of politicians by not only allowing unfunded spending, but recommending it. And, perhaps most importantly, he operated as if his presidency existed in a vacuum — that what he did would have no impact on future presidents or future generations.

In fact, LBJ abused future presidents by cramming into entitlement programs costs that could not be funded, and he set in motion a cycle of climbing debt that has become an international embarrassment.

From a fiscal standpoint, LBJ destroyed the pay-as-you-go philosophy of earlier years with his "charge it" attitude. The plethora of programs he introduced served as the honey that drew lobbyists to Washington, who proceeded to become a dangerous and corrupting part of the political scene.

From a judicial standpoint, the LBJ era will be remembered as one in which activist federal judges rose to power and prominence, and, through the use of imaginative prose, managed to muddle the meaning of the Constitution to such an extent that future Courts would be deluged with cases seeking to make new law, or trying to get clarification. Most importantly, the Court's decisions moved civil law farther away from the moral law that guided most Americans.

LBJ and his Court installed the federal government in the role of benefactor. State power was diminished and individuals became more dependent on programs, grants and aid.

Special interest groups, no longer required to persuade fifty states to adopt favorable courses of action, gratefully trained their guns on the power brokers in the increasingly centralized federal government.

The power of Washington's politicians grew geometrically. Spawned by Roosevelt, encouraged by Truman, suffered by Eisenhower, and led to the Promised Land by Johnson, they changed the face of America, which, as it became bigger and richer, borrowed more, all of this behind the convenient curtains of World War II, Korea, and Vietnam.

Roosevelt's political excesses were legendary. His policies did not fix the Great Depression, but his leadership in World War II redeemed his reputation.

LBJ's political excesses were also legendary. His policies did not establish the Great Society that he envisioned. And there was no great Vietnam victory to redeem his reputation. Failure in Vietnam, and the failure to create what he had set out to do as his life's mission, destroyed him.

9

Richard M. Nixon, 1969–1972

Lawyer, Representative, Senator, Vice President, President

Richard M. Nixon was born in 1913 in Yorba Linda, California. The year before his birth, William H. Taft, a member of the Nixon family tree, completed his term as the 27th president of the United States. Nixon was the second of five brothers, all supervised by Quaker parents with modest resources.

In 1932, Nixon, 19, was attending Whittier College in California when another member of the family tree, Herbert Hoover, completed his single term in office. Presidential blood flowed through Nixon's veins.

Nixon's presence at Whittier was directly related to his outstanding high school record (first in the class of 1930), an achievement that brought scholarship opportunities for higher education. At Whittier, he majored in history and graduated in 1934 second in his class.

Franklin D. Roosevelt was president.

Good grades, not personal or family wealth, fueled Nixon's academic career, this time qualifying him for Duke University Law School (1934–37).

Living off-campus in a farmhouse and working as a research assistant to cover expenses didn't deter the focused Californian from posting another personal and academic record of high achievement; he was an honor student and president of his class.

Nixon was admitted to the California bar in 1937. Roosevelt was still president.

For the next four years, Nixon experimented with a law career and a business venture. In 1942, he had his first taste of government work in the Office of Price Administration in Washington. He didn't enjoy it and he resigned to join the navy — he was a member of the generation that faced military service shortly after graduation from college and before their careers had taken root.

Nixon spent five years in a successful naval career that saw him rise from lieutenant junior grade to lieutenant commander. After a stint in the South Pacific, he was discharged in 1946 and he took a position with the Navy Department's Bureau of Aeronautics.

Harry Truman was president; public debt was $242 billion.

California politicians saw promise in the highly intelligent war veteran and, with their help, he began his long political career in his home district with a surprise victory in 1946 over Rep. Jerry Voorhis, winning 57 percent of the vote.

Four years later Nixon was a national figure because of his duties as chairman of the House Un-American Activities Committee, which, among other things, uncovered the Russian spy, Alger Hiss.

Friends of Hiss, and their allies in the media, chastised Nixon for decades for his part in that national drama but, in the 1990s, KGB information released revealed without doubt that Nixon's charges against Hiss were valid, and that his critics were little more than partisan character assassins.

Capitalizing on his enlarged reputation, Nixon sought the seat of the retiring senator from California, Sheridan Downey. In so doing, he defeated Downey's heir-apparent, liberal icon Helen Gahagan Douglas (wife of movie idol, Melvin Douglas), by a large margin. His hard-hitting tactics in this campaign earned him the nickname "Tricky Dick" that followed him thereafter.

These twin encounters with the liberal establishment (Hiss and Douglas) were critical to the formation in Nixon's mind of antagonistic and cautious attitudes toward the media.

Now 38, Nixon was the youngest man in the Senate chamber (1951). He served with distinction as a powerful critic of Truman until in 1952 Dwight Eisenhower invited him aboard his presidential ticket.

After eight years as vice president, Nixon attempted to succeed his old boss in a presidential race in 1960 against John F. Kennedy; he lost by fewer than 200,000 votes. In what may have been the finest hour of his political career, Nixon did not contest the result despite ample evidence that vote tampering, not Kennedy, had defeated him. His graciousness spared the nation endless quarrels over presidential succession.

Nixon retired to private pursuits after the election until in 1962 he made an unsuccessful bid for the governor's seat in California after which he bade what turned out to be a premature farewell to the press.

The retired and somewhat bitter politician thereafter practiced law and limited his political activities to supporting Senator Barry Goldwater (R–AZ) and other Republicans.

But in 1968, to everyone's surprise, he was back, stronger than ever, as his party's nominee for president. He ran against Vice President Hubert Humphrey and the war policies of Lyndon B. Johnson and he won by a half-million votes.

Nixon, with superb academic, military, legal and political credentials, was perhaps the best-trained man ever to assume the presidential reins. He was 56 when in 1969 he became the 37th president of the United States.

His margin of victory over Humphrey[1] was too small to support a change in congressional leadership that could possibly redirect the policies of the nation more rationally, and more responsibly.

Republicans gained a few seats in the House in the 91st Congress and lost a few in the 92nd.[2] And throughout the Nixon/Ford administration, Democrats held with 54–60 seats.[3] In other words, the size of Democratic majorities changed a bit with each election, but Democratic control was never seriously threatened.

Even so, conservatives in both parties were anxious about the reach of Lyndon B. Johnson's Great Society programs, and Nixon, allegedly a conservative, was expected to slow what many thought to be a runaway train toward socialism.

However else Nixon's presidency was to be evaluated, conservative followers expected him to make a strong effort to reestablish the values that had made America great, and to make sense out of government spending, deficits, and the rise in public debt. He would be judged by them accordingly at the end of his administration.

Nixon assumed a public debt of $289.5 billion,[4] a surprising portion of which, from a historical standpoint, was made up of unfunded operating expenses:

Table 9.1
Public Debt 1968 (in billions of dollars)

	Total	%
World War One	$ 18.3	6.3%
Great Depression:	24.5	8.5
World War Two	142.5	49.2
Korean War	6.6	2.3
Interest	5.6	1.9
Government	36.9	12.7
Human Resources	60.4	20.9
Treasury, net	-5.3	-1.8
Total	$289.5	100.0%

Source: Table 8.7, Chapter 8

The changed political philosophy advocated by Lyndon Johnson is reflected in the above table. Prior to his ascension to power as Majority Leader in the Senate, the common explanation for climbing public debt (wars, disasters, etc.) pertained.

Thereafter it did not.

Deficits beyond that point to the greatest extent represented an act of free will by LBJ and his followers in the Congress. And the result of this marriage of Utopian ministers was a steady increase in debt with no end in view.

Would Nixon change this trend? If so, how?

As assistant problem solvers, Nixon inherited two Democrats, McCormack and Mansfield, who had enthusiastically helped to create his biggest headache — the Great Society.[5]

Nobody was placing high odds that Richard Nixon would succeed.

Perspectives

GENERAL

If Lyndon B. Johnson was not the busiest president in modern history, Nixon was. He had to simultaneously deal with civil rights, the Vietnam War, war protesters, the Cold War, foreign affairs, a troubled economy and, a relatively new phenomenon, international terrorism. Wherever he turned, there were problems, serious ones.

Nixon's global world presented challenges from all directions. Terrorists, for example, feeling themselves aggrieved, engaged in an undeclared war against selected neighbors and they waged it in a gruesome way against civilians.

A prime example of this uncivilized behavior was the murder of eight Israeli athletes at the 1972 Olympic Games by Arab terrorists,[6] a signal that segments of the Islamic world were un-restful and, perhaps, eager to strike out and assert their value system. It was a movement that was to grow in momentum as the decades passed.

Nixon did well in Vietnam, steadily reducing the involvement of American troops. Under Lyndon Johnson, the buildup had reached 543,000 men. The number was down to 340,000 by the end of 1970, 177,000 in 1971, and 25,000 in 1972. This was a remarkable achievement, but not good enough to impress protesters or the elite media.

THE HOME FRONT

Nixon's reduction in the military involvement of the United States in Vietnam was appreciated by the people, but not by the students on the campuses of America, or by the liberal media that loved to bedevil him, and to inflame those who opposed him.

The war, started by JFK, and accelerated by LBJ, suddenly became Nixon's war, and his inability to undo in a weekend what others had been doing for eight years was regularly portrayed in the press as a failure in his leadership. Nixon's press coverage during those years did nothing to soften his already negative attitude toward the press.

Students across America, following the example of the civil rights movement, held protest marches, including some in Washington that sometimes culminated in tragedy as in 1970 when, on the campus of Kent State University (Ohio), four students were killed and nine others were wounded.

When Nixon put his international, civil rights and social problems aside, he still had the wobbly economy to deal with.

The Misery Index[7] remained fairly steady, but the single factor that went up, unemployment, was the most socially sensitive of all, and it did nothing to improve the national mood. A healthy increase in earnings per capita of

36 percent[8] combined with less inflation and lower taxes per capita helped out.

But these good signs hid the dangerous trend Nixon had inherited. Spending per capita was headed for the moon and, except for the cost of *Interest* in the budget, the taxpayer was not feeling the pain that should have been attached to it.

Another event took place in Nixon's first term that shocked Washington. In 1970, he, a conservative, introduced price controls.

Except for the World War II era and a modest blip in the 1950s, inflation had been a minor problem, seldom rising above 2.0 percent until under Johnson it rose to 4.2 percent (1968).

The rate increased to 5.7 percent in 1970[9] and seemed to throw the White House into a panic. Nixon froze wages and prices and imposed thereafter controls that lasted to a decreasing degree until the end of 1973. Inflation dropped in 1968 to 3.2 percent. In the short term, therefore, price controls did the job. But their long-term impact had yet to be seen. Normally they are followed by unleashed demand and even higher inflation, and time would test that proposition.

The American economy often prospers in times of war. Nixon was an apparent beneficiary of that phenomenon in the form of GDP growth of 36 percent,[10] but the growth was mostly inflation-driven funny money, and the adjusted growth rate was an anemic 12 percent.

This fact of life finally turned up in 1971 when an 11-year streak of positive federal receipts ended.[11]

Even with the dip in income, tax revenues in 1969–72 were 1.41 times higher than the previous four years,[12] an indication that the deficit for the period would be cost driven.

Supreme Court[13]

Chief Justice Earl Warren, appointed by Eisenhower, started the 1969 calendar year with three associates who were appointed by Ike: Stewart, Brennan and Harlan, and five appointed by Democrats: Douglas and Black (FDR), Marshall and Fortas (LBJ) and White (JFK).

Assuming each judge essentially held the same worldview of his nominator, one could expect a liberal majority on many decisions of 5–4. But the previous years had clearly indicated that, especially on social issues, Warren and Brennan would switch sides leaving, at best, Harlan and Stewart to carry the conservative flag.

Much new legal ground had been dug by this Court during the previous four years. Many wondered what the new Court would do, especially because four newcomers appeared on the scene: Warren Burger, Lewis Powell, Harry Blackmun and William Rehnquist.

- Warren Burger — Burger had a private law practice for over 20 years, and he dabbled in Republican politics until in 1956 President Eisenhower appointed him to the U.S. Court of Appeals, Washington, D.C., Circuit. Richard Nixon in 1965 lifted him to the U.S. Supreme Court as Chief Justice to replace the retiring Earl Warren, and between them they handled 44 cases in 1969–72.[14] On the surface, this left the Court in the same ideological balance; actually, it was a Republican gain because Warren had turned out to be much more liberal than anyone expected Burger to be. Ironically, Burger was the spokesman for the decision that brought President Nixon down. His Court ruled against Nixon's claim for Executive Privilege, and the tapes that demonstrated Nixon's complicity in the Watergate scandal were released. Nixon resigned soon after.
- Lewis Powell[15] — Powell received his graduate and law degrees from Virginia's Washington and Lee University, and later he earned his master's degree at Harvard. Powell, a partner in a successful Virginia law firm, was first approached in 1969 about a Supreme Court appointment. He turned down the first request, but in 1971 he accepted (replacing Hugo Black) when the offer was repeated. On the bench, Powell was less liberal than Black, but not as conservative as many hoped. On balance, his appointment was a plus for Republicans.
- Harry Blackmun[16] — Blackmun received his undergraduate and legal education at Harvard. After decades in private practice, he accepted from Eisenhower an appointment in 1959 to the U.S. Court of Appeals from which position in 1970 President Nixon sent him to the Supreme Court (replacing Abe Fortas). He was recommended by Chief Justice Burger. Blackmun's value to conservatives is summed up in one phrase: He wrote the *Roe v. Wade* opinion that made abortion legal in the United States, setting off a controversy that will linger for so long as there is a Christian religion. By the time of his retirement he was a predictable ally of Justice Brennan, also a renegade conservative.
- William Rehnquist — After his stint in the air force during World War II, Rehnquist earned his bachelor and Master of Arts degrees at Stanford, demonstrating early on a brilliant mind. He continued his education at Harvard and earned a second master's degree, this time in government. He then returned to Stanford Law School for his law degree — typically, he graduated at the top of his class (Sandra Day O'Connor finished third in the same class). After serving as a clerk for Supreme Court Justice Robert Jackson, Rehnquist moved to Phoenix, Arizona, started a private law practice and became active in Republican politics — among other things, he campaigned for Barry Goldwater. When Nixon entered the White House in 1969, he brought

friends with him, including his new deputy attorney general, William Rehnquist. In 1971, Rehnquist was lifted to the Supreme Court to replace John Harlan — both men conservatives, Rehnquist more so.

Nixon's judicial appointments, especially Rehnquist, were probably as good as he could get through a Senate controlled by Democrats. Blackmun was his worst choice.

Men selected for the Supreme Court often behave other than expected. By the end of Nixon's first term, the Court should have been tilted to the right.

But it wasn't.

Some men change on the bench. One never knows who they are until their decisions begin to roll in. That's where definition begins and ends.

A few sample cases below give an indication of the concerns of the day.

Tinker v. Des Moines, 1969. The Tinkers, parents of Christopher (16), John (15) and Mary (13), protested the Vietnam War, and they used their children as part of their protest by adding a black armband to their school clothing. The principals of the Des Moines public schools ruled that the armbands would provoke disturbances, and they outlawed them; violators would be suspended. The Tinker children violated the rule and were suspended. The issue: Were the armbands symbolic speech that has protection under the First Amendment? In a 7–2 decision (Black and Harlan dissenting) the Court ruled that the armbands were a form of protected speech, and that school officials had not presented persuasive evidence that the forbidden conduct would unduly interfere with appropriate school discipline. This is yet another example of the Court poking its nose into affairs that can, and should, be handled locally. This and similar decisions have made the job of imposing the simplest common sense disciplines by school officials so complex and legally burdensome that they avoid doing so, a reaction that, while understandable, has caused discipline itself to lag, and has promoted the out-of-control behavior currently found in many public schools. Additionally, such decisions placed the welcome mat before the Court for those who wish to make similar claims, and they have contributed to the steadily growing caseload of the Court.

Tilton v. Richardson, 1971. A new federal law provided construction grants to religious institutions that needed buildings for nonreligious purposes. It further provided that after twenty years the buildings could be used for any purpose. The issue: Did the law violate the religion clauses of the First Amendment? In a 5–4 decision (Black, Marshall, Douglas and Brennan dissenting) the Court ruled that the law was constitutional, except for the twenty-year clause, which it invalidated. This decision was not as narrow a reading of the church/state clause as antireligionists would have preferred; it would have gone the other way had Blackmun not succeeded Fortas, who most probably would have voted with the minority and made them a majority. Blackmun in this instance served as a checkmate against the renegade Brennan.

Miller v. California, 1972. Miller was convicted of violating a state statute that outlawed the distribution of obscene material. The issue: Is the distribution of obscene material through the mail protected speech under the First Amendment? In a 5–4 decision (Stewart, Douglas, Marshall and Brennan dissenting) the Court ruled that obscene material is not protected speech. Opening up this Pandora's Box of pornography cases is the legacy of the Court's original decision to be active in this area in the Roth case (1957).

Furman v. Georgia, 1972. Furman, while burglarizing a private home, was discovered in the act by a family member. Furman fell down while trying to flee, his gun discharged accidentally, and a member of the family was killed. He was convicted of murder and sentenced to death. The issue: Did the death sentence constitute cruel and unusual punishment in violation of the Eighth and Fourteenth Amendments? In a 5–4 decision (Powell, Burger, Blackmun and Rehnquist dissenting), the sentence was overturned as being cruel and unusual punishment (Brennan and Marshall believed it to be unconstitutional in all cases). This was a legitimate case for the Court dealing as it did with a subject that will probably be forever debated.

And so the judicial aspect of Richard Nixon's first term ended. The drift of the Court was toward more involvement in private affairs because of the activist nature of previous Courts that had removed from state and local governance certain types of cases dealing with private behavior that were destined to make the legal road to the Supreme Court more active than ever before. The legal tilt of the Court as 1969 came to a close was still — because of so many 5-4 decisions on critical issues — uncertain.

SOCIETY

When federal money is poured into purposes that impact the lives of Americans at an unprecedented rate in the form of social services, and when the Supreme Court issues edicts that reach down into classrooms in a manner that dismisses the relevance of local law, society is bound to change.

A thumbnail sketch of these changes can be identified by examining an array of social statistics.

Readily available data shown on Appendix 4.1 demonstrates that the rate of divorce in America since 1940 had practically doubled by the time Nixon's first term ended. And since it is generally accepted knowledge that weakness in the family is the formula that produces strength in crime, it isn't too surprising to see that the murder rate had also ballooned.

The deterioration of marriage had only a very indirect relationship to the federal government. Changes in state law, beginning in 1969[17] in California; a general relaxation of morals in the 1960s; the rise of feminism (*The Feminine Mystique,* by Betty Friedan, 1963)[18]; and the increased availability of birth control methods were the primary causes.

And as the popularity of enduring marriage diminished, the number of unmarried couples increased. What was once regarded as "shacking up," a practice frowned upon by society, was on the way in 1969 to becoming a respectable alternative lifestyle.

Change in Public Debt

Franklin D. Roosevelt was the first of the modern presidents to become known more by his initials (FDR) than by his name. The same practice didn't quite take hold with Harry S Truman, but it did with Kennedy (JFK), Johnson (LBJ) and Nixon (RMN).

On the surface, the increase in revenue by 1.41 times in 1969–1972[19] indicated that progress on debt or tax reduction could be made, a possibility that seemed even stronger when the slowdown of the war in Vietnam was fed into the equation.

But like most things that appear on the surface, the obvious can quickly disappear when one looks deeper and appraises LBJ's parting gift to RMN — a cost base that amounted to 76 percent of current revenue.[20] Given the recent spending history of Congress, this didn't leave him with much room to maneuver, and it seemed to guarantee another period of deficits.

The only question was: How much?

Table 9.2
Transactions (in billions of dollars)

		1969–72		1965–68
Taxes		$ 774.1		$ 549.4
Less:				
Defense	$322.3		$262.0	
Interest	57.4		39.4	
Total		379.7		301.4
Net		$ 394.4		$ 248.0
Less:				
Government	$ 99.7		$ 96.3	
Human Resources	340.8		190.6	
Total		440.5		286.9
Surplus/deficit		$ -46.1		$ -38.9
Debt, beginning		-289.5		-256.8
Total		$-335.6		$-295.7
Adjustment*		13.2		6.2
Debt, Ending		$-322.4		$-289.5

*Treasury cannot be exact when it finances a budget deficit and the difference between what is needed and the value of securities traded inevitably produces a relatively small variance.

Source: Historical Tables 2007, 1.1, 3.1

An examination of the transactions for the period reveals the answer to this question, and provides some of the answers to the question that normally attaches to a deficit: Which cost centers were responsible?

A quick glance at the numbers in Table 9.2 indicates that *Interest* was becoming an important and growing cost center, *Defense* and *Government* were under control and, again, *Human Resources*, the statistical home of the Welfare State, was wildly out of control.

TAXES

More than anything else, the private sector hates inconsistency with tax policy. Unlike government, it plans ahead, at least five years, and it is of critical importance to it to know how much of a slice the government is going to take from its hard-earned profits.

And if there's anything the private sector was not getting from the government, it was consistent tax policy. JFK lowered taxes, LBJ increased them, and RMN reduced them again (1972), except for the payroll tax that went up to 9.2 percent on a maximum payroll of $9,000.

Actual revenues in 1969–72 amounted to $774.1 billion, or 41 percent above the previous period. Revenues increased in each of the four years of Nixon's first term except for 1971.[21]

The surge of revenue during the subject period was well above average,[22] and cannot be identified as a contributor to the deficit.

DEFENSE

Nixon inherited a defense budget of $81.9 billion and in 1972 he spent $79.2 billion[23]; it didn't vary much during the interim years.

Now two factors were in place that should have brought improved budget performance — strong revenues and stable *Defense*.

Regarding *Defense,* RMN had a problem new to him, but one that would be commonplace for succeeding presidents. The cost of the Welfare State crowded the budget to an extent that made it difficult to protect the value of the dollar by controlling debt and interest costs, and, on the other hand, to maintain a military establishment of sufficient size to protect the nation.

The size and capacity of LBJ's military was less than circumstances called for. RMN had to rebuild that strength within the constraints of a normal budget. He did so, but cautiously. More needed to be done, but the funds had been deployed elsewhere because of mandatory spending requirements for social services.

For the four full years, *Defense* increased 23.0 percent, far less than the revenue rate of increase. It did not contribute to the deficit for the period.[24]

Those who constantly blame *Defense* for taking too large a slice of the revenue pie have no historical basis for their claims. *Defense* in 1969–72 was well below the rate of revenue increase. The conclusion was the same under Kennedy and Johnson. Since all but the final days of the Vietnam War took place during the regimes of Kennedy, Johnson and Nixon (first term), it follows that the total cost of it was financed with current revenues. Generally speaking, the same holds true of the Korean War. Only $6.6 billion of its total cost was funded with debt.

Citizens who believed that the high taxes of the 1950s and 1960s were needed to support troops will be dismayed to learn that, instead, they were used to pay for some of the cost (the rest of it ended up in public debt) that was associated with the creation of the new America of Lyndon Johnson.

INTEREST

Interest expense in any organization, public or private, should be a minimal cost. When it isn't, it is a clear sign that the institution involved is unable to support itself on its current revenues, and it may be unduly reliant upon outside financing.

In the private sector this could mean that the company is ripe for takeover or bankruptcy; in the public sector it means that the nation is approaching a serious fiscal crisis that could powerfully influence the well-being and the security of the nation, its currency and its people.

During World War II, *Interest was* one of the cost centers that contributed to the deficit.[25] This was not surprising, nor was it a matter of undue concern. America was at war, borrowings were unusually high to finance that effort, and the expectation that this situation would reverse when peace was restored was a valid one.

And that proved to be the case. *Interest* was not again a part of the annual deficit until the first term of RMN.[26]

During the subject period, *Interest* was 1.46 times larger than it was during the previous four years. Had its growth been limited to the rate of revenue growth, its cost in the subject period would have been $55.5 billion, or $1.9 billion less than actual. To that extent, *Interest* was underfunded in 1969–72.[27]

When *Interest* is underfunded *because of national security concerns, or because of some passing emergency*, there is no need for concern — with time it will disappear. But when *Interest* becomes a major expense *because operating costs are unfunded*, responsible politicians will rush to prevent such a phenomenon from becoming a trend.

Prime interest rates were down to 5.3 percent in 1972,[28] but in 1969 and 1970, they approached 8 percent before they headed down.[29]

The increased cost of *Interest* represents the marriage of two powerful factors: (1) Climbing debt; (2) a worsening money market at least partly caused by the powerful presence of the federal government in the marketplace competing with the private sector for investment capital

Interest was 7.4 percent of revenue in 1969–72 (Table 9.2). Commercial enterprises could not long exist with such an interest charge — only in government is such unproductive cost ignored. And given the spending philosophies in place, *Interest* would continue to grow even more.

Someday it will reach a level that inconveniences politicians. Maybe then they will investigate the cause.

Was unfunded *Interest* a reasonable addition to public debt? Yes and no.

• Debt caused by uncontrollable costs times interest rates would equal an amount that could be logically added to public debt.
• Debt caused by controllable costs times interest rates would equal an amount that should not have been added to debt.

As time passed, more and more debt was falling into the second classification (above) and the interest cost attached simply added to the overall problem of overspending.

GOVERNMENT

After dealing with primary costs, $396.3 billion of revenue remained to cover operating costs, or 1.38 times higher than the total of the same costs during the preceding period. Increased spending in *Government* beyond that level would contribute to the deficit for the period; increased spending below that level would be passed along to *Human Resources*, the final cost center.

Government increased by 1.04 times in 1969–72, well under the rate of revenue increase. For that reason, it did not contribute to the deficit for the period. It is prudent, however, to glance at the line items to maintain contact with the impact of policy decisions.

Revenue was 1.41 times higher than it was during the preceding four years. Revenue available to operating cost centers was 1.38 times higher than the costs of those centers during the previous period. Spending growth beyond 1.41 times indicates that the line item is growing faster than the revenue curve; growth beyond 1.38 times identifies the line item that contributes to the deficit.

Overall, the cost center was fully funded. But several line items deserve special attention: Energy, Community, Agriculture, Justice and General.

Energy cost in 1965 was $700 million; in 1968, $1.0 billion; in 1972, $1.3 billion.[30] Obviously, RMN inherited an upward cost trend that continued at a lower rate during his first term. This trend tracks well with the increased price for crude oil[31] that became a matter of growing concern during the 1960s and 1970s.

Community/regional development costs skyrocketed on a comparable basis. RMN inherited a cost in 1968 of $1.4 billion; in 1972, the cost was $3.4 billion, an increase of 143 percent. This increase can be traced to a surge in cost that began in 1970 on RMN's watch, and may be charged to him as an unwise increase in overhead costs. This increase attacked RMN's future budgets; it was but one example of how he had abandoned his conservative supporters.

Table 9.3
Government (in billions of dollars)

	1969–72	1965–68	% Change
Energy	$ 4.3	$ 3.1	38.7%
Natural Resources/Environment	14.1	11.1	27.0
Transportation	30.0	23.6	27.1
Community/regional development	10.3	4.7	119.1
International affairs	17.9	21.8	-17.9
Science/space/technology	17.9	24.1	-25.8
Agriculture	20.6	13.9	48.2
Justice	4.8	2.4	100.0
General	9.6	6.6	45.4
Total	$129.5	$111.3	16.4%
Commerce & housing credit*	6.6	12.7	-48.0
Total	$136.1	$124.0	9.8%
Offsetting receipts	-36.4	-27.7	31.4
Net	$ 99.7	$ 96.3	3.5%

*Made up of earnings from various federal housing and other programs—subject to major changes from year to year relative to market conditions. (Historical Tables 2007, 3.2)

Source: Historical Tables 2007, 3.1

Readers at this point are asked to recall that it isn't the purpose of this book to critique the worthiness of government programs and initiatives, but to limit comments to the funding characteristics of the line item, or the cost center. In this case, there was no evidence to indicate that an increase of this size in this, or any other, line item was affordable — it is an example of irresponsible fiscal management.

Agriculture increased 1.48 times during the subject period, more than the rate of total revenue, or available revenue growth. RMN inherited a 1968 cost of $4.5 billion; in 1972, the cost was $5.2 billion, up 16 percent. Obviously, the upward cost trend that began in 1968 (Johnson's last year) was mostly inherited by RMN, and it continued to increase under him at a modest rate.

Justice expense doubled in size in 1969–72, a reflection of the times. Much like *Defense*, the cost of this line item varies with the mood in the country. America was aflame from coast to coast with social and student unrest, and the cost of keeping the peace kept pace with the need for more enforcement.

The increase in General was for the most part caused by a 1972 charge of $7.4 billion for "general purpose fiscal assistance," a line item that had normally cost about 10 percent of that amount and one that is not further explained in budget documents. The amount continued at that approximate level until, in the 1980s, it dropped just as mysteriously as it had increased.[32] One can speculate that this is an uncontrollable cost related in some way to foreign affairs.

RMN was fortunate in 1969–72 that cost control of some line items was sufficient to overcome overspending he had approved. The overall performance of the cost center was commendable, but some of its inner activities were unsettling.

HUMAN RESOURCES

Because *Government* did not need the level of funding allocated to it, additional funds were available to this cost center and its allowable growth potential was lifted to 1.56 times, higher than the 1.41 increase in revenue.[33]

Actual four-year cost amounted to $340.8 billion, as opposed to $190.6 billion for the previous four years, an increase of 1.79 times, well beyond allowable tolerances. This growth progression was not just a matter of concern, it was frightening.

How, when, where and by what authority did those in power get the idea that the nation's resources should be spent in such an irresponsible way? Was there no such thing as "timing" in their minds as they reshaped America? Even assuming that everything they did was worth doing, was there no understanding that it must be paid for—that piling up debt was not the way to do it?

An examination of the line items will reveal whether RMN was a participant in this spending orgy, or just an innocent victim.

Table 9.4
Human Resources (in billions of dollars)

	1969–72	1965–68	% Change
Education, training, services	$ 38.4	$ 20.6	86.4%
Health/Medicaid	26.6	12.1	119.8
Income Security*	59.9	31.7	90.0
Social Security	133.8	83.8	59.7
Medicare	26.0	7.5	246.7
Unemployment compensation	19.3	9.6	101.0
Veterans	36.8	25.3	45.5
Total	$340.8	$190.6	78.8%

*Minus unemployment compensation

Note: There were few social program of consequence prior to the 1960s except for Social Security (started in 1935) and the GI Bill.

Note: Major federal programs since the 1960s—Food Stamps 1961 (pilot), Food Stamps 1964, Medicaid 1965, Student Aid 1966, Medicare 1967, Coal Miners Benefits 1970

Source: Historical Tables 2007, 3.1

The spending in this cost center had passed excessive and reached bizarre. Every line item grew faster than the rate of revenue growth; every line item increased by more than any reasonable projection of revenue growth[34]; every line item contributed to the deficit.

Education increased 1.86 times, well above the rate of increase of any supportive revenue, and well above the rate of increase of any expected revenue.

Had the growth in this line item been restricted to the allowable 1.56 times, the cost in 1969–72 would have been $32.1 billion, $6.3 billion less than actual.

The responsibility for this over-spending falls upon LBJ on whose watch the programs were hatched that gave rise to the current overspending, which was beyond the power of the president to control.

The increase in Health/Medicaid is largely the consequence of the Medicaid program. In 1968, for example, the cost of Medicaid was $1.8 billion; in 1972, it was $4.6 billion — 2.6 times higher.[35]

This is an example of a social program running wild. Programs must be realistically funded and debt is not the way to do it.

Income Security almost doubled, primarily due to the maturation of programs already in place. For example, the ingredients of this line item are: Retirement and disability benefits, food and nutrition assistance, family assistance and housing assistance. In 1964, this array of programs cost $28.5 billion; in 1968, $37.3 billion and in 1972, $67.9 billion. How could anyone ignore such a cost progression?

Social Security draws the usual attention. And once again the most unfair tax of all was increased[36] as a tepid response to a structural problem that no politician in power had the courage to face.

The payroll tax increase was the coward's way out because the stigma was eventually borne by employers who had to meet employee demands for larger take-home pay. It was also a way of raising general revenues behind the noble veneer of "saving Social Security." The increased funds, of course, were used, along with all other federal receipts, to pay for day-to-day expenses.

Medicare gave a hint during the subject period of what its future budget impact would be. The massive increase was but a first step in the development of a line item destined to become a budget monster.

RMN also had to deal with unemployment, the cost of which was somewhat dramatic in his first term. A cost variation in Unemployment Compensation is normal as the economy ebbs and flows.

The increase in Veterans Services is related to the costs of the Vietnam War, and of all the cost variances, is the least worrisome.

Few people have available to them more data dealing with demographics than federal politicians. They have easy access to those who can interpret data and who can extrapolate probabilities from them. How many of them, faced with such hearty early-warning signals, took the time to estimate where these popular programs were headed?

The numbers in Table 9.4 speak for themselves. They elicit the shock one *should feel* when faced with such eagerness to spend the mountains of dollars made available by American taxpayers.

There is no particular sign that RMN had much to do with the cost overruns in this cost center. Unfunded costs are mostly identified with programs already on the books.

RMN, given the fact that Democrats controlled Congress, could do little to change the status quo. But his protesting voice should have been heard more often, and more effectively.

SUMMARY OF DEFICIT ALLOCATION

When RMN's first four years ended, it turns out that his inherited cost structure did not allow him much wiggle room, given the recent spending record of Congress.

Debt increased again in 1969–72, and the increase had nothing to do with national security. Taxpayers had good reason to gripe because they were being asked to support the re-invention of America, not the defense of it.

Table 9.5
Summary of Deficit, 1969–1972 (in billions of dollars)

Cost Center	Amount
Defense	$ 0.0
Interest	1.9
Government	0.0
Human Resources	44.2
Total	$46.1

Sources: Exhibits 1, 11–1, 16

The deficit was, on one hand, unavoidable in the sense that social programs in place were destined to create it, but it was avoidable, on the other hand, in the sense that men had created these programs and men with the will to do so could have modified or eliminated them.

Conclusion

The Vietnam War plagued President Johnson and his successor, Richard Nixon, and it was still going on when in 1972 Nixon's first term ended.

The war brought with it lots of baggage — student riots, an inflammatory press and a rapidly changing culture. It would be surprising if the spending priorities of the government didn't change during such a hurly-burly period.

But did they change as one might have expected?

America had radically changed over 12 years. The world of Eisenhower — a reasonable facsimile of the world of the Founding Fathers — was rapidly becoming the world of Lyndon Johnson, whose programs littered the budget. Lobbyists flooded Washington, arms outstretched for the next handout.

With more social programs came more power to politicians who proposed or who supported them. The tone of politics changed. Arrogance, never hard to find in Washington, became commonplace as these princes of the Welfare State preened themselves before an increasingly avaricious public.

Table 9.6
Spending Priorities

	1960	1968	1972
Primary costs			
Defense	52.2%	46.0%	34.3%
Interest	7.5	6.2	6.7
Total	59.7%	52.2%	41.0%
Government	11.9	14.5	12.5
Education/services	1.9	4.3	5.4
Health/Medicaid	.9	2.5	3.8
Medicare	2.6	3.3	
Income Security	8.0	6.6	12.0
Social Security	12.6	13.4	17.4
Veterans	5.9	3.9	4.6
Total	100.0%	100.0%	100.0%
	(3)	(2)(3)	(2)(3)

1 = peace; 2 = war; 3 = cold war

Source: Historical Tables 2007, 3.1

Two sentences capture the essence of the difference between Ike's America and the America that RMN dealt with: (1) In a time of peace, Ike allocated 52.2 percent of the budget to *Defense* and, in a time of war, RMN allocated 34.3 percent; (2) Under Ike, 29.3 percent of the budget flowed to social services; under RMN, the allocation was 65.9 percent.

Public debt increased to $322.4 billion in 1969–72.[37] Large deficits caused by unfunded operating expenses, once unheard of, were now commonplace.

Table 9.7
Public Debt, 1972 (billions)

Event	Inherited 1968	Added 1969–72	Total 1972	%
World War I	$ 18.3	$	$ 18.3	5.7%
Great Depression	24.5		24.5	7.6
World War II	142.5		142.5	44.2
Korean War	6.6		6.6	2.1
Interest	5.6	1.9	7.5	2.3
Government	36.9		36.9	11.4
Human Resources	60.4	44.2	104.6	32.4
Treasury	-5.3	-13.2	-18.5	- 5.7
Total	$289.5	$ 32.9	$322.4	100.0%

Source: Exhibits 1, 11, 12, 16

Richard Nixon came into office with 43 percent of the popular vote to support him,[38] and a powerful Democratic Congress to oppose him. The world he faced was chaotic, and his budget contained spending mandates that he had no hand in creating and that were protected by those who had fathered the Welfare State until it had become firmly cemented into the affairs of Congress.

Out of this stew little reform could be expected. And the low expectations were realized. At the end of his first four years RMN could not only see an out-of-control Social Security Program on his political landscape but also a plethora of newer, smaller social programs that were eating budget dollars and making it impossible to fund the military improvements that world conditions mandated.

In short, as far back as the 1970s, the Welfare State had become a national security problem. Incoming revenues and borrowing capacity had been preempted by Congress in order to refurnish America according to liberal tastes.

The silent agreement between the political parties, to limit debt financing (for rare, huge and wartime causes) that had controlled the behavior of American presidents and Congresses for almost 200 years had been trashed.

The race was on. Who could be the most compassionate, the kindest and the most sensitive? Who could spend the most, thereby becoming the darling of the establishment, defeat-proof at the voting booth?

RMN was the last line of defense for conservatives who had hoped to restore fiscal sanity and the power of the presidency to function as a commander in chief should be able to function. They were disappointed. But a new, more popular Nixon was running again. Maybe next time things would get better.

10

Richard M. Nixon and Gerald R. Ford, 1973–1976

Second-Term President

Richard M. Nixon won handily his presidential race in 1972 over Senator George McGovern (D–SD). Criticism from the press and protesters kept the Vietnam War issue burning, but voters believed Nixon had retreated from the war with all possible speed, and they sent him back to the White House with a resounding 61 percent of the popular vote.[1]

One might have expected, with such a powerful vote of confidence, that Nixon's coattails would have been strong enough to cause a change in congressional power. But it was not to be. He gained votes in the House, but not enough to change the power structure,[2] and he actually lost seats in the Senate.[3]

So, popular or not, RMN faced the same opposition leaders as he did in his first term, Carl Albert (D–OK) in the House, and Mike Mansfield (D–MO) in the Senate.[4] And the Democratic majority increased as RMN's reputation was eaten away by scandal.

Ironically, RMN's enemies actually assisted in his reelection by assuming that the public believed what the press and the TV-heads endlessly repeated, namely, that his war policies were unpopular throughout the country.

McGovern's supporters attacked Nixon's measured retreat from Vietnam. But that turned out to be his strong suit with voters, and his weak suit, continuing deficits and growing debt, did not get the attention it deserved. Had McGovern and his supporters focused voter attention on them instead of a war that was yesterday's news, he might have done better, but, by muting economic issues, he protected Nixon's weakest flank.

No sooner was Nixon sworn in for the second time than the scandal known as Watergate surfaced, and it gained steady momentum. And if that weren't enough, Vice President Spiro Agnew was forced to resign in 1973 because of alleged financial misdealings.[5]

Pressures associated with Watergate drew closer to Nixon in 1973 even as he dealt with foreign affairs and other major matters of state. His original advisers were gone by 1974; he was surrounded by people he hardly knew.

The congressional investigation of Watergate reached its apex when Nixon refused to release tapes of presidential meetings that had been held with his associates in the Oval Office. He justified not doing so by claiming executive privilege. The case went to the Supreme Court, and there Nixon lost his final and determining battle before the Chief Justice that he had personally appointed, Warren Burger.

The tapes were released, Nixon's lies were revealed, and in August 1974, he resigned. Gerald R. Ford, who had succeeded Agnew as vice president, assumed the presidency.

GERALD FORD, LAWYER, NAVY, REPRESENTATIVE, VICE PRESIDENT, PRESIDENT

Gerald R. Ford was born in Omaha, Nebraska, in 1913, under the name of Leslie L. King, Jr. His parents divorced when he was two years old, and his mother moved to Grand Rapids, Michigan, where she in due course married a local businessman, Gerald Ford. Ford adopted the boy and named him Gerald R. Ford.

Woodrow Wilson was president.

Twenty years later Ford was a football star at the University of Michigan, where he graduated in 1935. Despite an active athletic schedule, he had maintained a B average.

Ford turned his back on a professional football career (he had contract offers from the Detroit Lions and the Green Bay Packers) and he went to Yale as its head boxing coach and assistant football coach. He also studied law part-time and in 1938 he became a full-time student. Ford graduated in 1941 in the top 25 percent of his class. He then returned to Michigan, passed the bar, and joined a law firm in Grand Rapids.

It was the first year of Roosevelt's third term as president.

Like Richard Nixon (they were the same age), Ford was a member of the generation that spent many years in uniform during World War II.

He locked the doors of his law office in 1942 and joined the navy as an ensign; he was eventually assigned as a gunnery officer to the USS *Monterey*, a light aircraft carrier in the fleet of Admiral Bull Halsey.

Ford took part in several great battles in the South Pacific, including Wake Island, Okinawa, and the recapture of the Philippines. He earned 10 battle stars and in 1946 he was discharged as a lieutenant commander. A bright man and a first-class World War II hero, Gerald Ford would later be unfairly and unkindly portrayed by the press as slow-witted and clumsy.

Ford joined a law firm in Grand Rapids after the war until in 1948 he defeated Rep. Bartell Junkman, a Republican, in the primaries; he went on to win the general election.

His political career was launched. Harry Truman was president; public debt was $216 billion.[6]

Ford brought the toughness and intelligence to the House that he had shown in football, the Navy, and his law career. He was one of two House members on the Warren Commission that investigated the assassination of President Kennedy; he was a critic of Lyndon Johnson's War on Poverty ("a lot of washed-up old programs"); by 1965, he was at age 52 the minority leader and potential Speaker of the House.

But fate decided otherwise.

Vice President Spiro Agnew resigned because of a financial scandal, and in 1973 Ford replaced him. Richard Nixon resigned in August 1974, and in September 1974 President Ford granted him a "full, free and absolute pardon," a brave and wise act of a man with a job to do. Brave because it jeopardized Ford's political future; wise because it took Nixonmania off the front pages (where it otherwise would have remained for years), thus permitting the political process to move forward.

The public debt inherited by Nixon was now Ford's to deal with. It had grown to $322.4 billion in 1972, and over 40 percent of it was related to interest charges and unfunded federal programs.

Table 10.1
Public Debt 1972 (in billions of dollars)

	Total	%
World War I	$ 18.3	5.7%
Great Depression:	24.5	7.6
World War II	142.5	44.2
Korean War	6.6	2.1
Interest	7.5	2.3
Government	36.9	11.4
Human Resources	104.6	32.4
Treasury, net	-18.5	- 5.7
Total	$322.4	100.0%

Source: Table 9.7, Chapter 9

Nixon was powerful before Watergate; weak after it. He left a humbled and shrunken presidency to Ford who, considering the makeup of the Congress, had no power to effect meaningful changes in the spending trends that had led to ever-increasing debt.

But the inability of Nixon/Ford to control the growth of the Welfare State went beyond political resistance. The cost of entitlements is not subject to the same scrutiny as are expenditures for, say, battleships. Once launched, welfare programs become entitlements that tend to sail unmolested, outgoing monies being limited only by eligibility criteria.

And there is no effective overall spending cap for the federal budget. Unlike states, which must operate within balanced budgets, the federal government's spending is controlled by the collective conscience of the Congress that, presumably, wants the best for America.

No president can halt the spending of an undisciplined Congress under such a system — overhaul is the only way to stop it or lighten it.

Perspectives

General

The shooting war in Vietnam was over for the United States when Ford assumed command, but tensions persisted at home, albeit at a subdued level, and one more major embarrassment remained to the international image of America.

In an attempt to defuse local tempers, Ford offered clemency in September 1974 (the same month he pardoned Nixon) to draft evaders and deserters.[7]

The idea met with mixed reviews.

The American Legion thought the terms too liberal; some malefactors considered them too tough; others accepted the chance to get square with the law.

Ford's political enemies, stunned by his decision to pardon Nixon, regarded his offer of clemency as blatant politics.

Trying to heal America's bruises, however, whatever the motivation, was worthwhile as a clear signal, if nothing else, that the federal government was hearing the voices in the streets.

The final major embarrassment related to Vietnam took place in the spring of 1975. Saigon, the capital city of South Vietnam, was taken by the Communists, the American embassy was ravaged, and television cameras worldwide were treated to a final view of Americans turning tail and running to safety. Vietnam was unified soon after. The Socialist Republic of Vietnam renamed the capital city Ho Chi Minh City after the country's esteemed leader.

It was over. Whatever America's objective had been in Vietnam, which was never clear, it had not been realized. The war that America never fought to win was lost. And that experience has affected the use of America's military power from that day until today.

President Ford's presidential plate was not as full or as varied as that faced by his two immediate predecessors, but it was far from being empty of considerable challenges.

This was a time when hijackers changed forever the casual serenity of airports. Pro-Palestinian forces, for example, took an Air France plane in July 1976[8] and held over 100 hostages until Israeli commandos freed them in a raid on Uganda's Entebbe airport.

And domestic turbulence continued despite the cutback in Vietnam, the civil rights legislation, and the flood of Great Society money that poured into federal programs, all of it designed by Washington's politicians to cure the nation's ills, and all of it demonstrating once again that human nature has flaws that cannot be cured by laws and dollars, which must be confronted from within.

As an example of the idiocy at large in society, in 1974 the 19-year-old daughter of William Randolph Hearst was first kidnapped by the Symbionese Liberation Army, one of several self-important black protest groups of the day, and later joined them as a willing member.

And this was a time that effluence from the Watergate affair poisoned the political process and, in particular, weakened the power of the presidency — John Mitchell, John Ehrlichman and H. R. Haldeman, Nixon insiders, were found guilty of coverup activity and they were jailed.

The mood in Congress toward President Ford was personally pleasant (Ford was a genuinely likeable and popular man) and professionally venomous; between the political parties, the mood was antagonistic.

This combustible environment partly explains why Ford exercised his veto power 66 times in 27 months.[9] His need to do so was not lessened by the defensive position he, the post–Watergate Republican president, had inherited.

The cost of Watergate in terms of the power of the presidency cannot be overestimated. With Nixon on the ropes, or with Ford hanging on with as much dignity as he could muster, Democratic opponents seized the moment to increase their power in the budget process.

A month before he resigned, for example, a subdued Nixon signed the Budget Control Act, which established the Congressional Budget Office (CBO-1974)[10] and eliminated the presidential power to impound (to hold back on the payment of approved expenditures), putting into place as a substitute the toothless power of recision (a proposal by the president to rescind spending after it has been enacted, a proposal that Congress can ignore).

CBO does for Congress what the Office of Management and Budget (OMB) does for the executive and (it was previously assumed) for the Congress. Its creation, at the insistence of Democratic power brokers, represented a statement by them to the effect that they didn't trust the administration to provide them with objective data. They didn't have the presidency, but they could, and did, chip away at presidential powers and, in the process, made themselves more powerful.

The inevitable result of this maneuvering was to politicize the fact-finding process — to put two research groups into competition, guaranteeing that basic information, upon which decisions are based, would thereafter be biased and, more importantly, would be of lower quality.

This competition lessened the power of the presidency, which was the only office that was responsible to all of the people, and it increased the power of the Democratic Congress, which was essentially loyal to some, but not all, of the people.

The de facto elimination of the power of the president to impound, partly due to the Watergate-weakened presidency, destroyed one of the few controls over spending that a president had.

Also, three other factors lessened control over spending and were now fixed elements of the budget process:

1. Attitude: Conservative fiscal policies of Adam Smith, once shared by both parties, had been replaced, or were at least challenged, by those of John Maynard Keynes—high spending and growing debt were supported by respected economic theory.
2. Entitlements: Lyndon Johnson's programs, once approved, escaped the regular review process; spending is automatic.
3. Seniority: The seniority system in the House eroded in the 1970s. The result has been an endless group of ungovernable committees and chairpersons.

Such things made it unlikely that Ford or future presidents would make inroads on the spending problem until the entire intellectual, emotional and political edifice that supported current procedures was revised.

Another sign of changing times was the two attempts to assassinate Ford in September 1975. The shooters were young women.

The New Age had arrived. Modern women, it was demonstrated, could be just as bad as old-fashioned men, an aspect of the Great Society that many could live without.

Home Front

President Ford presided over the last embarrassing days of the Vietnam War in 1973.[11] By 1975, he had reduced the number of active duty personnel by about one-third,[12] but the remaining cost, deceptively high, represented the impact of inflation that (predictably) took off when Nixon's wartime price controls were totally eliminated.

The Misery Index[13] reflected the same thing, and more. It increased by 49 percent to 20.4 percent — the highest in modern history to that point. Inflation was part of it, but interest rates and unemployment played their role as well. Together, these in-your-face economic factors gave to Ford a weak platform to run on in the 1976 election.

Earnings per capita gave the illusion of prosperity,[14] and for some it was real, even when inflation was considered. But lurking in the background was the great fiscal danger to Americans as individuals, to the health of the nation's currency and to national security itself—spending per capita in 1976 was 2.7 times higher than it was in 1968, most of it due to the runaway cost of the Welfare State.

Given this state of affairs, it isn't surprising to find that public debt in 1976 was 1.6 times higher than it was in 1968,[15] most of the increase the unfunded costs of operating expenses,[16] especially those related to the Welfare State.

Ford could and did dodge bullets during World War II, but he could not dodge economic problems that owed their birth to Johnson, that accelerated under Nixon and that exploded on his watch.

SUPREME COURT[17]

Chief Justice Earl Warren heard 13 cases in 1957–60. The case load over the next three presidential periods was more than double that amount, and in 1973–76 it reached 38 cases under Chief Justice Warren Burger,[18] a reflection of the Court's decisions about what to hear, and what not to hear — about its perception of what was federal business and what was private sector business.

> The enumeration in the Constitution of certain rights shall not be construed to deny or disparage others retained by the people.— Ninth Amendment, U.S. Constitution
>
> The powers not delegated to the United States by the Constitution, nor prohibited by it to the States, are reserved to the States respectively, or to the people.— Tenth Amendment, U.S. Constitution

Conservatives objected to activist judges who considered the Constitution a living document (to be interpreted by them in the light of current social and political circumstances). The increased case load was a clear signal that the Court had strayed beyond its ordained focus, moving into areas that were best settled in accordance with the division of power enumerated in the Constitution between the federal government (in this case, the Supreme Court) and the local legislative mechanisms that more immediately, and constitutionally, reflected the will of the majority.

Conservatives hoped that Burger would redirect the Court's business onto a more reflective and less intrusive course.

There was good reason, on the surface, to believe that this would be the case. Burger himself and three associates (Rehnquist, Powell and Blackmun) had been appointed by Nixon, and two others (Stewart and Brennan) had been appointed by Eisenhower. If all voted with judicial restraint, decisions of 6–3 favoring that worldview should be forthcoming.

But history has shown that judges can be unpredictable creatures. Nothing was sure. And when one new associate appeared on the scene, John Stevens, another question was raised: What will he become when the black robes cloak his shoulders, and the social pressures to conform are applied to him?

- John Stevens— Stevens, born in 1920, is still active (2007) in the Supreme Court; he is its oldest member. The privileged son of enormously wealthy parents, Stevens was graduated from the University of Chicago before he enlisted in the navy to become part of its code-breaking team. His excellent performance earned him the Bronze Star. Law school came next at Northwestern University; he distinguished himself by achieving the highest grades in the history of that school. Following graduation, he served as a law clerk for Supreme Court Justice Wiley Rutledge (an ardent supporter of FDR). Private practice came next, interlaced with special counsel work for the House and for the Attorney General's office. President Nixon in 1970 appointed him to the U.S. Court of Appeals, Seventh Circuit from which position President Ford plucked him for a Supreme Court appointment when, in 1975, Justice Douglas retired. One wonders what Nixon and Ford were thinking when they appointed Stevens. His impeccable liberal credentials were there to see for anyone who cared to look. And that's what they got. From a conservative point of view, Stevens ranks with Brennan, Warren and Blackmun as the worst judicial judgments ever made by a Republican president.

The appointment of Stevens was a net plus for liberals— they got a younger liberal for an older one.

A few cases from the period give readers a clue as to the types of decisions that were made by this collection of legal minds, and they provide some insight into why, in later years, caseload would explode.

Roe v. Wade, 1973. Roe wanted to terminate her pregnancy with an abortion. Texas law forbade abortions except to save the life of the mother. The issue: Does the Constitution protect a woman's right to terminate her pregnancy with an abortion? In a 7–2 decision (Rehnquist and White dissenting), the Court ruled that, based upon the *Griswold* decision (1965), a woman has total authority over her pregnancy during the first trimester, and it defined different levels of state interest over the second and third trimesters. This decision struck down abortion laws in 46 states, laws made by state legislators who had been elected by the people. Seven justices established a new moral law as well as a civil law with this decision — a law that soon exploded into abortions of unheard of frequency as too many women turned their newly found right into just another form of birth control.

Frontiero v. Richardson, 1973. A female lieutenant in the air force applied for a dependant's allowance for her husband. The wives of male members of the services are automatically considered as dependents as a matter of federal law, but husbands had to demonstrate a defined level of need before that status was granted. Frontiero's request was refused. The issue: Is it constitutional to have different qualifications for dependents depending on the sex of the petitioner? In a 9–1 decision (Rehnquist dissented), the Court ruled that there should not be a different standard for male and female military with respect to dependency allowances. This case is a reflection of the growing power of the feminist movement under which women were becoming more insistent on parity with men, irrespective of circumstances.

Bigelow v. Virginia, 1974. Bigelow, editor of the *Virginia Weekly*, ran an advertisement for an organization that referred women to clinics and hospitals for abortions. The state law forbade any person or organization to encourage abortion. The issue: Was the state law unconstitutional? In a 7–2 decision (Rehnquist and White dissenting), the Court protected Bigelow's right to advertise and, in effect, struck down state laws that attempted to thwart the advertising of abortion services.

U.S. v. Nixon, 1974. Throughout his presidency, President Nixon taped all conversations that took place in the Oval Office. He kept them from those who were investigating the affair on the grounds of executive privilege. The issue: Is the president's right to executive privilege immune from judicial review? In an 8–0 decision (Rehnquist excused himself because of his prior relationship with Nixon) the Court rejected Nixon's point of view. This legitimate question for the Supreme Court was rendered by men some of whom were inherently loyal to the president. But, to their credit, they were even more loyal to their sense of professionalism.

Political affiliation might provide reasonably valid assumptions about how a Supreme Court judge might rule when confronted with such things as commercial issues, but when subject matter moves into areas of human behavior, history says judicial behavior remains in the realm of the unknown and the undependable until the judge fully exposes his inner self in actual rulings made in a Supreme Court environment.

Supreme Court justices are appointed for life, protected from the press unless they choose to become active in some public way. Most withdraw into a private intellectual world and they live a quiet, unobserved and completely secure life, keenly aware that the next decision they make could affect the lives of millions of Americans for decades to come.

Eventually, some justices become involved in issues that have broad social impact, such as civil rights cases that became so common in the 1960s. The Burger justices, for example, dealt with a social issue in 1973 that had even more impact on society — abortion.

Their ruling on that hot-button issue influenced the laws of most states, and it dramatically affected the lives of most Americans, black and white, and the moral code under which they lived their lives.

The judges ruled in a way that confounded many observers. Oddly, only Rehnquist, a Nixon appointee, and White, JFK's man, opposed the decision to legalize abortion for the entire nation — the right and the left joining together in united resolve.

The Roe decision, made under the leadership of Chief Justice Burger (Nixon), had the support of justices Blackmun (Nixon), Powell (Nixon) Stewart and Brennan (Ike) plus two unsurprising allies, justices Marshall (LBJ) and Douglas (FDR).

This decision, fundamentally made by Republicans, proved once again that judges appointed for life to the Supreme Court function free of career or political concerns—they becomes totally unpredictable.

No better example of this can be found than the Burger Court in general, dominated by Republicans, or in the rulings on critical issues of the two recent occupants of the Chief Justice's chair, Earl Warren and Warren Burger. Whatever their personal brilliance or integrity, from a conservative standpoint they were unmitigated disasters.

SOCIETY[19]

Society changing from within was a growing phenomenon. Evolving sexual mores, feminism, homes without attending mothers, etc., were contributions to a social stew that, in total, synchronized perfectly with Supreme Court decisions on such things as prayer in school, pornography and abortion, and with the irresponsible use of public funds by federal politicians.

Up became down in this era; wrong became right. Today became all important; yesterday didn't exist. Where debate once existed about what was good and what was bad, modern debate questioned the validity of the distinction. Good became the pleasant; bad, the unpleasant. Pleasure was king; reflection was useless—as one thinks so one acts. And this changing philosophy of life began to show up in the social statistics of the day.

The stability of the home continued to deteriorate, a trend that is ongoing, and one that is at the root of most social problems. And the increase in abortions following the *Roe v. Wade* decision of 1973 is a striking example of how Supreme Court decisions of the 1960s and 1970s helped to form a new morality in the United States, one at odds with that upon which the Founders had established the nation, and one destined to turn loose on society the cost of undisciplined instincts. Abortions in 1975 were 46 percent higher than they were in 1972.

Violent crime of all kinds was on the increase in 1976, a silent testimony to what can happen when respect for life is diminished.

As 1976 came to a close it was clear that the second American Revolution had more than a political dimension led by LBJ and his followers. Judicial and social changes were just as dramatic, just as devastating.

These data do not neatly synchronize with presidential eras, but the information is adequate to support the dictum that LBJ's legacy, the Great Society, had not yet been realized; that money, helpful when prudently spent in a way that assists initiative and self-reliance, is not the primary answer to the problems of humanity. In fact, after almost two decades of unbridled social spending, more debt was the most significantly visible consequence.

Change in Public Debt

The first year of Nixon's second term was promising only in the sense that the deficit ($14.9 billion) was lower than the previous year ($23.4 billion). Ford saw the same deceptive occurrence in 1974 — the deficit dropped from $14.9 billion in 1973 to $6.1 billion.[20]

But the improvement was illusory. Spending, not revenue, had always been the core of the deficit issue, and it was apparent in 1974 that the major problem persisted. It showed itself with a large growl in the next two years when spending soared.

In Ford's final two years, total deficits were $126.9 billion; for the four years, they were $148.0 billion.[21]

The increase in revenue in 1973–76, not quite as hefty as it was during the previous four years, was still well above average.[22] The deficit was again apparently cost related, a hypothesis that will be explored below.

Table 10.2
Transactions (in billions of dollars)

		1973–76		1969–72
Taxes		$1071.2		$ 774.1
Less:				
Defense	$332.1		$322.3	
Interest	88.6		57.4	
Total		420.7		379.7
Net		$ 650.5		379.4
Less:				
Government	$166.3		$ 99.7	
Human Resources	632.2		340.8	
Total		798.5		440.5
Surplus/deficit		$-148.0		$ -46.1
Debt, beginning		-322.4		
Total		$-470.4		$-289.5
Adjustment*		-7.0		13.2
Debt, Ending		$-477.4		$-322.4

*Treasury cannot be exact when it finances a budget deficit and the difference between what is needed and the value of securities traded inevitably produces a relatively small variance.

Source: Historical Tables 2007, 1.1, 3.1

"A fool and his money are soon parted," some wise man once said. American politicians, as the above chart shows, seem determined to prove the wisdom of that observation.

TAXES

Tax income was 38.4 percent higher than in 1969–72, well above the normally expected rate of increase during a four-year presidency. This revenue increase was, for all practical purposes, heavily influenced by inflation rates that ran from 5.8 to 11.0 percent during the period.[23]

The combination of LBJ–imposed overhead and RMN's price controls had joined together to produce a faltering economy that featured a hidden and floating tax (the inflation rate) that threatened to turn the U.S. dollar into funny money.

The fate of future revenues was uncertain as 1976 closed — a troubling thought when combined with the near certainty that costs would continue to explode; a recipe for disaster.

To stay healthy, a reduction in the cost of government was as imperative as it was unlikely. Knowing nothing else, one could safely predict that deficits would zoom and the future Misery Index would become painful.

And, of great significance, deficits were now at a critical level. Soon they would be systemically unavoidable in any long term until the structure of the Welfare State was changed.

Cost reduction would no longer suffice; a tax increase large enough to overcome current deficit levels was highly unlikely and could have, if tried, a devastating effect on an already weak economy.

Cost elimination and program restructuring were the realities that had to be faced. And they were the realities that were ignored.

DEFENSE

Defense under RMN in 1972 was $79 billion; it was $90 billion in 1976[24] an apparent increase in readiness of 14 percent. But the increase was mostly an inflationary illusion. Troop levels were substantially lower now that the Vietnam War was over.

Over the four-year period, the rate of cost increase in the *Defense* cost center was less than the rate of revenue increase; it was fully funded and did not contribute to the deficit for the period.[25]

INTEREST

Higher interest rates[26] and higher debt[27] combined to produce a four-year cost of $88.6 billion in 1973–76, 1.54 times higher than the previous four years. Had this increase been limited to the rate of revenue increase (1.38), cost would have been $79.3 billion or $9.3 billion less than actual. To that extent, this cost center in the subject period contributed to the deficit.

Years of fiscal mismanagement reached a new plateau in 1973–76. *Interest* was almost as important in the budget as the total combined cost of international, agriculture, science/space/technology, justice, and general government activities.

GOVERNMENT

Primary cost centers did not require the funding available to them and, as a consequence, the flow through of funds increased allowable growth of remaining cost centers from 1.38 times to 1.50 times.

Had the rate of increase in this cost center been so limited, the resultant cost would have been $149.4 billion or $16.9 billion less than actual. To that extent this cost center contributed to the 1973–76 deficit.

Table 2.4
Government (in billions of dollars)

	1973–76	1969–72	% Change
Energy	$ 9.6	$ 4.3	123.3%
Natural Resources/Environment	26.0	14.1	84.4
Transportation	43.0	30.0	43.3
Community/regional development	18.6	10.3	80.6
International affairs	23.3	17.9	30.2
Science/space/technology	16.4	17.9	-8.4
Agriculture	13.4	20.6	-35.0
Justice	11.0	4.8	129.2
General	40.0	9.6	316.7
Total	$201.3	$129.5	55.4
Commerce & housing credit*	23.1	6.6	250.0
Total	$224.4	$136.1	64.9
Offsetting receipts	-58.1	-36.4	59.6
Net	$166.3	$ 99.7	66.8

*Made up of earnings from various federal housing and other programs— subject to major changes from year to year relative to market conditions. (Historical Tables 2007, 3.2)

Source: Historical Tables 2007, 3.1

The volatile Commerce and Housing Credit had unusually heavy costs associated with mortgages in 1973–76 that accounted for about one-quarter of the cost increase in this cost center.

The allowable increase from a deficit standpoint is a yardstick that is too kind when the focus switches to cost efficiency — the rate of revenue increase (1.38) is more useful.

Under that test, Energy, Natural Resources, Community Development, Justice and General deserve analysis.

The increase in Energy was actually mild when compared with the explosion of crude oil prices during the subject period. Overall, the price of crude during the subject period was 2.5 times higher than it was during the previous four years; in 1976, it was 3.8 times higher than the previous four-year average — bad news for the upcoming administration.[28]

Spending in Natural Resources/Environment was disproportionate to any reasonable cost growth test. The major reason for this is again tied to the prevailing attitude in Washington that approved programs or new departments without due regard for budget consequences. In this case the Environmental Protection Agency was formed in 1970. Its cost in 1971 was $701 million; in 1976, the cost was 4.4 times higher,[29] and climbing, a dangerous signal that President Ford could not control the spending virus that had driven the budget toward collapse for almost two decades.

The increase in Community and Regional Development represents the maturation of programs that expanded in 1970 and exploded in 1973–76.

The increase in Justice was tied to inflation, and to the mood of the times that required more law enforcement — in 1976 the cost of Justice was about twice as expensive as it was in 1972.[30] Liberty carries a price tag when personal responsibility ceases to function as it should. America was less disciplined than before and, as night follows day, law enforcement became more active.

The budget line item, General, contains a sub-line item called General Purpose Fiscal Assistance, which became consequential for the first time in the 1973 budget when its cost went up about 11 times in one year and continued at that approximate level for the final three years of the RMN/GRF presidency. Repetition, boring though it may be, comes into play again with this line item — no matter how worthy, it was not affordable as timed and as structured. Under the existing budget circumstances, it was almost criminal to add another expenditure of this magnitude to the federal budget.

In summary, a rationale can be advanced to defend the outsized cost growth in Energy and Justice, but other increases appear to be related to new and sizable projects that, under existing budget circumstances, should have been canceled or postponed.

HUMAN RESOURCES

Similar to *Government, Human Resources* in the context of a balanced budget could grow by 1.50 times in 1973–1976. Growth beyond that amount would make the cost center a contributor to the deficit.

Had the growth in *Human Resources* been so limited, its cost during the subject period would have been $510.4 billion, as opposed to the actual cost of $632.2 billion — a variance of $121.8 billion.

Such an ugly level of fiscal madness is no longer surprising by this time in the LBJ–sponsored cost escalation cycle, but its acceptance by the political leaders of the era makes it even more insulting.

Every line item in this cost center grew faster than any recent study in income trends to the U.S. government would justify.[31] What had begun in the 1960s was continuing apace, and the refusal of elected officials to confront damage being done to the fiscal integrity of the nation was abominable.

Education grew by 56.5 percent. The first jolt of cost came in 1966, when it more than doubled.[32] Cost increases related to existing programs were automatic until, in 1975, a new sub-line item, Training and Employment, became

Table 10.4
Human Resources (in billions of dollars)

	1973–76	1969–72	% Change
Education, training, services	$ 60.1	$ 38.4	56.5%
Health/Medicaid	48.7	26.6	83.1
Income Security*	128.5	60.0	114.2
Social Security	243.6	133.8	82.1
Medicare	46.4	26.0	78.5
Unemployment compensation	44.5	19.2	131.7
Veterans	60.4	36.8	64.1
Total	$632.2	$340.8	85.5%

*Minus unemployment compensation (from 1965–68 on)

Note: Major federal programs since the 1960s— Food Stamps 1961 (pilot), Food Stamps 1964, Medicaid 1965, Student Aid 1966, Medicare 1967, Coal Miners Benefits 1970, Commodity Donations 1973, Supplementary Security Income 1974, Supplemental Feeding 1976, Earned Income Tax Credit 1976, Legal Services 1976

Source: Historical Tables 2007, 3.1

the newest and latest fashion on how to spend money. In 1976, its cost ($6.3 billion) was double what it was two years earlier — the cost trend was up when President Ford left office, undisturbed by his many vetoes.

The surge in the line item, Health, is essentially rooted in the maturation of the Medicaid program approved in the 1960s. In 1969, its cost was $2.3 billion; in 1976, $8.6 billion[33]— another powerful budget line item at the end of the Ford presidency that was out of control.

The growth in Income Security is directly related to Richard Nixon's abandonment of his conservative base when, with the élan of LBJ himself, he introduced Supplemental Security Income to the ever-growing plate of welfare goodies.

In 1974, its first year as a budget item of consequence, its cost was $2 billion; in 1976, it was $4.6 billion and destined to become a major budget item.

Social Security costs were still exploding and the Washingtonocrats could think of nothing more imaginative to do than to add once again to the payroll tax. In 1976, the taxable base was lifted from $9,000 to $15,300 — a 70 percent increase.[34]

The line item cost of Social Security in 1976 was 84 percent higher than it was four years before.[35] And nobody talked about it.

Medicare had just begun its baby steps toward its final role as a budget buster. The idea behind it was welcomed by most, but the method of financing it (via the payroll tax), and its inherent structure, should have been items of lively debate during the period about a cost that threatened to double every four years if not placed under controls. There was no lack of ideas about how to structure a sensible health program for the nation, but there were few who would listen.

The increase in Unemployment Compensation was a consequence of the poor economy during the period and, along with the increased cost of Veterans Services, it represented the only defendable increases in the cost center.

SUMMARY OF DEFICIT ALLOCATIONS

The purpose of this study of public debt is to identify its source in terms of four cost centers, *Defense, Interest, Government and Human Resources.*

The results of these allocations are disturbing because they stray from conventional wisdom, and point directly at the irresponsibility of elected officials who swear to protect the nation when they assume office.

Instead, they switch their loyalties away from the national welfare and toward their personal job security, and to the support of those giveaway programs that bring popularity with voters who are being persistently trained to look to Washington for services once handled locally.

Deficits piled upon deficits as the spenders consistently violated a fundamental law of finance — never use long-term borrowings to finance daily operating expenses — and its corollary — keep operating expenses within range of reasonably expected income.

The patterns of irresponsibility continued in 1973–76 and produced the largest deficit to that point in modern history, $148.0 billion.

Table 10.5
Summary of Deficit — 1973–1976
(in billions of dollars)

Cost Center	Amount
Defense	$ 0.0
Interest	9.3
Government	16.9
Human Resources	121.8
Total	$148.0

Sources: Exhibits 1, 11–1, 16

Existing programs by themselves in 1973 were enough to guarantee a deficit for the period, but to add additional ones in the face of past history was an act of fiscal lunacy. Costly programs were piled on top of a Welfare State load that was already back breaking: Commodity Donations (1973), Supplemental Security Income (1974), Supplemental Feeding (1976), Earned Income Tax Credit (1976) and Legal Services (1976).

This was not the presidency of a conservative. Nixon and Ford, wittingly or unwittingly, actually contributed to a fiscal load that was destroying the federal budget.

Conclusion

Other presidencies have been faced with serious external challenges, but few if any were beset by so many at the same time as Richard Nixon and, to a lesser extent, his successor, Gerald Ford.

And everything that happened, especially Watergate, made it even more likely that the America of the Founding Fathers would continue to drift toward the second America that was set into motion by Lyndon Johnson.

Table 10.6
Spending Priorities

	1960	1968	1972	1976
Primary costs				
Defense	52.2%	46.0%	34.3%	24.1%
Interest	7.5	6.2	6.7	7.2
Total	59.7%	52.2%	41.0%	31.3%
Government	11.9	14.5	12.5	14.0
Education/services	1.9	4.3	5.4	5.1
Health/Medicaid	.9	2.5	3.8	4.1
Medicare	2.6	3.3	4.3	
Income Security	8.0	6.6	12.0	16.4
Social Security	12.6	13.4	17.4	19.9
Veterans	5.9	3.9	4.6	4.9
Total	100.0%	100.0%	100.0%	100.0%
	(3)	(2)(3)	(2)(3)	(3)

1 = peace; 2 = war; 3 = cold war

Source: Historical Tables 2007, 3.1

The Soviet Union was more mature and powerful in 1976 than it was in 1960, yet America devoted less thereafter to national defense, not because money wasn't available, but because the government was more interested in continuing its social policies begun by LBJ.

This second American Revolution, that turned America upside down, took place without a shot being fired — a legislator's pen and a judge's gavel were the only weapons needed to accomplish the *coup d'état.*

Before concluding this appraisal of the Nixon/Ford administration two major issues that commanded headlines of the day must at least be recognized: Vietnam and Watergate.

Vietnam preceded Watergate.

To begin with, the war was popular. Congress passed with overwhelming support, for example, the Gulf of Tonkin Resolution in 1964, an agreement that gave President Johnson full wartime powers.

When Richard Nixon became president, however, the war was unpopular, and those who had originally supported it were running for political cover — it was politically proper to be anti–Vietnam. Ex-supporters of Johnson pointed the finger at Nixon. Vietnam became, presto, Nixon's war.

The Vietnam War is important in the context of this book because it attached to Nixon an unpopular cause. And despite his successful plan for withdrawal from Vietnam, he was attacked until the end of his first term as if he had been the one who started the war in the first place, all of which made him an easy target when Watergate became front-page news.

Watergate was many things to many people. How did it relate to the topic of this book, the public debt? Not at all, in any direct sense. But indirectly it resulted in a much weaker presidency at a time when presidential power was the only remaining control over spending.

Nixon had, and he used (as had presidents before him), the power to impound — the power to delay expenditures. The threat of it was more powerful than the fact of it in the eyes of a Congress that wanted to eliminate it. A weakened Nixon gave them their chance and the Budget Control Act of 1974 was the result.

The meaning?

The presidency Ford inherited was weaker. Ford had fewer budget controls at his disposal, which made it less probable that he would have a positive influence on the deficit and debt problems of America.

The debt went up again in 1973–76, this time by 48 percent, to $477.4 billion, as follows:

Table 10.7
Public Debt, 1976 (billions)

Event	Inherited 1972	Added 1973–76	1976	%
World War I	$ 18.3	$	$ 18.3	3.8%
Great Depression	24.5		24.5	5.1
World War II	142.5		142.5	29.9
Korean War	6.6		6.6	1.4
Interest	7.5	9.3	16.8	3.5
Government	36.9	16.9	53.8	11.3
Human Resources	104.6	121.8	226.4	47.4
Treasury	-18.5	7.0	-11.5	- 2.4
Total	$322.4	$155.0	$477.4	100.0%

Source: Exhibits 1, 11, 12, 16

Nixon and Ford, it must be recognized, had to work with a Congress ruled by the philosophical brothers and sisters of Lyndon Johnson. But yelps of pain and anguish from the two presidents or from conservative congressmen of the day about excessive spending were not loud enough to be effective.

Nixon and Ford may not have been as distressed by additions to welfare menus as they wanted conservative backers to think. The 109 vetoes that they used during their eight years in office (more by Ford than by Nixon)[36] are not enough to escape the conclusion that they were not as much opposed to the growth of the Welfare State as were their supporters.

Political philosophy is eventually expressed in budget numbers. Liberals claim to be prudent money managers but deficits related to their decisions give a more informative reading of their true beliefs and goals.

Conservatives may bellow during heated election campaigns about tax-and-spend liberals, but their lack of effective, noisy, postelection resistance to unwise legislation uncovers the hypocrisy of their rhetoric.

The antics of both groups reveal a fundamental comradeship they enjoy as they run their hands through the wealth that brings them security and power in office.

This backstage alliance between major political parties, not the esoteric arguments over economic theory, is responsible for the shift in priorities shown since the 1960s.

Substantially improved social conditions at the expense of temporary economic troubles is a salable formula to many Americans. But the information displayed herein suggests that economic and budget problems associated with the Welfare State have not been, and will not be, temporary. And the condition of society after having had billions of social service dollars poured into it serves to demonstrate a truth that modernists have ignored: more money does not necessarily bring fewer problems.

It has been the fortunate history of the United States that the inherent strength of its economic system has always overcome the tampering of lawmakers who annually do their best to destroy its job-making growth, which is the characteristic of the system that feeds more mouths and warms more bodies than all federal programs that ever were or ever will be.

In nine administrations examined to this point, no president had back-to-back years as bad as Nixon/Ford's 1975 and 1976 with their combined deficit of $126.9 billion. From a budgetary standpoint, those were back-breaking years from which the administration could not recover.

Would such deficits frighten the big spenders? Would a sense of reality return to Washington?

Richard Nixon was the most controversial president of the twentieth century. Somehow it is fitting that his second term, shared with Gerald Ford, produced one of the weakest economic records of the last half-century. But at the end of it, a new president of sterling character was assuming office. Hope for America, as always, was alive and well.

11

Jimmy Carter,
1977–1980

U.S. Navy, Businessman, Governor, President

Jimmy Carter was the first president born in a hospital. He arrived on October 1, 1924, in Wise Hospital, Plains, Georgia.

The president of the United States was Calvin Coolidge. Public debt was $21 billion.

Little in Carter's quiet, courtly demeanor hints of his colorful family background. Great-grandfather Littleberry and paternal grandfather William were killed because of business disputes; Carter's father James would leave the house whenever wife Lillian, a midwife to black women, entertained a black guest.

Carter's parents were obviously not philosophical twins, but they were hard-working, conscientious people. Between the father and his peanut farm and the mother working as a registered nurse, the couple prospered according to the standards of Plains, Georgia, and they provided a stable home environment for their four children, two boys and two girls. James Earl Carter, Jr. (he later changed his official name to Jimmy) was the oldest of the Carter children.

Carter's education began in the local school system, where he is remembered as a well-behaved, bright student. He graduated from Plains High School in 1941, after which he attended Georgia Southwestern College.

Carter, from the beginning, was determined to have a naval career, an ambition stimulated by admiration for his maternal uncle, Thomas Gordy, a navy radioman. Accordingly, he applied to the U.S. Naval Academy in 1941 after which he studied hard at Georgia Institute of Technology in 1942 — a year later he reached the first step in his career dream by entering Annapolis.

Franklin Roosevelt was president; public debt was $128 billion.

Carter's seven-year (1946–53) naval career began in June 1946; in July he married Eleanor Rosalynn Smith.

Known by classmates as a casually bright student who got high grades (top

10 percent) with little effort, Carter embarked on a routine naval career until in 1951 the celebrated Admiral Hyman Rickover selected him to serve on one of the first atomic submarines, the *Sea Wolf.*

This adventure was cut short in 1953 when the death of his father caused Carter to resign his commission (lieutenant senior grade) and to return home to manage the family farm. He was about 30 when he returned to his home in Georgia.

Dwight Eisenhower was president; debt was $218 billion.

Ten years later, after upgrading methods and expanding the market for his peanut business, Carter was a millionaire seeking a challenge. Politics provided the outlet.

He ran for a seat in the state senate in 1962 and after a squabble over voter fraud, he won the race and began a new career as a lawmaker.

In 1966 the quiet man from Plains made an unsuccessful run for governor. Lessons learned, he tried again four years later and he won. He served as the state's chief executive for four years (1971–75).

Carter was a man with clear and large ambitions. When he entered state politics at the senate level, he cocked a speculative eye on the top job in the state. Eight years later he was governor.

When he grew comfortable in that position, he looked above the issues of his state, appraised the performance of President Gerald Ford, and concluded that he could do better. Four years later Carter was president of the United States.

To win the Democratic nomination in 1976 was a major coup for Carter on his road to the presidency. Men with large reputations fought for the opportunity to run against Gerald Ford, the man who had pardoned Richard Nixon. Governor George Wallace of Alabama; Senator Henry Jackson of Washington; Jerry Brown, governor of California; and Representative Mo Udall of Arizona, for example, were competitors—men of parts and men with impressive credentials.

Carter eliminated them and earned his spot at the starting line pitted against Gerald Ford. He was an unknown versus a president with a poor economic record and the legacy of Nixon's scandal on his back.

Fate was kind to Carter in the sense that he ran for the presidency at a time when almost any Democrat would have won. With Senator Walter Mondale at his side, Carter won a slim victory (50 vs. 48 percent) over the Republican ticket of Gerald Ford and Robert Dole.[1]

Many pundits credit the election victory to the debates (Carter did well) and the burden of the Nixon pardon. Some mention as contributing factors the deficits during Ford's years, or that the economy was not performing well. But the critical factor was probably quite simple: Voters were tired of Republicans and their scandals, and they hoped that this outspoken Christian from the South would bring a breath of fresh air to the contaminated politics of Washington.

Carter's presidential mandate was not strong. He walked into the same power structure that had controlled Washington since Lyndon Johnson became Senate Majority Leader in 1955.[2]

Thomas O'Neill (D–MA) was Speaker of the House, and Robert Byrd (D–WV) was Majority Leader in the Senate.

Control of the presidency and both houses of Congress is the dream of any political party. If one must choose, control of Congress is better than control of the presidency; control of the presidency and one house of Congress is about equal in power to control of both houses of Congress; control of the presidency is more valuable than control over one house of Congress.

These appraisals are general and volatile, depending upon the popularity and personality of a president. People respond to people, and a bright, articulate, and popular president is a powerful figure in the United States, but he can accomplish little in domestic affairs without some congressional support.

Carter was in the ideal position for a president.

Nevertheless, from a public debt viewpoint, the outlook was not positive when he was elected even though the power issue, which many presidents have to overcome, had been resolved in his favor.

Another issue remained: The across-the-aisle unspoken agreement to avoid deficits was history, considered by modernists as a quaint practice favored by antediluvian lawmakers, men who never had the imagination to reengineer the American lifestyle into the Welfare State that was presently, compassionately and brilliantly under construction, according to the New Testament written by LBJ and preached by his apostles.

And it did not seem likely that Carter, the new Democrat in the White House, would reignite the disciplines under which the United States had become the preeminent financial and military power in the world.

The public debt assumed by Carter had grown to $477.4 billion under Nixon/Ford, and deficits during their final two years were huge. Would Carter break the mold and turn America back to fiscal sanity?

Table 11.1
Public Debt 1976 (in billions of dollars)

	Total	%
World War I	$ 18.3	3.8%
Great Depression:	24.5	5.1
World War II	142.5	29.9
Korean War	6.6	1.4
Interest	16.8	3.5
Government	53.8	11.3
Human Resources	226.4	47.4
Treasury, net	-11.5	-2.4
Total	$477.4	100.0%

Source: Table 10.7, Chapter 10

One must attribute to Carter, as a former businessman, a facility with numbers. And his reputation as a detail man leads one to believe that he was keenly aware of the spending habits of his liberal brothers.

Unlike pre–Eisenhower years when debt increased because of wars or great emergencies, Carter knew that debt was currently rising because Washingtonocrats had more ideas on how to spend than they had money to spend.

Managing affairs of government as that role had been historically understood didn't satisfy New Age politicians; instead, managing the behavior of the people of the United States had become their focus.

Carter knew budget deficits would continue, big time, if these attitudes continued. If he didn't change them or, failing that, if he didn't make it perfectly plain to the people that they were being abused by their elected officials, his presidency would be rated as a failure.

Perspectives

GENERAL

Carter brought his own style to Washington, one that was disliked by Republicans, and one that rubbed many Democrats the wrong way. He had portrayed himself as an outsider who would go to Washington and clean up the mess caused by insiders. And his natural aloofness confirmed the notion that he was not a team player — that he didn't respect his political colleagues.

Carter alienated natural allies; he never fully garnered the support for him and his ideas that should have been his. He remains today a controversial character because of his one-man-gang approach to problem-solving.

On the social side, he offered amnesty to draft evaders (Vietnam), who, during World War II, would have earned harsh punishment. When President Ford made a similar gesture to those controversial cop-outs, much of the press questioned his motives. Predictably, the media were not so critical of Carter when he did the same.

Once America retired ingloriously from Vietnam in 1975, the guns of the nation were returned to their holsters and what constituted peace in 1977–80 became the order of the day, namely, nations snarling at one another but, for the most part, limiting aggression to barks and not bites.

Carter was not faced with the variety of flaming issues that had confronted Presidents Johnson and Nixon, but those that drew his maximum attention would have tested the mettle of any president.

The Cold War with the Soviets, negotiations between Israel and Egypt, the Soviet invasion of Afghanistan, the Iran/Iraq War and, especially, the hostage situation in Iran were all events that helped to define the Carter presidency.

Three international incidents, one positive and two negative, were definitive for Carter: (1) His role in negotiations between Israel and Egypt that finally led to a peace agreement; (2) his inability to free American hostages in Iran, and (3) his decision to release control of the Panama Canal to Panamanians.

Enmity between Egypt and Israel was deep and bitter since the day that Israel was given birth by the United Nations in 1948.[3] Hope for peace between the two came in 1977 when President Anwar Sadat accepted the invitation of Israeli prime minister Menachem Begin to visit his country. Negotiations stalled and resulted in an invitation in 1978 from President Carter to continue their talks at the presidential retreat, Camp David, using him as the mediator. The ploy met with success; the Camp David accords were the result; in 1979, a formal peace treaty was signed.

Iranian militants in 1979 took control of the American embassy in Tehran and held captive over 60 American hostages — some were later released and 52 remained until Ronald Reagan became president in January 1981. Carter's inability to free them earlier and to deal with Iran with a firm hand smirched his reputation, nationally and internationally.

Debate and negotiations over the Panama Canal began under LBJ and they concluded under Carter with the Panama Canal Treaty of 1978. The agreement was opposed by conservatives, including Ronald Reagan, and by military leaders who believed the arrangement compromised the security of the hemisphere. Time will tell if the deal was good or bad for the United States.

Except that such incidents pointed to the continuing need for a strong defense, they did not, for the most part, have a direct impact on the public debt — they did not require the extraordinary use of federal funds that would have been needed, for example, to finance a major shooting war.

But one event did drain the nation's resources to an extraordinary degree, directly and indirectly, namely, the oil embargo by OPEC (Organization of Petroleum Exporting Countries).

OPEC discovered that what it had levied as a punitive tax against nations that supported its genetic enemy, Israel, had in fact become a golden spigot through which the wealth of the West poured to the East in staggering amounts. This was enrichment not easy to turn aside even when emotions attached to the Arab/Israeli War (1973) subsided.

The temptation to OPEC nations was (and is) to milk the golden calf for as long as possible. Energy costs zoomed in the United States.

HOME FRONT

The Nixon/Ford regime had been characterized by a shooting war, the Cold War, social upheaval and economic hard times.

Under Carter, challenges were fewer, and different:

- There was no Vietnam War or any other foreign event with similar demands.

- The Soviets were a continuing threat made more dangerous because of the decreasing ability of the United States to afford an adequate defensive posture due to high debt and continuing deficits.
- Social unrest had settled down to the general feeling of unease and disunity that was kept alive by minority leaders who made a living out of criticizing America.
- The economy was even worse than it was in 1976–1979.

Carter's response to the Soviet threat was to maintain a steady, active force of 2.1 million men.[4] The increase in *Defense* dollars that will be later appraised was related more to inflation than it was to preparedness.

The Misery Index[5] gives the sad state of the Carter economy in a glance. It increased by 76 percent—from 20.4 percent to 36.0 percent. Interest and inflation rates more than doubled; high unemployment continued.

Income per capita increased by almost 49 percent, but inflation and increased taxes per capita diminished its impact.[6] The growth in GDP between 1975 and 1980 of 57 percent[7] melted down to 16 percent when adjusted for inflation.

A fact known by many, but acknowledged by few, is that Carter left as his economic legacy a nation teetering on the edge of bankruptcy, soon to be faced with the need to devalue the dollar unless something soon, and something dramatic, happened in America.

SUPREME COURT[8]

President Carter did not nominate a Supreme Court justice. Seven of the justices (Rehnquist, Stevens, Blackmun, Powell, Burger, Stewart, Brennan) were appointed by Republican presidents; two (White, Marshall), by Democrats.

Chief Justice Burger still led the Court and in the subject period he heard 61 cases—almost five times the number heard by Chief Justice Earl Warren in the pre–LBJ era.[9]

The increased caseload was the result of the Court's recent interest in incidents once handled locally, which was the direct result of the legal meanderings of activist judges.

And when conservatives take to criticizing the decisions that so distorted American society, they would be wise to recollect that those decisions would not have been forthcoming had it not been for the flawed judicial choices of three Republican presidents, Dwight Eisenhower, Richard Nixon and Gerald Ford.

A review of a few cases reveals some of the concerns of the time.

Regents v. Bakke, 1978. Bakke, a white male, had twice been rejected by the University of California Medical School. His qualifications exceeded those of hundreds of minority students who had gained admission under an affirmative action policy. Bakke claimed that he had been excluded because of his race. The issue: Does the policy of the university violate Bakke's rights under the Civil Rights Act of 1964, and/or his equal protection rights under the Fourteenth Amendment? Four justices (Rehnquist, Stewart, Burger and Stevens) disapproved of the university's actions; four justices (Marshall, White, Brennan and Blackmun) approved. And Justice Powell agreed with parts of each argument. It was a standoff. The result was this: Bakke was admitted but discrimination because of race was not completely outlawed. This inability or unwillingness to make a clear decision paved the way for another horde of cases to flow to Washington. The time had come for a decision; the Court ducked; the price tag on racial injustice went up.

Poelker v. Doe, 1977. The city of St. Louis enacted a policy that forbade nontherapeutic abortions in state hospitals. The issue: Does the policy violate the equal protection clause of the Fourteenth Amendment? In a 6–3 decision (Brennan, Blackmun and Marshall dissenting), the Court ruled that the city policy was constitutional — it didn't deny abortion rights; it dealt with the location of the act. This was a sensible decision but, in the process of making it, the legalization of the right to an abortion was once again enunciated.

Maher v. Roe, 1977. Connecticut law limited state Medicaid benefits to first trimester abortions that were medically necessary. The issue: Did the law violate the equal protection clause of the Fourteenth Amendment? In a 6–3 decision (Brennan, Blackmun and Marshall dissenting) the Court ruled that the law did not violate a woman's right to an abortion. It dealt with payment, not rights, and the state had a legitimate interest in protecting the use of its funds. This is another illustration of the havoc produced in the nation when the Court stripped states of their right to legislate about such matters. Grievances that once flowed to local politicians in fifty states now flowed in one direction — the Supreme Court.

Bellotti v. Baird, 1979. A Massachusetts law required parental consent before a minor could have an abortion, but it carried a provision that permitted a judge to overrule both parents for "good cause shown." The issue: Did the law unconstitutionally restrict a minor from having an abortion? In a 7–1 decision (White dissenting and Powell absent) the Court found the statute unconstitutional for three reasons: (1) It required parental notification in all cases; (2) it did not permit the minor to seek an independent judicial assessment of her competence to make an independent judgment; (3) it permitted a judge to deny an abortion to a minor who was competent to decide otherwise. With this, and similar decisions, the Court invaded the American home and the historical rights of parents to govern their minor children.

If it is true that the pursuit of LBJ's Great Society did lasting harm to the nation's fiscal soundness, it is also true that the Supreme Court eroded American institutions by assuming duties that nobody asked them to assume, by finding in the Constitution words that were never written.

Society[10]

Federal money in the form of programs and grants was pouring into society in the 1960s and 1970s, as were new laws that, on the surface, only governed civic affairs but which, below the surface, were collectively preaching a moral philosophy that had nothing to do with the religious values that motivated the Founding Fathers.[11]

> Reading, reflection and time have convinced me that the interests of Society require the observation of those moral precepts ... in which all religions agree.—Thomas Jefferson
> If men are so wicked with religion, what would they be without it?—Benjamin Franklin
> Religion and good morals are the only solid foundation of public liberty and happiness.—John Adams
> ... reason and experience both forbid us to expect that National morality can prevail in exclusion of religious principle.—George Washington

Sentiments such as these from strong-minded, independent-thinking and powerful men testify to the importance of the socially related subject matter that the Supreme Court has assumed unto itself.

The ultimate face of intrusive Supreme Court decisions can be found in the social statistics of the nation. About one-quarter of marriages ended up in divorce in 1960; in 1980, about 43 percent of them met the same fate. Abortions in 1980 were 121 percent higher than the year before the *Roe v. Wade* decision that legalized them.

In 1962 the federal cost of supporting public education was $1.2 billion; in 1980, it was $31.8 billion[12]; SAT scores, a generally accepted measurement of the quality of public education, were lower in 1980 than they were in 1972 — $30 billion down the tubes.

Murder, rape and assault crimes were on the rise in a society that was supposed to be kinder and gentler than before. The cost of the line item Justice in 1960 was $400 million; in 1980, it was $4.7 billion.

With such a report card, LBJ's Great Society didn't look so hot in 1980.

In 1960, the cost of Human Resources in the budget was $26 billion; in 1980, $313 billion. Human Resources is the budget line item that houses most (not all) of the costs related to the Welfare State. For this increased cost, and the increased debt and interest charges that went with it, the nation got the social statistics noted above.

Change in Public Debt

Having already been introduced to the Misery Index for 1980, one is prepared for a deficit during the period.

During Carter's years deficits were constant and large. The pattern he inherited had not changed. Spenders and those without the courage to resist were in control.

Nixon and Ford had tolerated them.

Carter joined them.

At the bottom end of the prevailing power structure, Americans yearned for a leader who would resist.

Within the numbers of the Transactions table, hard-edged political truths are found.

Table 11.2
Transactions (in billions of dollars)

		1977–80		1973–76
Taxes		$1735.6		$1071.2
Less:				
Defense	$ 452.0		$332.1	
Interest	160.5		88.6	
Total		612.5		420.7
Net		$1123.1		$ 650.5
Less:				
Government	$ 305.1		$166.3	
Human Resources	1045.2		632.2	
Total		1350.3		798.5
Surplus/deficit		$-227.2		$-148.0
Debt, beginning		-477.4		-322.4
Total		$-719.6		$-470.4
Adjustment*	7.3	-7.0		
Debt, Ending		$-711.9		$-477.4

*Treasury cannot be exact when it finances a budget deficit and the difference between what is needed and the value of securities traded inevitably produces a relatively small variance.

Source: Historical Tables 2007, 1.1, 3.1

A glance is sufficient to conclude that the revenue increase was substantial, and that the deficit was cost related.

The interesting question as one approaches the analysis of the transactions for the period is whether or not Carter was able to persuade fellow Democrats to restrain their spending, and to address the questions that past budgets had raised, for example:

- Is Social Security endangered because so many other social programs compete for the same dollars?
- Is there no answer for rising Social Security costs other than the raising of the payroll tax?
- Is the payroll tax the best way to finance Medicare? Is there no better way to structure its benefits?

- Is it not time to put all government fringes and social programs on the table for examination?

These are but some of the questions an alert president would have been asking in 1977–80. And if correct responses from Congress were not forthcoming, these are the issues that a thoughtful president would have placed before the American people.

If Carter did so, it will be detected in the upcoming analysis.

TAXES

Tax income for Carter went up in every year,[13] and he ended up with the largest four-year revenue increase in modern presidential history.[14] Ordinarily an observation like that would be followed by a sunny forecast about the deficit. Unfortunately, the impressive revenue increase was inflation driven.

Inflation, inflation, inflation.

Everything was up. Economists would give sophisticated reasons for the sorrowful condition. Humble and less-informed Americans would guess that it was caused to a large extent by a government that was out of control and by a rising debt that wouldn't stop.

Whatever the reason for the shaky value of U.S. currency, Carter had to pay his bills with it, and he didn't do well. His annual deficits were never less than $41 billion.

Most people have seen a magician rap a table with one hand to draw attention while with the other he prepares a new trick — now you see it now you don't. The American tax system operates the same way.

Periodically politicians with furrowed brows argue vociferously over amendments to the personal income tax code, a debate that draws wide media coverage while, with little fanfare, the payroll tax pokes its nose deeper into America's wallet.

- In 1960, payroll taxes were 15.9 percent of all tax revenue; 36.1 percent of personal income tax; 68.4 percent of corporate taxes.[15]
- In 1980, they were 30.5 percent of all taxes; 64.6 percent of personal income taxes; 144.3 percent of corporate income taxes.

This represents a sea change in tax policy that is especially reprehensible because:

- It is sneaky and hypocritical: It is sold to the public as a necessary method to protect Social Security, but the taxes collected are used to pay general government expenses, as well as benefit payments.
- The pressure normally associated with tax increases is shifted from the politician who levies the tax to the employer who must deduct it from wages.

- It represents a shift away from a progressive tax system that exempts some low wage earners, to a flat tax system that is inescapable.

Given inflation and interest rates during the Carter years, this persistent movement by the government to dependence on payroll tax revenue was especially burdensome in 1977–80.

And it became even more so in 1980 when Social Security benefits became taxable for the first time to middle-upper-class earners, the taxable wage base was lifted from $15,300 to $25,900, and the tax rate was lifted from 9.9 to 10.16 percent.[16]

If it walks like a dog, wags its tail like a dog, and barks like a dog, it's a dog. Social Security taxes are just another way for Washington to collect money.

DEFENSE

This cost center went up 1.36 times during the 1977–1980 period, well under the rate of revenue increase (1.62 times).[17] As noted before, the increases were inflation related.

Actually, Carter came late to the realization that the military services were in deplorable condition, having been cannibalized during the presidencies that followed Eisenhower, the last defense-conscious president who built the war machine that was later depleted in Vietnam.

Carter actually spent less than Gerald Ford and much less than Dwight Eisenhower, when measured as a percent of either GDP or total spending, at a time when international dangers were even greater.

There must have been a reason why a patriotic ex-navy officer would so limit his spending on national defense. And there was. Budget resources were gobbled up by the Welfare State; the ability of a president to adequately maintain a robust military, without going heavily into debt, was proportionately diminished.

Profligate spending in 1980 had become a national security issue that could no longer be ignored. The increased cost of *Defense* of $119.9 billion was fully financed, and it did not in any way contribute to the deficit for the period.[18]

INTEREST

Interest went up 1.81 times, well above the rate of revenue increase. Had its growth been restricted to the rate of revenue growth, its cost would have been $143.5 billion, or $17.0 billion lower than actual. To that extent, this cost center contributed to the deficit for the period.

Was unfunded *Interest* for the period a reasonable addition to public debt? Yes and no.

It has previously been noted that the portion of *Interest* related to the debt that was caused by the unfunded costs of the Welfare State is not a legitimate use of the nation's ability to borrow. Generally speaking, about half of the debt at the end of Carter's term fell into that classification.[19] There would have been no unfunded *Interest* had that problem not existed, and about half of the total cost of Interest ($80 billion) for the four-year period would have been available to other cost centers for more productive use.

Comments about the budget seldom linger on this nonproducing line item. Too bad. If the cost of Government in 1980 was important, the cost of *Interest* was more important; if the cost of Medicare in 1980 was important, *Interest* was more important. Over 10 percent of all taxes paid in 1980 went to the payment of interest — the average American would love to have a 10 percent wage increase.

Interest expense is important.

GOVERNMENT

Maximum funds available for *Government and for Human Resources* depend upon two factors:

- How much revenue was allocated to and used by primary cost centers (*Defense* and *Interest*)?
- The relationship of unused revenue to the total cost level of the remaining two cost centers during the previous four years.

In this case, if cost growth in Government and Human Resources had been limited to 1.43 times, it would not add to the deficit. Growth beyond that point would be unfunded spending.

Spending went up 1.83 times, well above the allocated amount. Had it remained within guidelines, cost would have been $237.6 billion as opposed to actual cost of $305.1 billion. The excess cost of $67.5 billion was unfunded, and it added to the deficit.

Washingtonocrats responded to the clarion call for cost reduction with their typical response — spending promiscuously increased by 83.5 percent.

Energy, Natural Resources, Community and Agriculture were well out of control, and they deserve further analysis.

Energy supply reflected the cost of the oil crisis that hit Gerald Ford's administration hard, and Carter's harder. The average four-year price of crude oil under Nixon/Ford was more than twice as high as it was under Nixon, and the average price under Carter was almost three times higher than it was during the prior four years.[20]

Energy costs were a headline concern. Carter's response was typically bureaucratic; he established the Department of Energy, a maneuver that was sure to add overhead to an already costly activity.

Natural Resources and Environment increased 80.8 percent, a good part

Table 11.3

Government (in billions of dollars)

	1977–80	1973–76	% Change
Energy	$ 33.2	$ 9.6	245.8%
Natural Resources/Environment	47.0	26.0	80.8
Transportation	69.7	43.0	62.1
Community/regional development	40.7	18.6	118.8
International affairs	34.1	23.3	46.4
Science/space/technology	20.6	16.4	25.6
Agriculture	38.2	13.4	185.1
Justice	16.2	11.0	47.3
General	50.1	40.0	25.3
Total	$349.8	$201.3	73.8%
Commerce & housing credit*	23.5	23.1	1.7
Total	$373.3	$224.4	66.4%
Offsetting receipts	-68.2	-58.1	17.4
Net	$305.1	$166.3	83.5%

*Made up of earnings from various federal housing and other programs—subject to major changes from year to year relative to market conditions. (Historical Tables 2007, 3.2)

Source: Historical Tables 2007, 3.1

of it caused by inflation, which made all departmental budgets swell. This line item embraces such things as water resources, conservation, land management, recreational resources and pollution control. The increase was fairly uniform throughout and does not indicate new, wild spending initiatives. Information suggests that the cost spike was temporary and would soon level off.

Carter's interest in Community Development (up 118.8 percent) before, during and after his administration exceeded his interest in controlling federal spending, and must have sent the comforting message to fellow Democrats that he was one of them, and that business as usual was the order of the day.

If the chief doesn't care, why should the Indians worry?

Carter was a peanut farmer. Somehow it wasn't surprising to find that under his administration the Farm Income Stabilization program drove the cost of Agriculture through the roof.

An acceptable budget system denies approval to projects that cost more than current revenues can bear. Absent such a shutoff mechanism, human nature remains as the only deterrent to overspending, a weak twig upon which to hang the fiscal sanity of a nation.

The American budget system is undisciplined. A complete overhaul is indicated.

HUMAN RESOURCES

Human Resources grew by 1.65 times over the expenditure level of 1973–76, well beyond the allowable amount in the context of a balanced budget. At its maximum allowable growth level, the cost of *Human Resources* would have been $902.3 billion, as opposed to actual cost of $1,045.2 billion. The excess cost of $142.9 billion was unfunded, and it added to the deficit.

Table 11.4
Human Resources (in billions of dollars)

	1977–80	1973–76	% Change
Education, training, services	$ 109.8	$ 60.1	82.7%
Health/Medicaid	79.5	48.7	63.2
Income Security*	219.5	128.5	70.8
Social Security	401.6	243.6	64.9
Medicare	100.7	46.4	117.0
Unemployment compensation	56.0	44.5	25.8
Veterans	78.1	60.4	29.3
Total	$1045.2	$632.2	65.3%

*Minus unemployment compensation (from 1965–68 on)

Note: Major federal programs since the 1960s— Food Stamps 1961 (pilot), Food Stamps 1964, Medicaid 1965, Student Aid 1966, Medicare 1967, Coal Miners Benefits 1970, Commodity Donations 1973, Supplementary Security Income 1974, Supplemental Feeding 1976, Earned Income Tax Credit 1976, Legal Services 1976, Energy Assistance 1977

Source: Historical Tables 2007, 3.1

Every line item in *Human Resources* but Veterans and Unemployment grew faster than revenue; all increases were huge and beyond the predictable ability of income[21] to cover for any prolonged period.

The increase in Education, etc. (82.7 percent), is a reflection of two major things:

- The maturing costs of inherited projects.
- The impact of inflation on a cost trend that was already out of control.

New initiatives were not so much the problem in Education as was the unwillingness here, and throughout the budget, to restrain spending to an affordable level.

Under Jimmy Carter, Health increased 63.2 percent. How many workers would like to have their paychecks increased by such an amount? Medicaid, of course, was the primary problem.

Income Security increased 70.8 percent. This catch-all title covers federal pensions, housing/food/nutrition assistance, supplemental security income (SSI), etc. Growth in such programs has been constant since the 1960s. SSI was Nixon's contribution to this menu of benefits— in 1980 it cost $5.7 billion,[22] a cost that didn't exist in 1973.

If one proceeds under the myth that Social Security and Medicare programs are not in trouble as long as payroll taxes for these programs exceed obligations and are deposited in the "trust fund," then the programs were fully financed in 1977–80.

But if one proceeds on the basis that Social Security taxes are just another form of taxation, that the funds are general funds, and that the "trust fund" is a charade supported by a ledger entry, then the programs stand at the welfare trough along with the others.

In such a light, they are growing too fast.

Under either proposition, programs must be modified because the concept of supporting payments to the old, solely by deductions from the young, is not a viable one that will stand the test of time.

Carter subtracted nothing from the welfare menu. His major influence on the budget was organizational, the Departments of Education and Energy, which characteristically loaded up with costs to prove they were needed.

Businessmen who permit the continuation of failed programs that lead their companies toward bankruptcy would be hanged on Wall Street with the approval of everyone with ten fingers, ten toes and the capacity to count.

But in Washington, politicians who sell themselves as the friend of the working man and who spend the nation's resources like idiots are applauded for their compassion, just as those who would restrain them are reviled as uncaring and cruel. Such has been the case since the 1960s; such will be the case until the axe inevitably falls.

SUMMARY OF DEFICIT ALLOCATIONS

When Jimmy Carter took office the hope was that his rapport with fellow Democrats, mixed with common sense, would bring sanity back to the budget. On his first day in the Oval Office one might have dreamed of a conference among leaders that would have resulted in the realignment of some welfare programs and the elimination of others as inefficient or as being redundant.

Certainly there was reason to do this because social statistics clearly indicated that if a Great Society were ever to come it would not be the result of programs administered from Washington.

Had this meeting taken place, the deficit would have been smaller. But it didn't happen.

The Welfare State, as is, continued to drive the nation deeper into debt, assisted by a crippled economy that, in part, reflected the lack of common sense in Washington.

Without a doubt, this budget was hammered by inflation. But one must remember that revenue was inflated too—that there is more to this deficit than bad luck.

The thing that stands out is that Carter did nothing to cure the spending virus that had been driving Congress for 20 years. In fact, he joined the spenders.

Table 11.5
Summary of Deficit — 1977–1980 (in billions of dollars)

Cost Center	Amount
Defense	$ 0.0
Interest	17.0
Government	67.3
Human Resources	142.9
Total	$227.2

Sources: Exhibits 1, 11–1, 16

Conclusion

Jimmy Carter arrived at the White House in a determined frame of mind. The first man from the Deep South since Zachary Taylor to be elected president, a deacon in his Baptist Church in Georgia, Carter hoped to restore the dignity of the wounded presidency and to bring to Washington some of the unadorned virtue and civility that was an inherent part of his nature. He cultivated his image as an "outsider," one determined to set things right for the people.

As a symbol of his determination to deflate the idea of a regal presidency, for example, he disposed of the presidential yacht.

Whatever his noble objectives, he did not accomplish the thing that most needed doing, namely, reversing the spending priorities of Congress and leading the nation back to a place that would enable future presidents to resolve their duties as commander in chief without, at the same time, driving the nation deeply into debt.

Table 11.6
Spending Priorities

	1960	1968	1976	1980
Primary costs				
Defense	52.2%	46.0%	24.1%	22.7%
Interest	7.5	6.2	7.2	8.9
Total	59.7%	52.2%	31.3%	31.6%
Government	11.9	14.5	14.0	15.4
Education/services	1.9	4.3	5.1	5.4
Health/Medicaid	.9	2.5	4.1	3.9
Medicare	2.6	4.3	5.4	
Income Security	8.0	6.6	16.4	14.7
Social Security	12.6	13.4	19.9	20.0
Veterans	5.9	3.9	4.9	3.6
Total	100.0%	100.0%	100.0%	100.0%
	(3)	(2)(3)	(3)	(3)

1 = peace; 2 = war; 3 = cold war

Source: Historical Tables 2007, 3.1

Priorities were worse after four years of Carter. *Defense, for example,* went up an affordable $119.9 billion. Nevertheless, during the same four years, the deficit was $227.2 billion.

This means that a deficit would have existed even if *Defense* had not increased — that in a troubled world, and in the midst of a Cold War with the Soviets, the United States could not modernize its military without going into debt.

Carter's deficit was the largest in modern history to that point,[23] and it took place during a period of modest *Defense* costs. He left behind a public debt of $712 billion.[24]

Table 11.7
Public Debt, 1980 (billions)

Event	Inherited 1976	Added 1977–80	Total 1980	%
World War I	$ 18.3	$	$ 18.3	2.6%
Great Depression	24.5		24.5	3.5
World War II	142.5		142.5	20.0
Korean War	6.6		6.6	.9
Interest	16.8	17.0	33.8	4.7
Government	53.8	67.3	121.1	17.0
Human Resources	226.4	142.9	369.3	51.9
Treasury	-11.5	7.3	-4.2	-.6
Total	$477.4	$234.5	$711.9	100.0%

Source: Exhibits 1, 11, 12, 16

The Washington establishment is deeply entrenched. Newcomers are greeted tentatively and appraised for how they might react to the game of you-support-my-bill and I'll-support-yours. Especially watched are reformers who brag about "outsider" status, an implied insult to "insiders." Carter was such a man.

He surrounded himself with trusted lieutenants from the South who served him well but who did not play ball with Congress.

As a result, Carter faced more resistance from a Democratic Congress than one would have expected. His energy bill was a notable exception.

Perhaps the American people were the beneficiaries of this tension between the White House and the Hill. As bad as things worked out, they might have been even worse if a love match had existed between the spenders and a liberal president.

Carter inherited a nasty economic situation that was born under Kennedy/Johnson, one that matured with Nixon, and worsened under Nixon/Ford.

Under Kennedy/Johnson — days of relatively low costs and high expectations— Great Society programs were hailed as noble acts of a benevolent government, the modern description of the wolf in sheep's clothing.

Under Nixon/Ford reality replaced expectations, entitlements seriously took hold and they demanded attention. They didn't get it.

Everything got worse on Carter's watch. He did not have a successful presidency. In foreign policy he had high moments, but the overriding memory of his international activities will be the hostage crisis in Iran and his ineptness at handling the situation.

Domestically, Carter did not scale down Great Society programs, and he enlarged the role of government by adding the Departments of Energy and Education, a sure way of increasing the cost of it.

Jimmy Carter ran again for the presidency in 1980 against Ronald Reagan, a figure from Western politics who had almost wrested the nomination from Gerald Ford in 1976. Reagan spoke a language that Washingtonocrats failed to realize was modern, overdue and up-to-date.

He talked about bloated government, runaway federal programs, and the like. His voice was a breath of fresh air blowing across the nation from west to east.

Carter, with Walter Mondale repeating as his running mate, lost by seven million popular votes. He retired to Plains, Georgia, and he has since lived a productive life, which, on a humanitarian scale, is more impressive than that of any modern president. In that respect, these are possibly his best years.

But he has also become politically meddlesome, forcing his way uninvited into delicate situations, and sometimes embarrassing the sitting president.

Spenders in 1977–80 caught a glimpse of what happens when the rosy scenario of unending good times does not transpire. In a very short time, a very wealthy nation can become very wobbly.

Unbeknownst to most Americans, and generally unreported, was this simple truth at the end of 1980: If the current trends in the economy and in Washington continued, the United States of America, the richest nation that the world had ever known, could crumble under massive debt that was stupidly put into place by selfish politicians with grandiose ideas.

In effect, Carter passed the nation's problems along to the next president, in worse condition than they were before.

12

Ronald W. Reagan,
1981–1984

Actor, Governor, President

Ronald Wilson Reagan, the oldest president in history when he retired, was born February 6, 1911, in Tampico, Illinois, in a five-room flat over a bakery, destined to be the 40th president of the United States. He was the second child of Jack (1883–1941) and Nelle (1883–1962) and he immediately, for unknown reasons, inherited the nickname "Dutch," thanks to his father.

William Taft was president at the time, and the public debt was $2.8 billion.

Jack Reagan, with a sixth-grade education, was one of many who were battered by the Great Depression. A shoe salesman until he was 50, he was an active supporter of Franklin Roosevelt during his later years and he caught on as a director of New Deal projects in Dixon, Illinois.

Jack Reagan's occupational and parental objectives were compromised by alcoholism, a condition that Nelle Reagan described to the children as a sickness. She supplemented her husband's income with wages earned at a local dress shop.

Whatever their personal and economic problems, Jack and Nelle Reagan provided a home life that Ronald Reagan later placed among his happiest days.

Education for Reagan was always in a state of tension with his other activities. In grade school, with few diversions to distract him, he was a high-level student. In Dixon High School (1925–28), sports entered his life along with politics (he was president of the student body), acting and writing; his grades dropped to average.

What he lost in grades because of extra-curricular duties, Reagan gained in opportunity. Eureka College (1928–1932) offered him a partial football scholarship. There he maintained his typical schedule in sports and other activities. For example, his interest in drama and writing surfaced, and he joined the debating team.

Reagan worked as a dishwasher to pay his bills; he majored in economics and sociology and he got by with below-average grades. He graduated in 1932.

Herbert Hoover was president; debt was $19.5 billion.

The Great Depression hovered over the land in 1932; it was a world of no jobs, and the chances of new graduates to find work were limited. But personality and leadership traits that Reagan had exhibited throughout his academic career continued to serve him well. He caught on with a radio station in Davenport, Iowa, as a sportscaster; he rose rapidly in his new profession.

Six years later Dutch Reagan was well known in the sports world of the Midwest, the voice of Big Ten Football and the clever broadcaster of telegraphed major league baseball games.

But he was restless too because the acting bug within him demanded expression; he constantly probed for a break into the profession and in 1937 it paid off. A screen test resulted in a contract with Warner Brothers at a guaranteed wage that permitted him to leave broadcasting.

In 1941, 30 years old with four years behind him as an actor in films, Reagan got more fan mail than anyone working for Warner Brothers, except for Errol Flynn. The world was a rosy place for him and for his bride of one year, actress Jane Wyman.

The president of the United States was Franklin Roosevelt; debt had risen to $48.2 billion[1] because of the Great Depression.

The years 1941 and 1942 were pivotal in Reagan's life. He reached the zenith of his acting career in 1941, a feat that pleased his father, who died in the same year; in 1942 he traded Hollywood for army life. Poor eyesight kept Second Lieutenant Reagan on stateside duty from which Captain Reagan emerged three years later (1945), a middle-aged actor in Hollywood terms with a questionable future. But his wife's career soared during the war; in 1948 Jane Wyman won the Oscar for best actress.

From his 20th to his 30th birthdays, Reagan's life was all upbeat. From the small-town college football player, recognized only within ten miles of Eureka, he became a radio and film star recognized anywhere in America.

The next decade was quite different.

Reagan's marriage ended in 1949 because of career strains, leaving him emotionally wounded. He rebounded in 1951 with renewed political interests, and with the reenergized talents that had made him a campus leader.

He was president of the Screen Actors Guild as his 40th birthday approached, a loyal Democrat, and a supporter of Helen Douglas in her senatorial race against Richard M. Nixon.

Harry Truman was president. The Korean War was in process; public debt was $214.3 billion.

The transformation of the 40-year-old Democratic actor to the 50-year-old conservative politician, and from unhappy bachelor to happily married man, began for Reagan in 1952. In that year he married actress Nancy Davis, which decision he would later say was the best he ever made, and he actively supported Dwight Eisenhower for president, a clear signal that the early influences of Rooseveltian charm had cooled.

In 1954, his film career on the wane, Reagan signed with General Electric as television host of GE Theater. In that role he traveled the country as GE's spokesman and he cultivated his already formidable speaking abilities.

He also did another hitch as president of the Screen Actors Guild (1959–60) and (a switch) he backed Richard Nixon in his unsuccessful presidential race against John Kennedy.

Reagan was 50 in 1961, happily married and already more politician than actor; John Kennedy was in his first year as president; public debt had increased to $238.4 billion, previewing a condition of continuing deficits and climbing debt that would, if not corrected, destroy the America that Dutch Reagan would one day serve.

When his television program phased out, Reagan signed on for another (*Death Valley Days*). He was in 1964 an active supporter of Barry Goldwater, Republican candidate for president (defeated by Lyndon Johnson). During the campaign he gave a nationally televised speech that drew more contributions than any political speech in history.

The stage was set. The potential candidate had been tested on the campaign trails. Reagan entered his first political race in 1967 and became governor of California with a 58 percent voter mandate; in 1971, he was in the first year of his second term as governor.

Richard Nixon was president; public debt was $303 billion.

A new era was underway in Washington, one in which deficit spending was touted as an absolute good; paying bills out of current revenue was discarded as a quaint, antediluvian philosophy.

Reagan glanced across the fruited plains to the Golden City and he saw in operation a political philosophy destined to drive debt ever upward.

The rocking chair beckons to many when the 60th birthday is passed. But Reagan wasn't ready for retirement. In a life filled with momentous decades, the 1970s was one of his most exciting. He was urged to run again at the end of his second term as governor — he refused.

Exposure to presidential politics in 1968 had whetted his appetite for greater things. Biding his time, Reagan polished his national reputation with a newspaper column, radio broadcasts, and speeches on the lecture circuit. Then, in 1976, he made his move and he nearly beat Gerald Ford for the Republican nomination.

Four years later he was not to be denied. The nomination was his by a landslide. He went on to win a big victory over Carter (51 percent of the popular vote vs. 41 percent for Carter)[2] in the general election.

Reagan's popularity had political coattails. Republicans also won control of the Senate,[3] and they decreased the size of the Democratic majority in the House.[4]

Howard Baker (R–TN) and Robert Dole (R–KS) were Senate Majority Leaders for six years until Democrats again won control, with Robert Byrd (D–WV) holding the position as Majority Leader for Reagan's final two years. Tip O'Neil (D–MA) and Jim Wright (D–TX) ran the House during the presidency of Reagan.

This split control was not an ideal situation for Reagan, but it was good enough to get the tax cuts that people, companies and the economy desperately needed.[5]

And Reagan needed all the help he could get because he was confronted by years of endless deficits and a climbing public debt that had reached $711.9 billion, as follows:

Table 12.1
Public Debt 1980 (in billions of dollars)

	Total	%
World War I	$ 18.3	2.6%
Great Depression:	24.5	3.5
World War II	142.5	20.0
Korean War	6.6	.9
Interest	33.8	4.7
Government	121.1	17.0
Human Resources	369.3	51.9
Treasury, net	- 4.2	-.6
Total	$711.9	100.0%

Source: Table 10.7 Chapter 10

The traditional explanation for public debt as a legacy of war, economic recession and inflation correctly described the accumulated debt of all presidents through Eisenhower. Otherwise, it does not apply to substantive aspects of the modern debt problem.

The analysis of three post–Eisenhower administrations (JFK/LBJ, RMN/GRF, JEC) has demonstrated that external events, which were fundamentally causative to the expansion of debt before 1960, retreated in importance after that year. Thereafter, high-spenders purposefully and deliberately caused debt expansion while pursuing their socialistic agenda for America.

The fundamental reason for the expansion of debt is the cost of the Welfare State. Contrary explanations are but one more example of the pabulum that is too often released to taxpayers to keep them unaware of what they are paying for as the expanding ship of state converts itself from the American Republic established by the Founding Fathers into the American Welfare State established by Lyndon Johnson.

Perspectives

GENERAL

The hostage crisis in Iran was headline news when Reagan took office. For reasons known to Iranians alone, the decision to release hostages was withheld while Jimmy Carter was in office. The mood changed when Reagan was elected; hostages were released.

Graciously, Reagan invited Carter to welcome them home, thus closing a difficult chapter in the life of America's 39th president.

Reagan was shot in March 1981, the bullet narrowly missing his heart (he was 70 at the time). He was discharged from the hospital 12 days later, and in a few weeks he was working a full day, his reputation even larger than before. Reagan added to his image of strength and determination in other ways before the year was over, a positive image that endured throughout his presidency.

Two events stand out: (1) Reagan proposed and Congress enacted the largest tax cut in history; (2) Air traffic controllers went out on strike and, when they refused to obey Reagan's order to return to work, Reagan fired them.

These actions, controversial with liberals, advanced Reagan's popularity. Love him or hate him, like Franklin Roosevelt and Lyndon Johnson, he stood for something. Americans respond to that; they expect presidents to be strong men of purpose.

The space program, a budget item of growing importance since the 1950s, received a meaningful lift in 1983 when Sally Ride, the first female astronaut, joined the crew on the space shuttle, *Challenger*.[6]

And in a different field, Reagan's appointment of the first female to the Supreme Court, Sandra O'Connor, also drew attention as being in step with the times. Women in the 1980s were increasingly found in high government positions and in the private sector, a welcome sign in a world starved for leaders of quality.

The relationship between Winston Churchill and Franklin Roosevelt became famous during World War II; so did that of Reagan and British prime minister Margaret Thatcher during their years of shared leadership.

It solidified in 1982 when Reagan backed Great Britain and Thatcher in the war with Argentina over the Falkland Islands, a British possession, an action consistent with Reagan's attitude toward the use of force. He would use America's might, given a just cause. Examples include: The deployment of missiles in Europe; the use of U.S. Marines in Lebanon (over 200 killed by terrorists); the invasion of Grenada to rescue Americans and to thwart plans to make it a base for the Soviets.

Such events didn't have an impact on the budget with the force of a major war, but their enumeration is needed to set the tone of the world in which Reagan operated.

The major external force, of course, was the Soviet Union. Reagan was relatively quiet on the diplomatic front during his first term in the sense that he avoided face to face confrontations with the USSR. But the American public was ever aware of his appraisal of the Soviet threat.

And the public was kept abreast of Reagan's plan to rebuild the military, despite congressional opposition, and to negotiate with the Soviets from a position of strength.

The chill between the two superpowers remained, and Reagan, with an increasingly powerful military presence behind him, watched and waited while the Soviet leadership changed from Brezhnev to Andropov (1982) to Chernenko (1984).

Despite the dangerous international mood, the deficit and the debt were influenced far more by the clash between Reagan (who wanted to win the Cold War, cut spending, and reduce debt) and liberals (who were satisfied with the status quo in the Cold War that they thought was unwinnable; and they thought it was unacceptably dangerous to try to win).

Above all, Reagan's opponents in Congress were determined to protect the Welfare State and to continue their spending habits regardless of the impact on the deficit. That is not what they said; it is how they acted with respect to the budget, a much more meaningful barometer of what politicians really believe.

Events would prove Reagan right about the war, the cost of which (improved Defense) was piddling compared with the unrecovered costs of the Welfare State and the countless billions that would have been spent in the future had not America prevailed in the Cold War.

HOME FRONT

George Washington, the first American president and indispensable leader of the brand new United States of America, brought stability and believability to the central government.

James Madison (1809–16) was the president who defended the Union against Britain's second attempt to bring the colonies to heel in the War of 1812 (one of the most important and least publicized events in American history).

Abraham Lincoln kept the Union together and set the stage for the integration of blacks into the mainstream.

Franklin Roosevelt in World War II protected the United States from the perils of a Hitler-dominated world that would have emerged from the conflict if America had not joined the Allies.

And Ronald Reagan brought a near-bankrupt America back to financial stability and, by his steadfastness against unremitting ridicule and criticism, brought the Soviet Union to its knees and the Cold War to a close.

These were America's greatest presidents because they protected the growing nation or because, through their unique vision, patriotism and decisiveness, they shielded and improved the Union and the country that exists today.

The national mood was low. Federal deficits had become systemic in the sense that no politically feasible cost reduction or tax increase could, by themselves, eliminate them.

The economy, a basket case when Reagan took over, was his domestic Cold War, as potentially destructive to the essence of America as any foreign enemy. Crippled as it was, it was the only engine strong enough to pull the United States out of the doldrums. Reviving it together with, at the budget level, cost *elimination* through program restructuring was the only sensible response to the spending problem.

Reagan reasoned that tax relief and deregulation were the remedies for the economic torpor, and he took advantage of his popularity and his limited congressional control to pass the largest tax relief bill in American history. He ignored the pleas of his critics to raise taxes.

His objective: Jump-start the economy and lower the Misery Index that, under Carter, has risen from 20.4 percent (already too high) to an unacceptable and devastating 36.0 percent.[7]

Federal tax receipts were pallid in 1982; they went down in 1983, but then the economy roared back and it provided a record-breaking year-to-year string of positive receipts until they dropped again in 2001.[8]

Reagan's tax policy was a resounding success. In 1984 the Misery Index had dropped to 23.6 percent, and the trend was downward.

Relative to debt reduction, the prime importance of a growing economy cannot be stressed too much. The complete turnaround in 1981–84 was impressive, but beyond that, *it is what had to happen if America was to survive as a major financial power.*

Americans to this day do not appreciate how close they were in 1980 to calamity or how valuable were the imposed Reagan cures.

They worked. They were imposed by a president who wouldn't veer from his stated belief that taxpayers needed relief, and they would respond with growth when they got it.

Reduced inflation went along with economic growth. From a startup point of 13.5 percent in 1980, the rate reached 4.3 percent in 1984, a benefit to taxpayers at least as valuable as the reduction in tax rates, especially when combined with the fact that the prime interest rate dropped from 15.3 percent in 1980 to 12.0 percent in 1984, and the trend was sharply downward.

Income per capita, from 1980 to 1984, increased by 37 percent, a benefit sweetened even more by the decrease in taxes per capita, which was not as powerful as it could have been because of the pre-programmed (Social Security Amendment of 1977) increase in payroll taxes.[9]

This continuing and unattractive phenomenon of increased payroll taxes was the result of Congress failing to confront the need to restructure Social

Security. Payroll taxes could not unendingly support its growing demand for cash.

Reagan's tax plan worked well; his deregulation process had good results. But his stated desire to modify entitlement programs fell on the deaf ears of the House Speaker, Tip O'Neil, as did his general appeal to control spending.

Spending in 1984, for example, was 28 percent above revenues,[10] a reflection of the struggle between Reagan and those who were determined to protect the programs they had developed since the 1960s.

Reagan had a Cold War to win and a government to trim. Congress bucked him every step of the way.

When campaigning for the presidency, Reagan promised to improve *Defense* and to cut spending. Once elected, he assigned top priority to *Defense* and he rebuilt the military despite the fact that Congress refused to cooperate by reducing the cost of the Welfare State.

Why were his critics so intransigent? Whatever the stated reasons, facts indicate that they placed a disproportionate value on social projects.

By claiming for *Defense* its rightful position in the hierarchy of cost centers, Reagan made it clear that entitlements had to be cut, and that the way to do it was to redesign them.

To do this, his opponents would have to admit that they had been wrong for twenty years, and they would have to share the unpopular responsibility for cutbacks.

They were not prepared for that. They preferred to underrate the Soviet problem and to blame Reagan for overspending.

Despite pressures to do otherwise, Reagan kept his pledge — he rebuilt the American military.

The result was the combination of irresponsible social spending and the necessary spending to build the military, a marriage destined to show itself in deficits and debt.

Supreme Court[11]

A president, by the things he supports and advocates, helps to set the tone of the nation and he can therefore indirectly influence the judicial positions of activist judges who are swayed by public opinion. Aside from that, however, there is little a president can do to influence Court opinion except to nominate people who, he believes, hold a worldview similar to his own.

Of the nine returning justices in 1981, led by Chief Justice Burger, all but two (Marshall and White) had been appointed by Republican presidents. Burger heard 65 cases in 1981–84, about the same number that he handled during the previous four years.[12]

Past Court opinions demonstrated that judicial restraint would not dominate despite the Republican orientation of most of them. Too many so-called conservative justices strayed from the farm, especially on social issues. That being the case, it was not expected that the decisions that had so upset and so divided American society would be repealed by the current Court.

There was one variable, however, that would have unknown impact. A woman, Sandra Day O'Connor, was nominated by Reagan to replace the retiring Potter Stewart. Stewart, appointed by President Eisenhower, was an unreliable conservative vote. History would reveal the leanings of Justice O'Connor, the first woman in history to wear the black robe.

- Sandra Day O'Connor — O'Connor originally earned a degree in economics at Stanford University; a latent interest took her to the law school at Stanford where she graduated third in her class (William Rehnquist was first). After graduation, O'Connor followed her husband to Germany where he served with the Judge Advocate General Corps for three years, and Sandra worked as a civilian lawyer in the Quartermaster Corps. O'Connor had difficulty finding work in the private sector because of her sex, and she struggled for a time with a private practice before she returned to public life as an assistant attorney general in Arizona. When a state senator resigned his seat, the governor of Arizona chose her to take his place in the world of politics. She eventually became Majority Leader of the Senate, the first woman in American history to do so. O'Connor returned to law in 1974 as a justice on the state Supreme Court; four years later she was appointed to the Arizona Court of Appeals and, two years later, Reagan nominated her for the Supreme Court. As a member, O'Connor often sided with conservative judges, but as time passed and the value of her vote in swing decisions increased, she became less reliable.

O'Connor, from a conservative point of view, was a marginal improvement over Stewart, the man she replaced.

A selection of cases shows that the interests of the day were much the same as before.

Lynch v. Donnelley, 1983. Donnelley objected to a Christmas scene erected for forty years in the shopping district of Pawtucket, Rhode Island. The display included depictions of Santa Claus, his house, a Christmas tree, a banner that said "Seasons Greetings" and a crèche. The issue: Did the inclusion of the crèche violate the establishment clause of the First Amendment? In a 5–4 decision (Marshall, Stevens, Brennan and Blackmun dissenting) the Court found that the display did not violate the First Amendment, that the crèche simply depicted the origins of a federal holiday, that showing it posed no danger of establishing a state church, and that it was "too late in the day to impose a crabbed reading of the First Amendment on the country." This was a close call made possible by the support of Byron White, a JFK appointee, who joined

Chief Justice Burger, and three other justices (Rehnquist, O'Connor and Powell) in forming the majority opinion, and it underlined the continuing national squabble over the true meaning of the First Amendment. *Did it forbid the establishment of a state religion? Or did it forbid the recognition of any religion?* This time, the Court narrowly favored the "state religion" concept. The next Court — who knows? This is the quandary that Supreme Courts create when they step into affairs that are best left to the states.

Palmore v. Sidoti, 1984. Anthony and Linda Sidoti, both Caucasians, divorced. Linda was awarded custody of their daughter. A year later she was cohabiting with a black man. Anthony sought and gained custody of the child because the child would be stigmatized by the interracial relationship. No evidence was presented to demonstrate that Mrs. Sidoti was otherwise an unfit mother. The issue: Did the removal of the child from the mother constitute a violation of the equal protection clause of the Fourteenth Amendment? In a unanimous decision the Court held that ethnic prejudices were not permissible considerations for the removal of the child from the mother. The decision was based upon the limited facts presented. But it was a sign of the changing times that a mother with a child, and living with another man was not, by itself, grounds for the removal of the child that should have been advanced by the father's attorney as evidence for the Court to consider.

Clark v. C.C.N.V., 1984. The Community for Creative Non-Violence had a renewable permit to hold demonstrations in Lafayette Park in Washington, D.C. The subject demonstration involved the creation of a tent city in the park to house overnight demonstrators. The Park Service, citing regulations, denied that aspect of the demonstration. The issue: Do the regulations curb symbolic speech in violation of the First Amendment? In a 7–2 decision (dissenters not identified) the Court supported the regulations: Expression is subject to reasonable time, place and manner restrictions, the protest was at odds with the government's interest in maintaining the condition of the parks, the dissenters had other ways to communicate the same message. It was a sign of the changing times that such trivia would ever reach a Supreme Court.

Bob Jones v. U.S., 1982. Bob Jones University, as a matter of religious belief, had a rule that required the expulsion of those involved in interracial dating or marriage. The Internal Revenue interpreted this rule as constituting racial discrimination, and it refused to continue tax-exempt status to the university. The issue: Can the government prohibit race discrimination at the expense of the free exercise clause of the First Amendment? In an 8–1 decision (Rehnquist dissenting) the Court upheld the decision of the IRS that the government may justify a limitation on religious liberties by showing it is necessary to accomplish an "overriding government interest" such as the elimination of racial discrimination. That racial discrimination should be eliminated as a matter of national interest is undeniable. But it is not the function of the Court to provide justice in a matter such as this. Congress defined tax-exempt status, and if it intended to deny it to schools like Bob Jones it should have said so or, failing that, it should correct its previous omission. This decision, a just one, was made by the wrong institution. It should have been made by Congress; it is another example of judicial activism.

These cases indicate several things:

- Trivia too often clogs the judicial system because the Court does not accept the authority of state courts (*Lynch v. Donnelley*; *Clark v. C.C.N.V.*).
- The Court has an uneasy relationship with religion (many cases).
- Behavior once generally accepted as improper has become, under the law, not worthy of consideration (*Palmore v. Sidoti*).

Reviewing such cases does not lead one to feel that constitutional law is, after over 200 years of argument, any more settled than it ever was, and the reason for this is the increasing tendency of modern judges to ignore the meaning of the Constitution when it doesn't meet with their personal sense of justice.

SOCIETY[13]

Some pundits say America was emancipated in the 1960s. Women were liberated. Civil rights, especially of blacks, were solidified. Objective morality gave way to individual choice. Government became the caring, cuddling force that protected the "victims" in America. LBJ's programs led the way to a new America that would be proud and strong — and very nice.

But social statistics of the day suggested that Nirvana had not yet arrived despite the fact that over two trillion dollars had been poured into society from 1961 through 1980 in the form of welfare payments.[14]

The divorce rate in 1984 was almost twice the size of the 1960 rate. Abortions, over a million in 1984, were more than twice as frequent as they were prior to *Roe v. Wade*.

The number of people never married, and the number of unmarried couples were on the rise, both testifying to the impact of the sexual revolution and the deterioration of what had once been a general consensus of what constituted proper sexual behavior.

All violent crime was on the rise, and the prison population was exploding.

When individuals try something new and projects they favor fail to yield promised rewards, they usually drop the project and rethink their objectives and resources. Corporations, sports organizations, and artists do the same. But not the federal government. By any objective measurement the Great Society, and its unbelievably expensive programs and its intrusions into the daily lives of people and businesses, was a flop. But the high spenders ignored the negative results and continued to push funding for social programs, a characteristic that postpones forever a day of reckoning.

For example, beginning in the 1960s, blacks were the target of many federal programs, and the subject matter of Supreme Court decisions that represented a powerful attempt to facilitate the integration of the American population, black and white, into a unified whole.

Blacks in 1985 represented 12 percent of the total population and 44 percent of America's prison population.[15] This was yet another demonstration that the whole of society, had much work to do to heal itself.

Change in Public Debt

Ronald Reagan inherited a cost structure of $1962.8 billion. Revenue for the previous four years was $1735.6 billion. This means he needed a revenue increase of 13 percent just to cover the costs that were handed to him.[16]

Under these circumstances, a deficit was probable. The only practical question was: How much?

Political warfare was in full swing in 1981–84. On one side were entrenched strong-minded Democrats and weak-kneed Republicans; on the other, the intrepid Reagan and the staunch fiscal conservatives from both parties who had, finally, a champion who would take their case to the people.

The principal issue of the day was Reagan's determination to rebuild the military and to win the Cold War versus the refusal of his critics to accept his cause as either necessary or possible, and their insatiable desire to protect and to expand the Welfare State.

Whatever LBJ's apostles said in public, their budget behavior clearly stated that they resented every dollar spent on *Defense* because it reduced their power to practice give-away politics, a budget-busting election tactic that had given them congressional control for the best part of twenty years.

The comparative transactions, shown in Table 12.2, silently report the result of the collision between these political forces.

The table immediately reveals that the remaining revenue, after primary costs are deducted, is approximately the same as the total cost of *Government and Human Resources* over the previous four years, meaning that there was no revenue to cover increases in those cost centers.

Given the fact that *Human Resources* alone had grown by an average of 77 percent over the past three presidencies, it is obvious that a serious deficit during the subject period was inevitable.

Since the days of LBJ, the question of most interest during each succeeding presidency was this: Will this president make a difference? Will he reform spending habits of Congress?

It was the same with Reagan. He came to town as a conservative who was

Table 12.2
Transactions (in billions of dollars)

		1981–84		1977–80
Taxes		$ 2484.2		$1735.6
Less:				
Defense	$780.0		$452.0	
Interest	354.7		160.5	
Total		1134.7		612.5
Net		$ 1349.5		$1123.1
Less:				
Government	$ 340.7		$ 305.1	
Human Resources	1608.8		1045.2	
Total		1949.5		1350.3
Surplus/deficit		$ -600.0		$-227.2
Debt, beginning		-711.9		-477.4
Total		$-1311.9		$-704.6
Adjustment*		4.9		-7.3
Debt, Ending		$-1307.0		$-711.9

*Treasury cannot be exact when it finances a budget deficit and the difference between what is needed and the value of securities traded inevitably produces a relatively small variance.

Source: Historical Tables 2007, 1.1, 3.1

determined to rebuild the military and to redirect the course of the government.

Did he?

TAXES

The top personal income tax rate went from a high of 94 percent during World War II to a low of 70 percent under JFK and subsequent presidents through Carter,[17] a confiscatory rate of taxation that said, in effect, that the government disapproved of moderate- to high-income earners because, presumably, they would not spend their money as efficiently as the government would, with its wealth transfer programs.

It was also a statement to the effect that the job-creating ability of the private sector was not as beneficial to the average people of the nation as were federal giveaway programs.

Then Reagan appeared with a different viewpoint and with the will to implement it. In his view, the job-creating potential of the private sector, combined with a smaller, less-intrusive government, was the road to success, with government programs reduced to the necessary level that would provide relief and security to the vulnerable without, at the same time destroying incentive, and the need to be self-reliant.

Apart from economic theory, Reagan realized that the only long-term way to eliminate deficits and, eventually, to reduce debt, was to call upon the most powerful engine available to him — the American economy. Cost control would help; cost cutting would help even more. But the fundamental road to success was to get the American economy going, and to get the American people spending.

For this to happen, he had to change the governmental attitude toward corporations and toward people with moderate to high incomes. They were not enemies of state who stood in the way of the government's charitable endeavors; they were, instead, the combined unit that, when healthy, provided the wherewithal for government to be charitable in the first place. And they represented the only force powerful enough to turn the nation away from bankruptcy, and toward growth.

Reagan accordingly cut taxes in 1981 as no president before him had; he cut them in the midst of the deficits that he inherited; he cut them despite the predictions of tragedy from persistent political opponents, like Tip O'Neil, Speaker of the House, and Ted Kennedy, a liberal leader in the Senate, both from Massachusetts.

The short-term impact delighted Reagan's enemies. Federal revenue increased an anemic 3 percent in 1982; it actually declined in the next year.[18]

Then the worm turned; the tax cuts took hold. The economy roared its approval and it delivered 17 straight years of revenue increases to the federal government, a string of success unmatched in the modern era — perhaps in any era of U.S. history.

Low- and medium-income people are hurt most by taxes from which there is no exemption. Corporate and payroll taxes fit that description.

The inclusion of corporate taxes in this definition will come as a surprise to some, but only because they haven't stopped to remember that all taxes are ultimately paid by people, not by organizations.

A corporate tax is actually a hidden sales tax from which there are no exemptions. Those who supply products or services recover their costs, plus (in most cases) a modest profit. One of their costs is the federal tax. Consumers, therefore, pay the business taxes of their suppliers every time they buy something; to the extent that they don't, employees pay the balance in the form of lower wages and fringes.

It would probably be useful and beneficial to the low-income class to eliminate corporate taxes completely, and to recover lost revenue in the form of a federal sales or a flat tax that had exemptions for low-income groups, and for basic products like milk and bread.

Payroll taxes continued to balloon in 1981–84 as an automatic consequence of the Social Security Amendment of 1977, which provided for rate increases and for the gradual increase in the taxable earnings base.

The share of Social Security taxes in relation to all taxes has changed radically. In 1960, prior to the Great Society, Social Security taxes were 15.9 percent of all federal income. In 1984 they were 35.9 percent.[19]

Social Security taxes hurt most the low-income workers of America. Social Security was in trouble when Reagan took office. It had reached the point in 1981 when it would have been *theoretically* wise to draw on funds that were in lusher times left on deposit with the U.S. Treasury.

Unfortunately, it was at the same point when many discovered for the first time that Social Security was a shell game — the "excess" funds were gone, merged with other taxes and routinely spent on the operating expenses of government.

The "Social Security Trust Fund" is an IOU from Treasury. There is no cash and there never has been.

Carter and the Democratic Congress didn't touch the problem. They turned it over to Reagan and in 1983 he organized a group to fix it. The immediate result was a change in the timing of the payroll tax increases already outlined in the 1977 amendment, bringing them on line faster than originally planned.

DEFENSE

Candidate Reagan pledged to rebuild America's military might. The Iranian crisis drew attention to the fact that the Vietnam War had depleted the powerful force created and maintained by President Dwight Eisenhower.

Nixon, Ford and Carter, besieged by cost increases in domestic spending, did nothing to restore America's power on land, sea and in the air. The active military in 1980, for example, was 400,000 below the 1960 force.[20] America had ships without sailors, planes without mechanics, guns without soldiers, and a mission without morale.

All of this Reagan promised to fix. He also aimed for a balanced budget but, unlike the three previous presidents, not at the price of *Defense*.

Battle lines were drawn between him and his congressional opponents. He was determined to rebuild and maintain the nation's military power; they were determined to expand and protect the Welfare State.

Much has been made by enemies of Reagan of his increase in *Defense* that, they claim, was one of the primary reasons for deficits during the period.

This is false.

In terms of manpower, there was little difference under Reagan in the size of the active force. But the cost of maintaining it, partly due to inflation, was more expensive. For example, the cost of military personnel in 1980 was $41 billion; in 1984, $64 billion, an increase of 56 percent.[21]

The only way to avoid such an increase would have been to reduce the size of the active force, an option no responsible president would have taken.

The major increase in *Defense* related to Reagan's intent to increase firepower per man, and to build or buy ships, planes and munitions needed to reequip the military so as to reestablish the nation's ability to defend itself with something other than the ultimate weapon, its nuclear arsenal.

The latter point is generally disregarded. But it shouldn't be. A nation, especially a powerful one like the United States that does not have a conventional deterrent, and that relies solely on nuclear weapons, is the most dangerous power on earth. The world is a less dangerous place when America's conventional armed forces are able, ready and willing to fight.

Reaching that goal was expensive. In 1980, for example, the United States spent $93 billion on such things as maintenance, procurement, research and development, etc. In 1984, $163 billion was spent for the same things, an increase of 75 percent. And the items that grew the fastest were procurement (up 114 percent) and atomic energy defense activities (up 110 percent).

Given Reagan's objectives and his follow-through, it is not surprising that part of the deficit was caused by *Defense*.

The other side of that coin was the belief (hope?) that nondefense spending would be cut back until the Cold War was resolved. Was this likely? Reagan's opponents could not afford to take his objectives seriously. To publicly do so would have forced them, as patriots, to control domestic spending while the commander in chief went about his business, a road they had refused to take during the Korean and Vietnam wars.

Perhaps that is one reason why war was never declared in those conflicts, and why U.S. participation in them was always described with weasel words like "police action."

With that as background, and with the wisdom of hindsight, it is apparent that Reagan's opponents were not about to cut spending during a nonshooting Cold War. The MAD doctrine (mutually assured destruction) had kept the peace between the United States and the Soviet Union for forty years, the argument went. There was no reason to change. Reagan's military buildup was arbitrary, unnecessary and useless.

The Cold War can't be won, they said. The USSR is too strong, they said. Anyway, America's resources, they said, are needed for social projects, not for guns.

Given this clash of views, it was inevitable that a deficit would result and that *Defense* would be part of it.

In 1981–84, *Defense* increased 1.7 times and revenue increased 1.4 times. Had the increase *in Defense* been limited to the rate of revenue increase, spending would have been $646.8 billion or $133.2 billion less than actual. To that extent, this cost center added to the 1981–84 deficit.[22]

Was the unfunded spending in *Defense* a legitimate addition to debt or another example of spending unwisely?

The Cold War victory was tied to military strength that Reagan created by his will and by his determination. As such, unfunded costs of it were legitimate additions to national debt, necessary costs that were ignored by previous administrations that had allowed America's military strength to decline to unacceptable levels. In short, as he had done with Social Security, Reagan picked up a check that others had ignored.

Those who see no relationship between Reagan's military program and subsequent international events regard unfunded costs of *Defense* as unwise expenditures that could have been better spent on welfare programs.

Evidence favors the acceptance of the unfunded costs as a reasonable addition to debt, and the costs of recovering what should not have been lost in the first place, America's military backbone.

Liberal politicians saw Reagan as a threat to their plans. They pounced on the 1981–84 deficits and blamed them on his military spending and tax cuts.

In fact, federal revenues blossomed under lower taxes,[23] and the charge that his military project was abnormal was poppycock. The cost of *Defense* in 1984 as a percent of GDP and as a percent of total spending, was less than it was under Presidents Truman, Eisenhower, Kennedy/Johnson and Nixon.[24]

And it's a good guess that the only reason it was higher than Ford and Carter is because those gentlemen did not have either the political will or the political support to spend what was needed to rebuild the military.

INTEREST

Federal revenue increased 1.43 times. Had *Interest* increased proportionately, its cost would have been $229.7 billion or $125.0 billion less than actual.[25]

Starting with the analysis of Nixon/Ford, the position has been taken in this book that *Interest* in post–Johnson administrations is largely the result of inherited debt that sitting presidents had no hand in creating, and new deficits over which, because of entitlement programs, they had little control.

All the more so with Reagan.

In addition to the usual inability to overcome past problems absent full cooperation from a liberal Congress (an unlikely development), he was also faced with a money market that featured prime interest rates that were almost twice the size of Lyndon Johnson's.[26]

Like a recession or a depression, these excessive interest costs with minor variations were caused by the uncontrollable costs of the Welfare State.

GOVERNMENT

Defense and Interest as primary costs are allowed the same rate of growth as that which was provided by revenue growth (1.43 times). But the maximum growth rate of other cost centers in a balanced budget is set according to the relationship between current revenue, after the primary cost centers are funded, and the total costs of those centers during the previous four years, in this case, 1.19 times. For all practical purposes, this says that these cost centers had a very modest growth potential. *Government* grew 1.12 times, well below the rate of revenue growth and within the allowable boundary.

Signs of intelligent, controlled growth in any aspect of domestic spending, given recent history, is a welcome phenomenon. For the first time since Eisenhower, the hand of a president exercising control over spending was apparent.

Table 12.3
Government (in billions of dollars)

	1981–84	1977–80	% Change
Energy	$ 45.2	$ 33.2	36.1%
Natural Resources/Environment	51.9	47.0	10.5
Transportation	89.0	69.7	27.7
Community/regional development	34.2	40.7	-16.0
International affairs	53.1	34.1	55.7
Science/space/technology	29.9	20.6	45.1
Agriculture	63.7	38.2	66.7
Justice	20.3	16.2	25.3
General	45.4	50.1	- 9.4
Total	$432.7	$349.8	23.7%
Commerce & housing credit*	28.1	23.5	19.6
Total	$460.8	$373.3	23.4%
Offsetting receipts	-120.1	-68.2	76.1
Net	$340.7	$305.1	11.7%

*Made up of earnings from various federal housing and other programs— subject to major changes from year to year relative to market conditions. (Historical Tables 2007, 3.2)

Source: Historical Tables 2007, 3.1

This was a surprisingly well-managed cost center from a cost control point of view. It represents the type of behavior one expects to find in a responsible government that is heavily involved in justifiable national defense spending.

All line items were reasonably well controlled, but two deserve further comment, International and Agriculture.

Within the line item International there is a sub-item called International Security Assistance.[27] It is here that spending was unusually high. International Security Assistance can be placed in the same category as *Defense*. It represents costs involved in training, advising and assisting military forces of other countries, thus diminishing the overseas need for U.S. forces.

Reagan put more emphasis on this than previous presidents and it appears to be another justifiable cost related to the Cold War. The cost overage was offset by efficiencies in other line items.

Evidence suggests that the excess growth in Agriculture was not a consequence of inherited cost structure but was directly related to, and chargeable to Reagan policies. Fortunately, other efficiencies within the cost center offset what would otherwise have been a small unfunded addition to the deficit.

Since this cost center stayed within the bounds of allowable growth, it added nothing to the deficit for the period.

HUMAN RESOURCES

Government did not fully use revenues allocated to it and the flow-through allocation system in use provided slightly more revenue to the remaining cost center, *Human Resources*, and lifted its growth potential to 1.21 times.[28]

It wasn't enough.

At a time when past history said that welfare programs were out of control, and when current history said that America was in fiscal, as well as military danger, *Human Resources* increased by 1.54 times, well above the rate of revenue increase (1.43), or the rate of increase that would have resulted in a balanced budget (1.21).

This is the type of unrestrained, almost juvenile, behavior that had made a mockery out of previous budgets, and was continuing to do so.

Table 12.4
Human Resources (in billions of dollars)

	1981–84	1977–80	% Change
Education, training, services	$ 115.0	$ 109.8	4.7%
Health/Medicaid	113.3	79.5	42.5
Income Security*	349.4	219.5	59.2
Social Security	644.5	401.6	60.5
Medicare	195.8	100.7	94.4
Unemployment compensation	93.4	56.0	66.8
Veterans	97.4	78.1	24.7
Total	$1608.8	$1045.2	53.9%

*Minus unemployment compensation (from 1965–68 on)

Note: Major federal programs since the 1960s— Food Stamps 1961 (pilot), Food Stamps 1964, Medicaid 1965, Student Aid 1966, Medicare 1967, Coal Miners Benefits 1970, Commodity Donations 1973, Supplementary Security Income 1974, Supplemental Feeding 1976, Earned Income Tax Credit 1976, Legal Services 1976, Energy Assistance 1977

Source: Historical Tables 2007, 3.1

All line items, except Veterans, grew disproportionately.

Health costs, dominated by Medicaid, were 1.43 times higher because of cost increases that took off in the 1960s and have not stopped since. The only way to stop this level of increase is to restructure Medicaid, something Congress seems unwilling to do.

Income Security cost increases were also fundamentally the result of maturing programs that came on line since the 1960s. A few items in the detail of this line item deserve attention:

- Federal employees, including elected politicians, take good care of themselves. In 1980, Federal Employee Retirement and Disability cost $27 billion; in 1984, $38 billion — a 41 percent increase. Vulgar demonstrations of the tendency of government employees to feed at the public trough whenever possible amplifies the need to periodically put all federal programs and fringes on the table for reevaluation and reprioritization.

• Housing assistance more than doubled in cost in four years. The combination of Reagan's push for home ownership and the hard times caused by the ongoing recession, made for a busy Housing and Urban Development Agency (HUD) in the early 1980s.

Social Security and Medicare runaway costs are directly linked to the payroll tax problem that was becoming an increasingly heavy burden for low-income workers to bear. There was no answer to that problem in 1984 that was any better than the obvious answers previously advanced: these programs and how they are financed must be restructured.

Unemployment compensation spending was a direct result of the economy that Reagan inherited. But there was light at the end of the tunnel on this one: In 1984, the cost of this line item was 55 percent of what it had been in 1983.[29] The back of the recession had been broken and the unemployment rate would soon drop for the first time in 12 years.

Under Presidents Nixon, Ford and Carter, the average increase in *Human Resources* for four years was 76.5 percent.[30] During the same period, the average increase in revenue was 47.1 percent.[31] In a nutshell, that is the basic explanation for rising debt.

Had growth in *Human Resources* been kept within bounds, the cost for the period would have been $1267.0 billion, or $341.8 billion less than actual, and to that extent it contributed to the deficit.[32]

Reagan did not unwind the Welfare State, but he did two great things about *Human Resources*. He halted the growth of new and substantial initiatives. And he complained, he talked about it, he shone the light of day on spending problems that he alone could not fix.

And during the course of his dialogue with voters, he changed the political agenda in Washington. For the first time since the days of Dwight Eisenhower, balanced budgets, spending controls and similar subjects were openly discussed by power brokers. A preference for deficit spending, once the mark of an economic sophisticate, was now admitted only in the dark corners of the most liberal cocktail parties.

SUMMARY OF DEFICIT ALLOCATIONS

The potential damage to the fiscal integrity of the federal budget was obvious during the first Nixon administration. Since that time, conservative budget watchers had been waiting for someone to take charge and to change spending habits of the Democratic-controlled Congress.

Nixon, Ford and Carter failed. They left behind the same problems they assumed, but older and deadlier than before. Reagan didn't stop the deficits. He couldn't. The causative agents— mandatory entitlement programs— were untouchable until, when and if Congress decided to do something about them. So he hunkered down, stayed true to his *Defense* objectives and waited.

Table 12.5
Summary of Deficit —1981–1984 (in billions of dollars)

Cost Center	Amount
Cold War	$133.2
Interest	125.0
Government	0.0
Human Resources	341.8
Total	$600.0

Sources: Exhibits 1, 11–2, 16

The clash between a defense-minded president and a Congress that valued the protection of their pet projects above the demands of security and fiscal responsibility is vividly shown in these few numbers.

Place the name Reagan next to Cold War; it represents the cost of his determination to build the military and to stop the Cold War the old fashioned way — by winning it.

Place the name Johnson next to *Interest,* the excess cost of which is directly linked to the unfunded costs of the Welfare State that he started, and that his apostles implemented.

Place the name Reagan next to *Government.* The zero symbolizes the work of an executive who tried to reduce the discretionary costs over which he had some control.

And place the name Johnson next to *Human Resources* because he was the father of the Welfare State that may one day bring to its knees the mightiest nation the globe has ever seen.

Conclusion

Every president wants to make a difference when he is in office, to do something that will linger when he is gone. Some do make a difference and some don't.

Reagan did. And some of it showed up in the spending priorities of his first four years.

The United States may never again see the day when it can afford to devote 52 percent of its revenue to *Defense* during a period of relative peace, but priorities under Reagan shifted. During a critical period of American-Soviet relations more revenue appropriately went to *Defense,* and the *Government* was run more efficiently at a lower cost.

Table 12.6
Spending Priorities

	1960	1968	1976	1980	1984
Primary costs					
Defense	52.2%	46.0%	24.1%	22.7%	26.7%
Interest	7.5	6.2	7.2	8.9	13.0
Total	59.7%	52.2%	31.3%	31.6%	39.7%
Government	11.9	14.5	14.0	15.4	9.8
Education/services	1.9	4.3	5.1	5.4	3.2
Health/Medicaid	.9	2.5	4.1	3.9	3.6
Medicare	2.6	4.3	5.4	6.7	
Income Security	8.0	6.6	16.4	14.7	13.1
Social Security	12.6	13.4	19.9	20.0	20.9
Veterans	5.9	3.9	4.9	3.6	3.0
Total	100.0%	100.0%	100.0%	100.0%	100.0%
	(3)	(2)(3)	(3)	(3)	(3)

1 = peace; 2 = war; 3 = cold war
Source: Historical Tables 2007, 3.1

The *Defense* portion of the deficit was a legitimate addition to debt because it fell to Reagan to absorb neglected costs of *Defense* as the necessary price of winning the Cold War and of making the world a more peaceful place in which to live.

Unfunded *Interest* and *Human Resources* portions of the deficit were avoidable costs that directly related to overspending that began in the 1960s; they are not legitimate additions to public debt because they do not represent non-recurring emergency costs.

An exception to this would be that portion of *Interest* that was caused by inflationary rates, a figure that could have been, but was not, estimated.

Reagan inherited a deficit and a congressional spending machine gone wild. Given these conditions, increased debt was almost guaranteed, and given the unrepentant attitude of Congress, a sizable increase was likely.

Table 12.7
Public Debt, 1984 (billions)

Event	Inherited 1980	Added 1981–84	Total 1984	%
World War I	$ 18.3	$	$ 18.3	1.4%
Great Depression	24.5	24.5	1.9	
World War II	142.5	142.5	10.9	
Korean War	6.6	6.6	.5	
Cold War	133.2	133.2	10.2	
Interest	33.8	125.0	158.8	12.1
Government	121.1	0.0	121.1	9.3
Human Resources	369.3	341.8	711.1	54.4
Treasury	-4.2	-4.9	-9.1	-.7
Total	$711.9	$595.1	$1307.0	100.0%

Source: Exhibits 1, 11, 12, 16

No amount of feasible tax increase or cost reduction is alone, or in combination, powerful enough to offset the built in cost momentum of existing federal programs, nor would they be capable of throwing the federal budget into a surplus position so that debt and tax reduction options are developed. Only a combination of cost control and robust economic growth is up to that task.

Reagan's first term saw these improvements: *Defense* stronger, interest and inflation rates lower, the recession ended, federal revenue up sharply, a major simplification of the tax code, spending in *Government* modest, spending in *Human Resources* less extravagant than before.

Such things highlight the accomplishments of Reagan's first term. But there was more to be done. The deeply entrenched problem of spending growth was unsolved, and the investment in *Defense* had yet to pay off.

In a larger context, Reagan's major contribution to the public debt problem was his insistent voice, heard over and over again, deploring spending habits of the government and tax burdens levied on ordinary citizens.

His effective, strong, and conservative voice educated the people. They listened. In 1984 Reagan, 73 years old, ran for a second term and won a landslide victory over Walter Mondale.[33]

As historians of the future look back on the twentieth century, they may well regard Roosevelt, Johnson and Reagan as its most significant presidents.

Roosevelt changed the way government dealt with people, but he did so in a way that didn't fundamentally change the form of government itself. Perhaps he would have, given the time, but in fact he didn't. Except for federal programs protecting the old, the unemployed and the war veterans, the America he left behind was much like the America of old.

Johnson took principles established by Roosevelt and expanded upon them beyond belief, substituting the American Welfare State. The America of today is nothing like the America of old.

Reagan stopped the welfare train. He did not fix it or send it back to its beginnings, but he did make apparent to the nation the cost of the journey to the Great Society and the price it was paying for the mismanagement of its "credit line."

Because of his popularity, tenacity, and oratory, for the first time in decades the concept of a balanced budget could be discussed in polite society.

Reagan changed the agenda in Washington, a major accomplishment.

13

Ronald W. Reagan, 1985–1988

Second-Term President

America was headed for a crisis.

The 1981–84 clashes between liberals and conservatives ended in a stalemate and a $600.0 billion deficit. Not even America could afford too many rounds of such a match.

Somewhere, somehow, the race to bone-crushing debt had to stop; recognition that America cannot afford everything had to begin. The ability to fund primary costs had to be preserved; agreement on how to manage debt had to be reached on a firm, bipartisan basis.

Reagan rebuilt the armed forces. Measured historically, cost was as modest as it was necessary. The logic of the project was pure: America must have the ability to expand its forces through taxes and debt when circumstances dictate; America should not accept as inevitable a life forever threatened by the Soviet Union, an international bully.

The problems?

Post-Eisenhower spending on the Welfare State had lifted tax rates to their practical maximum level; the national budget in peacetime was chronically out of balance; the nation's credit line was being used to finance yesterday's socialistic ideas.

America had spent itself into a position where it could not create and keep a military force that was appropriate for its responsibilities as a world power.

To rebuild the military *under such circumstances* was to guarantee continuing deficits. But it also put tremendous pressure on those who created and maintained the Welfare State.

Reagan's insistence on funding an adequate *Defense* forced into the open for everyone to see the inability of government to do so without at the same time incurring huge deficits. The easy escape routes were closed down; there was no shooting war to justify tax gorging; public debt could not climb much faster without causing alarm, and without turning the national spotlight onto the big spenders.

There is no doubt about it. Reagan caused his critics to lose sleep. Lyndon Johnson's "guns and butter too" formula did not work. Trying to make it work during the previous two decades had weakened the financial strength of the nation to the extent that it had become an issue of national security.

At the beginning of Reagan's second term, public debt was $1307.0 billion, as follows:

Table 13.1
Public Debt 1984 (in billions of dollars)

	Total	%
World War I	$ 18.3	1.4%
Great Depression:	24.5	1.9
World War II	142.5	10.9
Korean War	6.6	.5
Cold War	133.2	10.2
Interest	158.8	12.1
Government	121.1	9.3
Human Resources	711.1	54.4
Treasury, net	-9.1	-.7
Total	$1307.0	100.0%

Source: Table 12.7, Chapter 12

Ongoing federal programs piled on top of normal government activities were now so demanding that to add anything, no matter how worthy, was an invitation to increased debt. And as debt grew, so did its offspring, *Interest*. Yet, no matter how high *Interest* went, it was hardly mentioned by Washington's peerless budgeters or, worse still, by the major media.

Why? Was it not worth reporting that *Interest* in 1984 was more expensive than any line item under the heading Government?—that it cost more than any line item listed under *Human Resources*, except for Social Security, and Income Security?—that it was almost half as expensive as *Defense*?[1]

How big did *Interest* have to be to gain the attention of opinion movers, to guide their attention to the *cause* of the debt that gave birth to the *Interest*?

Whatever the critical size that would demand accountability by the politicians or by the media, it obviously hadn't been reached in 1984.

The media preferred to lambaste the president for deficits he couldn't control—to politicize the problem for ideological reasons. And with politicians, the pursuit of power trumped the pursuit of truth. They were delighted to have the debate carried on in those terms.

High deficit? High debt? High Interest? It's Reagan's fault! End of examination! Such was the defense of the liberal community in and out of politics.

Now a man with the philosophical bent of Reagan would have never initiated unfunded spending in *Human Resources* of $341.8 billion in four life-times, never mind in four years (1981–84), which makes the point that deficits assigned to each president in the post–Johnson era have little meaning.

To identify cause and to properly assign responsibility, variations in each cost center must be traced back to those who established and nourished the troublesome line items. With one partial exception: *Interest*.

Nobody invented programs for it; it just happens, like snow happens when temperature and moisture conditions collude. Some of it is normal. Excessive amounts represent flawed fiscal policy.

The unfunded costs of *Human Resources* (the Welfare State) were the largest component of public debt in 1984. Nothing else came close. Big Brother buying votes with a credit card, a heinous practice, was fully exposed for the first time in 1981–84.

Any president of course depends upon congressional support to implement his ideas. During his first term, Reagan had an ally in the Senate, Majority Leader Howard Baker (R–TN), and an implacable enemy in the House, Speaker Tip O'Neil (D–MA).[2] To his credit, Reagan was able to accomplish much, including tax cuts, in that environment.

Reagan began his second term with a situation that was much the same, but a trifle weaker because Baker's successor, Robert Dole (R–KS) was more of a centrist — more likely to cozy up to his colleagues across the aisle.

Tip O'Neil continued to rule the House in 1985–86 and then he gave way to Jim Wright (D–TX) for the last two years of the Reagan administration, during which control of the Senate also shifted to Democrats under the supervision of Majority Leader Senator Robert Byrd (D–WV).

This means that in 1987 Reagan dealt with an opposition Congress, which partly explains the plethora of hearings held during those years as opponents tried to sully his reputation.

One major question hung in the air as Reagan's second term began: Would his critics back off, given their recent ascendancy to power in the Senate, or would their high-spending revert to form?

Perspectives

GENERAL

Reagan rejuvenated the armed forces during his first term. His primary objective in 1985–88 was to finish the project because, as he looked at things, it was the only way to end the Cold War — it was the only way to win it.

No doubt at times Nixon, Ford and Carter believed the same, but they were caught between a rock and a hard place. Rebuilding *Defense* to a more appropriate level, absent balancing cutbacks in other cost centers, would increase the size of deficits. And taking the political heat that went with that scenario was something for which they didn't have the stomach.

But Reagan did.

It was right to restore America's military might, he reasoned; it was wrong to overspend on things that people or states could do for themselves, or could postpone to a more appropriate time.

So he forged ahead no doubt hoping that along the way enough liberals would help him to adjust the size and the shape of more affordable government programs.

He pursued an institutional approach in his search for fiscal sanity, approving in 1985 the Gramm-Rudman-Hollings Act that was supposed to lead in 1990 to a balanced budget.[3]

It missed by $221 billion.[4] But more importantly, the effort was an indication that conservatives on both sides of the aisle (Hollings was a Democrat) were trying to be constructive and they were speaking out, joining Reagan's loud voice of outrage.

Foreign affairs occupied much of Reagan's time in his second term; he sought to cash in on America's rebuilt military muscle.

With typical optimism, he set out to tame the Russian bear, to deal with terrorists who were committing senseless crimes all over the world and to keep Central America free from Soviet influence.

Mikhail Gorbachev took control of the Soviet Union in March 1985. The state of relations between America and the Soviet Union since President Carter's days was symbolized by the refusal of the Soviets to participate in the 1984 Olympic Games held in Los Angeles.

Reagan and Gorbachev first met in late 1985. At that time Reagan mentioned, as an alternative to the MAD doctrine, a program that would, in effect, put an anti-nuclear roof over both countries, one that could defend against nuclear weapons. And he proposed disarmament schemes that had at their core his "trust but verify" point of view.

Reagan's ideas were rejected by Gorbachev and by most of America's liberal politicians and journalists. Reagan ignored them. He persisted and he kept the heat on.

The leaders met again in October 1986. The meeting broke up when Reagan stuck to his bargaining positions, an attitude that angered Gorbachev. The American press and Reagan's political opponents went wild — they faulted the president for not being more conciliatory.

By the end of 1987, however, Gorbachev was ready to deal. Arms reduction agreements were signed. The destruction of many weapons with provisions for mutual investigation of military sites was agreed to.

The Cold War was over. America had won; the Soviets, the liberals and the elite American media lost. A new tone was set. The Soviet empire crumbled. Two years later the Berlin Wall, the most significant physical symbol of the Cold War, became a bad memory.

Never-ending strife between Israel and the Arab world gave birth to a campaign of widespread terrorism that was supported by rogue nations like Iran, Syria and Libya.

Reagan focused on Libya. He froze its assets in the United States early in 1986, and U.S. ships patrolled the Mediterranean Sea off the Libyan coast. There were clashes between American and Libyan forces. A GI hangout in Berlin was bombed in April. German authorities suspected Libyans. Soon after, a bomb exploded aboard a plane during a flight from Athens to Rome. An Arab group took responsibility and cited the harassment of Libya as the cause.

Reagan went to work. Eighteen American bombers left England. They joined other planes from American carriers that patrolled the Mediterranean Sea. They headed for Libya, where they flattened Tripoli, a nearby airport and a military installation.

Occasional incidents of terrorism thereafter continued, but the number of Arab-related incidents after April 1986 dropped to a trickle. (Years later, they would begin again, more lethal than ever.)

Home Front

Strife with Iran brought to the Reagan presidency its most serious political problem — the so-called Iran-Contra affair.

The USSR, before its demise, fomented revolution in the Americas, including Nicaragua, returning to memory the Cuban fiasco under President Kennedy, and bringing once more to the fore the Monroe Doctrine, which warned all foreign powers to stay out of the Western Hemisphere.

Cuba still existed as a thorn in America's side. But another Cuba would not rise on Reagan's watch. He immediately and consistently resisted the growth of communism in the Americas. He suspended aid to Nicaragua and he accused it of supplying arms to rebels in El Salvador. A revolutionary group, the Contras, was formed and it attempted to overthrow the ruling party in Nicaragua.

Reagan assisted them; Democrats objected. Reagan skirmished with Democrats over his aid program, but he did not stop. Some of his aides stepped over the boundaries of propriety when Congress refused to fund the program. In their eagerness to find money to support the Contras, they linked transactions with Iran to the problem of funding the Contras in a clever way that also violated the letter of the law and, more importantly, evaded the will of Congress.

The hostile Congress jumped at the opportunity to nail Reagan and his men, to destroy the man who so eloquently opposed the Welfare State.

Hearings were held, charges were brought and heads rolled. Reagan was found innocent of illegality, but his image was scarred.

Those were his darkest days, made darker by miscalculations of his staff and by the venom his opponents could effectively release against him because they once again controlled the Congress.

These years were momentous, and the battle for America's future between the conservative president and his liberal opponents changed again its financial profile.

After four straight fiscal years of pallid GDP growth (1980–1983), the American economy got rolling again; it was healthy in 1984 and for the balance of his administration.[5]

The large first step toward solving the debt problem had been taken — mission accomplished — a healthy GDP.

Tax cuts, the medicine of choice, had been fiercely resisted by Democrats. But Reagan had prevailed.

The flow of revenues during Reagan's second term was steady, a reflection of the improved GDP and the sharp drop in the unemployment rate. Revenue in 1988 was 76 percent higher than it was in 1980, the year before the first tax cut.[6]

The Misery Index in 1985–88 dropped by 21 percent to 18.7 percent, its lowest point since 1976, and 48 percent lower than it was under President Carter eight years before.[7] Interest, inflation and unemployment rates were all down — normalcy had returned.

Income per capita in 1988 was 26 percent higher than it was in 1984, and over 70 percent higher than it had been under President Carter in 1980.[8]

The tax load per capita in 1988 was also lower than it was in 1980. It was difficult to keep it that way. Pre-programmed increases in payroll taxes (1977) kept adding to the tax load under the radar. In 1988, for example, taxable payroll was up to $68,400.[9]

While the nation's attention was locked on the tax and other benefits coming from the Reagan boom, the best kept dirty secret in Washington was proceeding apace — spending per capita.

The difference between spending per capita and taxes per capita represents current costs not funded out of federal revenue, most of which were cost overruns approved by liberal congressional leaders.

Prior to the Kennedy and Johnson administrations, the net effect of debt control policies was to borrow to meet tragedies or emergencies and, otherwise, to basically operate a pay-as-you-go-government.

But from the time Eisenhower left office, administrations have spent more than they taxed,[10] mostly because entitlement programs authorized in the 1960s, and expanded thereafter, zoomed out of control.

SUPREME COURT[11]

The Supreme Court at the beginning of Reagan's second term was made up of Republican appointees except for justices Marshall (LBJ) and White (JFK). As mentioned before, this meant little because some Republican nominees, Brennan for example, were as liberal as Marshall.

Chief Justice Burger was initially in charge; Rehnquist was promoted to succeed him. Together, they were involved in 100 cases,[12] 54 percent more than in the previous four years and 669 percent more than Chief Justice Earl Warren heard during the four years before LBJ's second American Revolution took hold.

This increased workload is the natural consequence of the decision of the Court to hear issues that could have been kept at the state level — it is the reward of the activist judge who wants to remake the world.

Two new justices appeared on the scene, Antonin Scalia and Anthony Kennedy. A thumbnail sketch of each man appears below.

- Antonin Scalia — Scalia graduated from Georgetown University with an AB summa cum laude in history, and as the valedictorian of his class. Law school followed at Harvard, after which he tried private practice for a short period before accepting an offer to teach law at the University of Virginia. Four years later, Scalia served the Nixon administration as a general counsel and as a negotiator with leaders of the telecommunications industry as they and the government planned the growth of cable television. A nomination from Nixon next found him occupied as head of the Justice Department's Legal Counsel. President Ford later assigned him to the task of determining legal ownership of Nixon's tapes and documents. He ruled in favor of Nixon, an analysis that was later rejected by the Supreme Court. With the election of Jimmy Carter as president, Scalia left government service to work as a resident scholar at a Washington think tank. He also taught law at Georgetown, the University of Chicago and Stanford. Reagan in 1982 appointed him to the U.S. Court of Appeals, Washington, D.C., and in 1986 he nominated him for the Supreme Court to replace William Rehnquist — Rehnquist was replacing the retiring Chief Justice, Warren Burger. Since his appointment, Scalia has built a reputation as a brilliant, colorful and conservative judge.
- Arthur Kennedy — Kennedy completed undergraduate studies at Stanford, and at the London School of Economics (one year). His legal education took place at Harvard, after which he entered private practice in San Francisco and, after his father's death, as the owner of his father's law practice in Sacramento. A socially and politically active man, Kennedy formed a friendship with Ed Meese, a Reagan confidante, one that continued and intensified over the years, and one that brought him closer to Reagan himself. Gerald Ford in 1975 nominated Kennedy to the U.S. Court of Appeals, Ninth Circuit. During the Carter years, that court was dominated by liberal judges; Kennedy stood out as a bastion of conservative values. When the nomination of Robert Bork in 1987 drew fierce resistance, Reagan turned to Kennedy to fill the seat of the retiring Lewis Powell. As a functioning

jurist, Kennedy is not as conservative as Scalia but is probably more dependable than the man he replaced. It is said that he serves the Court well as a coalition builder.

By this time in the march of LBJ's second American Revolution, it had become apparent that the Supreme Court had separated the American government from the moral tradition established by the Founding Fathers, who had expressed firm and easy-to-understand principles on subjects that seem to confuse the modern Court.

> Religion and good morals are the only solid foundation of public liberty and happiness— Samuel Adams, 1778
> Our Constitution was made only for a moral and religious people. It is wholly inadequate to the government of any other.— John Adams, 1798.
> The foundation of national morality must be laid in private families.— John Adams, 1778
> How is it possible for children to have any just Sense of the sacred Obligations of Morality or Religion if, from their earliest infancy they learn that their Mothers live in habitual infidelity to their fathers, and their fathers in constant infidelity to their Mothers?— John Adams, 1778
> The sacred rights of mankind are ... written, as with a sun beam, in the whole volume of human nature, by the hand of the divinity itself; and can never be erased or obscured by mortal power.— Alexander Hamilton, 1775
> All, too, will bear in mind this sacred principle, that though the will of the majority is in all cases to prevail, that will to be rightful must be reasonable.— Thomas Jefferson, 1801
> The first and governing maxim in the interpretation of a statute is to discover the meaning of those who made it.— James Wilton, 1790
> On every question of construction carry ourselves back to the time when the Constitution was adopted ... and instead of trying what meaning may be squeezed out of the text, conform to the probable one.— Thomas Jefferson, 1823
> I entirely concur in the propriety of resorting to the sense in which the Constitution was accepted and ratified by the nation.— James Madison, 1824

The attitude of the Founders toward religion, families, human rights and constitutional interpretation was as clear to them as it is ambiguous in modern society thanks, in large measure, to decisions of the Court.

And since the majority of Americans still hold values that are in accord with those of the Founders, it isn't surprising to find that cases flow to the Court that repeatedly attempt to overthrow past decisions made on such sensitive personal matters as:

- To protect the liberty to reasonably express, in public, a belief in God.
- To protect the God-given parental right to reasonably control their children without interference from the state.
- To protect the right of the majority to form the moral environment in which they live.

• To protect everybody from the intellectual meanderings of activist judges who, for example, supported the *Roe v. Wade* decision that legalized abortion throughout the nation thereby forcing on a public a new morality that stood in contradiction to their own sense of values.

Decisions that offend the public and that try to re-form their consciences according to legalistic principles tend to be tested. That is why the same subjects have been adjudicated for decades. And it's why the same issues appeared in the cases shown below.

Wallace v. Jaffree, 1984. A state law authorized public school teachers to lead prayer during the school day. The issue: Is the state law in violation of the establishment clause of the First Amendment? In a 6–3 decision (Burger, White and Rehnquist dissenting) the Court ruled that the law was unconstitutional. This is another example of the Court's oft-expressed unwillingness to permit citizens, through their elected officials, to establish the moral environment in which they live. State law was thrust aside; the tyranny of the minority was given another foothold in constitutional law. An interesting side note: Justice O'Connor, new to the bench, voted against the conservative position and gave rise to the hope of liberals that, like Brennan, she was one of them in disguise.

Aguilar v. Felton, 1984. New York City used part of its federal Title I funding to pay salaries of parochial school teachers citing as authority a clause in federal law that authorizes assistance to "educationally deprived children from low-income families." The issue: Did the use of federal funds in this manner violate the establishment clause of the First Amendment? In a 5–4 decision (Burger, White, Rehnquist, O'Connor dissenting) the Court ruled that the state's use of federal funds was unconstitutional. The Court can't be criticized for accepting a case that dealt with the interpretation of a federal law and its decision is a matter of reasonable debate. Justice O'Connor demonstrated with her dissent, as opposed to her concurrence in the previous case (above), that she was not driven by principle and could be a loose cannon in the years ahead.

Bethel v. Fraser, 1986. A high school student in a speech before 600 students used graphic sexual metaphors to make a point. The school has a rule that prohibits conduct that interferes with the educational purpose, including such language as the student used. The student was suspended for two days. The issue: Does the First Amendment protect such speech? In a 7–2 decision (Marshall and Stevens dissenting) the Court ruled that the school regulation was constitutional, that the school had the right to prohibit lewd and vulgar speech that violated the fundamental values of a public school education. Conservatives had no trouble with this decision. The major questions that come to mind when reviewing the facts of the case are these: Why did the Court hear it? Is there no lower jurisdiction or institution that it trusts to make decisions about such trivia? An interesting side note: Justice Stevens, a Ford appointee, was now a senior member of the activist wing of the Court.

New Jersey v. TLO, 1985. A fourteen-year-old girl was found smoking in the girls' bathroom of her high school. The principal questioned her and emptied her bag, finding within drugs and drug paraphernalia. The issue: Did the search violate the Fourth and Fourteenth Amendments? In a 6–3 decision (Marshall, Stevens and Brennan dissenting) the Court ruled the search was reasonable. In so doing, the Court did not apply the "reasonable cause" standard for a search because it took place in a school and because under the cited circumstances, it met the lower standard of "reasonableness." The same questions arise after a review of this case. How did it ever get to the Supreme Court? Why was it accepted?

The role of the Supreme Court under the Constitution is not to adjudicate quarrels in public schools. But precedent upon precedent established by earlier Courts kept them coming. What a waste of legal talent.

SOCIETY[13]

Changes in society are partly brought about by internal attitudes that are formed, absorbed and triggered by education (parents, schools, churches) and life experience. But government and judicial activities also play an important role in the development of changes in how people think and act.

Expanding welfare programs for example, despite good intentions, also diminish the work ethic and the sense of self-reliance that distinguishes free people from those who are protected by (enslaved by) paternalistic governments.

And Supreme Courts that lift schoolroom spats about vulgar speech and dress to a level of national and constitutional importance raise havoc with the ability of school principals to maintain order, and they embolden the always adventurous youngster to misbehave.

These influences, internal and external, civic and judicial, were more powerful than usual in the last half of the 20th century. A sense of rebellion began in the 1950s, exploded in the 1960s, matured in the 1970s and was firmly implanted in the 1980s.

In short, American society had been turned upside down in a few decades, and that change was reflected in the social statistics of the 1980s.

In 1985, it was about twice as likely that a marriage would end in divorce than it was in 1960. Given that outcome, it isn't surprising to find that fewer people married, the number of couples openly living together had almost quadrupled, and the number of abortions escalated.

One of the saddest statistics that profile the America of the 1980s is the SAT scores. Despite billions of state and federal dollars being poured into the public schools, scores nationally were deficient, and they showed no signs of significant improvement for reasons too complex to appraise here.

Murder, rape and assault since the 1960s were all on the increase; prison population was exploding, a sign that follows a disintegration of the general sense of what is right and what is wrong. Confusion about moral values results in more laws that attempt to restore order but actually result in more confusion, more laws and more lawbreakers.

On and on it goes, an array of numbers that announce the arrival of a new America, one that falls short of the expectations that were created in the 1960s. The social experiment of LBJ and his supporters that changed America from what it was to something as yet undefined, had yielded troublesome results, especially for those it was designed to help.

Value and capacity are the tests of expenditures:

- Are they worth it?
- Are they affordable?

Certainly social programs on the books satisfy the first test —controlled sacrifice to achieve them is worthwhile.

Just as certainly, the same programs as structured, as timed and as financed are not affordable. To persist in imposing them is the equivalent of a hedonist writing checks on a shrinking bank account in order to possess pleasures that his income does not support, and turning his back on the reality that one day he will be financially busted.

The case has been made here that the Great Society is too expensive for America, and the ill-advised pursuit of it has not been worth the time and effort. Massive amounts of federal spending have not made Americans happier; they have made them weaker and, arguably, they have been a corruptive influence.

Reagan epitomized American hope, but there was little he could do to change the onrushing tide that was, governmentally and judicially, creating a nation divorced from the concepts of those who had founded and nurtured it for two centuries.

Change in Public Debt

When Reagan first took office in 1981, he assumed a cost structure that, relative to revenue, was extraordinarily troublesome. And his problem in 1985 was even worse[14] for two reasons:

- He had increased *Defense* himself, as he said he would.
- Congress did not restrain spending, an action that was long overdue.

A deficit was therefore inevitable unless Reagan secured a windfall of revenue, or a cost reduction gift from Congress, something no president in recent history could expect.

Political warfare was even more intense during Reagan's second term, especially during the last two years when Republicans lost control of the Senate.

Defense was still a major priority with Reagan and the struggle with Congress for control over federal dollars continued.

Reagan was willing to add the debt necessary to restore America's military might, an attitude he shared with historical presidents who had the courage (not all did) to face a similar problem.

Congress was willing to add to debt in order to protect and to add to the Welfare State, an attitude that was in accord with no presidents except Jimmy Carter and Lyndon Johnson.

Few expected a balanced budget or anything approaching it given that condition on the political battlefield.

Table 13.2
Transactions (in billions of dollars)

	1985–88		1981–84	
Taxes		$ 3266.3		$ 2484.2
Less:				
Defense	$1098.5		$ 780.0	
Interest	556.0	1654.5	354.7	
Total				1134.7
Net		$ 1611.8		$ 1349.5
Less:				
Government	$ 361.1		$ 340.7	
Human Resources	1989.1		1608.8	
Total		2350.2		1949.5
Surplus/deficit		$ -738.4		$ -600.0
Debt, beginning		-1307.0		-711.9
Total		$-2045.4		$-1311.9
Adjustment*		-6.2		4.9
Debt, Ending		$-2051.6		$-1307.0

*Treasury cannot be exact when it finances a budget deficit and the difference between what is needed and the value of securities traded inevitably produces a relatively small variance.

Source: Historical Tables 2007, 1.1, 3.1

A quick glance at the numbers reveals the situation graphically that has been predicted throughout the previous chapters, to wit: The creation of a Welfare State has resulted in a condition under which the United States cannot afford a *Defense* budget of modest proportions (when measured by historical standards),[15] without plunging the nation into serious debt.

After deducting the primary costs from current revenue, $1611.8 billion was available to the other cost centers (above). As huge as this amount appears to be, it fades in significance when the cost of *Government and Human Resources* for the previous four years—$1949.5 billion — is fed into the equation.

The resulting message to an analyst is as ominous as it is clear: If other cost centers do not grow at all a deficit will be inevitable, and to the extent that those centers do grow, the deficit will be even larger.

This, for Reagan, was a living definition of being between a "rock and a hard place." There was absolutely nothing he could do to avoid the fiscal blow that confronted him except to complain loudly about the unaffordable cost of government. He did that—constantly.

TAXES

Tax cuts of 1982 were followed in 1986 by another major reform of the tax code. The end product featured lower rates, fewer rates, and the elimination of bracket creep (the automatic tax increase levied by the old system that became odious under Carter when inflation moved wages into higher tax brackets).[16]

Tax revenue in 1985–88, despite lower rates, was 1.31 times higher than it was during the prior presidential period,[17] about 2 percent lower than the average four-year increase during the previous seven presidencies.[18] Had it grown at the normal rate as it was then defined, it would have amounted to $3425.7 billion, or $159.4 billion higher than actual revenue.

DEFENSE

The blame game is always active in Washington and one of the favorite ways to explain the deficits during Reagan's years in office was to point at the increases in *Defense* spending, the implication being that he threw money away on needless military projects.

Defense did have unfunded spending during Reagan's first term that was calculated in the previous chapter as $133.2 billion — about 22 percent of the $600.0 billion deficit, and an increase in public debt that was as legitimate as those that took place during World War II.

The major part of the 1981–84 deficit was nonmilitary in nature. In fact, Reagan had a smaller active force than Dwight Eisenhower had in 1960 (pre–Vietnam); he had about 5 percent more men in uniform than Jimmy Carter.[19]

Those who painted Reagan as another Attila the Hun with hordes of new soldiers at his back were guilty of demagoguery. The increased spending was mostly devoted to reequipping a demoralized organization and to modernizing its weapons capabilities.[20]

Thanks to his foresight, later presidents had at their disposal the most lethal military force the world had ever seen, lethal enough to turn the Soviet tiger back into the Russian pussycat.

Had the growth in *Defense* been limited to the rate of revenue increase, the cost would have been $1025.6 billion or $72.9 billion less than actual. To that extent, this cost center added to the deficit.[21]

Consistent with the practices of historic presidents who were required to rebuild the military, this was a legitimate addition to public debt.

INTEREST

Interest rates went down in 1985–88,[22] which helped to deflate *Interest* cost, but the upward pull of the sheer size of the debt was once again strong enough to put this cost center into an unfunded position.

Had *Interest* increased at the rate of revenue, its cost would have been $466.4 billion or $89.6 billion less than actual. To that extent, this cost center contributed to the deficit of the period.[23]

Interest, now a major budget item in its own right in 1988, was more expensive than the entire cost of *Government* or all Income Security programs. It cost twice as much as all Education and Health programs; it was almost twice as costly as Medicare.[24]

Yet when budget experts drone on about deficits, the same two chestnuts are trotted out for examination, *Defense* and Social Security.

"Let's cut the COL index, or cancel a submarine" is the typical budget war cry. The flim-flam game. Now you see it, now you don't.

These diversionary tactics are designed to move the eye away from entitlement programs (including retirement and health plans for federal employees and politicians). Why? Because to reduce *Interest*, debt must drop. And to reduce debt, spending must decrease — a fate comparable to death for some politicians.

Interest rates were on a downward slope in 1985–88 but were, nonetheless, well above average throughout the period.[25]

GOVERNMENT

The day of reckoning had arrived. When *Defense and Interest* fully utilized the funds to which primary costs were entitled, there was no room left for cost growth in any other cost center.

Congress over a period of approximately three decades had built an overhead structure into the budget so huge that it monopolized revenue to an extent that was not only unaffordable, it was dangerous.

To reach budget balance, *cost reduction* was now an imperative for *Government and Human Resources*, a feat that had not been accomplished for eons.

Had the cost of the *Government* been reduced to the level that would have permitted a balanced budget, it would have been $310.0 billion, or $51.1 billion less than actual.[26] To that extent, it contributed to the deficit.

Unusual costs, some related to disaster relief due to droughts, fattened the costs of Agriculture for Reagan in the first three years of the subject period, but had leveled off again in 1988. The unfunded cost increases were offset by

Table 13.3
Government (in billions of dollars)

	1985–88	1981–84	% Change
Energy	$ 16.8	$ 45.2	-62.8%
Natural Resources/Environment	55.0	51.9	6.0
Transportation	107.3	89.0	20.6
Community/regional development	25.3	34.2	-26.0
International affairs	52.5	53.1	- 1.1
Science/space/technology	37.6	29.9	25.8
Agriculture	100.7	63.7	58.1
Justice	29.7	20.3	46.3
General	41.3	45.4	-9.0
Total	$ 466.2	$ 432.7	7.7%
Commerce & housing credit*	34.1	28.1	21.4
Total	$ 500.3	$ 460.8	8.6%
Offsetting receipts	-139.2	-120.1	15.9
Net	$ 361.1	$ 340.7	6.0%

*Made up of earnings from various federal housing and other programs—subject to major changes from year to year relative to market conditions. (Historical Tables 2007, 3.2)

Source: Historical Tables 2007, 3.1

cost decreases in other line items of the cost center to the extent that the overall increase was less than the revenue increase.

America under a succession of presidents seemed to need more law enforcement. Reagan was no exception and the cost of Justice increased by an amount that was excessive by any measurement except necessity.

It may be a statistical curiosity, but the cost of Justice was increasing as the signs of a decaying civilization in the United States became more prevalent.

The unfunded cost of *Government* was not due to overspending in the subject period, but to the inherited overhead structure born in the 1960s that had matured during the decades that preceded Reagan's assumption of office.

HUMAN RESOURCES

The deficit of 1985–88 was primarily caused by the now familiar cash-eating federal monster, *Human Resources.*

The reason for this is not complex, nor is it difficult to understand.

When a major cost center in any budget consistently grows at a level that is in excess of revenue growth, a deficit will eventually appear. That is exactly what has been happening in the federal budget since the 1960s.[27]

Human Resources since the 1960s increased at ridiculous rates when compared to actual and expected revenues until Reagan took office and closed the spigot. The problem was not solved, but the devastating costs increases of the 1960s, 1970s and early 1980s were tamed.

Had this cost center been cut back to the level that would have permitted a balanced budget, its cost in the subject period would have been $1464.3 or $524.8 billion less than actual.[28] To that extent, it contributed to the deficit for the period.

Table 13.4
Human Resources (in billions of dollars)

	1985–88	1981–84	% Change
Education, training, services	$ 121.5	$ 115.0	5.7%
Health/Medicaid	153.9	113.3	35.8
Income Security*	433.0	349.4	23.9
Social Security	814.1	644.5	26.3
Medicare	290.0	195.8	48.2
Unemployment compensation	67.7	93.4	-27.5
Veterans	108.9	97.4	11.8
Total	$1989.1	$1608.8	23.6%

*Minus unemployment compensation (from 1965–68 on)

Note: Major federal programs since the 1960s— Food Stamps 1961 (pilot), Food Stamps 1964, Medicaid 1965, Student Aid 1966, Medicare 1967, Coal Miners Benefits 1970, Commodity Donations 1973, Supplementary Security Income 1974, Supplemental Feeding 1976, Earned Income Tax Credit 1976, Legal Services 1976, Energy Assistance 1977

Source: Historical Tables 2007, 3.1

Medicare was the most damaging cost center, but its overage was offset by the other line items to the extent that the overall increase was less than the revenue increase.

The cost performance in *Human Resources* would have been applauded in a normal period. But normal times had disappeared long ago. The problem was no longer: How much was spent? As it was: Why didn't you drop or reorganize old programs to fit new circumstances?

SUMMARY OF DEFICIT ALLOCATIONS

The bad news in 1985–88 was a new deficit that was the largest in history. The good news was that the primary source of continuing deficits, *Human Resources*, grew at a slower rate than revenue.

Table 13.5
Summary of Deficit — 1985–1988 (in billions of dollars)

Cost Center	Amount
Cold War	$ 72.9
Interest	89.6
Government	51.1
Human Resources	524.8
Total	$738.4

Sources: Exhibits 1, 11–2, 16

Any fair analysis of the Reagan deficit must take into consideration the fact that the rate of increase in federal income during his second term was lower than normal.[29] Had the increase been equal to that experienced during the previous seven four-year presidential terms, the result would have been $159.4 billion of additional revenue (see Taxes), and the deficit would have been reduced to $579.0 billion.

Those who would deny this on the grounds that his tax cuts were responsible for the revenue loss are also saying, in effect, that tax relief had nothing to do with the economic turnaround and that higher tax rates would have been more beneficial to the economy. This proposition, ridiculous on its face, needs no further analysis.

Place the name of Reagan next to the Cold War amount of $72.8 billion. He advised it, planned it and spent it. And it was the final installment on the payment due for ending the Cold War with the Soviet Union.

Place the name Johnson next to *Interest*. This isn't entirely accurate because Eisenhower and Reagan added legitimate military costs to the debt, and other presidents added a minor amount of unfunded costs in other cost centers. But compared to the total size of new debt caused by the Johnson-related Welfare State, these amounts are trivial. Johnson and his policies are the major culprits for unfunded *Interest*.

Place the name Reagan next to *Government*. This cost variance is explainable, but it happened on his watch, and it does not track back to the policies of any other president.

Finally, place the name Johnson next to *Human Resources*, as the symbol of his achievement as the father of this travesty, and as the leader of the apostles who followed him.

The turnaround in the economy under Reagan was nothing short of astounding. Why then the huge deficit? The answer is boringly repetitive: Revenue was no longer adequate to simultaneously pay for a robust military and unadjusted entitlement programs.

Until all federal fringes and programs are put on the table and sorted out in terms of value and priority, the federal budget is in a condition of systemic deficits for so long as presidents maintain an adequate military force.

Conclusion

Ronald Reagan, determined to change the priorities of government, was equally determined to win the Cold War with the Soviet Union. He had Senate control for six years under Baker and Dole, and he never had House control, which was in the hands of O'Neil and Wright.[30]

Spending priorities on his watch changed.

Table 13.6
Spending Priorities

	1960 Ike	1968 LBJ	1976 GRF	1980 JEC	1988 RWR
Primary costs					
Defense	52.2%	27.3%	24.1%	22.7%	27.3%
Interest	7.5	14.2	7.2	8.9	14.3
Total	59.7%	41.4%	31.3%	31.6%	41.6%
Government	11.9	8.4	14.0	15.4	8.3
Ed. /services	1.9	2.9	5.1	5.4	2.9
Health/Medicaid	.9	4.2	4.1	3.9	4.2
Medicare	0.0	7.4	4.3	5.4	7.4
Inc. Security	8.0	12.2	16.4	14.7	12.2
Soc. Security	12.6	20.6	19.9	20.0	20.6
Veterans	5.9	2.9	4.9	3.6	2.9
Total	100.0%	100.0%	100.0%	100.0%	100.0%
	(3)	(2)(3)	(3)	(3)	(3)

1=peace; 2=war; 3=cold war

Source: Historical Tables 2007, 3.1

Johnson, during a shooting war, reduced military spending from Eisenhower's 52.2 percent to 27.3 percent, signaling a mind-set that would in future years change the government from one that valued security and liberty first to one that saw it as the largest welfare agency in the world whose primary job it was to take care of its victim-citizens from cradle to grave.

After eight years of Kennedy/Johnson, this trend continued for twelve more years until Reagan became president. He once again, as Eisenhower did, asserted the importance of national security and he reversed to some degree the new priorities.

He also, in passing, slowed growth in other cost centers with the exception of *Interest* over which he, like presidents before him, was helpless to control.

It isn't the purpose here to evaluate the performance of presidents in the international arena. In the case of Reagan, however, some aspects of foreign affairs activities must be touched upon because of their close relationship to budgetary decisions.

The rebuilding of America's military, and Reagan's demonstrated will to use it, was the cornerstone of America's foreign policy during the subject era.

Let others make a hero out of Russia's Gorbachev for ending the Cold War. Here the position is taken that Reagan restored America's strength and the USSR went bankrupt trying to keep up.

With determination, steadiness, and Teddy Roosevelt's "big stick," Reagan convinced Gorbachev that he meant business and the Soviet leader, like the good salesman he was, put the best face on it that he could as the Soviet empire collapsed beneath him.

Gorbachev, a loyal Communist (promoted through the ranks), did not assume office to turn the USSR into a democracy. He loosened central controls because he had to, because President Reagan's policies made it impossible to continue the old ways.

America's elite media, perfectly willing to lionize Gorbachev, has been unwilling to decorate the chest of the old Cold War warrior who more than anyone else brought the Russian bear to heel.

Nor is it often mentioned that Arab-sponsored terrorism declined sharply after Reagan's approved air attack on Libya; or that Central America was saved from communist infiltration because of his policies relative to El Salvador, Panama, Grenada and Nicaragua, policies that were constantly opposed by liberals.

These accomplishments were directly related to Reagan's attitude toward spending for the military. Absent his determination on the budget front, there would not have been the same progress on the international front. America's ability to sleep without fear of nuclear attack is the result in no small measure to Reagan's spending priorities of 1981–88.

Names and faces have changed, but the dominant trend in Washington since Lyndon Johnson became Senate Majority Leader, and especially since his presidency, has been the expansion of federal power at the expense of states' rights and individual liberty.

Reagan inherited the new priorities and with them the leaders who had spent a lifetime turning Washington into a welfare agency. He threw the light of publicity on welfare programs and he unwaveringly wailed about the cost of them. Their growth was slowed, but the real cost cutting had not begun.

In 1985–88, public debt increased to $2051.6 billion, as follows:

Table 13.7
Public Debt, 1988 (billions)

Event	Inherited 1984	Added 1985–88	Total 1988	%
World War I	$ 18.3	$	$ 18.3	.9%
Great Depression	24.5	24.5	1.2	
World War II	142.5	142.5	6.9	
Korean War	6.6	6.6	.3	
Cold War	133.2	72.9	206.1	10.1
Interest	158.8	89.6	248.4	12.1
Government	121.1	51.1	172.2	8.4
Human Resources	711.1	524.8	1235.9	60.2
Treasury	-9.1	6.2	-2.9	-.1
Total	$1307.0	$744.6	$2051.6	100.0%

Source: Exhibits 1, 11, 12, 16

The huge deficit exposed a Washington secret: When *Defense* takes its necessary slice of current revenue, deficits explode and the costs of social engineering are exposed.

With the close of Reagan's second term, seven straight presidents had outspent their income, producing 28 profligate years of climbing debt.

Was this because of wars, recession and inflation? Hardly. Washington has a serious problem that no amount of "spin" will take away. Spin doctors work overtime to point the finger the other way, to change suspect "spending" into noble "investments," but excuses are wearing thin. The truth will surface. And if enough people care about preserving America and its institutions, maybe they will do something about it.

The world changed during the administration of Ronald Reagan.

- He did not reduce spending as much as he had hoped, but he slowed its growth considerably.
- He repaired America's powerful economic tool, the only one mighty enough to balance the budget and to reduce debt and taxes on a sustained basis. The American economy, in a shambles in 1980, was purring like a Mercedes Benz eight years later.
- The Cold War, at its peak in 1980, was over in 1988.
- Terrorism that frightened the world in 1980 was greatly muted in 1988.
- Central America was in turmoil in 1980. In 1988, Cuba was a client without a sponsor; democracy was beginning to thrive in Central America.

It will someday be more generally recognized that Ronald Reagan had a hand in these developments.

14

George H. W. Bush,
1989–1992

Businessman, Representative, UN Ambassador,
Director of CIA, Vice President, President

When George Herbert Walker Bush entered the world in 1924 in the Milton, Massachusetts, home of his parents, Prescott and Dorothy, he preserved Jimmy Carter's status as the only president of the first forty-one to be born in a hospital.

Calvin Coolidge was president when baby George uttered his first sound. Public debt was $21.3 billion.

Many presidents have had royal political blood in their veins, albeit remotely. Bush was no exception. The New England National Historic Genealogical Society has verified that names like Winston Churchill, Abraham Lincoln, Theodore Roosevelt, and Gerald Ford are found in distant branches of the Bush family tree.

The Bushes settled in Massachusetts in the 1600s. Great-great-grandfather James chased gold with the forty-niners and he bequeathed to Bush his taste for travel. Great-grandfather James, a minister, was a fitting ancestor for Bush, who is a devout Christian.

A successful businessman/civil servant, grandfather Samuel left behind enough money for the Bush progeny to enjoy a rich lifestyle, and the family fortune was increased even more by Bush's maternal grandfather, George Herbert Walker, founder of a prosperous investment banking firm. Athletic skills Bush demonstrated in later years may have had their origin in that talented man, who was an accomplished boxer and golfer.

Until one reaches the parental level, the background of the Bushes reads much like that of the Roosevelts. Family fortunes, in both cases, were established before the parents of the presidents-to-be were born.

Thereafter, there is no similarity.

The Roosevelts leaned back, put their feet up and enjoyed the fruits of wealth; the Bushes actively participated in the day-by-day affairs of the world.

Father Prescott Bush (1895–1972) went to Yale and served with distinction as a soldier in the expedition against Pancho Villa and in World War I. Duty to country behind him, he built a prosperous business career that peaked when he became a partner in a prestigious investment banking firm in New York. Then politics attracted his interest, and in 1952 he became a member of the U.S. Senate.

In his private time, Prescott was a golfer of almost professional skill. He died of cancer in 1972 when his son George was ambassador to the United Nations.

Mother Dorothy is the Maine influence in Bush's life that draws him back to the rocky New England coast every year. Born in Kennebunkport, she was an active woman, a remarkable athlete and a newspaper columnist during her husband's days in the Senate. Dorothy married Prescott in 1921. The couple had five children of whom George was the second.

Bush moved from place to place during most of his lifetime. As a child, his residence changed from Massachusetts to Connecticut. His was a privileged upbringing, his parents supportive and loving; servants eased the way. His activities were typical — studies, sports, games, and quiet time.

George attended private day school until he was 13, after which he studied at Phillips Academy in Massachusetts. He was an ordinary student, a great athlete, and a popular and active campus figure.

Bush was ready for Yale in 1942, but his genes got in the way. His father's son to the core, he joined the navy and developed a record of heroics and bravery that compares favorably with that of any veteran. He was the navy's youngest pilot when he won his wings in 1943, and he flew 58 combat missions from the deck of the carrier *San Jacinto* over hot spots like Wake Island, Guam, and Saipan.

Bush was once forced to land in the sea; a second time he had to bail out of his bullet-riddled plane. In the first case, he was saved by the USS *Bronson*; the second, by the *Finback*, a submarine that halted its own tour to pull him in. Bush stayed with the *Finback* on its combat missions before it returned to port.

He was ready to go again in December 1944 as a member of a bomber squadron assigned to assault Japan. Harry Truman's decision to drop the big bomb may have saved Bush's life and that of tens of thousands of other Americans who would have been part of the bloody battle to subdue Japan. He was one of four pilots of his original squadron to survive; he wore the Distinguished Flying Cross in 1945 when he was discharged.

Bush and Barbara Pierce were married in January 1945 while he was still in the navy, a union of love and wealth; her father was publisher of two popular magazines, *Redbook* and *McCall's*.

The marriage was blessed with six children — four boys and two girls. One girl, Robin, died of leukemia when she was four years old, a family tragedy that left enduring marks on both parents.

Bush was a mature 21 when he returned to Yale and it showed in his marks— he graduated with honors in 1948.

In his senior year, Bush realized a boyhood dream when, as captain of the baseball team, he rubbed elbows with Babe Ruth, the unforgettable Sultan of Swat — a visiting dignitary at the Yale/Princeton game.

Harry Truman was president. Public debt was $216.3 billion.[1]

Can a young man from a wealthy family with countrywide connections "strike out on his own"? Probably not. Like it or not, family name and reputation precede him. But Bush came close.

He passed up the chance to go into investment banking with his father, but he did take advantage of family influence to get himself into the oil business in Texas. He sold oil-drilling equipment from Texas to California until, in 1950, he started the Bush-Overby Oil Development Company with money raised by his uncle. This operation evolved into the Zapata Petroleum Corporation, which in 1953 struck it rich.

Other ventures followed into the 1960s; then Bush sold his holdings (1966) and turned his interests toward politics. He was by now a self-made millionaire.

Lyndon Johnson was president; public debt was $263.7 billion.

Bush's public career began in Texas a few years before he sold his businesses. He ran for the U.S. Senate in 1964 against the incumbent, Ralph Yarborough. He lost but did much better in his state than the presidential candidate, Barry Goldwater.

In 1966 he tried again, this time for a seat in the House of Representatives. He won and in 1968 he repeated his victory.

After that election, in a typically courtly show of loyalty, Bush passed up Nixon's inaugural parade so he could say good-bye, at Andrews Air Force Base, to the departing president, Lyndon Johnson, who had been helpful to Bush's father in the Senate.

Bush, responding to party pressures, ran again in 1970 for the U.S. Senate against Ralph Yarborough. His chances were rated high because of the liberal views of his opponent. But the strategy hit the rocks when Yarborough lost the primary to Lloyd Bentsen, a former congressman with a conservative reputation as good as Bush's.

Bentsen won and Bush's career in elected politics was temporarily over.

"Politicians take care of their own," is an observation that is hardly original. The Republican Party and Richard Nixon appreciated the fact that Bush had given up a safe seat in the House in order to run for the Senate. Bush was repaid in the form of an appointive career that would take him to the far corners of the earth. He served in a variety of positions from 1971 to 1977: ambassador to the United Nations (1971–73); chairman of the Republican National Committee (1973–74); ambassador (unofficial) to China (1974–75); director of the Central Intelligence Agency (1976–77).

Bush stepped down from the CIA post when Jimmy Carter defeated Gerald Ford, and he started to organize his most ambitious political effort — a run for the presidency.

Ronald Reagan was Bush's primary opponent for the 1980 Republican nomination. Reagan won; he picked Bush as his running mate. The two went on to serve for eight years at the top of the Golden City.

It was Bush's turn in 1988, with the full support of Ronald Reagan. His opponent, Michael Dukakis, was a liberal from Massachusetts. Bush won handily.[2]

Ronald Reagan slowed growth in domestic spending but did not solve the underlying problems that made continuing deficits inevitable. Bush inherited them (as had the four previous presidents) and an *Interest* cost that, by itself, was a major budget problem.

On the plus side, the Cold War was over and with it the surge of military spending. Bush controlled the most powerful military machine in the world, and there was no rival in view.

Public debt in 1988 was $2051.6 billion and growing, as follows:

Table 14.1
Public Debt 1988 (in billions of dollars)

	Total	%
World War I	$ 18.3	.9%
Great Depression:	24.5	1.2
World War II	142.5	6.9
Korean War	6.6	.3
Cold War	206.1	10.1
Interest	248.4	12.1
Government	172.2	8.4
Human Resources	1235.9	60.2
Treasury, net	-2.9	-.1
Total	$2051.6	100.0%

Source: Table 13.7, Chapter 13

To inherit a high public debt was tough enough to deal with, but to inherit one that was steadily increasing because operating costs were out of control was quite another thing.

The only good news for Bush in the above table was the unfunded costs of the Cold War. The war was over and there was nothing in view when he took charge to indicate that the kind of pressure that led his predecessor to rebuild the military would continue.

Outside of that, it was all bad news. His inherited cost structure was brutally high and guaranteed another substantial deficit.[3]

Interest, Government, and *Human Resources* were the cost centers of immediate concern.

Bush was helpless before the unfunded cost of *Interest.* The market determined the rates, and only deficit control would halt additions to the base debt. *Interest,* in effect, was a consequence of deficits, not a cause of them.

Government and *Human Resources* were targets for action. Fix them, fix the problem; ignore them, face fiscal ruin.

Under Reagan, costs of the Welfare State, buried in *Government/Human Resources,* were fully revealed for the first time.

The piper had arrived for payment. Somebody would be stuck with the bill. The policy of "charge it," finally out in the open, was exposed as an act of fraud against the American people and their children. And the inability of presidents to stop systemic deficits was increasingly understood.

Realizing he was a victim of circumstances before he walked into the White House didn't give Bush much comfort. He must have known that the media's practice of hanging each president with the numbers of his time would leave him looking like a failure unless he could build a coalition of reformers who would, at his side, broadcast that a change, painful for some, was in the making.

The chances for doing that ranged from slim to none because he was faced with political opponents in both houses of Congress, Jim Wright (D–TX) and Tom Foley (D–WA) in the House, and super-partisan George Mitchell (D–ME) in the Senate.[4]

Perspectives

General

Bush, one of the best-trained men ever to assume the presidency, knew what and who to know in Washington. Many things may have troubled him during his presidency, but not much surprised him.

It is understandable that Bush wanted to separate himself from the shadow of one of the most popular presidents in history and to make his own mark. But except for breaking his "no new taxes" pledge in 1990, he made his most strategic blunder when he did so.

He hardly mentioned Ronald Reagan, he gave him little public credit for the more peaceful world that he (Bush) inherited, and when he added the devastating mistake of breaking his tax promise ("read my lips— no new taxes"), his separation from the ex-president was complete, and his destruction as a continuing political presence was assured.

In June 1990, Bush indeed became his own man when he raised taxes. The price was ruinous; with that single act, Bush doubled the chances that a Democrat would be the next president — any Democrat.

Bush did not present the stern resistance to federal spending that had characterized Ronald Reagan's stance. A gentleman to the core, he bargained in good faith with Democratic leaders, trying to persuade them to adopt more conservative positions.

Typically, they ignored him because they didn't fear public debt as much as they desired to protect the Welfare State, which, they reasoned, had given them the popular support needed to rule Congress for most of a half century.

Bush slowed down the spending orgy with his veto power,[5] but the balance of power favored his opponents and they used it effectively, their greatest success his collapse on the tax issue.

Thanks to Ronald Reagan, Bush inherited a less stressful world, but it was hardly peaceful. Just prior to his inauguration, for example, American planes shot down two Libyan fighters in the Mediterranean skies, a final reminder to terrorists from Dutch Reagan to behave.

The Berlin Wall became a memory in 1989.[6] The media made much of meetings between Bush and Gorbachev, but they were all an aftermath to a Cold War that actually ended in 1988. Neither Bush nor Gorbachev had much influence over the inevitable collapse of the Soviet empire that followed its unsuccessful attempts to compete for world leadership with Reagan's America.

Gorbachev was a memory in 1991; Boris Yeltsin was the first freely elected president of the Russian Republic. The Russian problem had boiled down to one significant issue: What would they do with their weapons? It was a subject sure to keep Bush and future presidents busy and the world on edge.

Margaret Thatcher also played a part in the formation of Bush's budgets in the sense that before her resignation in 1990 she pledged her support to Bush when he warned Iraq of dire consequences if it did not retreat from Kuwait. Her support was especially valuable when Bush was organizing an international military force to deal with Iraq.

Out of the confrontation with Iraq came Bush's finest hour as president. It was almost sufficient to overcome his domestic mistakes, almost but not quite.

The Gulf War against Iraq began and ended in January 1991. The demonstrated power of the United States was of a mind-boggling variety. Saddam Hussein survived because America's license to pursue the war with Allied support expired when Iraq surrendered and left Kuwait. It is one of the miracles of international politics that he survived for many years after the war, as cruel and as despotic as ever.

HOME FRONT

The arrest (1990) and conviction (1992) of General Manuel Noriega, the strong man in Panama, as a key player in the trafficking of drugs, symbolized America's deep state of addiction to dream worlds, a curse that would keep high the budgets of Justice for years to come.

The use of illegal drugs at all levels of society was now common and it constituted one of the many signs of how much America had changed in a matter of a few decades.

Noriega's arrest demonstrated the continuing and necessary attempt of the government to eradicate this problem with money and guns, but it was an effort doomed to failure because it failed to address the spiritual component of the problem.

Indeed, the spiritual heritage of the nation, which supported the unwritten laws that govern personal behavior more effectively than civil laws, had been set aside, notably by the Supreme Court, as being out-of-date in a modern society. Drug abuse was just one of the consequences of the new hedonism that was being celebrated from coast to coast.

The Nicaraguan problem that had plagued Reagan's final years was resolved with free elections in 1990 that caused the downfall of the Sandinistas, the corrupt group that had been the source of the trouble in that nation. This was regarded as a foreign policy victory for the Bush administration.

Certainly the most expensive domestic problem that Bush faced was the Savings and Loan crisis.[7] Hundreds of banks were bailed out by the federal government in order to stop a potential collapse of a large sector of the banking industry. This emergency situation, and the cost that came with it, qualifies as the type of thing for which the use of public debt is allowed.

The growth in GDP faltered in 1989–92[8]; it was reflected as well in the unemployment rate[9] and in the growth of federal revenue compared with that experienced by previous presidents over the past several decades.

The Misery Index was down again, from 18.7 percent to 16.7 percent, but the unemployment rate, the member of the troika of rates that add up to the index (and the one that has the worst impact on voters) increased.

Most of the public absorbed, unthinkingly, the relatively hidden benefits of lower interest and inflation rates, but the unemployed spoke loudly, their plight bringing with them the double whammy of lower revenue (lower withholding taxes) and higher cost (unemployment compensation).

Income per capita in 1992 was about 20 percent higher than it was four years earlier, but the rate of increase was lower than that experienced under Reagan and Carter.[10]

Taxes per capita, despite the controversial increase authorized by the "no tax" president, were down, but they also represent about the same tax load as that which pertained during the three most recent presidential terms.

Taxes as a percent of personal income per capita had remained relatively steady for decades, and that would seem to be a sign of a stable government, a valid inference until the Kennedy/Johnson administration took over.

Ever since, spending has been consistently in excess of federal revenues,[11] and the real tax load on consumers was only being partially paid each year by taxpayers—the rest of it was borrowed.

Someday the younger generation will catch on to this shell game that asks them to support the older generation while at the same time erodes Social Security because it had never been honestly and durably financed and because those who support it in its current form refuse to fix it.

SUPREME COURT[12]

William Rehnquist was promoted to Chief Justice (replacing Burger) under Reagan; his position as associate justice had been filled by Antonin Scalia who, with the chief, thereafter formed the backbone of conservative opinion on the bench. The other justices, except for Marshall and White, had also been appointed by Republican presidents. Stevens and Brennan, however, turned out to be activists and Blackmun and O'Connor were loose cannons. White cast a conservative vote on some social issues; Marshall never saw a liberal cause he disliked. Out of this mélange, nobody expected many unanimous decisions on controversial cases.

It is also true that few expected, if the opportunity arose, that Bush would be able to get a conservative nominee through the Senate Committee for the Judiciary that was dominated by liberal Democrats for whom the protection of abortion rights was the highest goal.

Robert Bork, a Reagan nominee, had challenged that attitude headon during his nomination hearings and he, one of the most able judges of the century, was voted down after being confronted with an insulting examination by Sen. Ted Kennedy (D–MA), who led the charge to destroy Bork's character and his nomination.

Bush nominated two justices, Clarence Thomas and David Souter. Souter cleared the process without undue difficulty, but Thomas, a black man, just made it after enduring hours of insults and innuendos orchestrated by committee members like Senators Kennedy, Metzenbaum (D–OH) and Leahy (D–VT), and by the well-organized abortion lobbyists.

A thumbnail sketch of the two new judges appears below.

- Clarence Thomas—Thomas is a graduate of Holy Cross (ninth in his class with honors in English) and Yale Law School. He returned to Missouri after graduation to work for State Attorney General John Danforth. After Danforth's election to the Senate, Thomas worked for Monsanto as a corporate lawyer. Two years later he was in Washington working as Danforth's aide. That position brought him to the attention of Ronald Reagan, and he was made the assistant secretary for civil rights in the Department of Education. Soon after he became head of the Equal Employment Opportunity Commission, in which post he dramatically changed the practices of the agency in ways that pleased conservatives, but alienated civil rights groups. In 1990, President Bush appointed Thomas to the U.S. Court of Appeals, Washington, D.C., and, when Thurgood Marshall retired in 1991, he elevated him to the Supreme Court. He was confirmed in the Senate 52 to 48. As a Supreme Court justice, Thomas has become a reliable ally of Rehnquist and Scalia.

• David Souter — Souter is a graduate of Harvard College and a Rhodes Scholar who attended Oxford before returning to Harvard for his law degree. Throughout his academic career, Souter was an outstanding student. He joined a Massachusetts law firm but found himself called to public service. He became assistant attorney general in the New Hampshire criminal division. State Attorney General Warren Rudman, admired Souter's work and made him his assistant; when Rudman became a U.S. senator, Souter replaced him. Two years later he was a judge with a reputation as a tough-on-crime jurist. Governor John Sununu made him a Supreme Court judge. President Bush made him a judge on the U.S. Court of Appeals, and when, in 1990, Justice Brennan retired, he nominated Souter to replace him. Souter proceeded smoothly through the confirmation process. Conservatives thought they had another winner, an opinion that Souter soon changed. As a jurist he has been quixotic and unpredictable, often a companion in opinion with O'Connor and Kennedy, a trio that sometimes sees left and sometimes right. Unpredictable as he is, Souter is less of an activist than the man he replaced.

The judicial appointments of President Bush accrue to his benefit. Thomas, a conservative gem, is the direct opposite of Thurgood Marshall; Souter is more restrained than Justice Brennan, Eisenhower's worst judicial nominee.

Chief Justice Rehnquist's caseload dropped from 100 in 1985–88 to 79 in the subject period — about six times more cases than Earl Warren heard in 1957–60.[13]

Case content was familiar, largely because decisions of prior Courts on such matters as abortion, prayer and speech were not generally accepted. This dissatisfaction resulted in constant probes and tests from those who felt that the Court was establishing a new ethic that differed from theirs, one that was at variance with the ideas promulgated by the Founding Fathers.

A selection of cases appears below that gives a feel for the concerns of the day, and about the attitudes of those on the bench.

Martin v. Wilks, 1989. Decrees approved by a federal court in Alabama governed the hiring and the promotion of blacks. A county in that state promoted blacks following the rules and it freely admitted that it was making race-conscious decisions. A white firefighter claimed that less qualified men were being promoted ahead of him because of those rules that, he contended, violated Title 7 of the Civil Rights Act of 1974. The issue: Did the firefighter have the right to challenge the established decrees? In a 5–4 decision (Marshall, Brennan, Stevens and Blackmun dissenting) the Court ruled that the firefighter had the right to challenge the decree. This narrow decision did not rule on the substantive issue (Are the decrees constitutional?) and it constituted a laudable example of judicial restraint. It was asked a narrow question and it delivered a narrow answer. It did not go beyond the facts and the specific question, something earlier Courts might have been delighted to probe.

Webster v. Reproductive, 1989. Missouri restricted abortions with a law that began with the statement that life began at conception. The law also forbade the use of public facilities to perform or assist at abortions that were not necessary to save a woman's life and it forbade the encouragement or counseling to have an abortion. A lower court ruled that these requirements were unconstitutional. The issue: Did the restrictions violate the equal protection clause of the Fourteenth Amendment? In a 5–4 decision (Marshall, Stevens, Brennan and Blackmun dissenting) the Court ruled that the restrictions were constitutional. The preamble statement about life was not a constitutional issue; no law required the state to go into the abortion business or to participate in it; the state had no affirmative right to aid anyone in the pursuit of their constitutional rights. The narrowness of this decision reflected the split in the country over this issue. Had the Court honored states rights to begin with and allowed each state to reflect the will of its people, this case (and dozens of others) would never have been heard and the issue would have been a matter of local debate in state legislatures, where it belongs.

U.S. v. Eichman, 1990. The Flag Protection Act of 1989 made it a crime to destroy an American flag, or any likeness of the flag that may be commonly displayed. Eichman, during a protest in Washington, set a flag ablaze on the steps of the U.S. Capitol. The issue: Does the Flag Protection Act violate freedom of expression under the First Amendment? In a 5–4 decision (Stevens, Rehnquist, O'Connor and White dissenting) the Court ruled the 1989 act to be unconstitutional because it was designed to suppress free expression when the content of the expression was objectionable while, at the same time, it permitted the same expression under more palatable circumstances. For example, the act said it was a crime to burn a flag during a demonstration, but it wasn't a crime to burn it during a flag burning ceremony. The most interesting part of this decision was Scalia's joining with the most liberal justices—his was the swing vote that carried the day. When the Court first decided to broaden the meaning of "speech" to include almost any physical act, it set itself up for a deluge of cases like this.

Planned Parenthood v. Casey, 1992. Pennsylvania law required that a minor seeking abortion had to have the consent of at least one parent, a married woman had to inform her husband, and, after consent, a 24-hour waiting period was imposed. A lower court upheld the requirements except for the notification of the husband. Abortion clinics and some physicians challenged these provisions. The issue: Do the restrictions that require consent and a waiting period violate the right to abortion that was established under *Roe v. Wade*? In a 5–4 decision (White, Scalia, Rehnquist and Thomas dissenting) the Court affirmed *Roe v. Wade* but, at the same time, it offered a new standard for governing abortions: Does state law impose an "undue burden" (a substantial obstacle in the path of a woman who seeks an abortion before the fetus reaches viability). Under that standard, the restrictions (except for husband notification) were affirmed as being constitutional. It's this type of decision that left the nation in turmoil. Obviously, the Court didn't have the courage to overturn *Roe v. Wade*, so it found a way to preserve it and, at the same time, to allow restrictions for so long as they met the new test of acceptability, namely, undue burden. Given this indecisiveness, nobody was surprised when cases testing the boundaries of abortion law continued to appear before the court.

An interesting sidebar to this case is the decision of Justice O'Connor to desert her conservative colleagues. It wouldn't be the first time in a long career that she got wobbly when hot issues appeared on the docket.

SOCIETY[14]

The condition of society was far different under George H.W. Bush than it was under Dwight Eisenhower.

- The status of marriage as an institution, for example, had changed considerably. About one in four marriages failed in the 1950s; it was double that in 1992. Fewer people were getting married, and the number of live-in arrangements was seven times larger in 1992 than it was in 1960.
- In 1950 there were 310 thousand cases of venereal disease — 740 thousand in 1990.[15]
- The number of reported cases of AIDS went from 435 in 1981 to 80 thousand in 1992, and the number of deaths went from 158 to 42 thousand.[16]

There are but a few of the changes that took place since the 1950s, changes that announced the arrival of a new America with changed values.

Change in Public Debt

It has been noted that President Bush inherited a cost structure that would choke the proverbial horse.[17] Only the confluence of a few unpredictable factors could save him from another destructive deficit.

- Peace. Bush needed peace so he could stop the military buildup that had done its job, and that would provide him with the opportunity to save a few dollars.

- Revenue. Bush needed at least the average revenue growth of the most recent presidents— 37.1 percent.[18]
- Interest/GDP. Bush couldn't control either the loan base (inherited) or the interest rate (market driven); he couldn't control the business cycle that had a life of its own. But he could advocate policies that didn't hurt business and he could pray for a break in the business cycle.
- Cost control. Bush could control some government costs directly; he could try to influence spending habits of the liberal-dominated Congress.

If these things broke right for Bush, he could lower the size of an inevitable deficit; if they didn't, the deficit could be huge.

A president with control over both houses of Congress can effect great change. Truman, Kennedy, Johnson and Carter were in such a position. Eisenhower, Nixon, Ford, Reagan and Bush (41) never had equivalent power.

Bush had zero control over Congress,[19] not good news at a time when great reforms were needed and when congressional cooperation or the lack thereof could make or break him.

The analysis of the transactions for the period will provide insight into how President Bush negotiated his voyage of the impossible.

Table 14.2
Transactions (in billions of dollars)

		1989–92		1985–88
Taxes		$ 4166.8		$ 3266.3
Less:				
Defense	$1174.6		$1098.5	
Interest	747.4		556.0	
Total		1922.0		1654.5
Net		$ 2244.8		$ 1611.8
Less:				
Government	$ 528.1		$ 361.1	
Human Resources	2650.1		1989.1	
Total		3178.2		2350.2
Surplus/deficit		$ -933.4		$ -738.4
Debt, beginning		-2051.6		-1307.0
Total		$-2985.0		$-2045.4
Adjustment*		-14.7		-6.2
Debt, Ending		$-2999.7		$-2051.6

*Treasury cannot be exact when it finances a budget deficit and the difference between what is needed and the value of securities traded inevitably produces a relatively small variance.

Source: Historical Tables 2007, 1.1, 3.1

The Cold War ended with Ronald Reagan. The years of abrupt increases in military spending were over. Yet growth in public debt exploded again in 1989–92.

It was no longer possible for liberals to blame *Defense* for huge deficits. With no war to hide behind, even they were forced to look at other cost centers with a critical eye.

A quick glance at the numbers in the above table reveals a familiar situation, and how formidable a budget problem Bush faced. In a period where *Defense* remained essentially stable, revenue remaining after deducting primary costs was less than the cost of *Government* and *Human Resources* during the previous period.

The numbers demanded that these two cost centers, especially the latter, be cut back. The past had caught up rapidly. What had been a problem for Nixon/Ford became a monster under Carter and, under Reagan and Bush, it graduated into an impossibility.

Taxes

One thing that had to work for Bush in order to avoid an enormous deficit was a rate of revenue growth that was at least average. Under the previous eight presidents, four-year revenue growth had averaged 37.1 percent.[20] Bush didn't come close. His growth rate of 27.6 percent was the lowest in three decades.

Had revenue grown at the average rate, it would have amounted to $4478.1 billion, or $311.3 billion more than actual. This shortfall must be considered when appraising overall budget performance in 1989–92.

Continuing deficits plus deficient revenue flow were no doubt the stimuli for Bush's infamous 1990 tax increase.[21] In so doing he bought into the long-standing theory of liberals that increased taxes are the answer to revenue problems.

Actually, economic activity is the primary generator of tax revenue and Bush's central problem was a slowdown in the economy. Unlike Reagan, Bush didn't have the foresight to stimulate the economy with tax cuts, or the patience to allow the business cycle to change. For him, that was too dangerous. And one must accept his reservations with measured respect.

Past fiscal policies had generated a mountain of debt and they had also limited a president's options when confronted by such a situation. Bush didn't have the borrowing power to play with that had been available to others. And what he did have he knew he might need because of problems in the Middle East.

He was in a tough spot. He decided that taking flak for a tax increase was preferable to other options. Right or wrong, it's a decision that many believe cost him a second term, and made William Clinton the next president.

Payroll taxes, under an automatic increase system developed in the 1970s and refined in the 1980s, continued to increase under Bush. The revenue from this source in 1992 was 38 percent of tax revenue from all sources—in 1960, it was 16 percent of all revenue.[22]

This represents a sea change in tax policy, and it is directly traceable to the many decisions made since 1960 that created the Welfare State that exists today.

The cruelest tax of all, one from which there is no exemption and one that was a relatively minor part of the revenue stream just a few decades ago, had become in 1992 a dominant source of federal income, and it was being used not to build trust funds for future retirees but to pay day-to-day operating expenses.

DEFENSE

A second thing Bush needed to have a reasonably successful term in a fiscal sense was peace. The Cold War was over; peace could permit him to shave *Defense* somewhat or, at least, keep it steady.

He didn't get peace, but *Defense* did remain relatively steady.

Saddam Hussein, president in name of Iraq, but dictator in fact, invaded Kuwait in 1990 and threatened the oil fields of Saudi Arabia. After failing to budge Hussein diplomatically, Bush did a magnificent job of rallying allies, including Arab nations, to join him in a military operation designed to move Hussein back to where he came from. About 500,000 U.S. troops were eventually moved into the area.

The war began with aerial bombardment in January 1991; allied ground forces were attack-ready in February; the war was over in March.[23] The war was quick; it was successful.

Had this cost center increased as much as revenue, the cost in the subject period would have been $1401.7 billion. Actual cost was $1174.6 billion or $227.1 billion less than its assigned share of the budget.[24] *Defense* made no contribution to the deficit and the unused funds flow to the other cost centers under the flow-through allocation system being employed.

INTEREST

Bush needed a break in interest rates during the period, and he did get relief. Astronomical interest rates that peaked under Carter and then dropped under Reagan were still heading down under Bush.[25]

Had the growth in *Interest* been limited to the rate of revenue growth, its cost would have been $709.3 billion, or $38.1 billion less than actual.[26] To that extent this cost center contributed to the deficit of 1989–92.

Interest has historical rather than current roots. And it will continue under future presidents as a problem of major significance until debt is finally reduced.

Deficits matter. They are the parent of *Interest*.

In 1989–92, *Interest* was 64 percent of *Defense;* it was more expensive than *Government;* without it, the deficit would have been cut by 80 percent.

This is the case because debt is so high; debt is high because deficits are systemic; deficits are systemic because spending in *Human Resources* is out of control.

Government

Funds available after deducting the needs of primary cost centers were less than the cost of those centers during the previous period. Cost cutback was the budget requirement.[27]

With that in mind, concern is immediately raised when the increase in *Government* not only exceeded the rate of revenue growth but also any reasonably expected rate of revenue growth.[28]

Had *Government* downsized to the level demanded, cost would have been $350.8 billion, or $177.3 billion less than actual.[29] To that extent, this cost center contributed to the deficit in the subject period.

A cost variance of such a magnitude is not unusual in *Human Resources*, but to find it in *Government* indicates that something highly unusual happened, something that should be revealed in the upcoming comparative analysis.

Table 14.3
Government (in billions of dollars)

	1989–92	1985–88	% Change
Energy	$ 12.9	$ 16.8	-23.2%
Natural Resources/Environment	71.9	55.0	30.7
Transportation	121.5	107.3	13.2
Community/regional development	27.5	25.3	8.7
International affairs	55.4	52.5	5.5
Science/space/technology	59.7	37.6	58.8
Agriculture	59.3	100.7	-41.1
Justice	46.2	29.7	55.6
General	44.4	41.3	7.5
Total	$498.8	$466.2	7.0
Commerce & housing credit*	181.8	34.1	433.1
Total	$680.6	$500.3	36.0%
Offsetting receipts	-152.5	-139.2	9.5
Net	$528.1	$361.1	46.2%

*Made up of earnings from various federal housing and other programs—subject to major changes from year to year relative to market conditions. (Historical Tables 2007, 3.2)

Source: Historical Tables 2007, 3.1

Under Reagan, the rate of increase in this cost center was well controlled except for a three-year substantial increase in 1985–87 in Agriculture, much of it related to drought conditions. The cost of this line item retreated in 1988 to a more normal level and President Bush reaped the benefit over the next four years.

Spending in *Government* was well controlled overall, except for Commerce (discussed below). But two items are worth exploring further, Science and Justice.

Science/space/technology increased disproportionately during the subject period. Bush inherited a cost that in 1988 amounted to $10.8 billion. Actual cost for 1992 was $16.4 billion,[30] or 52 percent higher than the base. This increased cost began in 1989 and it systematically continued. This disproportionate increase is directly related to the Bush administration.

The line item Justice increased well beyond the rate of increase in actual revenue, or any reasonably anticipated increase in revenue.[31] Similar to Science (above), the increase had nothing to do with inheritance and everything to do with decisions made during the period.

The cause of the overage was not cost control but social control because Justice for Bush and his immediate predecessors had ceased to be a benign, controllable line item. The effectiveness of moral law in the nation had declined and, accordingly, the cost of enforcing civil law had grown. For so long as society continues to drift away from historical values, it is likely that the cost of this line item will continue to grow disproportionately.

The wild increase in Commerce was related to the Savings and Loan scandal that threatened the banking system. Through no fault of its own, the Bush administration had to pick up the tab for the cost of keeping the system solvent.

Although the above items were not well controlled, their unfunded costs were internally financed by other line items within the cost center and the overall increase of 7 percent would have been, under normal circumstances, an admirable feat.

Unfortunately, this was not a time when normal circumstances prevailed. Any cost increase was unaffordable because past spending decisions and the unavoidable needs of primary cost centers had created a budget that yielded no opportunity for cost growth in other cost centers, which sent a clear message that by this time anyone could read, to wit: Cut or eliminate cost.

This was especially hard to respond to in *Government*, the cost center that supported basic government functions. It was a message, therefore, that was essentially directed to the remaining cost center, *Human Resources*.

HUMAN RESOURCES

This cost center had to decrease about 3 percent in order to fit into a balanced budget. Recent history did not indicate that the penalties related to overspending had penetrated the moral center of the high-spending Congress.

And current history demonstrated that nothing had changed. The cost increase was above the rate of revenue increase,[32] but, as an indicator of some restraint, it was less than the normal rate of revenue during a four-year presidency.

Comparative analysis will reveal if this result represents a ray of hope, or if it's a statistical aberration.

Table 14.4
Human Resources (in billions of dollars)

	1989–92	1985–88	% Change
Education, training, services	$ 164.0	$ 121.5	35.0%
Health/Medicaid	266.8	153.9	73.4
Income Security*	549.1	433.0	26.8
Social Security	1037.8	814.1	27.5
Medicare	406.6	290.0	40.2
Unemployment compensation	101.2	67.7	49.5
Veterans	124.6	108.9	14.4
Total	$2650.1	$1989.1	33.2%

*Minus unemployment compensation (from 1965–68 on)

Note: Major federal programs since the 1960s— Food Stamps 1961 (pilot), Food Stamps 1964, Medicaid 1965, Student Aid 1966, Medicare 1967, Coal Miners Benefits 1970, Commodity Donations 1973, Supplementary Security Income 1974, Supplemental Feeding 1976, Earned Income Tax Credit 1976, Legal Services 1976, Energy Assistance 1977

Source: Historical Tables 2007, 3.1

The average revenue increase for a four-year presidency from 1957 through 1988 was 37.1 percent. Using that as a yardstick, an increase in the cost of *Human Resources* of 33.2 percent offered a ray of hope that, over time, deficits could decrease.

To do so, however, the average increase would have to be consistent, an outcome that was more a possibility than a probability. Of the eight presidential terms that made up the average, half did not meet that standard.

The strategy to debt reduction should have included:

- A pro-business government stance that featured minimum controls and low taxes so as to maintain at full throttle the job-creating, revenue-yielding capabilities of the American miracle that never stops giving, namely, its free enterprise system.
- A cost elimination stance demanding that government fringe and welfare programs be systematically examined, coordinated, cut and restructured until they fit a sensible budget scheme.
- A new tax system that *eliminated* corporate, payroll and inheritance taxes and substituted a national sales tax or a flat tax with appropriate exemptions for low-income groups.

In normal times, cost growth of 33.2 percent in *Human Resources* would have been admired. Until Reagan's second term, that had hardly been the case.[33] Now, it was too late to stop the upward march of debt because available revenues did not permit what would ordinarily be considered normal increases— available revenues insisted on a cost cutback.

Increases in line items Education, Medicare and Unemployment Compensation were troublesome during the subject period.

Many presidents have a signature line item that reflects their personal desires to make a difference in some area of American life. With George Bush, it was Education. For example, its 1988 cost was $31 billion and in 1992, $43 billion — 39 percent higher.[34]

When making the decision to propose and authorize this spending, the president must have known that he was simultaneously authorizing an increase in public debt. If he didn't know, somebody did, and they should have told him — if a cost-cutting president fails to swing the cleaver himself, his ability to persuade others to be more disciplined is minimized.

Medicare increased 40 percent, a rate of increase obviously unaffordable, and one that was built into the system. It was beyond the control of the president. It will continue to increase as rapidly as the population of its recipients grows.

Medicare, like Social Security, is improperly structured and inadequately funded. In terms of uncontrolled rate of growth, it is the new lion of the budget that, when combined with Social Security, Medicaid and *Interest*, could bankrupt the nation.

Had Human Resources reduced costs according to the budget demands imposed by limited resources, it would have spent $1932.1 billion during the subject period or $718.0 billion less than actual.[35] To that extent, it was responsible for the budget deficit for the period.

SUMMARY OF DEFICIT ALLOCATIONS

President Bush needed peace, an income increase that was average or better, interest rates that were no higher, a healthy GDP growth rate and a Congress that would control spending and restructure unaffordable programs attached to the Welfare State.

Out of this menu, Bush got a break on interest rates and spending was better controlled than ever. Otherwise, it was business as usual, and the deficit showed it.

Table 14.5
Summary of Deficit — 1989–1992 (in billions of dollars)

Cost Center	Amount
Defense	$ 0.0
Interest	38.1
Government	177.3
Human Resources	718.0
Total	$933.4

Sources: Exhibits 1, 11–2, 16

It would be a disservice to President Bush to leave unexplained a huge deficit that was, to a substantial extent, unrelated to his particular style. Two items previously unearthed, for example, make quite a difference in the overall results.

Under the Tax section of this analysis it was noted that the national income in 1989–92 was well below average ($311.3 billion), and the cost of the Savings and Loan debacle, which appears in the analysis of *Government*, had nothing to do with Bush and it was unusually expensive ($138.3 billion). Eliminate these two items of "bad luck" and the deficit is reduced to $483.8 billion.

Beyond this, since it was known up front that zero growth was available to the nonprimary cost centers for reasons that had nothing to do with Bush you end up with a presidency that is more accurately described as another victim of Lyndon Johnson's second American Revolution.

It has been determined in previous chapters that unfunded *Interest* since 1960 has been fundamentally caused by the need to support the appetite of the growing Welfare State. Small slices of it could be assigned to individual presidents, but that overall truth would remain — had social costs been introduced in a timely, efficient manner, debt would be lower and *Interest* would not be a significant cost in the budget.

It is much the same with the other cost centers. The unfunded amounts were not so much the consequence of wild spending during the subject period as they were a mature reflection of costs that were born decades before.

Social policies begun under Johnson, expanded and protected by his successors, had matured into a government that cannot, at the same time, defend itself and continue to provide existing services.

The nation's central problem can be summed up in one sentence: In 1992, the cost of *Human Resources* was 2.6 times higher than the cost of *Defense*.

The nation's new priorities, as they had evolved since the 1960s were clear — maintaining the Welfare State was more important than maintaining liberty.

Conclusion

President Bush did not unduly separate himself from the policies of Ronald Reagan except for the tax increase he authorized, a decision (justified or not) he learned to regret.

He maintained a strong defense posture[36] and, except for the nonrecurring expense of the savings and loan bail-out, control in nonprimary cost centers was better than usual.

Table 14.6
Spending Priorities

	1960 Ike	1968 LBJ	1976 GRF	1980 JEC	1988 RWR	1992 GHWB
Primary costs						
Defense	52.2%	27.3%	24.1%	22.7%	27.3%	21.6%
Interest	7.5	14.2	7.2	8.9	14.3	14.4
Total	59.7%	41.4%	31.3%	31.6%	41.6%	36.0
Government	11.9	8.4	14.0	15.4	8.3	8.1
Education/services	1.9	2.9	5.1	5.4	2.9	3.1
Health/Medicaid	.9	4.2	4.1	3.9	4.2	6.5
Medicare	7.4	4.3	5.4	7.4	8.6	
Income Security	8.0	12.2	16.4	14.7	12.2	14.4
Social Security	12.6	20.6	19.9	20.0	20.6	20.8
Veterans	5.9	2.9	4.9	3.6	2.9	2.5
Total	100.0%	100.0%	100.0%	100.0%	100.0%	100.0
	(3)	(2)(3)	(3)	(3)	(3)	(2)

1 = peace; 2 = war; 3 = cold war

Source: Historical Tables 2007, 3.1

Given the world situation, Bush's allocation of fewer resources to *Defense* may not have been wise, but given budget pressures and the absence of the Cold War threat, it is understandable that Bush did a bit of cutting. At the end of his term, however, Bush had a very impressive active force of two million, only 10 percent lower than it was in 1988.

The elements of a healthy fiscal period did not materialize for Bush, and since his inherited cost structure was so prodigious,[37] and since Congress was unwilling to rework social programs, a large deficit was inevitable and public debt climbed to $2999.7 billion, as follows:

Table 14.7
Public Debt, 1992 (billions)

Event	Inherited 1988	Added 1989–92	Total 1992	%
World War I	$ 18.3	$	$ 18.3	.6%
Great Depression	24.5	24.5	.8	
World War II	142.5	142.5	4.8	
Korean War	6.6	6.6	.2	
Cold War	206.1	206.1	6.9	
Interest	248.4	38.1	286.5	9.6
Government	172.2	177.3	349.5	11.6
Human Resources	1235.9	718.0	1953.9	65.1
Treasury	-2.9	14.7	11.8	.4
Total	$2051.6	$948.1	$2999.7	100.0%

Source: Exhibits 1, 11, 12, 16

This was the thirteenth consecutive four-year deficit. Obviously something was wrong with the system, and with the people who were in control of it.

When elected officials over a long period demonstrate that they can't (or won't) handle the taxpayer's money wisely, their power to cause further harm should be curtailed. Added to the list of things to do, therefore, is the need to pass laws that limit congressional power — that require responsible budget behavior, which permits deficits only by a super-majority, and only after public debate about the emergency situation that requires the assumption of more debt.

Foreign policies of presidents are not the subject matter of this book and are mentioned only to the extent that they round out the profile of the man and relate to the budget deficit.

The Gulf War symbolizes Bush's international face. More than the victory itself, the challenge of organizing a response to Saddam Hussein, which included Arab nations not normally counted as friends of America and always counted as enemies of Israel, was one that he manfully accepted and skillfully accomplished.

Bush suffered unexpected revenue losses and costs that inflated his deficit. It is for precisely such domestic emergencies that the power to borrow should be used. And it is because emergencies will surely arise that the borrowing capacity of the nation should not be utilized for operating expenses. This is a lesson of history that some political leaders refuse to internalize.

Public debt *is not* in trouble because of highway problems, wars, banking emergencies and economic vagaries. The portions of expanded debt related to such things that were confronted by several modern presidents was ultimately affordable — under a sensible fiscal system those unfunded costs could have been repaid over time.

Public debt *is* in trouble because federal politicians will not cut operating expenses, especially *Human Resources*, to the limits of a reasonable revenue stream from a sensible tax system.

President Bush was not the stonewall of resistance to the spending ways of Congress that one might have preferred, but it would be the height of unfairness to lay blame for ballooning debt on his shoulders— as a president with no congressional support, he did what he could. On a four-year comparative basis, for example, he exercised his veto power at a rate comparable to Reagan's.[38]

Actually, long-departed President Lyndon Johnson and congressional leaders Sam Rayburn and Mike Mansfield had more to do with the 1989–92 deficit and therefore the climbing debt, than Bush did.

To openly propose spending and to fund it with an effective and transparent tax policy is, in a fiscal sense, to act responsibly. And the popularity that accompanies such an open approach to governance justly belongs to those who practice it.

Of the Republican presidents, and the congressional leaders who served in minority positions since the 1960s, only Ronald Reagan lifted his voice loud enough and effectively enough to awaken the people to the disgrace that our tax system had become and to the burden of debt that was piling up on a daily basis because of uncontrolled spending.

Bush was unable to maintain the kind of corrective momentum that his predecessor had begun. He didn't have the personality to pull it off; he wasn't motivated by the gut beliefs that triggered Reagan's actions.

George Bush met international responsibilities well; he was a gentleman who brought credit to the office; and he represented America honorably and efficiently in the international arena. Domestically, he was a victim of bad luck and some bad judgment, notably his tax increase.

15

William J. Clinton, 1993–1996

Governor, President

William Jefferson Clinton, born on August 19, 1946, in Hope, Arkansas, is the first president born after World War II. Harry S Truman was president when Clinton's mother, Virginia Cassidy Blythe, saw, for the first time, her president-to-be. Three months earlier the father, William Jefferson Blythe, died in an automobile accident.

Clinton was mostly supervised by grandparents for the first four years of his life because his mother went to New Orleans to earn a nursing certificate. She returned to Hope in 1950 and took charge of her son; later that year, when he was four years old, she married an automobile salesman, Roger Clinton.

The Clintons remained in Hope until 1953, when they moved to Hot Springs, Arkansas, where opportunities for work were better. The move improved their economic standing. Roger became a service manager in an automobile dealership; Virginia found employment as a nurse.

Clinton was seven. Dwight D. Eisenhower was president; public debt was $218.4 billion.[1]

Clinton's home life was difficult. His stepfather, a drinker, abused his wife; this caused strain between father and son that continued until Clinton was a student at Georgetown. His father died in 1967, his mother in 1994.

The Clintons were Baptists, but Bill Clinton received his early training in Catholic schools. Then, after two years, he transferred to the public school system of Hot Springs. Biographies state that he liked school and his grades were good.

Bill Clinton was in elementary school in 1956 when his mother had a second son, Roger Jr. At about the same time, he started to use "Clinton" as his surname and, when he was 15, he had his name formally changed.

Clinton was known as a musician in high school (he played the saxophone);

he was also academically and politically prominent. In 1963, he was a delegate to a citizenship training program for young people (American Legion Boys Nation) when he shook hands with President John Kennedy, an encounter that increased his already evident political ambition.

Clinton graduated from high school in 1964; Lyndon Johnson was president and his Great Society was taking its first baby steps into the world of the federal budget; public debt was $256.8 billion.

Clinton finished high school with the fourth-highest academic rating in his class. That plus his musical ability brought scholarships that took him to Georgetown University in Washington, D.C. His financial strain at Georgetown was eased with income he earned as an intern to Senator William Fulbright (D–AR).

Clinton majored in international affairs and he was class president during his first two years. After graduation (1968), he qualified for a Rhodes scholarship and he studied government for two years at Oxford, after which he entered Yale Law School. Apparently, scholarships again paid his way, assisted by income earned from part-time jobs.

During those years Clinton met Hillary Rodham, his wife-to-be, and he got his first taste of presidential politics as part of George McGovern's 1972 campaign against Richard Nixon. He graduated from law school in 1973 and returned to Arkansas.

Richard M. Nixon was president. Public debt was $340.9 billion, not yet reflecting the matured fruit of the Great Society.

Clinton joined the faculty at the University of Arkansas Law School, obviously a temporary position because politics was his game. It was a question of when, not if, he would seek political office.

He ran against John Paul Hammerschmidt in 1974, a Republican, for a seat in the House of Representatives. Clinton lost but in 1976 he ran for attorney general of Arkansas, and he won.

He was at it again in 1978, a man in a hurry running for the governor's job. Clinton won and became the youngest governor in the country, serving in 1979–80. Two years later he lost the job but he won it back again in 1982 and served for a decade (1983–92).

Clinton, as a founder of the Democratic Leadership Council and as chairman of the National Governor's Association, gained national attention; nevertheless, he was relatively unknown when in 1992 he entered the presidential sweepstakes against a field of national politicians and personalities with far more name recognition, including Governor Jerry Brown, Senator Bob Kerrey, Senator Tom Harkin, and others.[2]

Despite the odds and, especially, despite scandalous allegations that dealt with his sex life, Clinton won the nomination and, assisted by the third-party candidacy of Ross Perot, he won against President George Bush, 43 percent to 38 percent,[3] hardly a ringing endorsement. He and Vice President Albert Gore assumed office in 1993.

From the time of Clinton's birth, public debt was climbing. When as a teenager he shook hands with John Kennedy, standing nearby was Lyndon Johnson, who would create the Welfare State that had driven debt, under five presidents, to historic heights, most recently to $2999.7 billion, as follows:

Table 15.1
Public Debt 1992 (in billions of dollars)

	Total	%
World War One	$ 18.3	.6%
Great Depression:	24.5	.8
World War Two	142.5	4.8
Korean War	6.6	.2
Cold War	206.1	6.9
Interest	286.5	9.6
Government	349.5	11.6
Human Resources	1953.9	65.1
Treasury, net	11.8	.4
Total	$2999.7	100.0%

Source: Table 14.7 Chapter 14

There was no good news in the above table for the new president. Like those before him, he saw a mountain of debt and, according to recent financial reports, a budget out of control.

On the other hand, the power structure was apparently organized for accomplishment. Tom Foley (D–WA) and George Mitchell (D–ME) ran the House and Senate, respectively. Democrats ruled from top to bottom.[4]

Was this good news? Time would tell. But some were uncomfortable with the thought that those who had created and protected the growth of enormous debt were back in charge.

If Clinton placed a high value on lowering deficits (an uncertain proposition when applied to Clinton), then he must have noticed that the previous deficit was caused by unfunded costs in every cost center except Defense.

There was little he could do about *Interest* because he couldn't eliminate inherited debt, and he had no direct control over interest rates.

The numbers that greeted Clinton on arrival assured him that the road to a successful fiscal term in office would not be an easy one. His inherited cost structure was even worse than that which was thrust upon the previous two presidents.[5] A deficit seemed inevitable, barring some unforeseen miracle — one that would not be diminished by the charming, outgoing personality of the new president.

Government and *Human Resources* were cost centers over which Clinton had some influence. *Government* could be controlled; Reagan and Bush had done it; *Human Resources* presented a different problem. Clinton had little control over the time-honored entitlement costs that were breaking the bank. To make a dent in them would first require great persuasive powers, which Clinton had, and the will and the courage to use them, which he did not have.

Instead, given his history of disrespect for the military, he was more apt to reduce resources currently dedicated to *Defense*, despite global conditions that argued against that approach.

That would be the political battleground during Clinton's first term. History has demonstrated America's ability to conquer international tension and domestic emergencies. But did it still have the character to turn away from the enticements of a Welfare State?

That was the question that greeted Clinton when he entered the Oval Office. Would he bolster or weaken that character?

Perspectives

General

Clinton, young but well trained when he assumed the presidency, had behind him years of service in high leadership positions. To be sure, governing Arkansas was a long way from ruling the United States, but he had long since broken through the barriers imposed by state government. His horizons had long before gone beyond the needs of Arkansas, and he was accustomed to and comfortable with the processes of governance at the national level.

Clinton was not a "foreign policy" president in the sense that he was the obvious, energetic force and strategist. The Department of State held the limelight in international affairs relying upon him for handshaking duties. But there were a few carefully orchestrated and dramatic instances when he moved center stage.

The reputation of the United States, thanks to stunning victories in the Cold War and the Gulf War, was at its peak. Demands placed on the U.S. military during Clinton's watch were less dangerous, but readiness in an unsettled world was still the watchword. Tensions continued in the Middle East, North Korea was volatile, and Cuba and Haiti were chronic itches. China was unfriendly.

For some reason, such things didn't internalize with Clinton and, under his leadership, the size and the capability of the military kept shrinking.[6]

Breakaway states from the Soviet empire drew nervous glances from Europeans old enough to recall that an incident in Serbia had touched off World War I.

With the fall of the USSR, Yugoslavia disintegrated into ethnic squabbles. The crisis engendered by the breakup of Yugoslavia was essentially a European problem, but America was nevertheless pulled into the peacemaking process with troops and supports. It was a costly enterprise, using 20,000 U.S. troops, with no end in view.[7]

And the continued viability in Iraq of Saddam Hussein kept American ships and troops in the Middle East on the alert. A fly over system (mostly American) that patrolled north and south Iraq kept Hussein in his cage.

Clinton, seeking to duplicate President Carter's road to immortality (a negotiated peace between Israel and Egypt) tried to negotiate peace between Israel and the Palestinians; he failed.

Ties between the United States and the United Nations grew closer, in part because of shared concerns, but also because of an alleged tendency of the Clinton administration to adopt UN objectives as cornerstones of American foreign policy. Globalists liked this drift; nationalists were appalled by it.

Home Front

On domestic matters, Clinton bewildered some and frightened others. His attempt, led by his wife, Hillary, to federalize health care failed, to the relief of most Americans.

But the effort to do so was revealing.

It defined Clinton, from the first moments of his presidency, as one who sought an expanded role for government, a bad omen for a time that needed a president who would lead the effort to move in the opposite direction.

Clinton increased taxes even though he had promised to reduce them. Such a turnaround became commonplace during his presidency, a trait that didn't trouble most voters, or perhaps their failure to take offense simply proved once again that they don't care about, or listen to, the political dialogue of the day.

On the other side of the ledger, Clinton placed several women in high government posts (cabinet, Supreme Court), a continuation of a trend that had made more inclusive the administrations of recent presidents.

Clinton had significant impact on prevailing social attitudes because of the nature of his political support, but also because of his personal leanings.

The far left-wingers provided Clinton with warm and wealthy support, including endorsements and contributions from leading entertainment personalities — he enjoyed their company and he basked delightedly in their admiration.

As one of his earliest acts as president, he challenged the policy of banning homosexuals from the services. Opposition from Congress, the military and the people significantly altered his proposal, which eventually ended up as the "don't ask, don't tell policy" that exists today.

Clinton's approval rating dropped during his first two years, setting the stage for midterm congressional elections in which Democrats lost control of both houses of Congress.

The previous analysis of deficits has made it clear that the cost of the Welfare State is at the heart of the deficit problem. And since the first step in problem solving is problem identification, it was heartening to see the Republican-led 104th Congress address that core issue.

A symptom of this took place in 1996 when a welfare reform bill was passed, inadequate but a step in the right direction.

Serious discussions dealing with Medicare and Social Security reform were also held, something new to a Washington that had been dominated for decades by liberals. Capable men and women developed plans for a complete revision of the tax system, the albatross, despised by all but power-hungry politicians who had been squeezing the necks of taxpayers for decades.

Such investigations were hopeful signs. But they must be viewed with suspicion until they embrace programs that provide aid or income to everyone, including federal employees and non-citizens.

Unfortunately, and typically, the spotlight that shone on Social Security and Medicare did not shine with equal intensity on other programs that fall under the rubrics of *Government* or *Human Resources.*

Absent such a review, priorities cannot be set. And especially in a system that can't live within its income, priorities are essential.

The Republican Congress and the Democratic White House engaged in prolonged debate in 1995 over budget matters. Republicans won the substantive battle; controls were imposed and some costs were cut. But Clinton won the political battle.

By the end of 1995, Republicans looked like mean-spirited men determined to impose ruinous spending cutbacks without regard to consequences; Clinton posed as protector of the people — defender of "investments" in health and children, and in America's future. He was believed; his popularity surged.

Clinton supported the expansion of government, but because of his cleverness and the conservatives' clumsiness, he was given some of the credit for the general fiscal and economic improvements that came from the new conservative agenda.

Because of this, many believe Clinton demonstrated he was a superior fiscal manager. Others say he is not driven by deep-seated principles that mandate behavior.

Whatever or whoever he really is, Clinton, instinctively liberal, has a reputation as a centrist largely because he, like Gorbachev in Russia, bent before the inevitable and then took credit for the consequences.

GDP in 1996 was 23 percent higher than it was four years before, the lowest four-year increase since the early 1960s.[8] The same can be said for federal revenue, which increased by 25.3 percent, well below the average increase of 36.2 percent of the nine previous presidential terms.[9]

Had federal income increased at the normal rate, it would have amounted to $5675.2 billion or $455.7 billion more than actual. Any fair analysis of the deficit in 1993–96 must take this comparative revenue shortfall into consideration.

Clinton reacted to this with the highest tax increase in history,[10] a policy that could increase short-term revenue flow, but one that could also have dire long-term consequences.

Two presidents in a row (Bush, Clinton) had increased taxes as a remedy for a slowdown in the Reagan boom (13 years of revenue growth and still ongoing), a boom triggered in the first place by a low-tax policy. Those tax increases, in effect, reversed the positive impact that Reagan's medicines had on the private sector. The long-term impact of this aggressive tax policy was, to some, worrisome.

The Misery Index did not worsen under Clinton during the subject period,[11] but there was a change in the mix of the ingredients that worked to the president's political advantage.

The interest rate is the element of the Misery Index that has the least emotional impact on taxpayers who, by and large, are oblivious to economic changes that do not immediately affect them or their friends. On the other hand, changes in inflation and unemployment rates are regularly reported by the media, and they are felt in the homes, neighborhoods and supermarkets of America — they are politically sensitive. Both rates were down as Clinton's first term neared its end, which bolstered his popularity.

Personal income per capita was $24.7 thousand in 1996, an increase of 20 percent — a smaller increase than workers had enjoyed during the three most recent four-year presidential terms — the tax load per capita increased modestly.[12]

Public debt grew 24.5 percent under Clinton,[13] a slower rate than usual. Growth in debt during wartime is expected — for it to do so during a relatively calm period is cause for alarm, more so when it grows faster than GDP.

America needed, when Clinton took office, a hard-eyed realist who could clearly see the cause of deficits and climbing debt and who had a broad vision of how to attack the problem. And America needed a president who continued the high personal standards of behavior that characterized the previous four presidents, Ford, Carter, Reagan and Bush. Clinton had the tools of success at his disposal — a devoted Congress under Democratic control.

History will record that he didn't meet the tests of his time.

SUPREME COURT[14]

The Supreme Court in 1993 had one judge, Byron White, appointed by a Democratic president. On the surface, this appeared to be judicial heaven to those who oppose activist judges.

But history proves the philosophy of the appointing president is a poor indicator for how a judge will perform. And, to be more precise, it is a poor indicator when the appointing president is a Republican.

Democratic presidents do better. It is highly doubtful, for example, that liberals regret the appointment of jurists like Clark, Douglas, Frankfurter, Black and Marshall. On the other hand, jurists like Brennan, Stevens, Souter and Blackmun haunt conservatives who ultimately could depend upon only three men to show judicial restraint, Rehnquist, Scalia and Thomas. Other Republican appointees like Kennedy and O'Connor, presumably conservatives, were actually loose cannons.

Chief Justice Rehnquist heard 133 cases in 1993–96, 68 percent more than he heard in the previous four years, and ten times more than Chief Justice Warren heard during the four years prior to the Johnson-led second American Revolution.[15]

This increased case load is, broadly speaking, attributable to three factors:

- Court behavior and decisions are considerably influenced by the activities of previous Courts. For decades, liberal-dominated Courts had meddled into affairs normally handled on the state and local level. As a result, cases that once went in fifty directions to fifty states now went to Washington.
- Activist groups prefer to concentrate on one federal court system as opposed to bringing issues to many state courts.
- The election of a liberal president, who for his success depends upon the support of special interest groups, energizes those organizations to come forth with their causes.

There was little Rehnquist could do once the dikes were opened, and he restricted himself to handling cases efficiently, and to the attempt to put a lid on an already bad situation. To assist him with this he had two new judges, Stephen Breyer and Ruth Ginsburg. A thumbnail sketch of both appears below:

- Ruth Ginsburg — Ginsburg graduated first in her class from Cornell. She married soon after graduation and followed her husband into army life for two years before returning to school, this time to Harvard. Her husband's illness and other factors caused Ginsburg to leave Harvard and move to New York, and to complete her law education at Columbia. She graduated at the top of her class. After graduation, Ginsburg remained close to the academic community. She also joined and represented feminist causes before the U.S. Supreme Court, and she served the ACLU as a director. Jimmy Carter in 1981 appointed Ginsburg to the U.S. Court of Appeals, Washington, D.C., and in 1993 President Clinton raised her to the U.S. Supreme Court to replace the resigning Byron White. Ginsburg, a certified activist when nominated, has functioned as such on the bench. From an ideological standpoint, her appointment was a win for liberals; conservatives would miss occasional alliances with Justice White on key social issues.
- Stephen Breyer — Breyer, after graduating from Stanford, won a scholarship to Oxford. Law school was next at Harvard after which he clerked for Associate Justice Arthur Goldberg (1964–65). The Justice Department for a few years, marriage, teaching at Harvard and occa-

sional assignments in Washington preceded a seat on a federal appeals court before President Clinton chose him in 1994 to succeed retiring Justice Blackmun. From a conservative standpoint, Breyer was worse than Blackmun, but at least he was true to his colors—nobody expected him to be much different than he was.

A sample of cases heard by Rehnquist's team of unpredictable jurists provides insights about issues of concern and about the attitudes of recently appointed judges.

Bray v. Alexander, 1993. Jane Bray and others conducted demonstrations around abortion clinics in Washington, D.C. The clinics claimed that in so doing demonstrators were denying women their right to an abortion. The district court agreed and it ordered the demonstrators to desist, and to pay the clinics' legal fees. The issue: Did the demonstration interfere with women's rights? In a 5–4 decision (Stevens, Blackmun, O'Connor and Souter dissenting) the Court supported the demonstrators. The most interesting position in this case was taken by O'Connor. She emerged as a pro-abortion jurist with strong feminist views that overcame judicial restraint.

Veronia v. Acton, 1995. A school district discovered that illegal drugs were being used by student athletes. Research indicated that risk of injury increased in such a situation. The school adopted a random test program as a protection process. One student refused to be tested; he was dropped from the football team. The issue: Does the drug-testing program violate the search and seizure provisions of the Fourth Amendment? In a 6–3 decision (Stevens, Souter and O'Connor dissenting) the Court supported the drug test. This case brings several reactions. Why does the Supreme Court bother with such trivia? Is there no such thing as local authority anymore? Curiously, Ginsburg joined the majority; O'Connor dissented.

Rosenberger v. Univ. of Virginia, 1995. A university provided funding for secular student-run magazines; it refused to fund a Christian publication. The issue: Does university policy abuse the First Amendment rights of its Christian staff members? In a 5–4 decision (Ginsburg, Stevens, Souter and Breyer dissenting), the Court ruled that university policy was unconstitutional—if it chooses to support some speech, it must support all speech. The split decision once again demonstrated how divisive religious issues were in the country, and on the Court.

U.S. v. Va. Military Institute, 1996. VMI had a long tradition of male-only students. The United States brought suit claiming the policy was unconstitutional. Virginia responded by offering to build a VWI for women. The issue: Is the offer to operate a VWI responsive to the Fourteenth Amendment's equal protection clause? In a 7–1 decision (Scalia dissenting) the Court ruled VMI's policy was unconstitutional. This decision marked the end of single-sex colleges.

After the appointment of Ginsburg and Breyer, the Court was stable for more than a decade. And the shape of rulings to come had formed: Rehnquist, Scalia and Thomas would resist activism; Souter, Stevens, Breyer and Ginsburg would promote it; Kennedy and O'Connor would swing most decisions one way or the other.

SOCIETY[16]

William Clinton was the first president to emerge from the Woodstock[17] generation, which was 25 to 30 years old when he became president. He was their moral revolution realized; he was their representative against the repressive forces that frowned upon and inhibited their lifestyle.

Politics, always a bare-knuckle game, became unusually personal under Clinton, not because he sponsored it, but simply because he is what he is. His history of sexual liaisons that surfaced during the presidential campaign only confirmed to the Woodstock generation that Clinton was one of them.

Significant social changes continued under Clinton. Marriage was in bad shape when he came to Washington and it got worse in 1993–96, the most obvious sign of this being the steady increase in those who never married, and the surge in those who openly lived together outside of marriage.

The public education system had leveled off at a point of mediocrity that was reflected in the relatively stagnant SAT scores, assisted no doubt by a 53 percent increase in the use of illegal drugs by high school seniors.[18]

Incidents of violent crime remained relatively constant, but the nation's prison population increased by 45 percent from 1990 to 1995.

These selected statistics indicate that social trends were continuing to drift in the same direction.

Change in Public Debt

Presidents Reagan and Bush inherited a cost structure that almost guaranteed a deficit. President Clinton was in the same boat and he either knew it, or he can be held responsible for knowledge of it.

Consequently, if he wanted to avoid or minimize deficits, his primary fiscal objective should have been the same as, say, Reagan's while, at the same time, he maintained an adequate military force that equated with the needs of the times.

To achieve a reasonable fiscal performance he needed:

- Peace. A military buildup to face the equivalent, say, of a Soviet Union threat, would break the bank.
- Normal revenue. The previous nine four-year presidential terms had produced an average revenue increase of 36.2 percent.[19]

- Cost control. Reduction in the cost of existing social programs would be welcome but inadequate. The pressing need was to dump duplicative inefficient programs; to prioritize and restructure the others, including federal retirement/health plans.
- Clamp down. The plate of social goodies was overflowing and unafford-able — nothing should be added.

These were not optional priorities; they were the mandated attitudes of any serious-minded president who hoped to reestablish logic into the federal budget system.

A review of transactions of the period will reveal whether or not Clinton was a serious-minded president, keeping in mind that he lost Congress to Republicans in the 1994 election, and the budgets after 1994 had to be approved by his political opponents.

Table 15.2
Transactions (in billions of dollars)

		1993–96		1989–92
Taxes		$ 5219.5		$ 4166.8
Less:				
Defense	$1110.4		$1174.6	
Interest	875.1		747.4	
Total		1985.5		1922.0
Net		$ 3234.0		$ 2244.8
Less:				
Government	$ 384.6		$ 528.1	
Human Resources	3579.0		2650.1	
Total		3963.6		3178.2
Surplus/deficit		$ -729.6		$ -933.4
Debt, beginning		-2999.7		-2051.6
Total		$-3729.3		$-2985.0
Adjustment*		-4.8		-14.7
Debt, Ending		$-3734.1		$-2999.7

*Treasury cannot be exact when it finances a budget deficit and the difference between what is needed and the value of securities traded inevitably produces a relatively small variance.

Source: Historical Tables 2007, 1.1, 3.1

Under Reagan and Bush, remaining revenue after deducting primary costs was less than the cost of the remaining two cost centers during the previous period. This meant that cost growth in *Government* and *Human Resources* was not possible in the context of a balanced budget — that some level of deficit was guaranteed until the cost of *Government* decreased and the cost of *Human Resources* was reorganized and cut.

Clinton's situation was not as dire, but it also foretold a sizable deficit absent radical budget reforms.

TAXES

Clinton faced huge deficits and a revenue stream that was not (and could not be) adequate to cover the cost of a bloated government.

Unlike Reagan, who faced the same problem, he saw higher tax rates as the road to higher federal revenues and deficit elimination instead of choosing as his *primary* economic tool the power to stimulate private economic activity through tax cuts.

Partly as a result of Clinton's aggressive tax policy, there was an immediate positive impact on the revenue stream — in 1996, federal revenue was 33 percent higher than it was in 1992, and in 2000 it was 39 percent higher than it was in 1996.[20]

Clinton's high tax policies were, arguably, politically imposed. Democrats historically take advantage of high deficit years (whatever the reason) to impose higher tax rates that, thereafter, they protect.

The same situation existed here. Deficits were large; they could be blamed on inadequate revenue. And a huge tax increase could be sold as part of an "economic recovery" package.

Actually, the Reagan boom, after a brief slowdown in 1991, was continuing in 1992 (GDP growth 5.1 percent[21]), and the medicine needed was patience and the protection of it, not a tax increase that sent the wrong message to the private sector.

The result?

Clinton's higher tax rates arguably eroded the triggers of economic growth that Reagan's low tax policies had implanted until, in 2000, recession clobbered George W. Bush like an economic sledgehammer.

The lesson?

Confiscatory tax rates may yield enough revenue flow to keep one or two four-year presidencies afloat, but eventually they minimize or destroy incentives that make the free economy vibrant and growing.

In addition to the general tax increase, the automatic payroll tax increase continued to operate under the radar. Tax revenue during the subject period increased 1.25 times,[22] well under the average increase for the nine previous presidents. Had its increase been average (1.362 times),[23] revenue would have been $5675.2 billion, or $455.7 billion more than actual. Such a shortfall must, and will, be considered when the deficit for the period is analyzed.

DEFENSE

Before appraising Clinton's approach to military matters, it is useful to examine the field. What did he know, and when did he know it?

Clinton assumed office in 1993. Certainly he was made aware of the most important events that took place during the previous decade that had current relevance to national defense matters. And stimulation to get up to speed on such things should have reached crescendo pitch when, during the month following his inauguration, a group inspired by Osama bin Laden bombed the World Trade Center in New York City, killing six and injuring 1,000 Americans—a tragedy that could have been, if better executed, a catastrophe.[24]

A review of similar terrorist incidents would have revealed several things to the president:

- There are more than a billion Muslims to be found in significant numbers all over the globe — the largest Muslim nation, for example, is in (of all places) Indonesia. About 83 percent of Muslims are Sunnis. Shiites (16 percent), the largest minority group, are found mostly in Iran, Iraq and Lebanon.[25]
- Muslims can be militarily mobilized under the banner of religion more than any other group, reminiscent of the political power of Catholics in the twelfth and thirteenth centuries.
- The global reach of Islam (the religion of Muslims) is such that the possibility of a culture war between it and the Western world must inform all relations with Muslim nations.
- OPEC, an organization of Arabian states, is the major supplier of oil to the Western world.
- Muslim nations in the Middle East are either controlled by radical Muslims or by political leaders who live in constant fear of radical groups in their midst.
- From 1980 through 1988, the American airline business was hit hard by hijackings (Pan Am and TWA are, for example, out of business).
- American embassies were bombed; American troops were bushwhacked throughout the Middle East and in Europe.
- Hizbullah, a Shia terrorist group based in Lebanon and sponsored by Iran and Syria, was the major threat to Americans stationed in the Middle East.
- In April 1986 President Reagan ordered the bombing of Libya; after that action, plane hijackings practically disappeared.
- In December 1988 (probably as an act of retaliation) Libya organized the bombing of another American airliner, an act that killed 270 people. Libyans who did the deed were charged and convicted in a Scottish court.[26]

Terrorist activity declined sharply thereafter until in 1993 Clinton assumed office — then things began to go the other way.

- During his first four years, Osama bin Laden, the brains behind the WTC incident, emerged as the major threat who, in addition to deadly activities within Saudi Arabia, had the reach to directly harm the United States.

- Hizbullah retained its position as the most efficient killer of Americans in the Middle East.
- Iraq, like Syria, was disclosed as the sponsor of the terrorist group led by Mohammed Rashid, the killer who operated from Greece to Hawaii.
- Iran continued as the major financier of Hamas (Palestine) and Hizbullah (Lebanon), the organizations most responsible for the failure to negotiate peace in the region.

From the above it can be concluded that Clinton's world was not a safe or a peaceful one; normal reaction to data on hand, and to the potential it represented would have been to retain, add to or redesign the military capability of the nation. But Clinton did not see terrorism; he saw crimes. He did not see terrorists; he saw criminals. He did not see war; he saw courtrooms.

In due course, some of these criminals/terrorists were captured and jailed in the United States or elsewhere. But bombers in Hawaii, Greece, Scotland, New York and elsewhere were simply agents who could, and who were, quickly replaced by others while, in the background, the terrorist groups who hired such people were not only untouched, they were unrecognized for what they were — the most serious threat to the United States since Hitler.

Clinton's disdain for the threat was dramatically evident in his handling of the military during the period.

- He was the first modern president to reduce the budget of the *Defense* cost center.[27] As a percent of GDP and of spending, Clinton's military budget was the lowest in modern history.
- Clinton dropped the size of active duty personnel by 25 percent (an action his successor would pay for, dearly).
- In addition to the cutback in personnel, the military budget for maintenance, procurement and research was similarly reduced, leaving the impression that the organization was being stripped of capability, much as Harry Truman had done in 1948, and something Eisenhower had to correct in order to show a strong military face to North Korea (and to the Soviet Union and China), which was key to ending the Korean War.[28]

Someone in desperate search of a rationale to defend a president who lowers his guard during a time of peril can point to the budget mess. Strictly from that point of view, lower spending in *Defense* could cut substantially into the inherited deficit, *if* all other cost centers operated prudently.

Had *Defense* increased at the same rate as revenue it would have amounted to $1471.4 billion[29] — more than the actual cost. This cost center, therefore, made no contribution to the deficit for the period, and by not using its full availability it passed along to other cost centers an improved opportunity to operate in the black and to produce, at the least, a smaller deficit.

The Cold War was over; the Gulf War was won. But North Korea with its drive for nuclear weapons was a real threat, especially when mixed with the attitudes and capacities of China.

Russia was tamed but armed. Iraq, Iran, Syria, Libya and other countries in the Gulf region represented danger. The Serb/Bosnian conflict was active and continuing. Terrorists were active from Russia to the Philippines.

When conflicts of any magnitude arose in the world, America was often called upon to serve in some capacity that usually involved the use of expensive resources.

Was this a time for a cutback in military spending?

Interest

Like presidents before him since debt began to steadily climb since the 1960s, Clinton had to live with the interest cost of inherited debt. His hope concerning it had to be that the rate of debt increase would be lower during his four years, and that interest rates would remain steady, or decline. He inherited a good interest rate that continued during his first year, but thereafter it climbed.[30]

Had *Interest* increased at the same rate as revenue, it would have amounted to $936.2 billion — more than actual. This cost center continued to dangerously increase but, during the subject period, it was fully funded.

The size of *Interest*, funded or unfunded, is a major problem. Its 1993–96 cost was about 80 percent of *Defense*. It cost more than twice as much as *Government* — about 25 percent of the cost of the Welfare State (*Human Resources*). Its cost had become ridiculous.

And *Interest* is something else too — something unmentionable.

The usual cry is heard every year at budget time to adjust *Defense*, Social Security, and Medicare as serious-minded politicians expound on their proposals to redo these programs, but not a word is said about *Interest*, a cost that literally dwarfs most line items in the budget.

America paid $67 billion in 1996 to all the troops[31]; in contract, Interest cost $241 billion[32] — 3.6 times more than the amount paid to the troops.

National perspective? Where art thou? How can political leaders remain mute before such fiscal looniness?

Who are these people who run the U.S. government? How can they tolerate such demented fiscal relationships? Is common sense against the law in Washington?

Government

Primary cost centers did not use available revenues; cost cutback was not demanded of the other cost centers in the context of a balanced budget for the first time since the first term of President Reagan.[33]

Had the cost of *Government* increased at the approved rate, its cost would have been $537.4 billion — more than actual cost. This cost center, therefore, made no contribution to the deficit for the period.

From whence does this unusual cost performance come? Analysis will disclose.

Table 15.3
Government (in billions of dollars)

	1993–96	1989–92	% Change
Energy	$ 17.2	$ 12.9	33.2%
Natural Resources/Environment	85.0	71.9	18.2
Transportation	152.1	121.5	25.2
Community/regional development	40.8	27.5	48.4
International affairs	64.1	55.4	15.7
Science/space/technology	66.5	59.7	11.4
Agriculture	54.5	59.3	-8.1
Justice	63.9	46.2	38.3
General	51.1	44.4	15.1
Total	$ 595.2	$ 498.8	19.3%
Commerce & housing credit*	— 52.7	181.8	129.0
Total	$ 542.5	$ 680.6	-20.2%
Offsetting receipts	-157.9	-152.5	3.5
Net	$ 384.6	$ 528.1	-27.2%

*Made up of earnings from various federal housing and other programs—subject to major changes from year to year relative to market conditions. (Historical Tables 2007, 3.2)

Source: Historical Tables 2007, 3.1

The general performance in this cost center was commendable, but it is usually the case that analysis will uncover interesting aberrations.

There were two sides, for example, to the Savings and Loan scandal. The first was the cost side, which Bush took (bad luck), and the other was the revenue side that came to Clinton (good luck) as various assets possessed by the government were sold. This provided Clinton with a huge windfall of revenue.

But apart from that benefit, the cost center operated efficiently at a rate of increase (19.3 percent) lower than the rate of revenue growth that could be reasonably expected in a four-year period.[34]

Three items in the body of the above table deserve comment: Energy, Community and Justice.

Energy supply costs increased sharply in 1992 and they remained so for three more years.[35] This resulted in unfunded costs for the period, but there is no sign here of frivolous spending. Consistent with the theme of this book, why these amounts were spent was not probed, but the decision to do so under current budget circumstances appears to be a reasonable one.

With a Democratic president and a Democratic Congress in charge for two years, one tends to look with suspicion at any line item with the word

"Community" in it. But in this case increased cost had nothing to do with give-aways. The cost blip was associated with disaster relief and associated insur-ance. Similar to Energy, there is no sign of frivolous spending here.[36]

Readers by this time have become familiar with unfunded Justice costs, which were predominantly affected by the increased need for law enforcement in a society that had lost its moral consensus and by the increased alertness of the government relative to the capture and trial of terrorists who, under Clin-ton, were treated as criminals.

A cost-conscious Republican Party in 1995 assumed control of Congress. The cost of *Government* in 1994 was $108 billion; in 1995, it was $88 billion; in 1996, $95 billion,[37] a sign of progress; a ray of hope.

HUMAN RESOURCES

Under the flow-through method of revenue allocation in play in this book, all unused allocations to other cost centers became available to *Human Resources*, which in this case provided it with growth income, modest in size, but larger than it had been during the most recent four-year administra-tions.[38]

Had this cost center restricted itself to available revenue, its cost would have been $2849.4 billion or $729.6 billion less than actual. To that extent, *Human Resources* is responsible for the deficit.

This cost center, the source of social programs, gives comfort to liberals; to conservatives it is the home of unaffordable programs that drive the deficit, expand the debt and threaten the fiscal viability of the United States.

When will high spenders place country first and ambition second? When will they begin to relate goals to available resources? Were there signs of this happening under Clinton?

We shall see.

Increases in Unemployment and Veterans can be dispensed with as spend-ing that is specifically and uncontrollably related to the events of the times.

But this is not true of the other line items that represent the cost of vol-untary programs pressed into the budget based upon a vision that did not con-template such mundane considerations as affordability.

There is no sign of reform in this table; there is no sign of a presidential hand holding back the spenders; there is no sign yet of the positive influence of a Republican Congress.

But there are plenty of signs of business as usual.

The first can't-deny-it-exists-sign of the change in America from Eisen-hower's free nation to Johnson's Welfare State came in 1971 (Nixon) when, in the middle of the Vietnam War and the Cold War, Washington spent more on *Human Resources* than it did on *Defense*.

That's when the brakes should have been applied; that's when America's

Table 15.4
Human Resources (in billions of dollars)

	1993–96	1989–92	% Change
Education, training, services	$ 202.6	$ 164.0	23.5%
Health/Medicaid	441.3	266.8	65.4
Income Security*	752.7	549.1	37.1
Social Security	1309.7	1037.8	26.2
Medicare	609.4	406.6	49.9
Unemployment compensation	115.0	101.2	13.6
Veterans	148.3	124.6	19.0
Total	$3579.0	$2650.1	35.1%

*Minus unemployment compensation (from 1965–68 on)

Note: Major federal programs since the 1960s— Food Stamps 1961 (pilot), Food Stamps 1964, Medicaid 1965, Student Aid 1966, Medicare 1967, Coal Miners Benefits 1970, Commodity Donations 1973, Supplementary Security Income 1974, Supplemental Feeding 1976, Earned Income Tax Credit 1976, Legal Services 1976, Energy Assistance 1977

Source: Historical Tables 2007, 3.1

patriotic politicians should have asked: "What are we doing to this wonderful country of ours?"

Other significant landmarks on America's march to mediocrity took place on Clinton's watch:

- In 1996, *Human Resources* was more expensive than running the entire 1996 military establishment for more than three years.
- In 1996, *Human Resources* was more expensive than the entire budget of the United States in 1985 — just eleven years earlier.
- In 1996, the *entire* cost of *Government* was $95 billion. Four *individual* line items in the *Human Resources* cost center were more expensive — Health (including Medicaid), Income Security, Medicare and Social Security.
- In 1996, Social Security alone was more expensive than *Defense, and it had been since 1993.*

Social Security was now so huge that its rate of change was coming down to earth, but the amount of change was crippling.

Health, Income Security and Medicare continued to run wild under Clinton, increasing at rates that no reasonably predictable revenue could long afford.

Perhaps it is fair to say that every president is ultimately judged not so much on what he does as on how he reacts to the demands of his time.

SUMMARY OF DEFICIT ALLOCATIONS

Despite the additional revenue available to *Government* and *Human Resources*, the deficit for the period was over $700 billion, as follows:

Table 15.5
Summary of Deficit — 1993–1996 (in billions of dollars)

Cost Center	Amount
Defense	$
Interest	
Government	
Human Resources	729.6
Total	$729.6

Sources: Exhibits 1, 11–2, 16

If cutbacks had not taken place in military spending and if the massive and nonrecurring cost break not materialized in the line item Commerce (within the Government cost center — Table 15.3), Clinton's deficit would have approached or exceeded one trillion dollars because he did nothing to tame the deficit machine, *Human Resources.*

Clinton's first term deficit of $729.6 billion must not be left without noting that his increased revenue was below normal (estimated at $456 billion). Had this not been the case, the deficit would have been about $300 billion, all other things being equal.

Despite a massive tax increase, and the above-mentioned cost breaks, huge deficits and their fundamental cause were still on the table when Clinton waged his second presidential campaign against a weak opponent, Sen. Robert Dole (R–KS), and he won with 49 percent of the vote.

Ross Perot, the minority candidate who had made possible Clinton's 1992 victory over George Bush with a meager 43 percent of the popular vote, was also a factor in 1996, but not to the degree that it made a difference in the outcome.

Conclusion

Lucky presidents get to choose most of their agendas when they enter office, but most are forced to deal with the crises of their time and they are content to add a few changes to the national face that might distinguish them from the pack.

So it was with William Clinton. He soon learned, for example, Americans did not elect him to take another giant leap into socialism by nationalizing the nation's healthcare system.

But he didn't learn this soon enough. And before he woke up, Republicans won control of the Congress.

Ordinarily, such a shift in congressional control would have been bad news for a Democrat, followed by an ineffective presidency. But these were strange times. Continuing Democratic control would have assured continuing deficits of back-breaking style that, eventually, would hang on the skeleton of Clinton's heritage with all the sparkle of a wet dish rag.

On the other hand, a conservative Congress could force him to do things that eventually would earn him the reputation of being an even-handed, middle of the road politician (something he was not), an image he cultivated and enlarged upon after his presidency.

And that's what happened after the 1994 election, too late to stop things already in motion, but early enough to be felt in the final two years of the subject period.

Changes in spending priorities could be seen in 1993–96, some of them new and all of them disturbing.

Table 15.6
Spending Priorities

	1960 Ike	1968 LBJ	1976 GRF	1980 JEC	1988 RWR	1992 GHWB	1996 WJC
Primary costs							
Defense	52.2%	27.3%	24.1%	22.7%	27.3%	21.6%	17.0%
Interest	7.5	14.2	7.2	8.9	14.3	14.4	15.4
Total	59.7%	41.4%	31.3%	31.6%	41.6%	36.0	32.4
Government	11.9	8.4	14.0	15.4	8.3	8.1	6.1
Education/services	1.9	2.9	5.1	5.4	2.9	3.1	3.1
Health/Medicaid	.9	4.2	4.1	3.9	4.2	6.5	7.7
Medicare		7.4	4.3	5.4	7.4	8.6	11.2
Income Security	8.0	12.2	16.4	14.7	12.2	14.4	14.7
Social Security	12.6	20.6	19.9	20.0	20.6	20.8	22.4
Veterans	5.9	2.9	4.9	3.6	2.9	2.5	2.4
Total	100.0%	100.0%	100.0%	100.0%	100.0%	100.0%	100.0%
	(3)	(2)(3)	(3)	(3)	(3)	(2)	(1)

1 = peace; 2 = war; 3 = cold war
Source: Historical Tables 2007, 3.1

The Clinton cutback in resources dedicated to the military, during a time of mounting danger to the United States, is a perfect example of the caliber of thinking that has controlled Washington since the 1960s, and it gives life to the old bromide: *It isn't the people who are bad, it's their leaders.*

Judging by his actions, Clinton's three major objectives were:

• To increase taxes.
• To champion homosexual rights, particularly in the military.
• To nationalize health insurance.

He achieved his first objective; his attempts to achieve the other two won him in 1994 a Republican Congress.

Despite his tax increases, despite his cutback in *Defense,* and despite substantial cost breaks that came his way, public debt in 1993–96 increased to $3734.1 billion, as follows:

Table 15.7
Public Debt, 1996 (billions)

Event	Inherited 1992	Added 1993–96	Total 1996	%
World War I	$ 18.3	$	$ 18.3	.5%
Great Depression	24.5		24.5	.6
World War II	142.5		142.5	3.8
Korean War	6.6		6.6	.2
Cold War	206.1		206.1	5.5
Interest	286.5		286.5	7.7
Government	349.5		349.5	9.3
Human Resources	1953.9	729.6	2683.5	72.0
Treasury	11.8	4.8	16.6	.4
Total	$2999.7	$734.4	$3734.1	100.0%

Source: Exhibits 1, 11, 12, 16

This was the fourteenth consecutive four-year presidency to generate a deficit,[39] an institutionalized fiscal cancer that was, among other things, making it impossible for a sitting president to operate with confidence in foreign affairs.

The dilemma can be summed up this way. Of the total debt in 1996, the unfunded cost of the Welfare State accounted for most of it, and most of the unfunded *Interest* was rooted in the same cause. In short, had the growth in social programs conformed to the nation's ability to pay, there would be no debt crisis, or national security crisis in the United States.

Clinton's character is not the subject matter of this book. Nobody will ever nominate him as a great moral leader. Myths about him will not grow, as they did around George Washington. Nevertheless, he was in 1996 reelected by a larger margin than before. Why?

- Clinton's opponent, Robert Dole (R–KS) was personally colorless in a television age, and he failed to make the available economic case against Clinton.
- Clinton was charismatic in a television age, especially to females, with political talent and a knack for expressing his views in the language of conservatives. On the stump, for example, he could sound as conservative as William F. Buckley, the renowned pundit.

Clinton emerged from his first term clearly defined as a liberal in both social and economic matters, with the dangerous ability to phrase ideas in ways that made him sound conservative. He was, arguably, the worst possible choice for a country whose economy and culture were in decline and whose debt was out of control.

But he looked good. He was the hero of the Woodstock generation; he survived the first four years.

16

William J. Clinton, 1997–2000

Second-Term President

President Clinton faced an array of major problems as he began his second term in office. But before discussing them, it is useful to comment upon the person who, more than any political opponent, would add immeasurably to the difficulty of his task as president.

Himself!

Clinton, similar to Nixon, brought serious personality flaws to the Oval Office that were poisonous to the productive problem-solving environment that he desperately needed.

With Nixon it was an attitude toward those who opposed him in the media, or in politics, that made him chronically suspicious, constantly insecure and, ultimately, too willing to test or to break the law in order to gain political advantage.

With Clinton, it was a juvenile libido that neither marriage nor the fear of career destruction was strong enough to tame.

It isn't the role of this book to probe the Clinton scandals, sexual or otherwise. But his behavior interfered with his ability to concentrate on his job, something Americans had the right to expect. For that reason, the major activities of the Clintons that served as distractions of consequence deserve mention.

- — When Clinton was governor of Arkansas his wife Hillary was a partner with the Rose law firm. Both were involved with a real estate deal, later to be known as the Whitewater scandal. This scandal continued throughout most of Clinton's two terms in office. Fifteen people, including two friends of the Clintons, and the governor of Arkansas were convicted of crimes. The final independent counsel, Robert Ray, in October 2000 announced that the Clintons had not "knowingly participated in a criminal act."

- — Jennifer Flowers claimed a 12-year affair with Clinton that nearly derailed his 1992 presidential campaign.
- — Paula Jones sued Clinton in 1994 for sexual harassment. She persisted in her cause until, in November 1998, Clinton paid her $850,000 to drop the charges. As collateral damage to this case he first lost his license to practice law in Arkansas and, as a result of Supreme Court action, he later surrendered his license permanently.
- — Monica Lewinsky was 22 when she went to work in the White House in 1995; she entered a sexual relationship with Clinton until, in 1996, she was transferred to the Pentagon.
- — Several other claims accusing Clinton of improper sexual conduct were raised and then dropped during his tenure in the White House.

Other scandals diverting an unknown amount of executive attention included Travelgate (improper behavior in the White House travel office), Filegate (improper use of personnel files allegedly for political purposes), fundraising practices and the use of the White House in a demeaning way.

Clinton, for example, hosted 938 overnight guests in the White House, including hundreds of contributors. His White House politicking was not illegal or, as a general proposition, unusual. But his systematic use of the White House to reward supporters went far beyond what others had done in the past. One pundit said: "It's like the difference between someone who likes to have a cocktail before dinner ... and a guy who downs a fifth every night."[1]

By contrast, President George H. W. Bush had 284 overnight guests, which included only a few major contributors; Reagan's family and a few close friends were the only overnight guests; a Carter spokesman said that Carter wouldn't even consider such a thing as making guests out of contributors; a presidential historian said of Clinton's White House practices: "It's the selling of the White House."

The scandals were many, but the ones that haunted Clinton all the way to an impeachment trial in the Senate were Whitewater, Paula Jones and Monica Lewinsky. But as troublesome as they were, the unlisted actions were, perhaps, the most important. They put the heat into the impeachment proceedings. And they were not presented to the Senate for a very good reason: They were personal not illegal.

Yes, he lied; yes, he obstructed justice; yes, he acted in a courtroom as no lawyer should, and for that he was disbarred for life.

So it was a beleaguered Clinton who faced the problems of his age in 1997, and a battered Clinton who had to deal with them on a daily basis for four years.

For a man with a healthy home life to which he could retire and rejuvenate, his was a momentous task; for one without such a blessing, the beginning public debt and all it portended must have seemed mountain high.

Table 16.1
Public Debt 1997 (in billions of dollars)

	Total	%
World War I	$ 18.3	.5%
Great Depression:	24.5	.6
World War II	142.5	3.8
Korean War	6.6	.2
Cold War	206.1	5.5
Interest	286.5	7.7
Government	349.5	9.3
Human Resources	2683.5	72.0
Treasury, net	16.6	.4
Total	$3734.1	100.0%

Source: Table 15.7 Chapter 15

The contents of this table gave Clinton little cause for relief, but it should have focused his attention.

World War II, the Great Depression, the Korean War and the Cold War were related to events that were over and done with. And there was only one thing about *Interest* that demanded his attention, to wit: He must pay it to protect the value of the dollar, which was one of his two primary responsibilities. To make this payment possible, every debt-ridden president must protect every tool available, including the magical American economy.

Clinton's major challenges were clear:

- Defense — The presidential oath always put this cost center on top of the priority pile. Clinton was aware of the dangers of terrorism that emanated from the Middle East. During his first term, the World Trade Center had been attacked, businessmen had been murdered in Pakistan, the Khobar Towers had been blown up in Saudi Arabia,[2] and the Middle East press was full of anti–American insults. This alone should have informed Clinton that his reduction in military strength during his first term[3] was ill-advised, and that he should reverse his course in 1997–2000.
- Energy — Clinton did not create the energy problem in the U.S. that featured an overreliance on oil from the unstable Arab nations that had the largest reserves. Crude oil prices during his first four years swung by as much as 31 percent, year to year,[4] an indicator of both the willingness and the capacity of OPEC (a group of oil-producing nations) to manipulate prices to fit its needs, political and economic. It was the indicated role of this president to do what his predecessors had not done, namely, to mount an energy development project, using as a model the Manhattan Project of World War II that produced the first atomic bomb.
- Government — This cost center essentially represents the price of run-

ning the federal government, except for *Interest, Defense* and *Human Resources*. Presidents have a direct impact on these costs and it was expected that Clinton would act appropriately, given the budget situation.

- Human Resources—This cost center was largely the cause of the rising debt since the 1960s, not because its programs were not laudatory in a Utopian sense but because their entry into the budget had been ill-timed, poorly structured and unaffordable. In an administration that had effective budget control for three of his first four years in office, Clinton did nothing to cure this problem. The passage of the Welfare Reform Act in 1996 through a Republican Congress gave hope that some change might come about.
- Society—American society was morally confused. No single president caused this; no single president could fix it. But a president in the same moral, dignified mold of Carter, Reagan and Bush could at least set a good example for the American people that might slow the rate of decay. Clinton's responsibility was to fill that role during the subject period. He failed.

To be truly effective, a president needs the support of both houses of Congress. To have a chance at effectiveness, he should have control of at least the House or the Senate.

Clinton had no support; he lost the Congress to Republicans in the 1994 election. As a consequence, Newt Gingrich led the House (R–GA) and Trent Lott (R–MS) led the Senate.[5]

Ordinarily such an alignment would sterilize the effectiveness of a president. But in this case it provided Clinton with the only positive memory of his presidency that he carries with pride in his post-presidential life—his undeserved reputation as a fiscal moderate who led the way to the first budget surplus (1998) in twenty-nine years.[6]

Actually, the budget magic was the 1994 election that put Republicans in charge of a Congress that pulled Clinton into middle-of-the-road positions that led to budget surpluses.

Perspectives

GENERAL

The political climate in Washington during Clinton's second term was difficult, made more so by the drumbeat of constant distractions that were related to Clinton's private life.

The Whitewater investigation and the Paula Jones trial were ongoing events. Then came a busy 1998: The Lewinsky scandal was aired in the press, Ken Starr broadened his investigation to include charges of obstruction of justice and perjury, Clinton lied to the public about the affair (wife Hillary blamed the accusations on a right-wing conspiracy), Kathleen Willey and Juanita Broaddrick leveled their charges of harassment and rape; impeachment hearings began in the House and at year's end two specific charges were on the way to the Senate for trial — perjury and obstruction of justice.

In the meantime, as Clinton's troubles persisted, the world did not stop turning.

The U.S. space program, a mystery to most Americans, moved ahead at times in concert with Russia. Also, for the first time an American female astronaut, Col. Eileen Collins, headed a space mission.

Speaking of Russia, the colorful Yeltsin stepped aside and in 2000 a young ex–KGB officer, Vladimir Putin, was elected president. Putin's ambitions had not externalized during the Clinton era, but time would show him to be less than enamored of the democratic process that had begun under his predecessors.

U.S. arms were brought into play as a result of NATO's involvement in Bosnia, and they were needed again to calm the Serbian/Albanian conflict in Kosovo. Otherwise, military activity compared to previous years was a relatively minor consideration for Clinton, an attitude that flowed from his approach to terrorism.

Clinton didn't add to military capability to combat terrorism; instead, he hired lawyers to prosecute lawbreakers, one by agonizing one. And while he did this, terrorists were at work, for example:

- 1997 — The Taliban, an extremist Muslim group, took over in Afghanistan and created a safe haven for Osama bin Laden's training camps for terrorists.[7]
- Iraq expelled American members of the UN arms inspection teams.
- 1998 — The U.S. Embassy in Lebanon was attacked by Hizbullah; U.S. Embassies were bombed by al Qaeda, the bin Laden-trained terrorists[8]; Iraq terminated all U.N. arms-inspection efforts.

Clinton's reaction?

Osama bin Laden, he said, was "perhaps the preeminent organizer and financier of international terrorism in the world today."[9] He used the right words; he formally recognized that organizations involved in international terrorism existed.

Also, his strong views about Iraq's Saddam Hussein were shared by some of his outspoken colleagues in words that, at a later time, they wished would be forgotten:

- "One way or the other, we are determined to deny Iraq the capacity to develop weapons of mass destruction and the missiles to deliver them.

That is our bottom line."—President Clinton, Feb. 4, 1998, *U.S. News*

- "If Saddam rejects peace and we have to use force, our purpose is clear. We want to seriously diminish the threat posed by Iraq's weapons of mass destruction program."—President Bill Clinton, Feb. 17, 1998, All Politics CNN
- "He will use those weapons of mass destruction again, as he has ten times since 1983."—Sandy Berger, Clinton National Security Adviser, Feb. 18, 1998, Associated Press
- "Hussein has ... chosen to spend his money on building weapons of mass destruction and palaces for his cronies."—Madeline Albright, Clinton Secretary of State, Nov. 10, 1999, *Washington Times*
- "We urge you, after consulting with Congress, and consistent with the U.S. Constitution and laws, to take necessary actions (including, if appropriate, air and missile strikes on suspect Iraqi sites) to respond effectively to the threat posed by Iraq's refusal to end its weapons of mass destruction programs."—Letter to President Clinton.—Democratic Senators Carl Levin, Tom Daschle, John Kerry, others, Oct. 9, 1998, CNN, Inside Politics
- "Saddam Hussein has been engaged in the development of weapons of mass destruction technology which is a threat to countries in the region and he has made a mockery of the weapons inspection process."—Rep. Nancy Pelosi (D–CA), Dec. 16, 1998, http://www.glennbeck.com/news/01302004.shtml

That's what Clinton believed. But what did he do?

He apparently believed black-robed judges would fix the problem. Some terrorists were captured and convicted and a few missiles were launched (to no effect).

Then came his knockout punch. He cut *Defense*—again. He reduced America's military capability to defend against a very likely terrorist attack in the U.S. that could be at least as large as the WTC bombing in 1993.[10]

The entire power structure of the Democratic Party believed that Hussein had stockpiles of chemical/biological weapons, that he had demonstrated a willingness to use them and that, at the least, he had an ongoing nuclear development program supported by the requisite technical know-how.

Every president since the 1940s had been involved with a shooting war until Clinton, who had a relatively peaceful eight years.

The Cold War was over and he refused to recognize that international terrorism was war of a different type, spasmodic in its deadly events, surreptitious in its tactics, without an easily detectable national origin and organized around a religious belief rather than the more conventional nationalistic agenda.

The closest thing Clinton had to warfare was the upset condition of relationships between Serbs, Croatians, Bosnians and the Albanian residents of Kosovo. This was essentially a European affair, but NATO got involved, which meant that the militarily bankrupt Europeans had to call upon American muscle in the form of occupying forces, and in the use of U.S. airpower.

Finally, it is worth noting that in 1998 India and Pakistan became nuclear powers. North Korea and Iran threatened to be next in line, a sobering thought because both were, for different reasons, regarded as rogue nations who could destroy world harmony.

These events had no impact on Clinton's decision to strip the military, but they did activate diplomatic initiatives with North Korea (that disintegrated a few years later).

Five nations were considered to be nuclear weapons states in 2000: the United States, England, France, China and Russia. Two other states had conducted nuclear tests—India and Pakistan. Israel, not listed as a nuclear weapons state, has, it is widely believed, a stockpile of hundreds of weapons.

It's safe to say that the United States of William Clinton was not a deterrent to the expansion of nuclear power.

HOME FRONT

Clinton's scandals dominated the news during his final four years. The Whitewater, Paula Jones, Travelgate and Filegate scandals were ongoing. The latter two issues gradually disappeared from view, but Whitewater and Jones issues endured.

The Lewinsky, Willey and Broaddrick scandals appeared in 1998. Then came the decision of the House to impeach the president, the endless public hearings, the payoff to Paula Jones and in early 1999, the televised trial and exoneration of the president in the U.S. Senate.

Throughout all of this activity, Clinton adopted the role of victim; his supporters viciously attacked the independent counsel, Ken Starr.

Clinton was charged with perjury and obstruction of justice. His public opinion machine ignored the charges and painted Clinton as a romantic who withheld the truth about his escapades in order to protect his family. The Woodstock generation found it easy to forgive their president.

So Clinton survived his scandals and today is supported by public appearance fees and book contracts, speaking authoritatively about how other people and other presidents should act.

GDP in 2000 was 26 percent higher than it was four years before, a rate of growth competitive with previous presidencies that weren't distorted by inflation.[11]

But that positive result, it turns out, was misleading. The Reagan 17-year boom, during which federal revenue persistently grew, ended in 2000.[12]

The Misery Index was about the same in 2000 as it was in 1996, but again the ingredients of the index shifted to Clinton's political advantage. The super-sensitive unemployment rate was down, while the less noticed interest and inflationary rates were higher — these were precursors of things to come.[13]

Personal income per capita was higher than it was four years before. But that wasn't the end of the story. The per capita tax load was the highest it had been since 1944, the days of World War II.[14]

Stop!

That statement demands reflection that can be summed up this way: FDR in 1944 was in the middle of World War II with 12 million men in uniform; Clinton in 2000 was a peacetime president with 1.4 million men on active duty.[15] And Clinton's per capita tax load was only a fraction lower.

Inflation up, interest rates up, and taxes at an all time high during peacetime. This was not the medicine for a healthy economy.

Reagan began the 17-year boom by lowering all elements of the Misery Index and by reducing taxes per capita. His legacy was intact when President Bush left office. Clinton reversed course; the boom ended.

SUPREME COURT[16]

When a Democratic president takes over in the White House, Supreme Court activity explodes; activists come out of the walls with various causes expecting, for some illogical reason, that a sitting president will influence day-to-day Court decisions.

Actually, presidential power in any significant sense is limited to the nomination of judges when vacancies occur. That is not to say that private conversations might not take place, but one would have to be a complete cynic to hold that these honorable people can be corrupted by a president for political reasons.

Nevertheless, partisans act as if this were not the case. In 1965–68, for example, the Supreme Court heard 154 percent more cases than it did under Eisenhower in 1957–60; it heard 39 percent more cases under Carter in 1977–80 than it did under Nixon in 1969–72. So, it isn't surprising to see that the Court in 1997–2000 heard 222 percent more cases under Clinton than it did under Bush in 1989–92.[17]

The Rehnquist Court continued unchanged to handle this regurgitation of cases with four liberal and three conservative votes assured, and with two justices, O'Connor and Kennedy, who could end up anyplace on the legal landscape.

A few cases provide insight into the minds of these justices and into the concerns of the people of the day.

Clinton v. Jones, 1997. Paula Jones sued President Clinton for sexual harassment that later resulted in economic and psychological harm to her. Clinton invoked his immunity as a president to get the case dismissed. The issue: Is a sitting president entitled to absolute immunity from charges related to events that took place prior to his presidency? In a unanimous decision the Court ruled that presidential immunity applied only in very unusual circumstances, a threshold that the Jones case did not meet. This case is an example of the legal maneuvering that took place behind the scenes as Clinton sought every possible way to avoid having this sordid affair exposed in a court of law. The decision is also a positive commentary on the judges who made it, especially those appointed by Clinton.

Gebser v. Lago, 1998. A teacher, discovered having sex with a student, was fired. The student claimed she was being harassed under Title IX of the Education Act and she claimed damages. A lower court ruled against her. The issue: Can a federally funded education program be required to pay damages to a student who is caught having sex with an employee? In a 5–4 decision (Souter, Ginsburg, Stevens and Breyer dissenting) the Court ruled against the student. The school knew nothing about the behavior until it was discovered and was in no way liable to anybody for anything. There are two aspects of this case that are confounding: (1) How did it ever get before the bench? (2) Four judges wanted to pay damages to a girl who was found having sex on school property.

Bond v. U.S., 2000. An immigration officer, while checking the status of passengers on a bus, squeezed a passenger's bag and felt a hard object. The passenger admitted owning the bag and consented to its search. The agent found a "brick" of an illegal drug. The passenger, indicted on drug charges, moved to suppress the evidence on the grounds that the intrusive squeezing was a violation of the search and seizure provisions of the Fourth Amendment. A court of appeals ruled that the agent's behavior was proper. The issue: Did the officer's manipulation of the baggage that resulted in the search constitute a violation of the Fourth Amendment? In a 7–2 decision (Breyer and Scalia dissenting), the Court ruled that the agent's search was improper, and that the passenger had a privacy interest in the bag and had a right to expect that employees would not grope it in an exploratory way. Three reflections follow a reading of this case: (1) Breyer and Scalia made strange bedfellows; (2) the decision of the appellate court (in favor of the agent) on this marginal case was reasonable. Why did the Supreme Court take it on? (3) In an age of terrorism, the limitation on an agent's rights imposed by the Court is frightening

Bush v. Gore, 2000. The presidential election had ended with Bush winning Florida by a small margin of votes. The Florida Supreme Court that had acted in an ugly partisan matter on all election issues ruled that every Florida county must recount so-called under-votes. Bush protested the decision. The issues: Did the Florida court violate the Constitution by making new election law? Do standardless manual counts violate equal protection and due process clauses of the Constitution? In a 7–2 decision (Breyer and Ginsburg dissenting) the Court ruled against the Florida Supreme Court. The 2000 election ended in an ugly legal mess because the Florida court tried to manipulate the results by imposing a new law that was completely impractical. Democrats yelled foul, and they never forgave Bush for winning or the Supreme Court for ruling. Postelection counts by several news organizations confirmed over and over that Bush had won. But emotions trumped facts and Bush assumed office with a sizable array of political opponents.

SOCIETY[18]

Social statistics contain good and bad news. Late arriving estimates suggest that the percentage of marriages ending in divorce is shrinking; the number of abortion and AIDS cases in 2000 was sharply down. But it is also true that fewer people are getting married and the number of households made up of unmarried persons is persistently growing.

Education quality in public schools improved marginally in 2000, but SAT scores were still lower than they were in 1972, a powerful and silent comment on the billions of dollars that have poured into the system in search of improved quality.

Violent crime was down in 2000, but the prison population continued to explode — 1.4 million people were locked up.

Change in Public Debt

President Clinton entered his second term with an inherited cost structure that appeared to give him an improved opportunity for deficit reduction.[19] There were two basic reasons for this:

- *Defense*— Clinton had unwisely cut *Defense* at a time when future troubles with terrorists, and with Iran, Iraq and North Korea seemed certain and imminent.
- *Government*— Clinton was the beneficiary in his first term of a surge of revenue related to the Savings and Loan debacle that lowered the cost of *Government*, a gift that would not be repeated during the subject period.

Clinton had another thing going for him that normally would be a liability, namely, Congress was controlled by the opposition party. From a deficit reduction and cost control standpoint, nothing better could have happened to him because out of this conflict came his reputation as an even-handed politician.

Clinton, to be responsible, had the same mandates that had been on the table since the 1960s: Restructure entitlement programs, trim operating cost, improve the business environment nationally and internationally, pray for healthy tax collections and maintain a military organization that meets the threats of the times.

A review of the transactions for the period will reveal how Clinton resolved these responsibilities.

Table 16.2
Transactions (in billions of dollars)

		1997–2000		1993–96
Taxes		$ 7153.8		$ 5219.5
Less:				
Defense	$1108.4		$1110.4	
Interest	937.8		875.1	
Total		2046.2		1985.5
Net		$ 5107.6		$ 3234.0
Less:				
Government	$ 489.6		$ 384.6	
Human Resources	4209.0		3579.0	
Total		4698.6		3963.6
Surplus/deficit		$ 409.0		$- 729.6
Debt, beginning		-3734.1		-2999.9
Total		$-3325.1		$-3729.3
Adjustment*		-84.7		-4.8
Debt, Ending		$-3409.8		$-3734.1

*Treasury cannot be exact when it finances a budget deficit and the difference between what is needed and the value of securities traded inevitably produces a relatively small variance.

Source: Historical Tables 2007, 1.1, 3.1

Shock! That is the first reaction to the numbers in the above table.

A budget surplus—for the first time since the days of Eisenhower.

What happened? An analysis of the transactions for the period should reveal the answers to that question.

TAXES

The normal revenue increase in the 10 four-year presidential periods that preceded this one was 35.2 percent. In the subject period, it was 37.1 percent; in the three most recent presidential terms it averaged 28.1 percent.

Had the revenue increase been normal, income for the period would have been $7056.8 billion or $97.0 billion less; had the increase been the same as that which was experienced during the three most recent presidential terms, income for the period would have been $6686.2 billion or $467.6 billion less than actual. This revenue differential will be considered when the results for the four-year period are summarized.

GDP growth, on the other hand, was about the same as the average GDP growth experienced during the previous three presidencies.[20] It follows that revenue growth was primarily due to increased tax rates and to higher employment,[21] not to robust economic growth.

Defense

Terrorists were loose. They had directly attacked the United States. The most dangerous one, Osama bin Laden, had been given safe haven in the Taliban-ruled Afghanistan where he was training followers in the art of killing Americans.

Hizbullah, a terrorist organization based in Lebanon, active and deadly, was a constant threat to any American stationed in Arabia.

Arafat, a terrorist in a peacemaker's clothing, continued to threaten Israel through his own organization and that of Hamas, another terrorist group based in Palestine.

Terrorists were being trained in Iraq, with the approval of Saddam Hussein. Hussein also subsidized Palestinian suicide bombers. He denied access to UN arms inspection teams. He shot at U.S. planes that were, with UN approval, flying over the northern and southern sections of Iraq in order to keep Hussein in his Baghdad cave.

Iran, Libya and North Korea were developing nuclear weapons. Syria and Iran supported the attempts of Hizbullah to control Lebanon and to continue its attacks on Israel.

What was Clinton's reaction to this pleasant worldview and its potential for mortal danger to the United States? He cut *Defense.*

President George H. W. Bush left office with two million people on active duty in the military; Clinton left an active force of 1.4 million — a 30 percent cutback.[22]

The cost of *Defense* was about the same. Had it increased at the same rate as revenue, cost would have been $1521.9 billion or $413.5 billion more than actual.[23]

This fact can be rephrased in more concrete form: If the active force had been returned to the level Clinton inherited, the cost of the increase would have been fully funded by the flow of revenue into the federal coffers during the subject period, and the budget surplus would have disappeared.

Clinton did not have a significant military confrontation, not because the United States was not in danger but because he didn't recognize the dangers that existed. He passed the military problems along to his successor.

Interest

Clinton could thank President Johnson, father of the Welfare State, for the growth in budget importance of *Interest.* Whatever the level of interest rates, cost was going to be high because the amount of public debt was high and still growing, largely due to the accumulation of unfunded costs related to Johnson's dream.

Interest during the subject period increased again, this time slower than the revenue curve — it was fully funded.

But that had long ago ceased to be the major consideration in budget terms. Any increase was unwelcome. The actual cost growth of $62.7 billion was just another load of dollars being spent to protect the value of the U.S. currency in world markets.

GOVERNMENT

Revenue was up; primary cost centers were less expensive. As a consequence, under the flow-through method of revenue allocation that has been employed in this book, remaining cost centers had room to grow in the context of a balanced budget to a degree that had not been seen since the 1970s.

Government spent less than its allowable allocation.

Table 16.3
Government (in billions of dollars)

	1997–2000	1993–96	% Change
Energy	$ 2.9	$ 17.2	-83.1%
Natural Resources/Environment	92.5	85.0	8.8
Transportation	170.5	152.1	12.1
Community/regional development	43.3	40.8	6.1
International affairs	60.7	64.1	-3.7
Science/space/technology	72.1	66.5	8.4
Agriculture	80.4	54.5	47.5
Justice	99.0	63.9	54.9
General	56.2	51.1	10.0
Total	$ 677.6	$595.2	13.8%
Commerce & housing credit*	-7.8	-52.7	-85.2
Total	$ 669.8	$542.5	23.5%
Offsetting receipts	-180.2	-157.9	14.1
Net	$ 489.6	$384.6	27.3%

*Made up of earnings from various federal housing and other programs— subject to major changes from year to year relative to market conditions. (Historical Tables 2007, 3.2)

Source: Historical Tables 2007, 3.1

Three cost breaks in Energy, International and Commerce were partly responsible for the budget success of this cost center.

The cost of oil spiked upwards in 2000, but Clinton overall had a cheap oil market in which to operate.[24] Also, other uninvestigated factors that decreased the cost of energy supplies in 1997[25] and thereafter provided a cost break that resulted in a relatively inexpensive energy cost.

Despite a world in turmoil, State Department activities were carried out in a relatively inexpensive way. Costs increased sharply in Clinton's final year, but they were essentially flat during the early years.[26]

The Savings and Loan debacle was a gift that never stopped giving to

Clinton. Once again, the cost of bailouts was more than offset by the revenue from asset sales. The volatile line item, Commerce etc., records this benefit.

On the negative side of things, Agriculture and Justice grew disproportionately.

The cost of Agriculture was fairly steady until the year 2000. At that time, procedures inspired by Clinton, indirectly tied to the Kyoto Treaty (that dealt with environmental issues), doubled the cost of the line item and passed along to the next president an abnormally high cost base.[27]

The nation had become more unruly as the national consensus about moral law became fragmented, partly because of controversial Supreme Court decisions. And since diminished personal control is ordinarily followed by increased civil control, the cost of Justice had, for that reason alone, been growing disproportionately for some time. That this was a losing battle has been regularly demonstrated by the growing population of prisoners in the United States.[28]

Also, law enforcement was Clinton's answer to the threat of terrorism, and there were costly successes as several bad guys were captured and jailed.

But terrorism, of course, marched onward. Perhaps it was inspired even more strongly to attack the United States and its people as it became known that America's response would be a legal strategy that was too little, too late and too timid.

Cost control of *Government* was commendable in 1997–2000, partly due to cost pressures applied by conservatives and partly to old-fashioned good luck with line items that, to other presidents, were very costly.

HUMAN RESOURCES

A welfare reform bill was passed in 1996, and there were other signs in that year that the results in this cost center could be more hopeful in future years. Did it turn out that way in 1997–2000?

Whenever a radical change takes place in anything, the first thing to look for is: What significant thing happened that didn't exist before? Chances are, if that thing can be identified it will also be found to be the fundamental cause of the change.

For example: The United States was in debt up to its ears in 2000, and that debt had been climbing for decades ever since the 1960s, a phenomenon that was new to American politics.

What happened?

Although the consequences have turned out to be complex, the answer to that question is simple. Political thinkers since Karl Marx have dreamt of creating the perfect society in which the difficulties of life are kept to the bare minimum as a result of enlightened social policy that features a benevolent government. Experiments with this idea have inevitably ended up as socialistic states being managed from on high by a special few.

Table 16.4
Human Resources (in billions of dollars)

	1997–2000	1993–96	% Change
Education, training, services	$ 203.8	$ 202.6	.6%
Health/Medicaid	550.8	441.3	24.8
Income Security*	855.8	752.7	13.7
Social Security	1543.9	1309.7	17.9
Medicare	770.3	609.4	26.4
Unemployment compensation	113.0	115.0	- 1.7
Veterans	171.4	148.3	15.6
Total	$4209.0	$3579.0	17.6%

*Minus unemployment compensation (from 1965–68 on)

Note: Major federal programs since the 1960s— Food Stamps 1961 (pilot), Food Stamps 1964, Medicaid 1965, Student Aid 1966, Medicare 1967, Coal Miners Benefits 1970, Commodity Donations 1973, Supplementary Security Income 1974, Supplemental Feeding 1976, Earned Income Tax Credit 1976, Legal Services 1976, Energy Assistance 1977, Welfare Reform 1996

Source: Historical Tables 2007, 3.1

The Soviet Union is the most recent example of the failure of this dream as a practical basis for governance that, at the same time, preserves liberty.

But the idea lives on and European nations, for example, are hurrying down the same road to ruin as if the meltdown in the Soviet Union had never occurred.

History's lesson is clear. A paternalistic government, no matter how well intended, is: (1) unaffordable, and (2) the enemy of personal liberty and initiative.

Many American political leaders have fallen for the same idea despite the clarity of the message, and despite the most recent example of European disintegration.

Led by Lyndon Johnson they introduced a new budget scheme, one that had not prevailed before under leaders who had made the nation great. It was this: Spend for what you think is good and worry about paying for it later.

American politicians since the 1960s did precisely that. They envisaged a certain world, they developed programs that would create it and they paid no attention to cost.

Out went the pay-as-you-go attitude of the first thirty-four presidents; in came the wisdom of the thirty-sixth president who set the nation on a course from which it has yet to recover, and one that has the capacity to destroy the richest nation on earth because it forgot how to count.

The major culprit in this sad budget drama is the cost center, *Human Resources*, home of the largest entitlement programs. Its cost over eleven four-year presidential terms has increased faster than the increase in revenue nine times, and deficits have occurred in every one of those periods.

So what happened in 1997–2000? What was different? The same president was in office? Most of the same congressmen were in place that served four years before.

The difference was in leadership in the Congress.

Conservatives and liberals are different kinds of people with different worldviews about money and morality. And in 1997–2000 conservatives with a desire to shrink government were in charge. This was the critical difference that kept the growth of the line items in this cost center within reach.

Had this budget center used its entire revenue allocation, its cost would have been $4618.0 billion, or $409.0 billion higher than actual, and to that extent it contributed to the budget surplus for the period.

SUMMARY OF BUDGET SURPLUS

This was, in terms of budget results, a successful presidential term that produced a surplus of $409.0 billion.

Table 16.5
Summary of Surplus — 1997–2000 (in billions of dollars)

Cost Center	Amount
Defense	$
Interest	
Government	
Human Resources	409.0
Total	$409.0

Sources: Exhibits 1, 11–2, 16

Before accepting this attractive result as an example of how the corner has been turned and that future surpluses and debt reductions are possible without tampering with entitlement programs, it's useful to revisit sections of the analysis that explain how the surplus was generated:

Revenue

The analysis of tax revenue revealed that the increase was unusually high. Compared to the average increase experienced during the previous 10 presidential terms, it was $97.0 billion too high; and compared with the most recent three presidential terms, it was $467.6 billion too high.

This means the surplus would have been reduced from $409.0 billion to $312.0 billion had revenue increased at the average rate experienced during the 10 previous presidential terms; or it means that the surplus of $409.0 billion would have become a deficit of $58.6 billion had revenue increased at the rate experienced during the previous three presidential terms.

In short, Clinton's unexpected revenue bonanza accounted for 24 percent to 100 percent of the surplus.

Concerning the future, which scenario is the more likely? (1) The revenue increase will continue at Clinton's 37.1 percent; (2) it will return to the average of 35.2 percent; (3) it will return to the pattern established during the most previous three presidencies at 28.1 percent.[29]

From Eisenhower (1957–60) through Clinton (1997–2000), a four-year revenue increase of more than 35 percent occurred five times, *four of which occurred during the inflationary years that began with Ford and ended under Reagan*; increases in the 30–34 percent range occurred twice; in the 25–29 perent range, twice, and below 25 percent, two times.

From the above it is clear that, except for periods when inflation distorts revenue growth, it is likely that future revenue increases will be below 35 percent unless higher taxes can be sustained without damaging economic growth.

The abnormal revenue increase in 1997–2000 was more related to Clinton's high tax policies than it was to economic growth. Taxes per capita were at their highest level since World War II.[30] And since there is no evidence that such an increase can be maintained over a period of years without causing economic damage, it must be concluded that the surplus for the period, on revenue grounds alone, was at the least overstated and, at the worst, a short-lived myth.

Defense

Clinton dramatically reduced the amount of budget resources devoted to the military. If the world was at peace and no consequential threats were on the horizon, some cutback could have been supported.

If the world was a troublesome place with danger lurking in every corner of the globe, and with historical alliances weakened (by the inability of nations like France and Germany to afford a robust military), then cutbacks in *Defense* approved by Clinton in 1993–96 should have been reversed and the active military that he inherited should have been restored. Had he done this, spending in the *Defense* cost center would have increased by an amount that could have wiped out most of the budget surplus.[31]

Interest

The *Interest* cost center did not need all of the funds allocated to it and, as a consequence, it passed along unused funds to *Government* and *Human Resources*.

How likely is it that the current rate of revenue increase will continue to fund the increase in this cost center?

Every president is at the mercy of money markets and the inherited level of debt, which long ago was determined by Johnson's plan to turn America into a Welfare State.

Interest rates in 1997–2000 were fairly steady and debt was reduced, a combination that resulted in a relatively modest overall cost of *Interest*.

How likely was it that this "bonus" would continue to be realized by future presidents?

If revenue continues to be abnormally high, if a minimum military capability continues to be presidential policy, and if interest rates do not increase, the chances of repeating some level of benefit from this cost center is good. If, if, if...

In the past 11 presidential terms, nine experienced unfunded *Interest*. Based upon this, the Clinton *Interest* bonus of 1997–2000 should not be depended upon to continue.

Summary

The surplus was essentially manufactured by President Clinton by increasing taxes and by castrating the military, and by the energetic efforts of a conservative Congress to control spending. It was an I-want-to-look-good-before–I-leave-town strategy that served Clinton well.

But the country was worse off. International threats were in place; entitlement programs were untouched. And a new problem had been introduced: How long will the economy continue to grow under the high-tax environment created by Clinton?

Conclusion

When a president with antimilitary leanings presides over a Congress controlled by conservatives, it would be surprising if the spending priorities of the government were not changed. And indeed they were.

Table 16.6
Spending Priorities

	1960 Ike	1968 LBJ	1976 GRF	1980 JEC	1988 RWR	1992 GHWB	2000 WJC
Primary costs							
Defense	52.2%	27.3%	24.1%	22.7%	27.3%	21.6%	16.5%
Interest	7.5	14.2	7.2	8.9	14.3	14.4	12.5
Total	59.7%	41.4%	31.3%	31.6%	41.6%	36.0	29.0
Government	11.9	8.4	14.0	15.4	8.3	8.1	8.7
Education/services	1.9	2.9	5.1	5.4	2.9	3.1	3.0
Health/Medicaid	.9	4.2	4.1	3.9	4.2	6.5	8.6
Medicare		7.4	4.3	5.4	7.4	8.6	11.0
Income Security	8.0	12.2	16.4	14.7	12.2	14.4	14.2
Social Security	12.6	20.6	19.9	20.0	20.6	20.8	22.9
Veterans	5.9	2.9	4.9	3.6	2.9	2.5	2.6
Total	100.0%	100.0%	100.0%	100.0%	100.0%	100.0	100.0%
	(3)	(2)(3)	(3)	(3)	(3)	(2)	(1)

1 = peace; 2 = war; 3 = cold war
Source: Historical Tables 2007, 3.1

No modern president has shown less interest in the relationship between America's influence and its military power than Clinton. And the difference between his America and the nation that existed 40 years before was never more evident than it was in 2000.

Eisenhower in 1960, spent about half of the people's money on security; Clinton in 2000 spent about 17 percent.

This was a world turned upside down. The America of 2000 was not what it used to be, and what it was few if any could define.

The Clinton presidency had two themes that ran on parallel tracts: Clinton the man and Clinton the president.

Clinton the Man

Charisma! What is it? How is it defined?

There are no true answers to these questions because they deal with the reactions that people have to other personalities. In the world of politics, Teddy and Franklin Roosevelt had it, Kennedy had it, Reagan had it, Margaret Thatcher had it.

But what is "it"?

A judge's comment when asked about pornography was: I can't define it, but I know it when I see it.

So it is with charisma. Some people have it; most don't. And you know it when you see it.

And Clinton had it.

Charisma is more than good looks or an engaging demeanor. It is total impression — an aura — that some people project. And it is a powerful tool for a political leader. With it, his rhetoric seems better and his errors more understandable; with it, his plans seem more acceptable and his mistakes more human.

Despite humble beginnings, Clinton is confident and at home in the power parlors of the world. He speaks well, he is bright, and he can appear to be quite sincere. On the surface he seems amiable, although rumors about his temper are occasionally reported; his ability and his willingness to take a hit was demonstrated when his seamy personal life was put on display for everyone to see.

Clinton's natural gifts have served him well; they helped him, for example, to defeat the impeachment that was mounted against him.

But Clinton used his charisma in destructive as well as constructive ways. Dating back to his days as governor of Arkansas there were stories about womanizing, rumors that were given life by the Paula Jones case and the Lewinsky scandal, events that eventually defined the man to his profession (the law) and to the people.

The reaction of the law profession was as final as it can get — he was permanently disbarred.

With the people it was (is) a different story. The Woodstock generation had adopted him as their political hero.

If the new way is in error, and if old values are a better foundation upon which to build a civil society, he was the worst possible president for his time.

When the Clintons left Washington there was a final scandal over furniture and decorations that they wanted shipped to their new home in New York. And the last no-class act was President Clinton's use of his commutation and pardon powers.[32] Among others he commuted the jail terms of:

- Benjamin Berger — With co-conspirators he stole $40 million in federal money. The powerful Hasidic Community in New York supported Berger. Mrs. Clinton was a candidate from New York for the U.S. Senate.
- Melvin J. Reynolds — ex-congressman from Illinois; bank fraud, sexual assault, child pornography.
- Dorothy Rivers — Stole $1.2 million in federal grants; a friend of Jesse Jackson.
- Carlos Vignari — cocaine trafficking.

And he pardoned the likes of:

- Nicholas Altiere — cocaine trafficking.
- Chris Bagley — cocaine trafficking.
- Pincus Green — tax evasion and illegal trades with Iran; a New York billionaire.
- Susan McDougal — refused to testify in the Whitewater scandal; a friend of Clinton's.
- Marc Rich — A partner of Pincus Green; a Swiss-based billionaire.

A charming rogue. An unrealized talent. These and similar phrases capture the Clinton who might have been but never was.

Clinton the President

Certainly the Clinton-approved biographies of the future will headline the news of his budget surplus in 1997–2000. And indeed there was a surplus and, therefore, a debt reduction from $3734.1 billion to $3409.8 billion, as follows:

Table 16.7
Public Debt, 2000

Event	Inherited 1996	Added 1997–2000	Total 2000	%
World War I	$ 18.3	$	$ 18.3	.5%
Great Depression	24.5	24.5	.7	
World War II	142.5	142.5	4.2	
Korean War	6.6	6.6	.2	
Cold War	206.1	206.1	6.0	
Interest	286.5	286.5	8.5	
Government	349.5		349.5	10.2
Human Resources	2683.5	-409.0	2274.5	66.7
Treasury	16.6	84.7	101.3	3.0
Total	$3734.1	$324.3	$3409.8	100.0%

Source: Exhibits 1, 11, 12, 16

In Chapter 15 of this book the genesis of the surplus was explored. It was the result of confiscatory tax policies and unwarranted cutbacks in *Defense,* neither of which figured to endure without penalty for many months or years. Manipulated or not, the surplus was real and Clinton's hand could be seen on it.

Every president, however, is ultimately measured not by personal skills, but on how he handles the problems of his time — not by his personal initiatives to impress his stamp on the office, but by his willingness and his ability to resolve the nation's difficulties.

It is common in life for people to postpone what must be done by becoming furiously busy at something that is more pleasing and less difficult.

Such was the case with Clinton. While Clinton fiddled, Washington continued to burn. The terrorist threat was unanswered; Saddam Hussein was as dangerous as ever; international nuclear capability, actual and imminent, was successfully expanding; energy dependence of the United States was untouched; causes of continuing deficits and climbing debt were hidden behind a manufactured surplus.

Clinton did have accomplishments. For example, the North American Free Trade Agreement opened commercial doors with Canada and Mexico. But overall, he was a political failure. His party controlled everything when he entered office and nothing when he left it.

Most important of all, he left the presidency in a state of disrepair. His use of America's sacred physical symbol, the White House, and his personal behavior was unbefitting a president. His use of a president's pardon and commutation powers was highly controversial.

17

George W. Bush, 2001–2004

Businessman, Governor, President

George Bush is the first of six children that mother Barbara delivered to George H. W. Bush, the forty-first president of the United States. One child, Robin, died at the age of three with leukemia; the other four are alive and well, Jeb, Neil, Marvin and Dorothy, Jeb prominently so as ex-governor of Florida.

George was born in New Haven, Connecticut, in 1946. His father, 22 at the time and a highly decorated hero of World War II, was in his second year at Yale.

Harry Truman was president; public debt was $241.9 billion.[1]

Father George moved to Texas after he graduated from Yale, and he entered the oil business.

Young George spent most of his early years in the Lone Star State, which explains why he is often quoted as saying that he was born and educated in the East, but his heart is in Texas.

George Bush in many respects followed in the footsteps of his dad. He attended Phillips Academy in Andover and graduated from Yale in 1968 with a BA in history. During the same period he worked in his father's political campaign for a seat in the House of Representatives, thus following a long tradition in the family of activism in Republican politics (grandfather Prescott Bush was a distinguished U.S. senator).

And it must be noted—for those who are enamored of conspiracy theories about the political power wielded by secret societies—that George Bush (like his father) joined Yale's Skull and Bones, a society with many historically distinguished members.

Lyndon Johnson was president in 1968; the bricks for his new Welfare State were in place; public debt was $289.5 billion, still under control but needing adjustment by any group of politicians with the imagination, desire and the power to do so.

The Vietnam War was ongoing when young George graduated from Yale and he became a fighter pilot with the Texas Air National Guard. His assignments kept him stateside and critics have suggested that his father's prominence was responsible for this. No credible evidence has been presented to prove this charge, and those who have followed his father's distinguished and patriotic career doubt he would ever be party to such a deal.

George Bush's military career ended in 1974, at which time he attended Harvard Business School; he emerged with a Master of Business Administration Degree (the only president with that type of education background).

Bush graduated into a turbulent political period. Richard Nixon had resigned; Gerald Ford had ascended to the White House. Bush's father was chairman of the Republican National Committee, one of the toughest jobs in politics at the time because the reputation of the Republican Party, through no fault of his, was headed for the Dempsey Dumpster.

Public debt in 1975 was $394.7 billion; the budget was out of control. Ford was a weakened president reeling from the scandal with only his veto power to express his resistance to congressional spending (he used it 66 times in less than three years[2]); budget deficits had become endemic; Johnson's programs were unaffordable and in need of trimming.

Meanwhile, Bush looked at his father's former career, liked what he saw and, once again, he copied a winning act; he entered the oil business.

Bush has been quoted as saying that when he was young and foolish, he was young and foolish. His reference is to the years that followed his discharge from the navy. But these were also eventful years for him, so partying was, by definition, a diversion, not a preoccupation:

- After he entered the oil business he eventually became a partner or the chief executive officer of several ventures, involving himself in various mergers and acquisitions.
- He met and married Laura Welch in 1977; four years later they had twin daughters, Jenna and Barbara.
- He ran for the U.S. House of Representatives in 1978 and lost by 6,000 votes.
- He got his first insight into presidential politics in the primary campaign of 1980, which his father lost to Ronald Reagan, a national experience that was deepened during his father's eight-year vice presidency.
- Billy Graham, the esteemed evangelist, in 1986 entered Bush's life. As a result of that encounter, and reflection about where he had been, who he was and where he was going, Bush recovered his religious roots and he became the settled, focused man he is today.

Bush, after his father's unsuccessful campaign for a second term in 1988, organized several investors who bought the Texas Rangers baseball franchise, and he was made managing partner.

Politics beckoned once more in 1994; Bush threw his hat into the guber-natorial race against the popular Ann Richards. He wasn't given a chance to win but, assisted by his friends, Karen Hughes and Karl Rove (who followed him to Washington), he mounted an effective campaign that ended up in an impressive 52 to 47 percent win for Bush.

He was on his way. George Bush was an effective governor, the only one in Texas history to be elected to two consecutive four-year terms (prior to 1975 the governor served only two years). He made a major impact on issues deal-ing with tort law, education and criminal justice, and he was the pivotal force behind the largest tax cut in Texas history.

Bush's religious side, which proved to be a matter of concern during his presidency, was made apparent to his supporters, and to his detractors, during his years as governor. He pioneered faith-based welfare programs, for exam-ple, and he tested his opponents to the core when in his final year he declared June 10 to be "Jesus Day," a day to celebrate giving to the needy.

But, from a political standpoint, the most important thing is that Bush emerged from the political battles of his state as a well-grounded, popular and conservative politician with a track record of working well with opponents. He could cut through partisanship and get things done.

For a man with presidential ambitions, this was an attractive résumé, espe-cially when one added to it the family name, which had, for good reason, a blue-ribbon reputation.

And that's the way the Republican Party saw things when Bush threw his Texas Stetson into the presidential primaries.

With Karen Hughes, Karl Rove and his family at his side, Bush demon-strated he was as skilled and as tough in a national campaign as he had been in state politics. Funds poured into his campaign chest and intimidated most of his opponents, who quit, with the well-known exception of Sen. John McCain (R–AZ).

McCain, a war hero, spent over five years in the prison camps of the North Vietnamese. He became a senator in 1987 and his ambition for higher office bloomed in the 2000 campaign as he sought to be the man to replace William Clinton as the forty-third president — he was 64 at the time (Bush was a decade younger).

Support for McCain broke through in the New Hampshire and Michigan primaries, which he surprisingly won. But Bush rallied and one by one he added primary wins, forcing McCain to quit the race and, later, to (reluctantly) offer support to the Bush presidential campaign.

Known as a political maverick with a short fuse, McCain's appeal during the primaries was based essentially upon the support of some Democrats and Independents to whom he represented the "straight-talking" politician who bucked the system. He was the prototypical insider who portrayed himself as the outsider in order to gain the "I'm-against-all-government" voters.

That profile worked for a while but, unfortunately for him, he was running in a Republican primary, not in a national election. And Republicans did not want a maverick as their representative in a presidential contest.

To understand the tone of the 2000 presidential campaign, it is necessary to describe the feelings of both sides toward the incumbent, William Clinton, whose place was sought in the race by his vice president, Al Gore.

Clinton, to Democrats

Democrats had to defend Clinton because the failure to do so would validate the criticism of his personal behavior, besmirch the reputation of their party (which had supported him throughout the many scandals) and ruin their chances to retain control of the presidency, the only level of political power in Washington that was under their thumb (Congress was controlled by Republicans).

They had no positive arguments that could convincingly explain and defend Clinton's behavior; therefore, to reach their objectives, they had to (and did) demonize Clinton's critics in a way that would appeal to his basic constituency, the Woodstock generation, the major media and the liberal establishment.

Clinton, perhaps the most famous member of the Woodstock generation, had defeated in presidential campaigns two prototypical members of the old value system, George H.W. Bush and Bob Dole. His victory to his supporters validated their worldview. His presence in the White House was, to them, an unmistakable sign that the old ways were out and the new ways—their ways— were in.

Clinton, to Republicans

Republicans were deeply offended by the unpresidential behavior of Clinton who, they felt, had cheapened the White House and the presidency, using both as political tools, or as instruments of power that could be used to his personal advantage.

Those opposing forces were at work throughout the presidential campaign. Given these conflicting viewpoints, is it any wonder that the political campaign was one of the hottest?

This emotional baggage was intensified by the well-publicized fact that the political campaign ended with a decision by the U.S. Supreme Court, which ultimately hastened but did not change the final results of the election.

Like all presidents before him, Bush was presented with the problem of public debt that had risen to $3409.8 billion, an amount that minimized his ability in national or international affairs to operate with efficient freedom.

Table 17.1
Public Debt 2000 (in billions of dollars)

	Total	%
World War I	$ 18.3	.5%
Great Depression:	24.5	.7
World War II	142.5	4.2
Korean War	6.6	.2
Cold War	206.1	6.0
Interest	286.5	8.5
Government	349.5	10.2
Human Resources	2274.5	66.7
Treasury, net	101.3	3.0
Total	$3409.8	100.0%

Source: Table 15.7 Chapter 15

Managing a debt of this size was a considerable responsibility, one that could be made easier or harder by the level of available congressional support.

The House of Representatives was safe for Bush; it was under the control of Newt Gingrich (R–GA). The Senate was different. Tom Daschle (D–SD) was the Senate Majority Leader.[3] A highly partisan politician, Daschle could be depended on to block many initiatives.

The most positive thing about the public debt to Bush was the fact that it had dropped during the previous period. But someone in his administration must have called to his attention that the surplus during Clinton's final term had been manufactured by circumstances that weren't likely to repeat.[4]

In short, the essential problem that had built the debt in the first place, namely, poorly structured and unaffordable entitlement programs, remained untouched, and other major problems that were not confronted by Clinton, such as terrorism and energy, could require expensive cures in the months ahead.

But Bush was confident in 2000, holding a Reagan-like belief in the ability of Americans to overcome obstacles. Given a few years of peace, and at least minimum congressional support, maybe he could make a difference; maybe he could not only reduce debt but also reach and modify the sources of it.

Perspectives

General

Jimmy Carter, whatever his failings as a president, is an honorable man and in his four years he restored the dignity and the moral authority of the office. His successors, Ronald Reagan and George H. W. Bush did the same.

Then came Bill Clinton. His many detractors believed that his presidency lowered the dignity of the office. The moral authority normally attached to the presidency that had been recovered by Ford, Carter and Reagan was gone; Bush would have to re-create it through his behavior and that of his wife.

There was also a sense of incompletion about the Clinton presidency that hung in the air when Bush moved in. Clinton had been weak on the nuts and bolts issues of the time, and Bush paid the price:

- The energy problem was untouched; America was too dependent on foreign oil imported from unstable states.
- Most of the improperly financed and unaffordable entitlement programs that had driven public debt sky-high were untouched.
- Clinton's reaction to the threat of international terrorism was to strip down the military preparedness of the nation.[5]

Added to such problems was the onset of a recession that seemed to begin the minute Clinton left town.

Federal revenues in Bush's first year in office were 2 percent lower than the year before, marking the end of a 17-year Reagan boom and beginning the longest stretch of diminishing revenues in the history of the modern presidency,[6] something difficult to separate from the fact that Clinton raised per capita taxes to their highest level since World War II.[7]

Fate deals graciously with some presidents and devastatingly with others. Clinton, for example, was extremely lucky because unlike his predecessor, George H. W. Bush, who had borne the full cost of the Savings and Loan scandal, he received none of the net cost and all of the bonus from asset sales. He became president during the Reagan boom and had eight years of steady income growth. There were no shooting wars, the Cold War was over and he had a Republican-controlled Congress that provided him with his reputation as a budget deficit buster.

Herbert Hoover, on the other hand, a brilliant man, walked straight into the Great Depression in 1928 and never had a chance to succeed.

And so it was for George Bush (43). He was hit with a series of events that would have floored a lesser man:

- September 2001— Four planes were hi-jacked by Arabian terrorists. Two planes flattened the twin towers in New York's World Trade Center; a third crashed into the Pentagon and the fourth plane (thought to be headed for the White House) crashed in Pennsylvania when brave passengers attacked the hijackers. Total deaths were 2,792, including 343 firefighters and 75 policemen who met their fate trying to help or to find victims, and over 2,000 additional people were injured.[8]
- December 2001— Enron filed for bankruptcy.[9]
- January 2002 — Ken Lay, chairman of Enron, resigned.
- June 2002 — Arthur Andersen, prestigious CPA firm, convicted of destroying Enron documents.

- July 2002 — WorldCom filed for bankruptcy after misstating profits.
- September 2002 — Tyco executives guilty of stock fraud.
- October 2002 — ImClone CEO guilty of fraud and perjury.

The effect of these events on a recession that was underway was devastating to the economy, to people and to the inflow of federal revenues.

The Dow Jones Industrial Average of selected stocks dropped from 11,723 in January 2000 to its low point of 7,286 in October 2002[10]; the unemployment rate increased from 3.9 percent in 2000 to a high of 6.3 percent in 2003 before it dropped again to 5.4 percent in 2004.[11]

The decrease in federal revenue attached to the overall recession and to the loss in confidence in the American system will be dealt with more specifically in a later section of this chapter. It is sufficient to say at the moment that no president has been hit as hard on the revenue side of the budget equation than Bush was in his first term — not once was his annual revenue as high as it was in 2000, the last year of William Clinton's presidency.

To the horror of Democrats, Bush's response to the slowdown in federal receipts was to lower tax rates.[12] Like Reagan before him, he knew his best hope for a long-term revenue stream adequate to cover federal expenses was a healthy economy. Clinton's high-tax policy had, arguably, been one of the major reasons for the recession; lower rates could, as they did under Reagan, turn things around.

And indeed they did.

Not in time to bail out Bush's first four years, but in 2004 the trend was positive[13] and the future looked bright.

The attack of 9/11 brought terrorism front and center to Bush. His reaction was the opposite of Clinton's. He did not see gangsters to be brought to trial; he saw terrorists who, in or out of uniform, attached or unattached to a nation, were at war with the United States.

Osama bin Laden, based in his training camps in Afghanistan, took credit for the 9/11 tragedies in the United States. President Bush contacted the Taliban, the ruling group in that country, and demanded that bin Laden be produced.

The Taliban failed to respond. In October, the United States attacked. By the end of December, the Taliban was gone; bin Laden was hiding in a cave somewhere (his training camps destroyed); a new government was installed in Kabul, the capital of Afghanistan; and 31 million people were liberated.[14]

President Bush, in his 2002 State of the Union address, made it clear he wasn't through with terrorism. He defined the scope of the danger, he identified known terrorist groups and, in particular, he cited three nations as the axis of evil — Iran, Iraq and North Korea.

> States like these, and their terrorist allies, constitute an axis of evil, arming to threaten the peace of the world. By seeking weapons of mass destruc-

tion, these regimes pose a grave and growing danger. They could provide these arms to terrorists, giving them the means to match their hatred. They could attack our allies or attempt to blackmail the United States. In any of these cases, the price of indifference would be catastrophic.— President George W. Bush, State of the Union, 2002

Saddam Hussein had never ended the Gulf War according to the agreed upon terms. As a consequence, American planes were engaged in regular and expensive overflights of north and south Iraq to make sure that Hussein did not again attack his own people (Kurds and Shiites) or anyone else.

Weapons inspectors had been in and out of Iraq trying to verify that Hussein had destroyed his weapons of mass destruction (WMD), including his nuclear capability. The effort had not been successful because Hussein had refused to cooperate. As a consequence, world opinion, confirmed by U.S. intelligence services, held that Iraq had WMD, and history made it clear that Hussein would use them.

Also, Hussein permitted Osama bin Laden's al-Qaeda training camps to operate in Iraq; he provided safe haven for some al-Qaeda leaders and he subsidized suicide bombers in Palestine.

Pulling all this information together led Bush to the conclusion that Iraq was a rogue nation that, if stabilized, could immediately reduce the threat of terrorism in the Middle East, and in the world. Turning Iraq from a belligerent to an ally, or at worst a neutral, was considered by him to be a key element in the war against terrorism.

Bush appeared before the United Nations in September 2002 and called for an accounting from Iraq after noting its many violations of UN mandates over the past decade. Then the slow, steady march toward war with Iraq began:

- October 2002: The U.S. Senate passed a resolution that gave broad war powers to the president[15]:

    SEC. 3. AUTHORIZATION FOR USE OF UNITED STATES ARMED FORCES. (a) Authorization.— The President is authorized to use the Armed Forces of the United States as he determines to be necessary and appropriate in order to—
    (1) defend the national security of the United States against the continuing threat posed by Iraq; and
    (2) enforce all relevant United Nations Security Council resolutions regarding Iraq.

- November 2002: The UN Security Council passed a unanimous resolution demanding that Iraq disarm or face "serious consequences."[16]
- January 2003: The UN report on arms inspection was highly critical of Iraq.
- January 2003: Bush announced in his State of the Union address that if the UN refused to act against Iraq, the United States and its friends would.

- February 2003: Secretary of State Colin Powell presented the case for war against Iraq to the UN. (It was later determined that some of the information dealing with Iraq's WMD capability was incorrect).
- February 2003: France, Germany and Russia resisted the attempts of the U.S. and Britain to get the UN to move on its latest mandate to Iraq, and on the many other UN resolutions that Saddam had ignored over the years. (It was learned after the fact that Saddam had depended on one or more of these "friendly" nations to pacify the United States in the UN.)
- March 2003: The attack on Iraq began. In a month, Baghdad fell; in December, Saddam Hussein was in jail, and his two sons were dead.

The war was over in 2003 in every traditional sense, but actually it was the beginning of a problem that would dominate the Bush agenda for years to come — the inability or unwillingness of Iraqis to form a government that was acceptable to the major ethnic/religious groups, Kurds, Sunnis and Shiites.

It is not the purpose in this book to examine in detail the war against terrorism, or the troubles the United States has had since the formal war ended. But a few points can be made to make more understandable the need for a continuing U.S. presence in that land, an understanding of fundamental importance to anyone who attempts to make sense out of the politics of the time.

- After the fact it became fashionable for Democrats to deny that they supported the October 2002 resolution of war. Actually, 29 of them voted for it, including prominent figures such as Tom Daschle, Senate Majority Leader; Harry Reid, who was to succeed Daschle and John Kerry, presidential candidate in 2004. Based upon the same fundamental information that the president had, it can be said that the motion to go to war with Iraq, if the UN once again got wobbly, had substantial support in the Senate.
- The war plan was brilliantly executed, but the political plan was not. Kurd, Shiite and Sunni factions had not reconciled as the first term of the Bush administration ended, and cells of al-Qaeda operatives were trying to keep it that way.
- The entire liberal establishment, almost as soon as it became clear that Iraq would not be a quick and bloodless victory, with enthusiastic support from the media turned antiwar to the extent that it bordered on being the most valuable propaganda weapon of the enemy.

Goodwill that existed after 9/11, and nonpartisan support in the Congress that followed, began to melt away as body bags arrived and Americans began to realize that people were getting hurt in this war — that it wasn't going to end overnight.

The war was the central issue during the election of 2004. But underneath the rhetoric and behind the debates a haunting question repeatedly asserted itself: Are Americans tough enough to fight a war against an enemy that can fight back for an extended period of time?

The terrorists were betting in Iraq and elsewhere that America would fold.

HOME FRONT

"George W. Bush, go to hell!"— Maxine Waters (at the televised March for Women's Lives, Washington, D.C., April 24, 2005)[17]

The above comment, made years after the 2000 election, catches the attitude toward George Bush from the first day that he set foot into the Oval Office that is shared by many Democrats, especially members with Ms. Waters of the Black Caucus, a group of 43 black Democrats who seem to share a special dislike for the president.

It made no difference to these politicians that repeated postelection counts of votes in Florida, the state that pushed Bush over the top, clearly indicated that Bush won the presidency. In a political environment where some questioned his right to the position, Bush could avoid virulent attack only if he had the best of luck. And that is exactly what he did not have.

- There was a recession.
- Federal revenues dropped precipitously.
- Unemployment increased.
- Corporate scandals broke out.
- The "Clinton" budget surplus leaked away.
- France, Germany and Russia refused to enforce UN resolutions.
- The decision to go to war resulted in casualties.
- The Iraq phase of the war against terrorism did not end in a minute.

In other words, Bush's political opponents had a field day during Bush's first term. Everyplace they looked there was a problem they could hang on him.

How disturbing it must have been when Republicans in 2002 recovered the Senate[18]— and gained additional seats in the House.[19]

With everything going for them, with issues galore to complain about, Democrats lost again.

The result?

Hatred for Bush intensified. Rhetoric became more inflammatory. Politics in Washington, always somewhat gruesome, became nastier than ever.

And citizens too were beginning to feel the pressures of the time. In addition to the antiwar hammering that confronted them in the daily media blitz (that seemed determined to break the American will), people were increasingly concerned about the safety of their jobs and their savings.

The Misery Index in 2004, despite the problems in the economy, was 25 percent lower[20] than it was four years before, which was the good news; but there was bad news, too. The most politically sensitive element of the index, the unemployment rate, was up.

This reflects the hardship that had stricken America's middle class, just as the precipitous drop in the stock market (previously mentioned) ruined the retirement plans of some and frightened others who were trying to plan for the future.

The increase in income per capita was predictably tepid,[21] but that was relieved somewhat by lower interest and inflation rates, and by the drop in taxes per capita, all of which helped somewhat to alleviate the economic blows of the time.

These were tough times for the people in general and for Bush in particular. Recession, plus corporate scandals, plus the need to go to were was tough medicine. But these were the tests of the times that the president and the nation survived.

And Bush, to his credit, confronted them. Critics may deplore his tactics; nobody can deny his courage.

In 2004, GDP increased by a healthy 6.3 percent.[22] The economy, assisted by the president's tax program, was moving into a higher gear. Improved federal revenues were destined to follow.

SUPREME COURT[23]

The Rehnquist Supreme Court that operated intact during the past four years did the same in 2001–04. Three judges were approaching an age when retirement would at least be considered — Chief Justice Rehnquist (77), and Associate Justices Stevens (81) and O'Connor (71). None did so.

This was a difficult Court to predict: Four activists, Stevens, Breyer, Ginsburg and Souter; three conservatives, Rehnquist, Scalia and Thomas; two pragmatists, O'Connor and Kennedy.

For strict constructionists to prevail they needed the support of both pragmatists; for activists to prevail they needed only one more vote. Obviously, a unanimous opinion from this Court would not be common, and, on social issues, would be rare.

Chief Justice Rehnquist heard 327 cases in 2001–04, about 28 percent more than he heard during the previous four years and 25 times more than Chief Justice Warren heard in 1957–60 during Eisenhower's final years.[24] The explosion of cases began under Kennedy/Johnson; it has continued ever since, especially so when a Democrat has been president.

A sampling of a few cases provides insight into the concerns of the day, and of the leanings of the judges:

Ashcroft v. ACLU, 2004. The Child Online Protection Act prevented minors from accessing pornography online. Online publishers and the ACLU sued to prevent enforcement, arguing that it violated the free speech clause of the First

Amendment. The lower courts agreed, ruling that the law was "overbroad" and applied to too much protected material that adults had a right to access. The issue: Does the law violate the First Amendment by using a method that is not the least restrictive available? In a 5–4 decision (Rehnquist, Scalia, O'Connor and Breyer dissenting) the Court ruled that the law was unconstitutional — less restrictive means to the same end were available. Two observations flow naturally from this case:

- The judicial alignment is strange — Breyer sided with conservatives; Thomas, with activists.
- Something strange is happening in the United States when the U.S. Supreme Court exercises its brainpower to assure adults that they will not be deprived of their right to view pornography.

Ashcroft v. Free Speech Coalition, 2002. The Child Pornography Prevention Act prohibits any visual depiction of a minor engaging in sexually explicit actions, or any image that gives that impression. The FSC argued that the terms of the act are too broad and violate the free speech clause of the First Amendment; also, the act is overbroad because it bans material not found to be obscene in two previous Court cases. The issue: Is the act overbroad because it bans speech that was not found to be obscene under two previous cases? In a 6–3 decision (Rehnquist, Scalia and O'Connor dissenting) the Court ruled that the act is unconstitutional because it is overbroad and because it bans material that was previously found to be protected speech. An interesting aspect of this case is that it shows a willingness on the part of three judges to overturn precedent. The case also shows, once again, the slippery slope that was created when the definition of "speech" went beyond the ordinary and became almost any form of human expression.

Elk Grove v. Newdow, 2004. Newdow's daughter attended a public school that began the day with a voluntary recitation of the pledge of allegiance. Newdow protested the inclusion of the phrase "under God," and the requirement that his daughter, at the least, had to listen to the pledge. The U.S. Ninth Circuit court ruled that the 1954 act of Congress that added the disputed phrase, and the practice of voluntary recitation were both unconstitutional. Newdow, a divorced father, did not have custody of his daughter. The issues: Does Newdow have standing to bring the issue since he is not the custodial parent? Is the school practice of voluntary recitation unconstitutional? In an 8–0 decision (Scalia absent) the Court ducked the constitutional question by ruling that Newdow did not have standing. In a separate opinion, Rehnquist, Thomas and O'Connor defended the school practice.

Gratz v. Bollinger, 2003. Gratz applied to the University of Michigan's College of Literature, Science and Arts with superior scores and was denied admission because it was the practice of the college to enter virtually all qualified African Americans, Hispanics and Native Americans because "it serves as a compelling interest in achieving diversity among the student body." The issue: Does the college's use of racial preferences violate the equal protection clause of the Fourteenth Amendment or Title VI of the Civil Rights Act of 1964? In a 6–3 decision (Stevens, Souter and Ginsburg dissenting) the Court ruled that the college's practice was unconstitutional. The Court reasoned that the practice of awarding 20 points to every single member of the stipulated minority groups "is not narrowly tailored" to meet the college's "compelling interest." The Court did not rule on the merits of the "compelling interest" theory. While the nation in general was sympathetic to outreach programs that brought minority groups into the fold, it did not approve of overaggressive affirmative action processes that increasingly and unfairly denied to other Americans the legitimate fruit of their efforts. This decision reflected the tension between inclusiveness and fairness.

Grutter v. Bollinger, 2003. Grutter, a white resident of Michigan with superior test scores, was denied admission to the University School of Law because the school used race as an admission factor in the belief that it served a "compelling interest in promoting diversity" in the student body. A district court held that the "compelling interest" was not compelling and enjoined its use of race in the admissions process. The Michigan Supreme Court overruled citing the *University of California v. Bakke* (1978) as justification for the use of racial preferences in making admission decisions that were entitled to strict scrutiny. The Michigan court also ruled that the college practice did not, in effect, amount to a quota system. The issue: Does the college practice violate the equal protection clause of the Fourteenth Amendment or Title VI of the Civil Rights Act of 1964? In a 5–4 opinion (Rehnquist, Scalia, Thomas and Kennedy dissenting) the Court ruled that "in the context of its individualized inquiry into the possible diversity contributions of all applicants, the Law School's race-conscious admissions program does not unduly harm non-minority applicants." In this case, as opposed to Gratz, above, preferences were not allowed to groups, but to applicants after individual review. The Court avoided the "compelling interest" issue. *This and similar cases were gradually burying the dream of Martin Luther King, Jr., of a society when men and women would be judged by the quality of their character, not the color of their skin.*

These sample cases reveal the changes taking place in society as the original contract that brought them together was attacked by special interest groups and their allies in the judiciary. Activists had long ago learned to avoid state legislatures (the voice of the people), and to seek their goals through the courts—to impose by law what they couldn't win through argument.

Society[25]

The fiscal and judicial aspects of the second American Revolution were no longer evolving. They had become the norm of the times.

- Entitlement programs that never before existed dominated the federal budget.
- The nation could no longer afford a robust military.
- The U.S. Supreme Court had legalized abortion, a decision that remains controversial.

The America of Eisenhower no longer existed. The separation from the lessons of the past that began in the 1960s had come to full flower, to the delight of some, and to the dismay of others. Particularly disappointing was the corruption of the public school system.

As George Bush's first term came to a close it was reasonably clear that two items of social importance would dominate in the near term, marriage and stem cell research.

Congress had seen this coming and it passed the Defense of Marriage Act in 1996, which stated that, for purposes of federal law, marriage was defined as a union between a man and a woman.

Stem-cell research is the abortion issue grown large. Those who regard a fetus as a life, deserving protection, oppose it; those who don't, favor it. The issue is technical and beyond the scope of this book to probe, except to indicate that it may be the most important moral issue mankind has ever faced.

Change in Public Debt

The budget surplus of the previous administration seemed to offer a ray of hope that the long history of continuing deficits was over. But in the summary of the budget surplus of chapter 16 it was made clear that the surplus was a manufactured one that cynics could describe as short-term window dressing for President Clinton's last term that could not be repeated.

In addition to this, the immediate onset of a recession, followed by the attack of 9/11 and the corporate scandals, were enough to throw a cloud over the fiscal prospects of the new president, and to return to attention the scary relationship between the needs of national defense, the structural unsoundness of the federal budget and the size of the public debt.

Only one thing was sure: The recession would have a negative impact on federal revenue, and the 9/11 attack would require more spending for national defense, a combination bound to add to the already significant pressures posed by a budget that had been out of control for most of a half-century.

How these pressures were or were not resolved will become apparent as transactions for the period are analyzed.

A glance at the numbers provides a feel for what is to come. The revenue increase was low; the increase in *Defense* draws attention, as does the decrease in *Interest*.

Table 17.2
Transactions (in billions of dollars)

		2001–04		1997–2000
Taxes		$ 7506.8		$ 7153.8
Less:				
Defense	$1514.2		$1108.4	
Interest	690.4		937.8	
Total		2204.2		2046.2
Net		$ 5302.2		$ 5107.6
Less:				
Government	$ 706.5		$ 489.6	
Human Resources	5415.0		4209.0	
Total		6121.5		4698.6
Surplus/deficit		$ -819.3		$ 409.0
Debt, beginning		-3409.8		-3734.1
Total		$-4229.1		$-3325.1
Adjustment*		-66.4		-84.7
Debt, Ending		$-4295.5		$-3409.8

*Treasury cannot be exact when it finances a budget deficit and the difference
between what is needed and the value of securities traded inevitably produces a relatively small variance.

Source: Historical Tables 2007, 1.1, 3.1

Revenue remaining after deducting primary costs versus the total cost of
Government and *Human Resources* in 1997–2000 permitted cost growth opportunity but, since the ultimate deficit was huge, it is obvious that the cost growth
opportunity was not sufficient to satisfy the cost needs of those centers.

TAXES

Revenue in 2001 was less than it was in 2000. The 17-year Reagan boom
was over and for the first time in almost two decades a president suffered a
year-to-year revenue loss.[26]

For those who believe there is no difference between political parties, one
need only look at behavior to demonstrate the untruth of that position.

Clinton faced what he considered to be lower-than-necessary revenue
growth (actually, 1993 revenue was 5.8 percent higher than the year before and,
arguably, no tax increase was necessary), approved a huge tax increase[27] that
lifted taxes per capita to levels that hadn't been seen for decades.[28]

Bush, on the other hand, faced with a far more serious situation, looked
to the economy for the sustainable income needed by the government, just as
Reagan did when he struggled with an economy that was nearing collapse. The
recession was the problem, so Bush needed to stimulate the economy with every
tool at his command. An active economy would provide more jobs, higher
wages and fewer layoffs, all of which would eventually show as higher federal
revenue.

This contrast in style underlines a fundamental difference between the political parties: Republicans prefer high economic activity at low tax rates; Democrats prefer high tax rates, which, they insist, do not harm economic activity (but even they will agree that high tax rates are not good for the economy).

Bush's approach to the recession was a success by any measure in the sense that things could have been much worse if the government had not adopted policies that stimulated economic growth. But no approach was possible that could have avoided *all* penalties associated with the recession.

And in terms of revenue, they were expensive indeed.

Under the previous 11 presidential terms, the average four-year increase in revenue was 35.4 percent; under the three most previous presidential terms, the average revenue increase was 30.0 percent.[29]

Had tax income increased by 35.4 percent over the previous four years, it would have amounted to $9686.2 billion, or $2179.4 billion more than actual; if it had increased by 30.0 percent, revenue would have been $9299.9 billion, or $1793.1 billion more than actual.[30]

This means the deficit (like those experienced during the Great Depression) was fundamentally caused by a recession that was deeper, longer and more punishing than anything experienced since those dark days of pre–World War II.

It is to finance uncontrollable events, like recessions, that public debt should be used, and the subject deficit was an issue only because the nation's credit line, so to speak, had been extended by the unfunded costs associated with the unaffordable Johnson revolution, and, more importantly, because the media conveniently overlooked the punishing loss of revenue suffered by Bush through no fault of his own.

DEFENSE

Terrorism is the systematic use of terror to gain political power. Its special characteristic, namely, that which brings terror, lies in the fact that its targets are the innocent, those who are at work, at rest or at play when they are brutally attacked, tortured or killed by a zealot they didn't know and probably had never met.

The violence of terrorists is opportunistic; their goal is specific. They hope that an environment of fear and distrust will cause political pressures that will result in broad media coverage, political unrest and, eventually, the surrender of political leaders to their will.

Terrorism motivated purely by an appetite for political power is loathsome and dangerous, but it is also usually geographically limited. Drug kings of South America, for example, use it to keep the government weak and out of their business.

But terrorism motivated by religious belief carries with it an especially lethal attribute if the religion is broadly held. It becomes a threat wherever its practitioners are found.

Islam is the second largest religion in the world with more than a billion adherents located all over the globe, including Europe and the United States.

The brand of terrorism that threatens the United States is the worst kind. It is organized, sponsored, supported or, at the least, tolerated by the Islamic leaders of the world.

- Most 9/11 terrorists came from Saudi Arabia.
- Saudi Arabia supports Islamic mosques all over the world that preach Islamic superiority and anti–Western, anti–Jewish filth.
- Afghanistan was ruled by Muslim extremists until the United States cleaned them out.
- Saddam Hussein supported Palestinian terrorists and allowed terrorist groups to train in Iraq.
- Iran and Syria support terrorists.
- Libya was found guilty of the same.
- Governments of Pakistan, Turkey, Jordan and Egypt live in daily fear of an extremist takeover.
- Hamas and Hizbullah practically rule Palestine and Lebanon.
- The Middle East, in general, is virulently anti–Western.

The United States is not at war with terrorism because George W. Bush became president; it is at war because Bush acknowledges a reality that Clinton ignored — terrorists are at war with the United States.

The war against the United States actually began in the 1980s but, except for Ronald Reagan's attack on Libya (1986[31]) only the terrorists acknowledged it.

Attacks against America's global assets and its people[32] during the Clintons years were treated as if Al Capone had formed a new gang that had to be locked up, not as a systematic attack of an enemy against a culture they intended to dominate.

Accordingly, Clinton hired lawyers and he fired soldiers.

Clinton entered office with an active military force of two million; when he left, 600,000 troops had been fired and he transferred to Bush the smallest military force since Truman unwisely stripped the size of it, an action Eisenhower soon corrected in order to face the Korean War and the Cold War.[33]

Yes, there was a budget surplus in 1997–2000. But a major reason for that was the unwise and unwarranted cutback in the military that left the succeeding president in a weakened condition to fight the war that Clinton had ignored.

Had *Defense* increased at the same rate as revenue, the cost in 2000–04 would have been $1163.1 billion, or $351.1 billion less than actual.[34] To that extent, this cost center was responsible for the deficit for the period.

The ability to borrow, a priceless asset for any government, should be reserved for wars and other calamities, economic or natural. That had been the case until the Kennedy/Johnson era. Thereafter, under the watchful supervision of Democratic congresses, the availability of this national asset was abused, and debt grew because uncontrolled spending never ended.

The borrowing power Bush needed to rebuild the military was not available to him. Despite this, he prepared for war as best he could.

Bush did not increase the size of the military[35] but he radically improved its neglected readiness. Compared to the year 2000, spending in 2004 for operations/maintenance, procurement, and research was 64, 47, and 62 percent higher, respectively.[36]

No doubt Bush and Secretary of Defense Donald Rumsfeld would have, if possible, recalled the 600,000 well-trained troops dismissed by Clinton, but they were confronted by the budget reality that had loomed since the 1960s: The borrowing power of the United States had been dissipated by profligate spending. The beleaguered Bush could not turn to it for the support he needed without breaking the bank in the process.

America's claim to superpower status was coming to an end because of the actions of self-indulgent or power-hungry politicians who had never learned one of life's primary lessons, usually taught on mother's knee — always pay your bills.

The unfunded cost of expansion of the military was a legitimate addition to public debt since it was caused by a response to an act of war against the United States.

INTEREST

George W. Bush no sooner reached the Oval Office than he was hit by a recession. This was followed by the 9/11 attack and by corporate scandals that shocked the nation and sent the stock market into a spin.

But one thing broke his way. Inflation was low, and it dropped even lower during his term,[37] and — of more importance to the federal budget — interest rates dropped precipitously.

If the opposite had been the case, the deficit for the period could have been considerably larger.

Had *Interest* grown at the same rate as revenue, its cost during the subject period would have been $984.1 billion, or $293.7 billion more than actual.[38] For that reason, this cost center made no contribution to the deficit.

This was a fortunate break for the president, and it underlines the precariousness of the self-caused budget problem in the United States: Reasonably probable circumstance working in concert (for example, high interest rates plus high military costs) could cause deficits of unsustainable size or, alternatively, they could cause the United States to unilaterally disarm (as much of

Europe has come close to doing) because it no longer can afford a military establishment.

This fact, never mentioned in the major media, represents the greatest danger to the American way of life that exists in the modern world.

America, like Rome, will destroy itself in the foreseeable future if the quality of its national management, as demonstrated over the last half-century, does not radically improve.

GOVERNMENT

An early review of the numbers in Table 17.2 indicated that a major part of the deficit for the period would be found in *Government* and *Human Resources.*

Under the flow-though method of revenue allocation being employed in this book, *Government* could expand by 20.3 percent within the context of a balanced budget.

One would expect to find in wartime an increase in the cost of Justice and, perhaps, other department line items related to national security. Otherwise, one would expect a prudent Congress to be applying the spending brakes. Analysis will locate offending line items in the *Government* budget.

Table 17.3
Government (in billions of dollars)

	2001–04	1997–2000	% Change
Energy	$- .4	$ 2.9	-113.8
Natural Resources/Environment	115.5	92.5	24.9
Transportation	247.9	170.5	45.4
Community/regional development	59.5	43.3	37.4
International affairs	87.0	60.7	43.3
Science/space/technology	84.6	72.1	17.3
Agriculture	86.2	80.4	7.2
Justice	146.1	99.0	47.6
General	76.1	56.2	35.4
Total	$902.5	$677.6	33.2%
Commerce & housing credit*	11.3	- 7.8	144.8
Total	$913.8	$669.8	36.4%
Offsetting receipts	-207.3	-180.2	
Net	$706.5	$489.6	

*Made up of earnings from various federal housing and other programs— subject to major changes from year to year relative to market conditions. (Historical Tables 2007, 3.2)

Source: Historical Tables 2007, 3.1

The percentage change in the line item Energy draws the eye, but the cost significance is minor and attention quickly shifts to more costly line items like Transportation, Community, International, Justice and General, each of which expanded well beyond the limits of the approved multiplier (1.203).

Oil prices had a great deal to do with the cost of anything that moved. During Clinton's last four years, the price of crude oil per barrel averaged $18.63. Under Bush, the cost in an average year never went below $22.81 and in 2004 it had climbed to $37.66 per barrel.[39] And in addition to the cost of fuel, people and things during wartime move more often. This marriage of price and use yielded transportation costs of unusual size that can be logically tied to the war effort.

The temptation exists to label as a liberal project any increased costs in the line item Community and Regional Development. But in this case it isn't true. The distorted cost increase was specifically related to disaster relief and insurance, a line item of varying importance from administration to administration depending upon the whims of Mother Nature.

President Bush had a bad streak of luck that hit the budget hard in 2003 and 2004 — a massive failure in the power grid in the Northeast; hurricanes hit the southern states, especially Florida, with unusual ferocity; a gigantic tsunami struck Asia and the United States poured billions into the region.

One expects the State Department to be more active during a time of war. And it was. The line item International expanded by 43.3 percent — every subelement of this line item went up significantly.

It is no surprise that Justice increased abnormally. In addition to social pressures that had caused cost variances in this line item for years, there was added the beefed-up costs of all security systems in the United States because of the peculiar nature of an enemy that was more inclined to infiltrate than to attack.

The increase in the line item General wasn't probed in any depth except to note that cost remained relatively normal until the war in Iraq began in 2003. From this, and from the description of the sub-line items, it is estimated that the cost surge was war related.

If the total of all line items in Government had increased at the approved amount, the total in the subject period would have been $589.1 billion or $117.4 billion less than actual; to that extent this cost center contributed to the deficit for the period.[40]

This unfunded increase was not the result of mindless spending but, rather, was related to war for the most part. In normal times it would have been recognized as a legitimate addition to public debt.

HUMAN RESOURCES

For the first time since the 1960s, some level of self-restraint was demonstrated in this cost center in 1997–2000 thanks to four full years of Republican leadership in Congress. The importance of that control cannot be overestimated since it is runaway spending in this cost center that was the primary cause of the size of the debt in 2004.

The analysis of *Human Resources* for 2001–04 is approached with hope, but also with caution because the question is: Did politicians who preached smaller government when they were out of power continue to practice what they preached when they were in power?

Four years of affirmative response to that question was not enough to bring optimism. The same entitlements in the same form were still in place. There was much work — hard political work — to be done. Did they do it in 2001–04?

Table 17.4
Human Resources (in billions of dollars)

	2000–04	1997–2000	% Change
Education, training, services	$ 298.1	$ 203.0	46.8%
Health/Medicaid	828.5	550.8	50.4
Income Security*	1063.7	855.8	24.3
Social Security	1859.2	1543.9	20.4
Medicare	967.1	770.3	25.5
Unemployment compensation	185.6	113.0	64.2
Veterans	212.8	171.4	24.2
Total	$5415.0	$4209.0	28.7%

*Minus unemployment compensation (from 1965–68 on)

Note: Major federal programs since the 1960s— Food Stamps 1961 (pilot), Food Stamps 1964, Medicaid 1965, Student Aid 1966, Medicare 1967, Coal Miners Benefits 1970, Commodity Donations 1973, Supplementary Security Income 1974, Supplemental Feeding 1976, Earned Income Tax Credit 1976, Legal Services 1976, Energy Assistance 1977, Welfare Reform 1996, No Child Left Behind Act 2002, Medicare Prescription Drug Modernization Act 2003

Source: Historical Tables 2007, 3.1

The rate of cost increase in this center, by historical standards was not exorbitant.[41] But this was a time of war, a time when one would expect belt tightening — a time to park the imagination and to activate cost control procedures.

The increases in the line items Unemployment Compensation and Veterans escape criticism because the first was related to the recession and the second to the war, neither of which could be blamed on U.S. politicians.

But concerning other line items the kindest thing that can be said is that this was not the time to be expanding social services absent reasons of undeniable importance and urgency.

Education etc. is the first item to fall under the analytical microscope. The cost of this line item in 2000 was $54 billion; actual cost in 2004 was $88 billion[42]— 63 percent higher.

For some reason known only to President Bush, he chose this time of recession and war to collaborate with Ted Kennedy, the most partisan Democrat in the Senate, on the No Child Left Behind Act and on other education initiatives.

Productive education initiatives are indeed needed, and chief among them should be the establishment of standards and testing requirements designed to identify troubled schools and students, and to provide help for both. But as worthy as these aims are, they do not deal with cost-free deterrents to quality education such as immigration policy, union control, teacher certification requirements, the quality of teachers, etc.

Bush, in other words, fell into Washington's typical problem-solving trap, to wit: When a problem occurs invent a federal program.

Kennedy and his followers were complicit in this cost explosion but they are excused because they don't know better. But Bush does know better, and he was wrong to choose this particular and expensive road to education reform during a time of war.

Health/Medicaid increased more than 50 percent, an inexcusable rate of increase during a time of war, and during a time when no health menace was attacking the nation's citizens. The most important reason for this distorted increase was the growth in Medicaid, a program that dates back to the 1960s. In 2000, the cost of this line item was $118 billion; in 2004, it was $176 billion—a 49 percent increase.[43] The nation cannot afford huge programs that grow faster than the ability to pay.

The rates of growth in Income Security, Medicare and Social Security were not by themselves outlandish. But the danger these three ancient and unaffordable line items pose can be likened to a huge, out-of-control tanker carrying explosives, one that is unavoidably headed for New York harbor at a steady and irreversible pace. Sooner or later it will hit shore. And the explosion will be monumental.

So it is with this gathering of entitlement programs. If this ship can't be stopped and redirected, the United States is going to go BOOM.

Had the growth in *Human Resources* been limited to the allowable amount, cost would have been $5064.2 billion or $350.8 billion less than actual.[44] To that extent this cost center is responsible for the deficit for the period.

President Bush and his Republican colleagues in Congress did not attack the problems that beset this cost center. The things that have caused the growth in public debt were still in place in 2004.

SUMMARY OF BUDGET DEFICIT

Perception is almost everything in politics. Each political party on Election Day presents to the electorate the face of what it claims to be, a visage that too often bears little relationship to reality.

Some voters buy into disingenuous political speeches because they are politically illiterate, a condition that is growing alarmingly.

> If a nation expects to be ignorant — and free — in a state of civilization, it expects what never was and never will be.— Thomas Jefferson, 1816[45]

Jefferson, as usual, said it well. And reflection on his words brings one to a frightening recognition that the ultimate security of the greatest governmental experiment in history — the United States— depends upon the wisdom of its citizens, a wisdom based upon knowledge of, and appreciation of, freedoms organized by the Founding Fathers in the form of a Constitution that emerged from their collective mind, one that recognized that it worked under the direction of the hand of God.

The security of this grand experiment becomes compromised if one substitutes political illiterates for such dedicated citizens.

Lincoln's government of the people, by the people and for the people cannot be run by those apathetic and uninformed.

President Bush was measured in 2001–04 against the false impression of Clinton as a moderate who skillfully led the nation to its first budget surplus in decades.

On that yardstick he didn't fare too well — a surplus of $409.0 billion versus a deficit of $819.3 is a swing from bad to good that had many scratching their heads in bewilderment.

Table 17.5
Summary of Deficit — 2001–2004 (in billions of dollars)

Cost Center	Amount
War on Terror	$351.1
Interest Government	117.4
Human Resources	350.8
Total	$819.3

Sources: Exhibits 1, 11–2, 16

The cost of the War on Terror is an addition to public debt that was not caused by irresponsible behavior, but by the viciously effective behavior of an enemy that had finally been recognized as such by the U.S. Government.

Similarly, the unfunded cost of *Government* represents a legitimate increase in public debt because it was caused by such uncontrollable external events as the inflation in oil prices,[46] natural disasters in the United States and the South Pacific, accelerated State Department activity related to the war, increased Justice Department activity related to national security and, finally, the increased cost of services rendered that were war related.

Concerning *Human Resources*, however, responsibility for this cost overrun is shared between the Congress and the president, on two counts.

First, entitlement programs were not effectively restructured. An excuse for this can be found in the fact that power in the U.S. Senate was never decisive (veto proof). Republicans held power in January 2001, with 50 of 100 seats and Vice President Cheney casting the decisive vote. But in June 2001, Sen. Jeffords (R–VT) became an Independent who caucused with Democrats — and control went to Democrats (50 + 1–49).

Republicans reassumed control in November 2002, with the same tenuous 50 seats — their margin increased to 51 seats in the 108th Congress.

Second, it is understandable that Bush could not modernize federal programs, but it is not understandable why he was intent on expanding some of them, especially when other approaches less costly and more effective (and undeniably, more confrontational) were available to him.

His objectives in education, for example, were laudable, but it was a terrible time to expand the cost of a center that was already out of control.

Obviously his concerns about education quality outweighed his fear of deficits as he made clear in a succession of speeches, for example:

> Good jobs begin with good schools, and here we've made a fine start. Republicans and Democrats worked together to achieve historic education reform so that no child is left behind.... We must upgrade our teacher colleges and teacher training and launch a major recruiting drive with a great goal for America: a quality teacher in every classroom.[47]

Similarly, the president was concerned about the affordability and the durability of the nation's health care system and of Social Security, something he made clear as far back as his inauguration speech in January 2001:

> We will reform Social Security and Medicare, sparing our children from struggles we have the power to prevent.

These were braves words from a president who gained office by the slimmest of margins and who knew that the mere mention of Social Security in such a way threw most federal politicians into a state of shock.

But he couldn't do what he hoped to do with Social Security, and to make things worse, he added to the costs of other programs that were breaking the bank — during a time of war.

Finally, and importantly, one must not overlook the fact that compared to other presidencies George Bush had worse economic luck than any president since Herbert Hoover in the 1930s.

It wasn't his fault that he walked into a recession; it wasn't his fault that Arabs decided to attack America; it wasn't his fault that corporate scandals worsened an already difficult economic situation. Yet he paid for each of these things in terms of collapsing federal revenue.

Under the Taxes section of this chapter it was noted that had tax income increased at anything approaching normal, there would have been no deficit at all, despite his adventures in education and health care.

Conclusion

With revenue so low and *Defense* so high, the spending profile of the United States was bound to be much different from what it was before. This was the budget of a new president with a relatively new Congress operating under radically different circumstances.

Table 17.6
Spending Priorities

	1960 *Ike*	1968 *LBJ*	1976 *GRF*	1980 *JEC*	1988 *RWR*	1992 *GHWB*	2000 *WJC*	2004 *GWB*
Primary costs								
Defense	52.2%	27.3%	24.1%	22.7%	27.3%	21.6%	16.5%	19.9%
Interest	7.5	14.2	7.2	8.9	14.3	14.4	12.5	7.0
Total	59.7%	41.4%	31.3%	31.6%	41.6%	36.0%	29.0%	26.9%
Government	11.9	8.4	14.0	15.4	8.3	8.1	8.7	8.3
Education/ services	1.9	2.9	5.1	5.4	2.9	3.1	3.0	3.8
Health/ Medicaid	.9	4.2	4.1	3.9	4.2	6.5	8.6	10.5
Medicare		7.4	4.3	5.4	7.4	8.6	11.0	11.7
Income Security	8.0	12.2	16.4	14.7	12.2	14.4	14.2	14.5
Social Security	12.6	20.6	19.9	20.0	20.6	20.8	22.9	21.7
Veterans	5.9	2.9	4.9	3.6	2.9	2.5	2.6	2.6
Total	100.0%	100.0%	100.0%	100.0%	100.0%	100.0%	100.0%	100.0%
	(3)	(2)(3)	(3)	(3)	(3)	(2)	(1)	(2)

1 = peace; 2 = war; 3 = cold war

Source: Historical Tables 2007, 3.1

Under Eisenhower, with a robust military of 2.5 million men,[48] 28 percent of spending went to social services. From that time on, the slice of spending that went to social services steadily inclined until, in 2004 under Bush, it amounted to 65 percent and a nation that could not afford a military that was much smaller than Ike's.

Those are the broad and most dramatic comparisons that are disclosed in the above table. And they should make every American pause.

It has always been the case that war requires more resources than an economy usually provides. For that reason, the United States prior to 1960 developed a strong credit reputation that it made use of during times of stress. And because the ability to do so was of such importance to all presidents, care was taken not to abuse the borrowing capacity of the nation.

That policy for reasons elsewhere described changed after President Johnson inaugurated his Great Society programs.

President Bush has been one of several presidents who have been punished by this unaffordable policy that has led to excess debt. Bound on one hand by his presidential oath to defend the nation, Bush on the other hand was confronted by a credit line already overextended.

In practical terms, this meant his ability to build a military force adequate to meet the global threats of terrorism and nuclear expansion had been unduly and dangerously circumscribed.

During the subject period, the unfunded *Defense* and most of the increase in *Government* were unfortunate, but necessary; the increase in *Human*

Resources (more than 40 percent of the total increase in debt) represented the cost of a problem that the nation's politicians were afraid to face.

Had it not been for the fact that interest rates had sagged,[49] the deficit for the period could have exceeded a trillion dollars.

Table 17.7
Public Debt, 2004 (billions)

Event	Inherited 2000	Added 2001–04	Total 2004	%
World War I	$ 18.3	$	$ 18.3	.4%
Great Depression	24.5	24.5	.6	
World War II	142.5	142.5	3.3	
Korean War	6.6	6.6	.2	
Cold War	206.1	206.1	4.8	
War on Terrorism	351.5	351.5	8.2	
Interest	286.5	286.5	6.7	
Government	349.5	117.3	466.8	10.8
Human Resources	2274.5	350.5	2625.0	61.1
Treasury	101.3	66.4	167.7	3.9
Total	$3409.8	$885.7	$4295.5	100.0%

Source: Exhibits 1, 11, 12, 16

The only real criticism of the budget performance of the Bush administration in 2001–04 is the administration's failure to convince the American people that entitlement programs had to be changed for a simple and understandable reason — absent change, the nation would go broke; absent change, the cost was destined to overwhelm the budget.

The president's concentration on education costs can be criticized on several counts, but it is also true that education is one of the nation's nastiest problems, one that demands aggressive leadership. If history rules that Bush's judgment was flawed in this respect, it was an honorable error.

From a political standpoint, opponents of Bush during the 2004 election had plenty to blame him for. But fortunately for him, his faults were shared by his opponents and they couldn't use them against him.

For example, he didn't overhaul entitlement programs, but his opponents didn't want him to; he didn't fix the immigration problem, but his opponents didn't want him to do that either; his spending on education and health care may have been ill-timed and excessive, but his opponents approved of it.

This being the case, Democrats mounted a personal attack against Bush, rather than a substantive one during the election campaign.

It didn't work, and it also helped that his opponent was Senator Kerry of Massachusetts. This time there was no doubt: Bush won the election.

The questions?

Would America remain strong in what appeared to be a war of cultures? Would Bush break through Democratic resistance on problems like oil dependence and, especially, on the cost of entitlement programs?

18

George W. Bush,
2005–2008*

Second-Term President

George W. Bush's first day in the Oval Office was cursed by the onset of a recession but it was blessed with the gift of peace. On the last day of his first term, recession was a memory, but he found himself in the middle of the nation's most dangerous war since FDR in 1941 joined the Allies in a battle for Western civilization against Adolf Hitler's Nazi Germany and its allies, Japan and Italy.

The Korean and Vietnam wars were important, and they were costly in terms of treasure and life, but neither realistically threatened the United States as we know it. Even during the Cold War against the USSR with the deadliest weapons ever devised by man aimed at the United States 24 hours a day, only the most timid Americans believed the Soviets would pull the trigger while knowing that, as soon as they did, they would be annihilated by return fire. As bad and as frightening as Soviet leaders were, they were not mad, but ideologues seeking worldly power and wealth at an acceptable price.

But in the war against terrorism, like World War II, America's essence is at stake. Had America lost FDR's war, it would have earned freedom, as defined by Hitler. And if it loses Bush's war, it will earn freedom, as defined by Islam.

What does that mean? To find out, ask German Jews who survived the death camps to define Hitler's freedom for non–Germans; ask Christians who live in Saudi Arabia today to describe Islamic freedom for non–Muslims.

Hitler's freedom and Islam's freedom are not — to understate — America's freedom. Hitler was a menace, but even in victory he too was an ideologue driven by ambition for wealth and power. It would not have been in his interest to destroy America's infrastructure. Freedom would have crumbled under

*Numbers for 2007 and 2008 are estimates provided by the Office of Management and Budget, Historical Tables, Fiscal Year 2008.

him, but most American cities and wealth-building institutions would have been spared. Ironically, Hitler's ambition would have protected America's assets had he been victorious.

Not so with terrorists. And that is why the war against terrorism is even more threatening to the continuation of the American dream than Nazi Germany was in World War II. It is a different kind of war for reasons unique to the attackers and to the times.

The attackers do not represent a nation, but an extreme Islamic ideology that is shared by a large minority of Muslims, and is tolerated by the majority of Muslims to an unknown and varying degree. These zealots seldom frontally attack the U.S. military, but they will attack America's will to fight by killing innocents at random, and by destroying infrastructure without regard for consequential human suffering.

Terrorists enjoy economic and political fruits of victory but they are not satisfied by them. Their objective goes deeper: They insist upon conversion or subjugation — they intend to destroy the American way of life.

The times during which this latest uprising of Muslims is taking place are also unique. Communications, transportation and weaponry now make it possible for a relatively small group of activists to deal crippling blows that take thousands of lives and cause billions in damage in a matter of minutes.

And seven hours later they could be having lunch thousands of miles away.

Fifty years ago men like Ahmadinejad (Iran), Nasrallah (Lebanon), al-Sadr (Iraq), al-Assad (Syria) and Haniya (Palestine-Hamas) would have had zero international clout. But today they have the civilized world tied up in knots because of their willingness and their ability to destroy for the sake of destruction.

Another characteristic of the times is unique in terms of its impact on the exposure of the United States to international dangers. Western Europe is not what it used to be. Years of socialism, accompanied by a retreat from its Christian heritage, have left once proud and strong nations like France and Germany in a weakened condition. They are today what the United States could be tomorrow if it doesn't get its budget priorities and its values straightened out.

Countries with neither the resources to field a formidable military force nor the will to use it if it magically appeared will not be the allies of the future that they were in the past.

The appraisal of Western Europe by some terrorists as being a paper tiger unless supported by the United States is uncomfortably close to the truth. Except for Britain (to a declining degree), the United States can no longer depend upon the support of Western Europe. Indeed, one sometimes wonders if France, for instance, in its desperate eagerness to protect itself, hasn't become an enemy rather than a friend.

FDR, in the middle of his presidential crisis, was surrounded by allies. President Bush, in the middle of his, finds America's usual allies weak, resistant and obstructive. But he plods on, seeking new alliances with nations that have strange names, hoping to find a friend here and there to fight the fight that must be fought.

During his first four years, one could say that the United States came out ahead in the war against terror, but not by much. Initial military victories were eye-openers, but the difficulties of penetrating the cultures of the region had proved to be an enormously difficult and bloody task.

There were more questions than answers when Bush began his second term. Domestic issues like energy, immigration and Social Security had to be faced, but above everything else two questions loomed:

- Would the fortunes of war reward the United States in 2005–08?
- Would the American people and the Congress continue to support the war?

The size of public debt at the end of 2004 didn't make the latter question any easier. The United States hadn't yet reached the point where debt could go no higher, but any violent surge in spending or in interest rates would, as the saying goes, make the cheese more binding.

Table 18.1
Public Debt 2004 (in billions of dollars)

	Total	%
World War I	$ 18.3	.4%
Great Depression:	24.5	.6
World War II	142.5	3.3
Korean War	6.6	.2
Cold War	206.1	4.8
War on Terrorism	351.5	8.2
Interest	286.5	6.7
Government	466.8	10.8
Human Resources	2625.0	61.1
Treasury, net	167.7	3.9
Total	$4295.5	100.0%

Source: Table 17.7 Chapter 7

Budget discipline cannot be separated from public policy without causing trouble. That had been the lesson of the previous fifty years, one that Bush learned during his first four years, but one he forgot when he not only failed to correct the problems presented by improperly structured entitlement programs, but he added to them, not critically, but noticeably, during a war.

His priorities in 2005–08 were much the same as they had been four years before:

- Defense — Maintain a force equal to the task at hand. This meant during the previous four years refitting a neglected military and the reorganization of its components so as to make the smaller force combat-ready and efficient.

- Homeland security — Link it with immigration policy.
- Interest — Promote policies that encourage economic growth.
- Control spending so as to keep debt under control, and as an assist to monetary policies designed to control inflation.
- Government — Control costs in this cost center that is most responsive to executive command.
- Human Resources—*Restructure entitlement programs! Nothing new!*
- Legislation — Energy, immigration and entitlement program reforms were at the top of the list.

On the surface, it appeared that Bush had the congressional power to get legislative movement.[1] But appearances were deceptive. It was common for several Republicans, mostly from the Northeast, to jump ship on crucial votes, and Sen. John McCain (R–AZ) could often do the same. There was no reason to believe, therefore, that the heavily partisan politics in Washington would change much during Bush's last term in office.

Perspectives

GENERAL

Presidents are usually hung with the numbers of their time, and most Americans are more attracted to a politician's style than they are to his record of performance. Because of this, Bush seemed a pushover in the election of 2004 for any worthy candidate from the Democratic Party. Then Democrats made three mistakes that cost them the election:

- They nominated Sen. John Kerry (MA), a well-known but vulnerable Massachusetts politician.
- They underestimated George Bush.
- They misread and miscast the primary issues. The Kerry campaign had two primary components: Blame the poor economy on Bush — and portray Bush as a lightweight incapable of handling the presidency.

Unfortunately for Kerry, voters, with the memory of Clinton in their minds, were more interested in leadership and character than the economy and claims of superiority. They basically liked and trusted Bush.

Bush won the election by a three-point margin (51 to 48 percent). Kerry won 19 states plus the District of Columbia — in 14 states he drew less than 40 percent of the vote. Bush won 31 states — only Massachusetts and Rhode Island gave him less than 40 percent of the vote.[2]

The war, since 9/11, was the central issue of the times. Voices of dissent were muted immediately after 9/11 because a retaliatory fever had gripped the nation. But as time passed, as casualties mounted and as the memory of 9/11 faded, heel biting began.

The justification for the war was questioned during the election contest; liberals labeled the president a liar who led the nation into war for personal reasons, an insult that made even the most experienced watchers of political campaigns wince.

Slowly at first, then more quickly as time passed, support for the war became politicized. Democrats opposed it; Republicans supported it. On both sides of the aisle, an occasional maverick disputed the party line. Joe Lieberman (D–CT), for example, was a steady supporter of the war from the beginning.

The two political parties moved through the second term of George Bush with Democrats saying in a dozen subtle ways that America should get away from an Iraq that had nothing to do with 9/11, and Republicans saying that to prevail in Iraq is to sink deep pillars of freedom in the Middle East that will have a pacifying impact on the entire region — the region that grooms international terrorists who threaten America and its allies.

Needless to say, the cost of war added to the anger of liberals who see the price of every bullet as a dollar that could be flowing into a welfare program.

"Acidic" is a word that accurately described the 2004–08 political environment.

In the always rough world of politics, the president was personally and publicly insulted by the highest and the lowest in the liberal constellation who regularly broke another of America's great traditions (politics end at the shoreline). Democratic leaders, past and present, spoke out against the president and against American policy when visiting foreign countries, even when visiting the troops.

Patriotism as practiced by liberal politicians, especially those with presidential aspirations, and by their supporters in the elite media gave comfort to America's enemies, an unintended consequence that made life more difficult for the president and his men, and for the troops in the field.

But Bush plodded on. And there were successes in 2005 that were heartening.

An Iraqi election created a National Assembly of 275 people; in October, a new constitution was approved; the first parliament was voted on before the year ended, despite threats and the killings that intimidated the 70 percent of voters who participated in the election; the trial of Saddam Hussein began.[3]

But the year 2006 was a tough one for the United States.

Insurgents, led by al-Qaeda representatives, took advantage of the animus between Sunnis and Shiites and sparked a sectarian war that put blood on the street every day, too much of it American blood.[4]

The Iraqi government seemed unable to bring Kurds, Sunnis and Shiites together in common cause. Increasingly and violently, the factions retreated to tribal and religious loyalties. Civil war became a possibility, an eventuality that would profit nobody.

While America's immediate involvement in the War on Terror was the main news, it was not the only critical international event with which the Bush administration had to contend. Three others have been chosen for comment: Rogue nations and nuclear power; the Arab/Israeli conflict; Iran/Syria/Iraq.

Rogue Nations and Nuclear Power

Iran

During Carter's years, Iranians attacked the American embassy and took hostages in retaliation for America's support of the former shah, Mohammad Reza Pahlavi (deposed in 1979).[5] The hostages were released under President Reagan, but relations between the two nations had ever since been brittle.

The government is a Shiite theocracy that is ultimately led by Ayatollah Khamanei. President Mahamoud Ahmadinejad is the day-to-day face of Iran.

Iran seeks the unsupervised development of nuclear power in violation of UN mandates; it openly predicts the eventual destruction of Israel and the United States; it openly cultivates relationships with Cuba, Venezuela and North Korea, acknowledged enemies of the United States.

Iran has been in a tense relationship with the International Atomic Energy Agency (IAEA) of the UN during which its program to develop nuclear power (allegedly for peaceful purposes) has moved forward, with interruptions — but ever, and cleverly, forward[6]:

In December 2006, the UN agreed to impose sanctions against Iran. They are regarded as symbolic out of deference to Russia and China, who have important economic ties with that government.

The Iraqi relationship with the UN is being replayed under the name of Iran — warning after warning; refusal after refusal, followed by more warnings, etc.

North Korea

It is generally agreed that the leader of North Korea, Kim Jong IL is, at the least, a cruel dictator or, at the worst, mentally deranged (because no normal man would treat his people as he does). The United States and North Korea have been antagonists since the Korean War.

In the late 1980s or early 1990s, Jong began developing a nuclear capability that, if realized, would completely destabilize the region. He refused to allow the IAEA to inspect its development facilities; he withdrew from the Nuclear Non-Proliferation Treaty.

Former president Carter in 1994 arranged meetings with officials from the Clinton administration and from Korea to discuss the problem. The United

States struck a deal in 1995; North Korea was supposed to be out of the nuclear business.

North Korea admitted in 2002 that it lied; its nuclear program had continued; U.S. monitors were expelled; it has aggressively pursued its nuclear program ever since. Informed observers believe it possesses nuclear weapons, or at the least, it has the capacity to do so.

In October 2006, North Korea exploded a nuclear device; in the same month, the UN approved of sanctions against the rogue nation. Talks continue on a spasmodic basis between North Korea and China/Japan/South Korea/United States.

Absent an overthrow of the present government, the prognosis for stopping nuclear development is poor, unless the United States acts militarily.

If Iran goes nuclear, so will the world of Arabia (mostly Sunni) that fears the ambitions of a militant Iran (mostly Shiite); if North Korea goes nuclear, so will Japan and, perhaps, South Korea. In short, if these two nations go nuclear, where will it stop?

Arab/Israeli Conflict

The Arab/Israeli conflict is too often described in terms of the fight between Palestinians and Jews. And Palestinians are held up as impoverished victims of Jewish imperialism.

Palestinians live in a crowded, impoverished condition. The reason for this is not because Israel insists upon its legal right to live in 8,000 square miles of territory in western Asia; it is because most Arabs refuse to recognize the Jewish state and have cynically used Palestinians as a never-ending irritant designed to wear Israel down.

Arabs have plenty of land to which Palestinians could relocate; the internal problems in Palestine between the central government and Hamas (the armed terrorist group) are not so large that united Arab support could not quell them, given the will to do so.

In other words, the Palestine/Israel friction continues because Arabs want it to.

There is little chance that this conflict will end unless the rest of the world says to Muslim nations, especially Arabs, in one determined voice: Leave Israel alone! Or else!

Iran/Syria/Iraq

The Baker-Hamilton report, released in December 2006, suggests that the United States must become diplomatically aggressive in order to gain the victory that the president seeks in Iraq, including talks with known enemies like Iran and Syria. The inference is that the United States has some goodies in its diplomatic kit that will persuade known enemies of the United States to allow Iraq to form itself as a nation that is independent and friendly toward the United States and to other Western nations.

The year 2006 ended with the Baker-Hamilton report. It represented the work of a bipartisan committee that had studied the War on Terror and its ramifications for months. It contained little that was original; it expressed the hope that U.S. troop involvement would be minimal by January 2008; some referred to it as a prescription for defeat because it de-emphasized the military option. Others applauded it as bipartisan wisdom.

President Bush took it, and other information, under advisement in preparation for an announcement of new war policy.

The election of 2006 changed many things. Democrats recovered control of the House and the Senate[7]; Robert Gates replaced Donald Rumsfeld as secretary of defense; Bush shuffled the command structure in Iraq, and he announced a new strategy to win that involved sending over 20,000 additional troops to Iraq.

Democrats yelped at the president's determination to win a fight that they wanted to quit. History would declare the winner.

HOME FRONT

War news swallowed every other topic. Some progress, most of it unobserved by the war-conscious public, was made on the energy front; there seemed to be agreement that the U.S. dependence on foreign oil had to end. How to go about achieving energy independence, however, collided with other issues, such as the environment, that continued to separate Democrats and Republicans.

Given the results of the 2006 election, hope for a sensible reform of Social Security went out the window. Bush couldn't sell it when he had congressional control; without it, he didn't stand a chance.

The ever-so-important immigration problem got caught up in partisan politics because both sides wanted to curry the Hispanic vote, which was of growing importance. With the election over there was a chance for an immigration bill because both sides agreed on one important thing — a leaky southern border was bad for homeland security.

Nature played a part in defining the size of the deficit[8]:

- Federal (and private) funds began to flow in early 2005 to the Asian victims of the tsunami that hit the area at the end of 2004.
- August 2005 — Hurricane Katrina inundated southern states — New Orleans was especially hard hit.
- September 2005 — Hurricane Rita hit the United States; Pakistan (2005) and Indonesia (2006) suffered earthquakes that were followed by U.S. aid.

Supporting such things placed additional pressures on an already strained budget.

The economy recovered during Bush's second term, vindicating his tax policy and setting the stage for continued growth if he could protect the nation against the anticipated demands of Democrats for more taxes.

The GDP in 2008 (estimated) was up 26 percent over 2004,[9] and federal revenue for the period (estimated) was up 30 percent (in 2001–2004 it grew by less than 5 percent).[10]

The Misery Index was politically satisfying in that the unemployment rate was down, but the other two rates (interest and inflation) were up.[11] From the standpoint of the national budget and public debt, a high interest rate is always a matter of great concern.

High debt plus high interest rates plus high defense costs can be a deadly trio.

Conservatives were rightly concerned when mid-term elections approached. The improved economy was a plus, but they had made little headway on energy, immigration, and entitlement reforms and, worst of all, the war effort was not going well and the president's popularity had dropped precipitously.

The patience of the American people for losing causes is limited; there was a growing perception that the nation's problems were not being solved by the Republican majority; aliens were overrunning the borders; the war had become a partisan wrangle.

The voters acted.

Out went Republicans in 2006, in came Democrats. Goodbye Dennis Hastert in the House; welcome Nancy Pelosi (the first female Speaker of the House); goodbye Bill Frist in the Senate; welcome Harry Reid, the new Majority Leader.

Would the election make a difference?

SUPREME COURT[12]

President Bush did not have an opportunity to nominate a Supreme Court justice in his first term; in his second term, two seats opened up: Associate Justice O'Connor (resigned July 2005); Chief Justice Rehnquist (died September 2005).

And the battle began.

Rehnquist had been as reliably conservative as any justice ever appointed; O'Connor had been unreliable on social issues, including abortion and affirmative action, and she was often the deciding vote on other cases.

If activist justices replaced both Rehnquist and O'Connor, the Court would become overwhelmingly liberal, and the social revolution during which long-standing American values were demolished would continue at an accelerated pace.

If both of the new justices were conservatives, the net effect would be to (at least) slow down the social revolution because the new Court would have four justices on both sides of the activist fence, and Kennedy, who was not a knee-jerk activist, as the swing vote.

Abortion was the critical issue to Democrats, especially to those who sat on the Judiciary Committee (the Committee) of the U.S. Senate, Patrick Leahy (VT), Edward Kennedy (MA), Joseph Biden (DE), Herbert Kohl (WI), Dianne Feinstein (CA), Russ Feingold (WI), Charles Schumer (NY), and Richard Durbin (IL).

Parenthetically it must be noted that half of the Democrats on the committee were Catholic (Leahy, Kennedy, Biden, Durbin), a religion that represents the most intractable anti-abortion position in the nation. Each of these allegedly Catholic men embraces the pro-abortion position of the Democratic Party. They openly and vigorously do so in direct violation of the principles of life protection, which are regularly and irreversibly enunciated by their religion. Their public behavior is yet another demonstration of how some politicians show one face to the public during election campaigns, and another when they return safely to Washington for another term in office.

John Roberts was nominated by President Bush to replace the retiring O'Connor. But Rehnquist died before Committee hearings began, and the president switched signals — John Roberts if confirmed would replace Rehnquist, and he would nominate another to replace O'Connor.

Harriet Miers, a White House attorney, was his first choice. But conservatives rebelled. They wanted someone of the stature of Scalia or the departed Rehnquist, someone who could match wits with the best of the activist judges and she (Miers) did not, in their opinion, fit the bill. Bush listened to his colleagues. Miers gracefully withdrew in favor of Samuel Alito.

Roberts and Alito, highly qualified judges, bumped into a powerful judicial wall of obstruction designed to protect a woman's right to an abortion, which is the calling card of any politician who expects to succeed in the Democratic Party.

Both Roberts and Alito (unlike the equally qualified Robert Bork in 1987[13]) survived the attack. The former was approved by the Senate (78–22) in October 2005, and the latter (58–42), in January 2006 — 22 Democrats voted for Roberts and 4 voted for Alito.[14]

Neither Roberts nor Alito are activist judges, and the chances were better that the decisions of the new Roberts Court would be less radical.

A review of some cases heard by the Court in 2005–06 follows that yields a sampling of the concerns of the times, and the thinking of the judges.

McCreary v. ACLU, 2005. Three Kentucky counties displayed the Ten Commandments in courthouses and in public schools. The ACLU argued that showing them violated the establishment clause of the First Amendment. Two lower courts agree with the ACLU. The issues: (1) Does the showing of the Commandments violate the establishment clause? (2) Was a determination by a lower court that the purpose of the display was to promote religion sufficient to invalidate the exhibits?

In a 5–4 decision (Rehnquist, Scalia, Kennedy and Thomas dissenting) the

Court sustained the ACLU position on both issues. The vote of Justice O'Connor is but one more reason why conservatives welcomed her retirement.

Georgia v. Randolph, 2006. Police found cocaine in Randolph's home. They did not have a warrant but the wife authorized the search; Randolph was present and he objected. It was argued that the search was illegal because Randolph objected. A lower court supported the police and an appellate court and the State Supreme Court supported Randolph. The issue: Can police search a home when one resident approves and another resident objects? In a 5–3 decision (Roberts, Scalia and Thomas dissenting, and Alito absent) the Court ruled that the objection of one resident renders the search unconstitutional. This was a reasonable decision over which reasonable people can disagree.

Beard v. Banks, 2006. Pennsylvania houses incorrigible prisoners. Those in the level 2 classification (the most dangerous) are denied newspapers, magazines and photographs. Banks claimed that the policy was a violation of First Amendment rights. The District Court approved of the prison policy; the Appellate Court did not. The issue: Does prison policy violate the First Amendment? In a 6–2 decision (Stevens and Ginsburg dissenting; Alito absent), the Court sided with the prison. Past Courts had done much to destroy discipline in public schools, but in this case they supported it in prisons.

Kelo v. New London, 2005. The city of New London, Connecticut, used its power of eminent domain to take private property and make it available to a developer on the grounds that the move would create jobs and increase city revenue. Property owners argued that their Fifth Amendment rights were violated because taking private property for the convenience of private industry was not "public use" as described in the Fifth Amendment. The issue: Did the city violate the Fifth Amendment when it took private property for the designated purpose in order to get the designated benefits? In a 5–4 decision (Rehnquist, O'Connor, Scalia, Thomas dissenting), the Court ruled in favor of the city. In an act of unabashed activism, the Court argued that "public use" in the Fifth Amendment does not mean what it says, that a broader interpretation is needed to incorporate such things as the development plan of the city of New London. It is out of such fundamental rulings that "slippery slopes" are created. *Private property is now more vulnerable than before to any wily public official with the imagination to take advantage of the logic that is set forth in this decision.*

In 2006, Democrats won control of the Congress and Patrick Leahy replaced Arlan Specter as chairman of the Judiciary Committee. During the upcoming months, and well before the election of 2008, one can expect Associate Justice Stevens (86) to resign so as to give liberals the opportunity to fill his seat with a copy of himself. It is hardly likely that any replacement judge will be more liberal than Stevens, and might be somewhat more conventional in temperament. The tilt of the Court will not appreciably change after Stevens resigns.

Society[15]

The impact of the fiscal, judicial and social revolutions was a mature reality in 2004; during Bush's second term nothing radically changed. But two issues loomed large that, when resolved, would change things for better or for worse: homosexual marriage and embryonic stem cell research.

Homosexual Marriage

Canada broke the ice in 1999 in North America when it approved civil unions. This led in June and July of 2003 to the approval of homosexual marriages in two provinces, and in 2005 to the legalization of all homosexual marriages.[16]

Vermont (home of the new chairman of the Senate Judiciary Committee, Patrick Leahy) led the way in the United States when in 2000 it legalized same-sex civil unions.[17] Massachusetts followed in 2003 when, borrowing on the language of Canadian judges, it legalized marriage in that state.[18] No other states have legalized homosexual marriage, but several others have approved variations of the civil union.[19]

Embryonic Stem Cell Research

Embryonic stem cell research is the abortion debate in a different form. The research in this early stage has yet to cure anything and may never live up to its promise. From an ethical standpoint, it is controversial. On the other hand, adult stem cell research has had many successes, is not controversial and shows signs of being able to do much more.

Embryonic stem cell research in the United States is not illegal. The debate is over the willingness of the federal government to fund it.

Change in Public Debt

Nothing went right on the economic front for the Bush administration in 2001–04, and the peace that greeted it in January 2001 ended with the fires of war in December, an expensive war that placed even more pressure on an already stressed federal budget.

There was a bright side as the second term began. Low tax policy had worked and was one of the major reasons for the economic recovery that brought with it higher federal revenues.

But the costs of war continued, the budget benefit of low interest rates was a thing of the past and Bush's second term figured to be a tough one. One could only hope that Congress would not worsen the problem by overspending.

The war in Afghanistan had begun in 2001; action in Iraq began in 2003. The transactions of 2005–08 reflect a nation at war during a time of high debt, a debt so high that it inhibited the ability of the president to implement the most effective war policy.

Table 18.2
Transactions (in billions of dollars)

	2005–08 Estimated		2001–04
Taxes		$ 9763.8	$ 7506.8
Less:			
Defense	$2195.5		$1514,2
Interest	911.1		690.4
Total		3106.6	2204.2
Net		$ 6657.2	$ 5302.2
Less:			
Government	$ 858.3		$ 706.4
Human Resources	6849.0		5415.1
Total		7707.3	6121.5
Surplus/deficit		$-1050.1	$ -819.3
Debt, beginning		-4295.5	-3409.8
Total		$-5345.6	$-4229.1
Adjustment*		-.2	-66.4
Debt, Ending		$-5345.4	$-4295.5

*Treasury cannot be exact when it finances a budget deficit and the difference between what is needed and the value of securities traded inevitably produces a relatively small variance.

Source: Historical Tables 2007, 1.1, 3.1

When one sees a deficit in the trillions, warning bells sound and invite a fresh examination of debt as measured against GDP.[20]

Public debt in 2008 (estimated) was 37 percent of GDP. It has been at least that high before, for example, during the World War II and Korean War eras.

Under Kennedy, Johnson, Nixon, Ford and Carter, debt decreased to 26 percent of GDP largely because federal funds allocated to *Defense* (during the Vietnam War and the Cold War) shrunk from 52 percent under Eisenhower to 23 percent under Carter.[21]

This was a demonstration of a dangerous new aspect of modern politics, to wit: Debt cannot be reduced unless *Defense* is cut, a frightening precedent to pass along to succeeding presidents.

TAXES

The average four-year increase in revenue over the previous 12 presidential terms was 33.0 percent. The increase was 30.1 percent in 2005–08, well below the average.[22] Had his revenue been historically normal, it would have been $9,984.0 billion or $220.2 billion more than actual.[23]

The recession cost Bush about $2.0 trillion during his first term, and lower than normal receipts in his second term cost him another $200 billion, a total of $2.2 trillion, more than the combined deficits for both terms.

In other words, the Bush deficit in his first term would have been a surplus, it would have been about half as large in his second term, and over both terms he would have had a surplus if revenue had been normal. When the ultimate appraisal of his efficiency is made, this revenue shortfall must, in fairness, be considered.

Revenue in 2005 was for the first time higher than it was during Clinton's last year in office (2000), and the increase was steady thereafter,[24] good enough had spending been under reasonable control, but inadequate in a time of a war that was not treated seriously by bill-passing, program-loving Washingtonocrats who, apparently, will not be happy until they have spent the nation into bankruptcy.

Bush successfully fought to keep tax cuts in place and Democrats, despite evidence to the contrary, were equally determined to fight tax cuts, to increase tax rates on the always-hated "rich." And since they won the mid-term election, one can expect to see proposals for a tax increase in 2007–08 that will be stopped only by presidential veto.

DEFENSE

Some Republicans and most Democrats have opposed the war in Iraq since it became obvious that pacification of that nation would be a slow and bloody job. The form of the opposition has, in the view of some, given comfort to the enemy.

But there have also been those who have insisted that more troops should be assigned to the effort while, at the same time, complaining that National Guard units are being overused.

Nowhere in the debate has it been loudly mentioned that President Clinton reduced the size of the active military by 600,000,[25] troops, which, if present today, would make life much easier for the president, troops that would be the answer to questions dealing with underdeployment and an overused National Guard.

The election of 2006, and facts on the ground in Iraq, indicated that something different had to be tried to recover public support and to increase the chance of establishing a free Iraq that could govern and defend itself.

The importance and the scope of the War against Terrorism was ignored by most Democrats, and it was not yet internalized by the American public largely because the elite media devoted its primary coverage to body bags and seldom mentioned either the long-term consequences of defeat or victory.

One anticipated presidential reaction to the election is a request to restore some of the personnel cutback that took place in the 1993–2000 period, a time when the terrorist threat existed but was not faced.

Had *Defense* in 2005–08 increased at the same rate as did federal revenue, the cost would have been $1970.0 billion or $225.5 billion less than actual.[26] To that extent this cost center contributed to the deficit and, given the instability of the Middle East, there was no indication that military expenses were going to drop any time soon.

INTEREST

Bush had luck with interest rates during his first term, and that helped to soften the blow of higher expenses elsewhere. But in 2005–08, his luck ran out. Interest rates jumped[27] and when joined with the rising base of debt helped to create a budget expense that was partly unfunded by the revenue flow.

Had *Interest* increased at the same rate as federal revenue, cost would have been $898.2 billion or $12.9 billion less than actual. To that extent this cost center contributed to the deficit for the period.

In 1960, *Interest* was 14 percent of *Defense*; in 2008 (estimated) it was 43 percent.

Such was the world of Eisenhower during which he fought the Korean War; such is the world of Bush as he fights the War against Terrorism.

And America sleeps on.

GOVERNMENT

In the context of a balanced budget, the maximum growth allowed to *Government* and *Human Resources* was 1.126 times.[28]

Had growth in *Government* been restricted to the allowable amount, cost would have been $795.4 billion or $62.9 billion less than actual. To that extent, this cost center contributed to the deficit during the subject period.

The unfunded cost of *Government* during Bush's first term was mostly related to war and disasters. A comparison of item costs during the subject period will reveal if unfunded costs in 2005–08 were caused by similar events, or if profligate spending had again raised its expensive head.

Energy as a line item has seldom been a decisive cost relative to the size of the budget, or to the size of the deficit. For that reason, the cost increase was not probed except to note that the most recent surge of cost began in 1996, and it has continued ever since, albeit to a different degree in the subject period. The current cost surge was relatively large, but substantively of little importance.

The line items that strike the eye are Community and International, both of which were high in the previous period as well.

The cost increase in Community is centered in the same sub-line item, Disaster and Relief Insurance,[29] and it was caused by an onslaught of natural disasters in and out of the country.

No nation in history has been as generous with its resources and capabil-

Table 18.4
Government (in billions of dollars)

	2005–08*	2001–04	% Change
Energy	$ 4.4	$-.4	%
Natural Resources/Environment	129.2	115.5	12.8
Transportation	292.0	247.9	17.8
Community/regional development	138.1	59.5	132.1
International affairs	135.3	87.0	55.5
Science/space/technology	98.7	84.6	16.7
Agriculture	92.6	86.2	7.4
Justice	173.3	146.1	18.6
General & Allowances	84.3	76.1	10.8
Total	$1147.9	$902.5	27.2%
Commerce & housing credit†	12.0	11.3	6.2
Total	$1159.9	$913.8	26.9
Offsetting receipts	-301.6	-207.3	45.5
Net	$ 858.3	$706.5	21.5

*Estimated — Historical Tables 2008, 3.1

†Made up of earnings from various federal housing and other programs—
subject to major changes from year to year relative to market conditions.
(Historical Tables 2007, 3.2)

Source: Historical Tables 2007, 3.1

ities as the United States. Judging by the animosity toward the United States that is regularly seen in the United Nations, one doubts that it gets much credit from the takers, yet the giving continues—but it is expensive.

In a peaceful 2000, the cost of the line item International was $17.2 billion; in 2008 the cost was $36.1 billion (estimated),[30] an increase of 110 percent.

The reason?

War and the consequential costs that go with it, namely, assistance and a hyperactive State Department.

In 2006, the average price of oil reached $60 per barrel—about three times higher than it was in January 2001,[31] the first year of the Bush administration. There is no separate line item in *Government* for the price of fuel, but the various departments operate fleets of cars and the cost of running them influenced the cost of all departments.

The unfunded costs in *Government* in the subject period were not caused by uncontrolled spending. Nature and war did the damage; unfunded costs were legitimate additions to the public debt.

HUMAN RESOURCES

Education, Health and Unemployment Compensation caused the most trouble in 2001–04, the first caused by a new education initiative in which the president was a full participant, the second caused by the growth in Medicaid, and the third being caused by economic recession.

Human Resources increased 26.5 percent during the subject period, hardly an indicator of the belt tightening expected from serious-minded politicians during a time of war.

Table 18.4
Human Resources (in billions of dollars)

	2005–08 Estimated	2000–04	% Change
Education, training, services	$ 392.9	$ 298.1	31.8%
Health/Medicaid	1052.5	828.5	27.0
Income Security*	1304.1	1063.7	22.6
Social Security	2270.8	1859.2	22.1
Medicare	1392.4	967.1	44.0
Unemployment compensation	140.5	185.6	-24.3
Veterans	295.8	212.8	39.0
Total	$6849.0	$5415.0	26.5%

*Minus unemployment compensation (from 1965–68 on)

Note: Major federal programs since the 1960s— Food Stamps 1961 (pilot), Food Stamps 1964, Medicaid 1965, Student Aid 1966, Medicare 1967, Coal Miners Benefits 1970, Commodity Donations 1973, Supplementary Security Income 1974, Supplemental Feeding 1976, Earned Income Tax Credit 1976, Legal Services 1976, Energy Assistance 1977, Welfare Reform 1996, No Child Left Behind Act 2002, Medicare Prescription Drug Modernization Act 2003

Source: Historical Tables 2007, 3.1

Relative to the normal ability of federal revenue to support cost growth (33 percent),[32] Medicare and Veterans were the most out of line.

The Medicare Prescription Drug Act of 2003 was the most important element that led to the unfunded cost increase. For example, in 2003 the cost of Medicare was $249.4 billion; in 2008, $391.6 billion (estimated)— an increase of 57 percent.[33]

Similar to the No Child Left Behind Act of 2002, Bush promoted this initiative, something that should never have been done to a line item already out of control.

Bush had confused his constituents. On the one hand, he outdid President Reagan in his attempts to restructure Social Security and to inform the public that Medicare needed the same treatment. Then he worked hard to get a new Medicare initiative passed. His constituents may have responded positively to benefits associated with the new programs had they been couched in bills that changed the federal edifice of health care to a more affordable form. But to add cost without reform was anathema to them. When searching for reasons for the failure of Republicans to retain congressional control during the

2006 election, this unconservative approach to Medicare did not help Republican candidates.

The increase in the line item Veterans is explained by one word. War!

It is an oversimplification to say that cost increases in *Human Resources* were, except for two major items, reasonable. The time had passed when reasonable rates of increase would suffice, or when a balanced budget was an adequate target. Costs had to be cut in order to generate surpluses with which debt could be reduced, thereby ridding the budget of the unproductive stranglehold that *Interest* represented, and restoring to the presidency the ability to expand military spending without, at the same time, causing a fiscal crisis.

Social programs must be cut. The only question is: Will they be cut intelligently so as to cause the least amount of harm? Or will Congress wait until the pantry is empty, forcing abrupt withdrawal of benefits in a way that will maximize pain?

SUMMARY OF BUDGET DEFICITS

This presidential period demonstrated once again that Congress will not cut spending, even in the darkest times. And despite an intensive campaign by President Bush, and the fact that conservatives controlled Congress in 2005–06, entitlement programs remained in unaffordable condition protected as usual by the Democratic Party.

As a matter of fact, before Democrats assumed control of Congress in 2007, the menu of federal services was worse than before. President Bush's attempts at bipartisanship in the fields of education and health care earned him nothing but continued scorn from the left, and added to the budget busters already in place.

The deficit exceeded $1 trillion for the first time in history. The myth was allowed to stand (by the elite media) that it was caused by war. But the costs of battle have never been the primary reason for deficits that have gone up and up and up since the 1960s,[34] nor were they the major problem in the period 2005–08.

Table 18.5
Summary of Deficit — 2005–2008 (in billions of dollars)

Cost Center	Amount
War on Terror	$ 225.5
Interest	12.9
Government	62.9
Human Resources	748.8
Total	$1050.1

Sources: Exhibits 1, 11–2, 16

Unfunded costs related to the war were about 22 percent of the deficit, a legitimate and modest use of the ability to borrow that would have been shrugged off as irrelevant during an era in which the budget was in reasonable control.

The unfunded cost of *Interest* was a reminder that past fiscal mistakes reappear as current burdens. Had the debt base been made up only of additions caused by past *emergencies, Interest* would not be a budget problem of consequence.

The unfunded cost of line items in *Government* were directly related to natural disasters and to war — proper additions to public debt that in circumstances of budget control would be recovered over a short period of time.

The unfunded cost of *Human Resources* reflects the core of the fiscal problem in Washington that no group of politicians has had the power or the will to correct, although the need to do so has been apparent for a half-century:

- The majority of Democrats don't want to fix it.
- Republicans have not had the veto-proof power to do so.
- President Bush has sent mixed messages on the need to do so, preaching against excess cost on the one hand and approving additional costs without reform on the other.

The above cost variances played their part in the formation of the deficit. However, the most significant single factor was not cost but revenue.

The average rate of increased revenue from decade to decade[35] has been decreasing for decades, and Bush had been extremely hard hit by this phenomenon. As noted in a previous section of this chapter (Taxes), the deficit in the subject period would have been decreased substantially, and for both Bush terms would have been eliminated entirely had revenue been historically normal.

It's time for politicians, the media and the people to grow up and to face the new economic realities, instead of beating up on each president as deficits endlessly repeat for causes that are never fixed and are seldom discussed.

Conclusion

During his eight years in office, Bush had less that 12 months of peace, and he was confronted by natural disasters and economic crises that, by themselves, would have been difficult to handle. Under such circumstances, it would have been surprising if the fiscal profile of the United States remained stagnant.

Table 18.6
Spending Priorities

	1960 Ike	1968 LBJ	1976 GRF	1980 JEC	1988 RWR	1992 GHWB	2000 WJC	2008 GWB*
Primary costs								
Defense	52.2%	27.3%	24.1%	22.7%	27.3%	21.6%	16.5%	20.9%
Interest	7.5	14.2	7.2	8.9	14.3	14.4	12.5	9.0
Total	59.7%	41.4%	31.3%	31.6%	41.6%	36.0%	29.0	29.9%
Government	11.9	8.4	14.0	15.4	8.3	8.1	8.7	7.0
Education/ services	1.9	2.9	5.1	5.4	2.9	3.1	3.0	2.8
Health/ Medicaid	.9	4.2	4.1	3.9	4.2	6.5	8.6	9.7
Medicare		7.4	4.3	5.4	7.4	8.6	11.0	13.5
Income Security	8.0	12.2	16.4	14.7	12.2	14.4	14.2	13.1
Social Security	12.6	20.6	19.9	20.0	20.6	20.8	22.9	21.1
Veterans	5.9	2.9	4.9	3.6	2.9	2.5	2.6	2.9
Total	100.0%	100.0%	100.0%	100.0%	100.0%	100.0%	100.0%	100.0%
	(3)	(2)(3)	(3)	(3)	(3)	(2)	(1)	(2)

*Estimate, Historical Tables 2008

1 = peace; 2 = war; 3 = cold war

Source: Historical Tables 2007, 3.1

The picture is complete. The current situation may be framed in numbers, but the meaning is clear:

- Defense — It approaches the humorous to hear politicians blame continued deficits on wars. Only 18 percent of the total deficits accumulated since 1941 can be fairly assigned to Defense.[36]
- Interest — The cost of money should never be a dominant number in a federal budget. It was too high in 1960 because debt was too high (some World War II debt was still outstanding), and it was even higher in 2008 for the same basic reason. The only way to substantially decrease its cost is to substantially reduce the size of debt.
- Government — With some exceptions, succeeding presidents did a good job of controlling the cost of *Government* despite the fact that 10 percent of the accumulated deficits came from this cost center. Generally speaking, uncontrollable external events caused the unfunded spending to a degree that would have been recoverable in a saner budget environment.
- Human Resources— This cost center is the core of the budget problem. Accumulated unfunded costs represent 66 percent of the additions to public debt since 1941. Absent this level of spending, public debt of $5.3 trillion in 2008 (estimated) would have been $3.4 trillion lower (70 percent) and Interest cost of 2008 would have been about 3 percent of all spending.

Table 18.6 tells a simple story. Eisenhower, the presidents who preceded him, and the Congresses that supported them took the oath to defend America and its Constitution seriously, in the sense that, to them, national defense was the priority line item in the budget — debt and tax rates were managed in such a way that emergency funds could be attracted during times of war.

Kennedy/Johnson introduced a new theory that was supported by Democratic Congresses. Their iron grip over congressional power was unbroken until 1994. Lip service was still given to the oath to defend America, but the new budget priority became the creation of a new and a better society. A succession of programs was progressively formed and introduced and protected until the Welfare State that exists today was firmly in place.

The simplistic result of this collision of worldviews can be phrased in a few words. In 1960, a time of peace, Eisenhower spent 52 percent of federal funds on *Defense*, and he ended up with a small budget surplus; in 2008, a time of war, Bush spent 21 percent on *Defense* and ended up with a huge deficit. Under Eisenhower, public debt was dropping; under Bush, public debt is increasing.

Table 18.7
Public Debt, 2008* (billions)

Event	Inherited 2004	Added 2005–08	Total 2008	%
World War I	$ 18.3		$ 18.3	.3%
Great Depression	24.5		24.5	.5
World War II	142.5		142.5	2.7
Korean War	6.6		6.6	.1
Cold War	206.1		206.1	3.9
War on Terrorism	351.5	225.5	577.0	10.8
Interest	286.5	12.9	299.4	5.6
Government	466.8	62.9	529.7	9.9
Human Resources	2625.0	748.8	3373.8	63.1
Treasury	167.7	- .2	167.5	3.1
Total	$4295.5	$1049.9	$5345.4	100.0%

*Estimated, Historical Tables 2007, 7.1

Source: Exhibits 1, 11, 12, 16

President Bush was partially responsible for some of the unfunded costs in *Human Resources* because he sponsored an increase in the Medicare program without the balance of offsetting reforms. But the basic reason for the huge amount of unfunded costs is the unavailability of funds to cover the full cost of the Welfare State.

On the judicial front, the U.S. Supreme Court levied another blow against the basic principles established by the Founders when it put economic development ahead of a person's right to own land without interference from the state. And it muddied church/state issues even more with other rulings that should have been left for the states to decide.

The Bush era ended with questions that few thought would ever be asked: Can America ever reduce debt to a sensible level? Is America a nation based upon Judeo-Christian morality, or is it the Rome of the twenty-first century? Has the American Constitution become a mere symbol instead of the protector of freedom it was meant to be?

Conclusion

This book examined the growth of public debt over 68 years under 12 presidents covering 17 four-year presidential terms. It began with the work of a patrician, Franklin D. Roosevelt, from a blue-blood New York family, and it ended with George W. Bush, from another great American family. Both were war leaders, both confronted dangerously weak economies and both were required to make decisions that made memorable history.

Roosevelt has been enshrined as a national hero because the United States and its allies prevailed over the threat of world domination posed by Adolf Hitler's Nazi Germany and its allied powers.

Bush's reputation (he is currently unpopular) depends upon the ultimate end of the War against Terror, which is more properly titled the War against Islam, whose extremists leaders are once again attempting to conquer Western civilization, that is, Judeo-Christian civilization.

It is fitting to begin this conclusion with a review of each president's contribution to the current size of the public debt.

The Presidents

FRANKLIN ROOSEVELT AND HARRY TRUMAN

Roosevelt bears remote responsibility for public debt in the sense that he showed how a tax base could be created, how the private sector could be invaded, and how certain social programs like care for the aged, veterans and the unemployed could bring great popularity to a politician.

His Social Security program quickly became an accepted part of the federal landscape. It would be a stretch however, to hang the existing strain of high debt around his neck — those who disagreed with him, after all, had more than a half-century to undo his alleged mischief.

But FDR did do the spadework that got Americans accustomed to an intrusive government — that whetted the appetite of Americans for the goodies that could be dispensed from Washington. Deliberate or not, he served as the seducer who invited Americans to trade liberty for security, a bargain, time would tell, that far too many were willing to make.

FDR's reputation as a war leader overwhelmed any negative comments about his skills as a manager of the Great Depression, or as a steward of American liberty.

Harry Truman headed the nation from 1945 to 1952 and is probably best remembered for his surprisingly effective leadership during the war, for his decision to end World War II with the atomic bomb, and because of his association with the Marshall Plan that saved Europe.

Public debt was about $235 billion when Truman succeeded FDR in 1945, and it was $215 billion when he left office in 1952.[1] He was the only president covered in this book to pass on less debt than he inherited.

This would seem to indicate he was a conservative leader. This is not true.

The debt reduction was natural. The war had ended and military spending dropped faster than tax rates; some of the budget surplus was directed to debt.

Presidents more liberal than Truman might have plowed surpluses into new programs faster than he did; presidents more conservative might have reduced debt even faster. Truman did a little of both.

Harry Truman doubled the cost of Social Security in 1951 by adding beneficiaries, and to that extent he can be remotely identified with the public debt problem. But, as with FDR, those who followed had plenty of opportunity to reshape social programs into a more durable structure.

Blaming FDR and Truman for modern debt problems is a weak crutch upon which to build an argument for responsibility. Both were liberals and in an environment unrestricted by wartime needs, they might have led the charge to a socialistic state. But they *were* so restricted; and they did not plant the seeds of socialism so deeply that they couldn't be rooted out by successors who were so inclined.

DWIGHT EISENHOWER

A responsible government was in place when Dwight Eisenhower took office in 1953; when he left it in 1960, the same America was still in place.

Eisenhower is the stand-alone president who served as the bridge between the America that was and the America that was to follow. He headed a conservative government and when he left office in 1960 public debt was only 10 percent higher than the one he assumed; as a percent of GDP it was significantly lower.[2] The United States, its budget, its military and its growth were under control. It was the last period of "normalcy" that America would experience in the twentieth century; the attitude of political leaders toward debt was orthodox.

JOHN F. KENNEDY

Kennedy, like Eisenhower, was a stand-alone president, but for a different reason. His tragic assassination after less than three years in office makes it impossible to identify him in any final and fair way to the climbing debt that followed his untimely death.

Were the programs introduced after his assassination on his agenda before it? If so, would he have implemented them at the same time in the same form?

The answer to those questions will never be known for certain and, therefore, Johnson gets the credit/blame for the fiscal revolution that split America into competing groups and that progressively brought the crushing burden of debt without end.

This may not be entirely fair. The famed and well-oiled Kennedy public relations apparatus carefully screens what can and what cannot be attributed to members of that anointed clan. And it isn't difficult to imagine that the president who signed Food Stamps into law (1961)[3] would have also approved of other programs later advanced by Johnson, at the pace that Johnson insisted upon.

That is the rub — the pace.

Kennedy might have approved of the goals (as most theoretically did) but he might have been unwilling to destroy the budget to get what he wanted, a price Johnson was willing to pay.

That being the case, it is reasonable and safe to label Johnson as the father of the Welfare State and to treat Kennedy as a short-term player who will forever be defined by his admirers in terms of what might have been.

LYNDON JOHNSON

Did Lyndon Johnson implement Kennedy's agenda or his own? Was he the loyal soldier who carried forward the Kennedy dream or did he cynically use the emotion that surrounded the assassination as a tool to get his own creative ideas passed into law (the "Let's do it for Jack" syndrome)?

It will never be known for sure who created the notion that the Founders had it all wrong — that socialism was the preferred governmental form of modern man. But it is certain that total breakaway from past fiscal disciplines didn't begin until Johnson became president (November 22, 1963). On that day, the public debt problem of the twenty-first century was born — it is 45 years old.

The forward momentum of Johnson's plan (never expressed as such) to convert freedom-loving America into a Welfare State was thereafter unchecked until Ronald Reagan entered the Oval Office in 1981. And it remains as a viable force in 2008; one that is defended and expanded upon by current Democratic leaders whenever they have the power to do so.

Public debt has grown from $254.0 billion to $5.6 trillion since 1963.[4] Subsequent presidents, caught in the tight grip of entitlement programs, have been little more than spectators watching debt mount and, with the exception of Reagan, making no effective protest.

Johnson didn't act alone. The 87th through the 96th Congresses[5] fixed the Welfare State so firmly into the budget — and the national psyche — that it will take fiscal dynamite to get it out.

This was done deceitfully under the cover of war, allowing the myth to float that external events, not social spending, caused deficits. Americans never had a chance to vote up or down on the Welfare State — it was slipped into their homes through the cellar door.

The public unthinkingly, unquestioningly and selfishly took the benefits but never paid the piper as the excess costs attached to Johnson's Utopia slid into debt unnoticed, and onto the backs of their children.

A few wise men recognized what was happening, among them the esteemed scholar and philosopher Russell Kirk who wrote: "Johnson ... piled the tremendous cost of the war ... upon the staggering cost of the welfare state at home. One might have thought he could not do sums. He ruined the dollar and bequeathed to the nation an incomprehensible national debt."[6]

The old consensus to balance budgets was destroyed under Johnson and his chief congressional allies; honored practices of lowering taxes and debt, after emergencies had come and gone, were abandoned.

Eisenhower's doctrine relative to Vietnam (stay out of it) was ignored; Kennedy and Johnson wasted America's military power in a war that they never allowed the military to fight with vigor.

The Founding Fathers headed America down the road of liberty. Their inspiration guided the first 34 presidents through more than 150 years of expansion and war.

Then came Johnson.

He planted the seeds that, at the least, sent America on a path to an idealistic destination at a financial cost it cannot afford and at a spiritual cost that, as it has before, leads to self-indulgence and internal decay to a degree that could eventually destroy it as a major world power.

Marx and Lenin were the ideological icons who led the Russian nation into the dreary unproductive state it is today. Johnson and his men may one day be similarly recognized in American history.

NIXON/FORD/CARTER

These presidents, two Republicans and one Democrat were victims of Johnson's fiscal revolution. In the case of Nixon and Carter, they were willing victims.

Nixon, a generally acknowledged expert in foreign affairs, was a complete bust as a manager of national affairs who, among other unwise decisions, added

Supplemental Security Income to the already bloated menu of social programs, an innovation that in 2008 cost (estimated) $32 billion.[7]

The hapless Carter, totally miscast as the President of the United States, did nothing to persuade fellow Democrats that entitlements needed reform. Additionally, when faced with a big-time energy crisis, he showed his bureaucratic colors: Instead of mounting a national effort with Democratic colleagues to free the nation from the grip of foreign oil, he formed a new federal department to supervise what was being done incorrectly.

Gerald Ford was a double victim: He had the Welfare State to contend with and he had to do so in a presidency that had been severely weakened by Richard Nixon and the Watergate affair. In his case, there was some sign of resistance to the Democratic hegemony — he exercised his veto power a vigorous 66 times during his relatively short presidency.[8]

Nixon was the great disappointment during these twelve years. He followed directly the father of the Welfare State, Lyndon Johnson. It had already been demonstrated that the social programs in place were not affordable. True, he had no congressional support.[9] But he was brilliant; he was supposed to be a conservative and he did have veto power to be used as a symbol of protest. He also had the bully pulpit.

He exercised his veto power a limp 43 times — Eisenhower did so 181 times. Instead of preaching against irresponsible spending in his eloquent voice, he added irresponsible spending of his own. He was (apart from Watergate) a crushing disappointment to conservatives.

Public debt was $290 billion when Nixon took office in 1968; when his successor Gerald Ford left office in 1976, it was $477 billion — a 64 percent increase, none of it caused by military spending.[10]

When Carter left office in 1980, debt was $712 billion — another increase of 49 percent, none of it caused by military spending.

Controlling the cost of the Welfare State was no longer an issue — restructuring was the need. That these three presidents failed to finish such a prodigious task is easy to understand, but for them to fail to begin the process, or to speak loudly against the paralysis that gripped Washingtonocrats, is unforgivable.

The condition causing these problems was easy to identify. *Human Resources*, budget home of the Welfare State, had grown at a rate[11] that no predictable revenue stream could afford,[12] a fact that was not even a topic of conversation in the major media, which was too approving of the movement toward socialism to worry about such a mundane thing as the cost of it.

In the meantime, Iran thumbed its nose at Washington and held American hostages apparently unafraid of what the toothless tiger from the West could do to make them regret it.

RONALD REAGAN

Ronald Reagan did many things during his presidency but, relative to the public debt problem, his major contributions were:

- A revised tax policy that energized the economy and eliminated some unfairness and inefficiency in the system.
- The Cold War victory that benefited future presidencies in the form of lower *Defense* costs.
- A loud, insistent and articulate voice describing over and over, to the American people, the fiscal mess in Washington.

The radical, Lyndon Johnson, started the downhill direction in America that brought the nation to the unfortunate debt position that exists in 2008.

The defender, Ronald Reagan, brought the deficit/debt problem into the open and he forced everyone to look at it — he removed denial as an option.

During Reagan's years, public debt increased from $712 billion in 1980 to $2.1 trillion in 1988,[13] an increase of $1.4 trillion. About 15 percent of the increase was due to the military buildup that defeated the Soviet Union; another 15 percent was due to high interest expense caused by inflationary rates and by the huge amount of inherited debt; the overwhelming cause of the increase (62 percent) was the unfunded costs of *Human Resources*.[14]

Reagan wielded his veto pen 78 times[15]; he spoke endlessly about the dangers of big government and big spending.

As Johnson constructed the foundation of the Welfare State, so did Reagan construct the walls with which to defend against it.

But an uncomfortable, lingering question remained in the Washington air when Reagan removed his personable, charismatic presence from the scene. Would his conservative apostles be as effective at defending the America of the Founding Fathers as Johnson's apostles had been at tearing it down?

History will, as always, provide the answer.

George Washington was the great war leader who led the colonies to freedom. James Madison led America in the War of 1812 as Britain once again tried to bring the "colonies" to heel; Abraham Lincoln protected the Union during the Civil War at a time when the danger of a split nation was as real as it is today in Iraq (2007); Franklin Roosevelt was America's champion during World War II.

With the exception of Madison (an underrated leader), these men are highly honored presidents mostly because of their critical relationship to shooting wars fought in defense of American liberty.

Saving America from financial ruin and leading America to victory in the Cold War were accomplishments of Ronald Reagan that will one day cause historians to group his name with those listed above — with the names of America's greatest presidents.

George H. W. Bush, William Clinton

Bush (41) and Clinton were more victims than they were contributors to the public debt problem. Clinton participated in welfare reform with his Republican Congress, but under both men the major entitlement programs emerged essentially intact. Their deficits were built into a system that was born decades earlier and would continue until pain was felt.

George W. Bush

"The operation was a success, but the patient died."

That old remark captures the results of Bush's attempts to reform the Welfare State.[16] Even more than Ronald Reagan, the president traveled across the nation trying to educate the people about the inevitability of change in entitlement programs because of structural problems that need to be intelligently fixed while there is still time to manage the crisis in a humane way.

He failed for four primary reasons:

- The public has grown accustomed to federal benefits; they fear politicians who try to change them; they believe politicians who deny the need for change.
- Bush is Republican. Democrats have successfully demonized Republicans as enemies of entitlements, a hurdle difficult to overcome absent, as an ally, a supportive, prominent Democratic face.
- The war in Iraq was going poorly; the public had lost confidence in Bush's credibility, a trend worsened by the tentative way the federal government responded to damage caused in New Orleans by hurricane Katrina.
- Bush weakened his case as a reformer when he added cost to the Medicare system, another program that is not structured to endure.

Relative to public debt, Bush has a mixed record. His outstanding and courageous attempt to alert the public to a system that is nearing collapse was unprecedented. In this, and in many other ways, he has demonstrated political courage to a degree seldom seen. And for that he deserves high marks.

On the other hand, he approved cost increases in programs that are already going broke.

Bush was not responsible for most of the unfunded spending that took place on his watch. Spending on *Defense* was justified; unfunded *Interest* was not avoidable; most of the increase in *Government* was war or disaster related.

Unfunded spending in *Human Resources* was built into the system and was born in the 1960s—it has plagued every president since.

But more than any of these things, important as they are, Bush was deprived of the normal revenue that previous presidents enjoyed, and that alone was enough to explain his deficits.

History will judge Bush and, like FDR, the outcome of a war, not the condition of the budget, will probably be the yardstick applied.

What has come of this insane fiscal journey of four decades?

John Steele Gordon said it well: "In this period we increased the size of the national debt by a factor of seventeen. And for what? ... The answer, I'm afraid, is little more than the political self-interests of a few thousand people, Democrats and Republicans alike, who held public office during this period."[17]

Camouflaged Development

The argument developed in this book says that men, not events, caused the astronomical increase in debt. Of the $5.1 trillion of accumulated deficits over the 68-year period, at least $3.4 trillion (66 percent)[18] was caused by men with a political agenda that, to them, was apparently more important than the protection of the nation, and the protection of the dollar.

How did it happen? How did it escape the attention of the American public?

First, it was Vietnam, then recession under Nixon/Ford, including oil inflation.

Under presidents Johnson, Nixon and Ford, debt grew substantially (101 percent).[19] While this was happening, Americans read headlines about the war and worried about the cost of gasoline. Subliminally, they heard about deficits and assumed they were caused by military spending. But that wasn't the cause. *Defense* was fully funded by normal revenue; the unfunded spending was mostly related to the growing Welfare State.[20]

Under Carter appeared the energy problem, roaring inflation and the hostage crisis in Iran. That's what the media reported; that's what the people accepted as the reason for continued deficits and for climbing debt. That was partly correct, but only partly; the unfunded spending for *Human Resources* under Carter caused most of the deficit (63 percent).

Then came Ronald Reagan. Camouflage was wearing thin, but it held up one more time. Deficits could no longer be blamed on a shooting war or a recession, but there was always Soviet activity to blame, and Reagan's reaction to it. Why didn't he spend less on *Defense*? Why didn't he increase taxes? Because he didn't, liberals claimed, deficits persisted.

That spin continued until the end of Reagan's eight years. The media cooperated. Headlines featured foreign affairs. And the flimflam might have worked again but for three things:

- Thanks to the military strength of America, reborn under Reagan, the USSR collapsed, terrorism declined, and Central America stabilized.
- Reagan's economic policies worked. The economy was humming.

• Reagan would not allow media to bury the budget/debt issue. He spoke out. Truth surfaced. When he left town, the nation knew it had a fiscal problem.

Large deficits accumulated under Reagan, most (67 percent) caused by unfunded spending in *Human Resources*. The military spending that liberals claimed was breaking the bank caused 16 percent of the deficit; it was the bargain-basement cost of winning the Cold War with the Soviets. Not a bad deal.

By the time George Bush (41) and Clinton appeared, deficits were no longer news, apathetic Americans ignored them in part because the media did the same. America was drifting toward big-time budget problems on the ship of the Welfare State that had developed serious leaks. An additional $1.2 trillion was added to debt, 80 percent of which was related to the unfunded cost of *Human Resources*.

George Bush (43) did his best, to no avail, to wake America up to the peril that entitlement programs represented. The reaction of politicians has been denial — more of the same; the reaction of the public has been ineffective. Another $1.9 trillion (estimated) has been added to debt, 59 percent of which was related to the same cause, namely, unfunded spending in *Human Resources*.

What is there left to say in the face of this stubborn unwillingness to face reality, this eagerness to hide responsibility behind external events, or this practice of destroying each president who doesn't solve that which others did not confront?

Wars, recessions and inflation served for a time as the camouflage behind which the development of the Welfare State was hidden from public view. But since Reagan that excuse for public ignorance and inaction no longer exists. True, the major media has been no help. It has almost been complicit with the developers of the Welfare State. But that too has run dry as an excuse for inaction.

The public is silent today because it wants to be. And it won't change until the pain begins.

Is the Size of Public Debt Important?

In his work *Redeeming the Time*, Russell Kirk (1918–94) wrote: "Economically, the position of the United States is more precarious than it was in 1929; our debt is astronomical in quantity."[21]

There is no shortage of concerns expressed about the condition of the public debt, or about the flawed system and philosophy that feeds it. But the opinion of Russell Kirk, quoted here, is of special importance because, to many, he was a great intellect of the twentieth century and a powerful apologist for the American system of government. One can be sure that he wrote those words with a heavy heart.

One can only imagine what he would say today about a $5.6 trillion debt in 2008.[22]

NATIONAL SECURITY

No democracy will ever maintain a military force capable of handling all contingencies. Instead, the goal is to have enough force at the ready to hold the line until the nation mobilizes resources required to meet immediate threats.

America's wartime strength significantly depends upon its ability to tax and borrow. To the extent that presidents have that full power, they are able to protect the nation; to the extent this isn't true, the power of presidents is diminished and the nation is exposed to avoidable dangers.

> "A national debt, if it is not excessive, will be to us a national bless-ing."—Alexander Hamilton[23]

Hamilton, the brilliant Founder who realized the inestimable value of a good credit reputation, spoke sensibly. And America realized the merit in his opinion when it came time to fund, for example, World War II.

Could America similarly expand in 2008?

First of all, before getting lost in the game of what might be, it's worth examining *need*: Would any modern war require the same kind of a build-up?

The answer is no. The day of pitched battles between dug-in forces of millions of men is over. This is the era of terrible weapons, huge kills and, perhaps, guerrilla warfare. The FDR military in 1945 of 12 million Americans[24] is a dinosaur not to be seen again.

But some significant expansion of the military is needed, and it's worth examining the nation's ability to handle expansion as it once did.

Active duty forces during the Korean War went as high as 3.6 million; 3.5 million in Vietnam.[25] Reagan and Bush (41), facing the Cold War and the Gulf War, had over 2.0 million troops.

Active forces (2007) currently amount to 1.4 million, thanks to cutbacks ordered by Clinton. *Direct costs* for 1.4 million troops (without considering supplies, training, etc.) in 2008, were $136 billion.[26] At the 2.0 million force level, it would be $194 billion — a $232 billion cost increase over four years on top of a $1 trillion deficit.

Given a throat-choking level of interest cost, a level of taxation already historically high, a huge deficit and a congressional attitude that balks at the historically low level of military spending under Bush, the environment, to say the least, is not hospitable to the notion that the size of the military should be significantly expanded.

In summary, America's future security depends no longer on its internal ability to fund the necessary level of military strength (as was the case under

Eisenhower), but on the hope that the military strength needed in the future will be affordable.

THE DOLLAR

The increase in public debt experienced since the 1960s attacks the value of U.S. currency.

America has an unanswered deficit problem that keeps pushing its debt skyward. At some point investors in U.S. securities will become concerned about the value of their holdings because of the size and the cause of America's debt. Any condition, like exploding debt, that has that *potential* impact on investors is a threat to the value of the dollar.

All debt in all cases represents potential pressure on the lender, and not all debt is always held by friends. To the extent that America constantly needs to go to the market for funds to cover uncontrolled deficits, to the same extent it is vulnerable to pressure from debtors, some of whom are not, or may not be, friendly.

In 2006, 53 percent of public debt was owned by foreigners.[27] A decade ago, it was 32 percent. This means America is more vulnerable to fiscal intimidation than ever before.

Some of the more interesting owners who have invested more than $10 billion in the securities of the U.S. Treasury include China and Japan (the biggest — six-figure investors), South Korea and Taiwan ($50 billion range), and dozens of smaller investors ($10–50 billion) like France and Germany and the oil exporters from the Middle East.

To keep U.S. securities attractive, the rate of return must be competitive. And for so long as deficits drive the need for more and more debt, the need to keep interest rates high will continue. No system with such a built-in inflationary characteristic is good for the American dollar.

The costs of the Welfare State have been the source of runaway debt for four decades. If uncorrected, they will endanger the future value of America's dollar, just as they have eroded confidence in currencies of socialistic nations around the globe.

The Average American

Americans care about national security issues and, in a vague way, identify with the need to maintain sound money. But their relationship to an esoteric concept like a public debt measured in trillions escapes most. Washingtonocrats spend little time educating them, and for good reason — they created the debt, they continue to add to it and, like anybody who has created something shameful, they don't want to talk about it.

The problem of high public debt affects Americans personally in four very important ways: (1) jobs, (2) wages, (3) taxes, and (4) prices.

Jobs

The private sector is deprived of capital to the extent that government competes for available funds (this assumes the Federal Reserve isn't playing games with money supply); the government has been pulling increasing amounts of capital away from the private sector since the 1960s. It can be argued that there has been less investment in the private sector than there might otherwise have been and, as a result, fewer jobs are available.

To what degree — who knows with any specificity? But the obvious point is made. Excessive government borrowing depresses private investment and job creation.

Wages

Most businesses use short- and long-term loans to provide capital during cyclical periods and for long-term needs. High public debt sustains high interest rates in the marketplace. High interest rates increase the cost of business, and they decrease the profits out of which higher wages are paid.

That which decreases profits (like high interest costs) is an enemy of the wage earner. And since interest is the inevitable companion of borrowing, a public debt that spurs an increase in all interest rates is the working man's enemy.

Taxes

In 2008, *Interest* was 9.8 percent of all taxes collected by the federal government.[28] If there were no *Interest*, taxes could have been 9.8 percent lower to produce the same budget result.

But some level of *Interest* is natural.

If *Interest* in the federal budget were half as expensive, taxes could be reduced by about 5.0 percent.

A 5.0 percent change in income isn't much money to politicians who squander the nation's wealth, but it's an important sum to the worker who is raising a family.

Prices

The average worker spends most of his or her earnings and uses credit to finance major purchases. Using credit means exposure to interest rates.

The prime interest rate was 4.8 percent in 1960; in 2006 it was 8.0 percent.[29]

A climbing public debt breeds high interest rates. The penalty to consumers relative to high interest rates can be a severe one, especially to a generation of consumers that, unlike its forebears, lives day-to-day on credit.

A 30-year mortgage for $100,000 at 5.0 percent, for example, would cost $505 per month — at 8.75 percent the cost would be $787 per month.[30]

The difference in rates causes an annual cost *increase* of $3,384 — over the life of the mortgage, $101,520. In terms of average income per capita,[31] that's more than two years of work sacrificed on the altar of high interest rates.

Apply this analytical approach to the number of credit transactions that the modern consumer conducts and the meaning of interest rates begins to assume the level of importance that it deserves.

Is the debt that tends to keep interest rates high important to the average American?

Yes!

The security of the nation and its currency are weakened by it. The job market is less robust and taxes are inflated because of it. And the chance of most Americans to build savings is practically destroyed by it.

Who Did It?

Twelve presidents, 34 congresses, six chief justices and about three dozen associate justices of the U.S. Supreme Court were involved in this analysis. All left footprints on the second American Revolution that produced the Welfare State and the social upheaval that identify the America of 2008. Those who have been identified as leading men in this drama will be discussed below under the headings, the executives, the congressmen and the judges.

The Executives

LYNDON JOHNSON

Total breakaway from past disciplines began when Lyndon Johnson became president. His no-holds-barred approach to spending what he wanted, when he wanted led to the debt we have today.

Under him, Food Stamps (1964), Medicaid (1965), Student Aid (1966) and Medicare (1967) went on the books, and his congressional team added to the menu over the next decade.

By 1980, the full Johnson dream was in place, and public debt increased from Eisenhower's $237 billion to Carter's $712 billion, an increase of 202 percent.

There have been many greater men than Lyndon Johnson in American politics, but nobody had more far-reaching influence than he.

RONALD REAGAN

Ronald Reagan bucked the momentum of the Johnson steamroller. He didn't have the veto-proof clout that it took to reform entitlements, but he did take deficits out of the shadows and explained their cause loudly and often.

If climbing debt is a problem, if the social programs were weaved into the federal budget too hastily and if they have been protected too vigorously, then Ronald Reagan is the hero of this book. The truth is out because of him. Voters and their politicians must do the rest.

GEORGE W. BUSH

George W. Bush tried to do something about entitlements; he served as a courageous war leader who faced up to the challenges of his time. History will judge how well he did.

The chief executives covered in this book ranged from great to mediocre when measured against the challenges of their time. FDR, Truman and Ike served before the seeds of socialism were planted and debt began its irreversible incline. Of the three, FDR can be, and usually is, regarded as great.

John Kennedy was an interim figure who did little to influence anything in any meaningful way, through no fault of his own. A bullet ended his promising career.

The story of public debt is, at the same time, the story of all presidents from Lyndon Johnson to George W. Bush. And of these eight men two stand out and one awaits the verdict of history: Johnson and Reagan, ideological opposites, and George W. Bush who is fighting the battles of his time.

Johnson, the radical; Reagan, the defender; George W. Bush, the contender. They wrote the history of life in America during the last half of the twentieth century.

The Congressmen

Presidents lead America, but it takes a team to get things done; a president's power is defined by his congressional clout. And Democrats had all of it from 1960 to 1994, except for six years of Senate control under Reagan.[32]

The America of the Founding Fathers became the America of Lyndon Johnson during these years. After Johnson retired, his work was continued by his loyalists: Coal Miners Benefits (1970), Commodity Donations (1973), Supplementary Security Income (1974), Supplemental Feeding (1976), Earned Income Tax Credit (1976), Legal Services (1976) and Energy Assistance (1977) were typical additions to the Welfare State that year after year kept adding to public debt.

The great enablers who protected, nurtured, expanded and protected this march to socialism were Sam Rayburn, John McCormack, Carl Albert, Tip O'Neil, Jim Wright and Tom Foley in the House; in the Senate, Mike Mansfield, Robert Byrd and George Mitchell.

Highest honors go to those who hammered the entitlement programs into place so firmly that they may never be dislodged: *Rayburn, McCormack, Albert and Mansfield*. The others saw to it that the plan of the master, Lyndon Johnson, was followed, and that the usurpers were kept at bay.

HOUSE SPEAKER SAM RAYBURN (D–TX)

Rayburn was Speaker of the House under presidents Roosevelt, Truman, Eisenhower and Kennedy. He lived through the growth of the Social Security program under Truman and he saw the introduction of the Food Stamp program under Kennedy.

There is little doubt that Rayburn would have been as enthusiastic a supporter of the expansion of the Welfare State under Lyndon Johnson.

JOHN MCCORMACK (D–MA)

John McCormack joined the Kennedy/Johnson team in 1963, and he served as speaker of the House through 1969, the first two years of the Nixon administration.

He saw the core of the Welfare State slide into the budget while America watched the Vietnam War — Food Stamps, Medicaid, Student Aid, Coal Miner Benefits and Medicare — programs that would revolutionize the budget process and generate federal debt for decades to come.

CARL ALBERT (D–OK)

Carl Albert served two presidents during his term as Speaker of the House (1971–76). He saw the Nixon presidency crumble under the weight of the Watergate scandal; he joined enthusiastically with his colleagues in adding more programs to the already unaffordable Welfare State — Commodity Donations 1973, Supplementary Security Income 1974, Supplemental Feeding 1976, Earned Income Tax Credit 1976, Legal Services 1976.

MIKE MANSFIELD (D–MT)

Mansfield served with House Speakers Rayburn, McCormack and Albert. And during his unmatched years as Senate Majority Leader, he served presidents Kennedy, Johnson, Nixon and Ford. He saw, supported and fought for the entire spectrum of the Johnson program; he was the most enduring supporter of the Johnson ideology.

Lyndon Johnson's second American Revolution hit a wall when Ronald Reagan became president. But all of the pieces of the Welfare State were already in place. In little more than two decades Johnson and his key men (especially Mansfield) led the charge for a new America that was up to its hips in debt — an America that could no longer mount a credible military force that, apart from nuclear weapons, met the needs of the day without, at the same time, adding to public debt.

Democratic leaders who would thereafter step forward were stewards, not creators — disciples, not apostles.

Tip O'Neil, Jim Wright and Tom Foley in the House together with Robert Byrd, George Mitchell and Tom Daschle in the Senate thereafter served as care-takers and protectors of past victories against the attempts of conservatives like Reagan who were gradually persuading people that the free lunch Democrats had sold for decades was not so free after all.

One politician stands apart, *Mike Mansfield,* the always dependable part-ner who for 17 years carried the ball for Johnson personally, or for his pro-grams.

The Judges

According to an ABC poll of January 26, 2006, 43 percent of Americans disagree with the *Roe v. Wade* decision that made abortion legal, 57 percent are opposed to abortion as a birth control procedure, 69 percent are against par-tial-birth abortions and 86 percent oppose them when the woman is pregnant for six or more months.

The *Roe* decision is more than 33 years old. It has split America as no other issue. It continues to do so, and poll numbers say that it is a case that should never have been decided at the federal level in the first place.

If this is so, activist judges who supported the *Griswold, Roe* and *Doe* deci-sions (the ones that established and then extended the right to an abortion) deserve special status on the list of those most responsible for the judicial/social aspects of the second American Revolution.

Earl Warren and *Warren Burger* head the list, because they were at the time the Chief Justices that led the others to the decision that upset the moral val-ues of the United States in such a broad way that the damage cannot be calcu-lated.

They were not alone. Associate Justices *Douglas, Brennan, Stewart, Mar-shall, Blackmun and Powell* were enthusiastic supporters of those decisions with-out which the nation would not have suffered more than three decades of sometimes fierce division.

Another supporter of abortion, who came along after the *Roe* decision, was Justice *Stevens* (still active) who has demonstrated in several cases his kinship with the original "abortionists." He also stands out as the judge who would give you and your children the least amount of protection against pornography.

If you'd like to eliminate anything that smells of religion in the public square or in its schools, Judges *Stevens, O'Connor, Souter* and *Blackmun* would qualify as advocates for your cause.

The worst/best (depending on your point of view) judge across the board most likely to upset American values was *Stevens* — *Blackmun, Brennan* and *Marshall* fit the same general mold.

Finally, *Souter* is the top candidate on the current Court for "most radical" status.

Remember their names: *Warren, Burger, Douglas, Brennan, Stewart, Marshall, Blackmun* and *Powell,* the foundation judges who had the most negative impact on the values of America as they had been defined before the 1960s. None are active today.

And remember too: *Stevens, O'Connor,* and *Souter.* O'Connor, retired, can do no more damage to the church/state argument, but Stevens and Souter are active and threatening. *Stevens* will probably resign before 2009, but *Souter* will continue for a time to come.

A WORD

The spending splurge since 1960 has been supported by taxpayer dollars, much of the money coming from wage earners who own little more than a house, a car, and (maybe) a small nest egg, men and women living from paycheck to paycheck, faced with parental costs increasingly beyond their ability to pay, dreaming of vacations they can't afford, and dreading retirements they don't dare face.

These people are described by some as "undertaxed" because their rates are the lowest in "the Western world," a designation that has little meaning for any individual who will lose the house if he/she is unemployed for six months. He/she does not feel undertaxed.

More meaningfully, he/she is not undertaxed.

Just exactly who are these thinkers from Olympus who decide that 21 percent of per capita income[33] is a fair average level of federal taxation?

Who are these people who say that redistribution of wealth is a function of government? That penalties associated with progressive tax rates are morally justified?

Who placed the scales of godlike justice in their hands?

What is the relationship of such ideas to those of the Founding Fathers — to those of Karl Marx?

When did these men stop managing the American government and start managing the lives of its citizens?

And given the results of their programs, how dare they hold themselves up as qualified to manage anything?

Taxes paid by the average person are more than mere dollars. Of the average man and his money, Petronius said: "Have and you shall be esteemed."[34] He knew that a dollar in the pocket supports one's ego.

George Bernard Shaw said: "Money ... enables life to be lived socially."[35] Shaw knew that those with a dollar can mix with others; those without are outsiders.

"Money is time," said George Gissing.[36] He was right. Without it there is no leisure to enjoy those things that nourish the soul.

America's political leaders have been for 50 years unthinkingly, even stupidly, spending the esteem, the pride, and the leisure of Americans in pursuit of a social dream that has eluded the followers of Marx since the publication of his "Communist Manifesto" (1848).

Shrouded though it might be in the language of compassion, Lyndon Johnson's Great Society was nothing more or less than the most recent failed attempt to enslave people in a bureaucratic quagmire, which, when successful, reduces them to the status of dependent cogs in a well-oiled centralized machine.

The Great Society has been a monumental waste of time and money. Federal politicians of the last half-century have violated the work of their predecessors; they have abused the trust placed in them by their constituents; they must be stopped.

Only the voters can do so.

Voters must get angry. They must vote. They must remove from office those who do not talk straight and elect those who will cut spending, reduce the size of government, lower debt, and return to Americans the right to live their own lives.

"Though I am an enemy to the using of our credit but under absolute necessity, yet the possessing a good credit I consider as indispensable in the present system of carrying on war. The existence of a nation having no credit is always precarious," said Thomas Jefferson.[37]

Amen, and amen.

Appendices

1. Summary of Federal Deficit/Surplus by Cost Centers,[1] 1941–2008 (in billions of dollars)

President	Years	Total	Defense	Interest	Govt.	HR
FDR	1941–44	$-127.8	$-127.8	$	$	$
FDR/HST	1945–48	-47.6	-37.4	-5.4		-4.8
HST	1949–52	2.0	22.8		-5.6	-15.2
Ike	1953–56	-6.6	-6.6			
Ike	1957–60	-12.1			-4.4	-7.7
JFK/LBJ	1961–64	-21.0			-12.8	-8.2
LBJ	1965–68	-38.9		-.2	-14.1	-24.6
RMN	1969–72	-46.1		-1.9		-44.2
RMN/GRF	1973–76	-148.0		-9.3	-16.9	-121.8
JEC	1977–80	-227.2		-17.0	-67.5	-142.7
RWR	1981–84	-600.0	-133.2	-125.0		-341.8
RWR	1985–88	-738.4	-72.9	-89.6	-51.1	-524.8
GHWB	1989–92	-933.4		-38.1	-177.3	-718.0
WJC	1993–96	-729.6				-729.6
WJC	1997–2000	409.0				409.0
GWB	2001–04	-819.3	-351.1		-117.4	-350.8
GWB	2005–08	-1050.1	-225.5	-12.9	-62.9	-748.8
Totals		$-5135.1	$-931.7	$-299.4	$-530.0	$3374.0
Percent		100.0%	18.1%	5.9%	10.3%	65.7%

2. Profile of Political Power, 1941–2008

Congress	House	Senate	President
77	Rayburn (D)	Barkley (D)	FDR (D)
78	Rayburn (D)	Barkley (D)	FDR (D)
79	Rayburn (D)	Barkley (D)	FDR/Truman (D)
80	Martin (R)	White (R)	Truman (D)
81	Rayburn (D)	Lucas (D)	Truman (D)
82	Rayburn (D)	McFarland (D)	Truman (D)
83	Martin (R)	Taft (R)[a]	Eisenhower (R)
83		Knowland (R)	
84	Rayburn (D)	Johnson (D)	Eisenhower (R)

Congress	House	Senate	President
85	Rayburn (D)	Johnson (D)	Eisenhower (R)
86	Rayburn (D)	Johnson (D)[a]	Eisenhower (R)
87	Rayburn (D)[b]	Mansfield (D)	Kennedy (D)
87	McCormack (D)		Kennedy (D)
88	McCormack (D)	Mansfield (D)	Kennedy (D)[c]
88			Johnson (D)[d]
89	McCormack (D)	Mansfield (D)	Johnson (D)
90	McCormack (D)	Mansfield (D)	Johnson
91	McCormack (D)	Mansfield (D)	Nixon (R)
92	Albert (D)	Mansfield (D)	Nixon (R)
93	Albert (D)	Mansfield (D)	Nixon (R)
94	Albert (D)	Mansfield (D)[a]	Ford (R)[d]
95	O'Neil (D)	Byrd (D)	Carter (D)
96	O'Neil (D)	Byrd (D)	Carter (D)
97	O'Neil (D)	Baker (R)	Reagan (R)
98	O'Neil (D)	Baker (R)	Reagan (R)
99	O'Neil (D)	Dole (R)	Reagan (R)
100	Wright (D)	Byrd (D)	Reagan (R)
101	Wright (D)[a]	Mitchell (D)	Bush I (R)
101	Foley		
102	Foley (D)	Mitchell (D)	Bush I (R)
103	Foley (D)	Mitchell (D)	Clinton (D)
104	Gingrich (R)	Dole (R)[a]	Clinton (D)
104		Lott (R)	
105	Gingrich (R)	Lott (R)	Clinton (D)
106	Hastert (R)	Lott (R)	Clinton (D)
107	Hastert (R)	Daschle (D)	Bush II (R)
108	Hastert (R)	Frist (R)	Bush II (R)
109	Hastert (R)	Frist (R)	Bush II (R)
110	Pelosi (D)	Reid (D)	Bush II (R)

a) Resigned. b) Died in office. c) Assassinated. d) VP succession.

Sources: www.senate.gov; http://clerk.house.gov; *New York Times Almanac 2006*, pp. 124–129.

3.1. U.S. Population, 1800–2008 (millions)

Year	Pop.	Year	Pop.	Year	Pop.
1800	5.3	1810	7.2	1820	9.6
1830	12.9	1840	17.1	1850	23.2
1860	31.4	1870	39.8	1880	50.2
1890	63.0	1900	76.2	1910	92.2
1920	106.0	1930	123.2	1940	132.2
1950	151.3	1960	179.3	1970	203.3
1980	226.5	1990	248.7	2000	281.4
2004	293.9	2006	298.2	2008	303.6

Notes: 1) 2008 is estimated; 2) White population in 1990 was 80% of the total — 75% and dropping in 2000. In the same period Hispanic population increased 58 percent.[1]

Source: Statistical Abstract of the United States.

3.2. U.S. Population, Over 65, 1940–2030

Year	Total	% of Total Pop.	10-year Change
1940	9.0	6.9%	
1950	12.4	8.1	17.3%
1960	16.7	9.2	13.6
1970	20.1	9.8	6.5
1980	25.5	11.3	15.3
1990	31.2	12.5	10.6
2000	35.0	12.4	-1.0
2010	40.2	13.0	4.8
2020	54.6	16.3	25.4
2030	71.5	19.7	20.9

Source: New York Times Almanac 2006, p. 285.

3.3. Black Population, 1980–2003

Year	Total pop.[2] (mil)	Black pop.[3] (mil)	%	Prison Pop. (000s)[4]	Black Prisoners (000s)[4]	% of prisoners
1980	226.5	26.7	11.8%	329.8	146.9	44.5%
1985	237.9	29.0	12.2	502.5	220.7	43.9
1990	249.4	30.5	12.2	773.9	360.0	46.5
1995	262.8	33.1	12.6	1125.9	541.7	48.1
2000	281.4	34.7	12.3	1391.9	610.3	43.8
2003	291.0	35.8	12.3	1470.0	621.3	42.3

4.1. American Social Statistics, Family, 1940–2005

	Divorce[1]	Abortion (000s)[2]	Never Married[3]	Unmarried Couples (000s)[4]	AIDS Cases[5]	SAT Score[6]
1940	16.5%					
1950	23.1					
1960	25.8		23.3%	439		
1970	32.7		25.1	523		
1972		587				1039
1973		616[a]				
1974		763[a]				
1975	48.1	855[a]				1010
1980	43.3	1,298	26.1	1,589		994
1981					435	
1985	49.3	1,329[a]			12,035	1009
1990	48.0	1,430	26.4	2,856	49,669	1001
1995	50.0	1,211			70,220	1010
1997						
2000		858	28.2	4,736	41,239	1019
2002	43.0 e					
2003	42.0 e		28.8	4,622	43,171	

	Divorce[1]	Abortion (000s)[2]	Never Married[3]	Unmarried Couples (000s)[4]	AIDS Cases[5]	SAT Score[6]
2004						
2005			29.2			1028

a) CDC — abortion.

4.2. American Social Statistics, Crime, 1964–2004 (000s)

	Murder	Rape	Assault	Prisoners
1964	8.0			
1975	20.5	56.1	492.6	
1980	23.0	83.0	672.7	329.8
1990	23.4	102.6	1,054.9	773.9
1995	21.6	97.5	1,099.2	1,125.9
2000	15.6	90.2	911.7	1,391.9
2003	16.5	93.4	857.9	1,470.0
2004	16.1	94.6	854.9	1,497.0

Source: New York Times Almanac 2006, 2007, pp. 311, 318, 319; 1964 infoplease.

5.1. Supreme Court Justices, 1941–2008

FDR 1941–44	*FDR/HST 1945–48*	*HST 1949–52*	*Ike I 1953–56*
Wiley Rutledge	**Fred Vinson**	Sherman Minton	Wm. Brennan
Robert Jackson	Harold Burton	Tom Clark	John Harlan
James Byrnes[c]	Wiley Rutledge	**Fred Vinson**	**Earl Warren**
Harlan Stone	Robert Jackson	Harold Burton	Sherman Minton[c]
Frank Murphy	**Harlan Stone**[b]	Wiley Rutledge[b]	Tom Clark
Wm. Douglas	Frank Murphy	Robert Jackson	**Fred Vinson**[b]
F. Frankfurter	Wm. Douglas	Frank Murphy[b]	Harold Burton
Stanley Reed	F. Frankfurter	Wm. Douglas	Robert Jackson[b]
Hugo Black	Stanley Reed	F. Frankfurter	Wm. Douglas
Owen J. Roberts	Hugo Black	Stanley Reed	F. Frankfurter
	Owen J. Roberts	Hugo Black	Stanley Reed
			Hugo Black

Ike II 1957–60	*JFK/LBJ 1961–64*	*LBJ 1965–68*	*RMN 1969–72*
Potter Stewart	Arthur Goldberg	Thurg'd Marshall	Wm. Rehnquist
Chas. Whittaker	Potter Stewart	Abe Fortas	Harry Blackmun
Wm. Brennan	Chas. Whittaker[a]	Arthur Goldberg[c]	Lewis Powell
John Harlan	Wm. Brennan	Byron White	**Warren Burger**
Earl Warren	John Harlan	Potter Stewart	Thurg'd Marshall
Tom Clark	**Earl Warren**	Wm. Brennan	Abe Fortas[c]
Harold Burton[c]	Tom Clark	John Harlan	Byron White
Wm. Douglas	Wm. Douglas	**Earl Warren**	Potter Stewart
F. Frankfurter	F. Frankfurter[c]	Tom Clark[c]	Wm. Brennan
Stanley Reed[c]	Hugo Black	Wm. Douglas	John Harlan[c]
Hugo Black		Hugo Black	**Earl Warren**

Ike II 1957–60

JFK/LBJ 1961–64

LBJ 1965–68

RMN 1969–72
Wm. Douglas
Hugo Black[c]

RMN/GRF 1973–76
Wm. Rehnquist
John Stevens
Harry Blackmun
Lewis Powell
Warren Burger
Thurg'd Marshall
Byron White
Potter Stewart
Wm. Brennan
Wm. Douglas[c]

JEC 1977–80
Wm. Rehnquist
John Stevens
Harry Blackmun
Lewis Powell
Warren Burger
Thurg'd Marshall
Byron White
Potter Stewart
Wm. Brennan

RWR I 1981–84
Wm. Rehnquist
Sandra O'Connor
John Stevens
Harry Blackmun
Lewis Powell
Warren Burger
Thurg'd Marshall
Byron White
Potter Stewart[c]
Wm. Brennan

RWR II 1985–88
Anthony Kennedy
Wm. Rehnquist
Antonin Scalia
Sandra O'Connor
John Stevens
Harry Blackmun
Lewis Powell[c]
Warren Burger[c]
Thurg'd Marshall
Byron White
Wm. Brennan

GHWB 1989–92
Clarence Thomas
David Souter
Anthony Kennedy
Wm. Rehnquist
Antonin Scalia
Sandra O'Connor
John Stevens
Harry Blackmun
Thurg'd Marshall[c]
Byron White
Wm. Brennan[c]

WJC I 1993–96
Stephen Breyer
Ruth Ginsburg
Clarence Thomas
David Souter
Anthony Kennedy
Wm. Rehnquist
Antonin Scalia
Sandra O'Connor
John Stevens
Harry Blackmun[c]
Byron White[c]

WJC II 1997–00
Stephen Breyer
Ruth Ginsburg
Clarence Thomas
David Souter
Anthony Kennedy
Wm. Rehnquist
Antonin Scalia
Sandra O'Connor
John Stevens

GWB I 2001–04
Stephen Breyer
Ruth Ginsburg
Clarence Thomas
David Souter
Anthony Kennedy
Wm. Rehnquist
Antonin Scalia
Sandra O'Connor
John Stevens

GWB 2005–08
Samuel Alito
John Roberts
Stephen Breyer
Ruth Ginsburg
Clarence Thomas
David Souter
Anthony Kennedy
Wm. Rehnquist[b]
Antonin Scalia
Sandra O'Connor[c]
John Stevens

a) Disabled. b) Died in office. c) Resigned.

Source: www.oyez.org.

5.2. Supreme Court — Chief Justices
Case Activity, 1941–2006

Chief	41–44	45–48	49–52	53–56	57–60	61–64
Harlan Stone	11	2				
Fred Vinson		6	11	2		
Earl Warren				7	13	31

	65–68	69–72	73–76	77–80	81–84	85–88
Earl Warren	33	9				
Warren Burger		35	38	61	65	38
Wm. Rehnquist						62

	89–92	93–96	97–00	01–04	05–06
Wm. Rehnquist	79	133	254	327	70
John Roberts					

Source: http://www.oyez.org.

6.1. Federal Tax Income Trend, By Decade,
1941–2009 (billions of current dollars)

Yr.	1940s	1950s	1960s	1970s	1980s	1990s	2000s
0	6.5	**39.4**	92.5	192.8	517.1	1032.1	2025.5
1	8.7	51.6	94.4	**187.1**	599.3	1055.1	**1991.4**
2	14.6	66.2	99.7	207.3	617.8	1091.3	**1853.4**
3	24.0	69.6	106.6	230.8	**600.6**	1154.5	**1782.5**
4	43.7	69.7	112.6	263.2	666.5	1258.7	**1880.3**
5	45.2	**65.5**	116.8	279.1	734.1	1351.9	2153.9
6	**39.3**	74.6	130.8	298.1	769.2	1453.2	2407.3
7	**38.5**	80.0	148.8	355.6	854.4	1579.4	2540.1
8	41.6	**79.6**	153.0	399.6	909.3	1722.0	2662.5
9	**39.4**	**79.2**	186.9	463.3	991.2	1827.6	2798.3
Total	301.5	675.4	1242.1	2876.9	7259.5	13525.8	22095.2
Up	123.6%	83.9%	131.6%	152.3%	86.3%	63.4%	

Source: Historical Tables 2007, 1.1, 1940–2005; Historical Tables 2008, 2006–2009.

6.2. Federal Tax Income Trend, By Decade, 1940–2009 (billions of *indexed* dollars, 2000 = base)

Yr.	1940s	1950s	1960s	1970s	1980s	1990s	2000s
0	66.5	241.0	440.5	713.3	973.8	1270.3	2025.5
1	85.8	299.5	443.2	659.3	1027.8	1251.6	1945.5
2	134.1	369.4	462.9	697.5	991.8	1262.8	1776.6
3	206.4	381.4	488.8	743.8	922.7	1306.3	1674.8
4	361.5	377.6	510.2	791.1	988.3	1394.2	1972.8
5	364.8	351.8	520.3	759.9	1054.3	1466.6	1914.4
6	295.9	390.4	570.4	757.0	1079.9	1546.8	2075.6
7	262.6	403.4	628.6	840.1	1168.6	1652.3	2103.3
8	259.0	389.6	624.0	884.5	1205.8	1779.8	2188.2
9	237.3	381.7	729.2	949.0	1265.3	1864.5	2246.4
Total	2273.9	3585.8	5418.1	7795.5	10678.3	14795.2	19923.1
Up		57.7%	51.1%	43.9%	37.0%	38.6%	34.7%

Source: Historical Tables 2007, 1.1, 1940–2005; Historical Tables 2008, 2006–2009; Price index Table 10.1.

6.3. Federal Tax Revenue by Source (in billions of dollars)

Year	Total	Income Tax	Corp.	Soc. Sec.	Excise	Other[a]
1941p/w	$6.5	$.9	$1.2	$1.8	$2.0	$.6
1944w	43.7	19.7	14.8	3.5	4.8	.9
1948p	41.6	19.3	9.7	3.8	7.4	1.4
1952w	66.2	27.9	21.2	6.4	8.9	1.8
1956p	74.6	32.2	20.8	9.3	9.9	2.4
1960p/w	92.5	40.7	21.5	14.7	11.7	3.9
1964w	112.6	48.7	23.5	22.0	13.7	4.7
1968w	153.0	68.7	28.7	33.9	14.1	7/6
1972w	207.3	94.7	32.2	52.6	15.5	12.3
1976cw	298.1	131.6	41.4	90.8	17.0	17.3
1980cw	517.1	244.1	64.6	157.8	24.3	26.3
1984cw	666.5	298.4	56.9	239.4	37.4	34.4
1988cw	909.3	401.2	94.5	334.3	35.2	44.1
1992p	1091.3	476.0	100.3	413.7	45.6	55.7
1996p	1453.1	656.4	171.8	509.4	54.0	61.5
2000w	2025.5	1004.5	207.3	652.9	68.9	91.9
2004w	1880.3	809.0	189.4	733.4	69.9	78.6
2008[a]w	2662.5	1246.6	315.0	927.2	68.1	105.6

a) Estimate, Historical Tables 2008. P = mostly peace; w = mostly war; cw = cold war

Source: Historical Tables 2007, 2.1; Appendix 6.

6.4. "Other" Federal Tax Revenue by Source
(in billions of dollars)

Year	Total	Estate/Gift	Customs Duties/Fees	Fed. Reserve Earnings	All Other
1941	$ .8	$ .4	$ .4	$ .0	$ .0
1944	1.0	.5	.4	.0	.1
1948	1.5	.9	.4	.1	.1
1952	1.7	.8	.5	.3	.1
1956	2.3	1.2	.7	.3	.1
1960	3.9	1.6	1.1	1.1	.1
1964	4.7	2.4	1.2	1.0	.1
1968	7.6	3.1	2.0	2.1	.4
1972	12.4	5.4	3.3	3.3	.4
1976	17.3	5.2	4.1	5.4	2.6
1980	26.3	6.4	7.1	11.8	1.0
1984	34.4	6.0	11.3	15.7	1.4
1988	44.1	7.6	16.2	17.2	3.1
1992	55.8	11.2	17.3	22.9	4.4
1996	61.5	17.2	18.1	20.1	5.1
2000	91.9	29.0	19.9	32.3	10.7
2004	78.7	24.8	21.1	19.7	13.1
2008[a]	105.6	25.7	29.2	36.1	14.6

a) Estimate, Historical Tables 2008.

Source: Historical Tables 2006, 2.5

6.5. Presidential Tax Income, FDR to GWB

President	Term	Current Revenue[1]	Prior Period	% Change	Moving Avg
FDR	1941–44	91.0	26.0	250.0	
FDR/HST	1945–48	164.6	91.0	80.9	
HST	1949–52	196.6	164.6	19.4	
Ike 1	1953–56	279.4	196.6	42.1	
Ike 2	1957–60	331.3	279.4	18.6	18.6
JFK/LBJ	1961–64	413.3	331.3	24.8	28.5
LBJ	1965–68	549.4	413.3	32.9	29.6
RMN	1969–72	774.1	549.4	40.9	31.9
RMN/GRF	1973–76	1071.2	774.1	38.4	32.9
JEC	1977–80	1735.6	1071.2	62.0	37.1
RWR 1	1981–84	2484.2	1735.6	43.1	37.9
RWR 2	1985–88	3266.3	2484.2	31.5	37.1
GHWB	1989–92	4166.8	3266.3	27.6	36.2
WJC 1	1993–96	5219.5	4166.8	25.3	35.2
WJC 2	1997–00	7153.8	5219.5	37.1	35.4
GWB 1	2001–04	7506.8	7153.8	4.9	33.0
GWB 2	2005–08	9763.8	7506.8	30.1	32.8

6.6. Presidential Tax Income vs. Inherited Cost Structure, FDR to GWB

President	Term	Current Revenue	Inherited Costs[2]	% of Revenue
FDR	1941–44	91.0	38.0	42
FDR/HST	1945–48	164.6	218.8	133
HST	1949–52	196.6	212.1	108
Ike 1	1953–56	279.4	194.6	70
Ike 2	1957–60	331.3	286.0	86
JFK/LBJ	1961–64	413.3	343.4	83
LBJ	1965–68	549.4	464.3	85
RMN	1968–72	774.1	588.3	76
RMN/GRF	1973–76	1071.2	820.2	77
JEC	1977–80	1735.6	1219.2	70
RWR 1	1981–84	2484.2	1962.8	79
RWR 2	1985–88	3266.3	3084.2	94
GHWB	1989–92	4166.8	4004.7	96
WJC 1	1993–96	5219.5	5100.2	98
WJC 2	1997–00	7153.8	5949.1	83
GWB 1	2001–04	7506.8	6744.8	90
GWB 2	2005–08	9763.8	8326.1	85

7.1. Growth/Decrease in Defense Spending FDR to GWB (billions of dollars)

President	Term	Current Defense[1]	Prior Defense[1]	% Change
FDR	1941–44	177.9	6.8	2516
FDR/HST	1945–48	147.6	177.9	-17
HST	1949–52	96.6	147.6	-35
Ike 1	1953–56	187.3	96.6	94
Ike 2	1957–60	189.3	187.3	1
JFK/LBJ	1961–64	210.1	189.3	11
LBJ	1965–68	262.0	210.0	25
RMN	1968–72	322.3	262.0	23
RMN/GRF	1973–76	332.1	322.3	3
JEC	1977–80	452.0	332.1	36
RWR 1	1981–84	780.0	452.0	73
RWR 2	1985–88	1098.5	780.0	41
GHWB	1989–92	1174.6	1098.5	7
WJC 1	1993–96	1110.4	1174.6	-5
WJC 2	1997–00	1108.4	1110.4	-
GWB 1	2001–04	1514.2	1108.4	37
GWB 2	2005–08[2]	2195.5	1514.2	45

7.2. Active Military Personnel — Cost Per Person, FDR to GWB (billions of dollars)

President	Year	Defense Cost (billions)	Personnel (millions)[3]	% Change
FDR	1945	83.0	12.1	
HST	1950	13.7	1.5	-88
Ike 2	1960	48.1	2.5	67
JFK/LBJ	1965	50.6	2.7	8
RMN	1970	81.7	3.1	15
RMN/GRF	1975	86.5	2.1	-32
JEC	1980	134.0	2.1	0
RWR 2	1985	252.7	2.2	5
GHWB	1990	299.3	2.0	-9
WJC 1	1995	272.1	1.5	-25
WJC 2	2000	294.5	1.4	-7
GWB 1	2004	455.9	1.4	0
GWB 2	2008[2]	606.5	1.4[4]	0

8.1. Per Capita — Federal Tax Income vs. Personal Income (population in millions; tax income in billions)

President	Year	Pop.[1]	Fed. Tax Income[2]	Fed. Tax Income Per Capita	Personal Income Per Capita	% Taxed
FDR	1940	132	$ 7	$ 53	$ 849	6.2
FDR	1944	138	44	319	1149	27.7
FDR/HST	1948	147	42	286	1391	20.6
HST	1952	158	52	329	1653	19.9
Ike	1956	169	75	444	1949	22.8
Ike	1960	179	92	514	2219	23.2
JFK/LBJ	1964	192	113	589	2663	22.1
LBJ	1968	201	153	761	3445	22.1
RMN	1972	210	207	986	4677	21.1
RMN/GRF	1976	218	298	1367	6663	20.5
JEC	1980	227	517	2278	9910	23.0
RWR	1984	236	666	2822	13585	20.8
RWR	1988	244	909	3725	17052	21.8
GHWB	1992	255	1091	4278	20576	20.8
WJC	1996	265	1453	5483	24651	22.2
WJC	2000	281	2025	7206	29845	24.1
GWB	2004	293	1880	6416	33050	19.4
GWB 4	2008	304	2663	8760	41566	21.1

8.2. Per Capita — Federal Spending, Excluding Defense (billions of dollars)

President	Year	Pop (mil)[1]	Spending Minus Defense (bil)[3]	% Change	Per Capita
FDR (1,4)	1940	132	$ 7.8		$ 59
FDR/HST (1)	1948	147	20.7	165.4	141

President	Year	Pop (mil)[1]	Spending Minus Defense (bil)[3]	% Change	Per Capita
HST (2)	1952	158	21.6	4.3	137
IKE-(1,3)	1960	179	44.1	104.2	246
JFK/LBJ (2,3)	1968	201	96.2	118.1	479
RMN/GFR (1,3)	1976	218	282.2	193.3	1294
JEC (1,3)	1980	227	456.9	61.9	2013
RWR (1,3)	1988	244	774.1	69.4	3173
GHWB (1)	1992	255	1083.2	39.9	4248
WJC (1)	1996	265	1294.8	19.5	4886
WJC (1)	2000	281	1494.7	15.4	5319
GWB (2)	2004	293	1837.1	22.9	6291
GWB (2)	2008	304	2295.4	24.9	7551

1 = peace; 2 = war; 3 = cold war; 4 = Great Depression

2008 = estimate

8.3. Defense vs. GDP and Total Spending, 1941–2008

Pres.	Year	Defense	Spend	GDP	D vs GDP	D vs S
FDR	1944	$ 79	$ 91	$ 209	37.7%	86.8%
HST	1948	9	30	256	3.5	30.0
HST	1952	46	68	349	13.2	67.6
Ike	1956	43	71	427	10.0	60.6
Ike	1960	48	92	518	9.3	52.2
LBJ	1964	55	119	640	8.6	46.2
LBJ	1968	82	178	867	9.5	46.1
RMN	1972	79	231	1178	6.7	34.2
GRF	1976	90	372	1737	5.2	24.2
JEC	1980	134	591	2727	4.9	22.7
RWR	1984	227	852	3840	5.9	26.7
RWR	1988	290	1065	5009	5.8	27.2
GHWB	1992	298	1382	6240	4.8	21.6
WJC	1996	266	1561	7694	3.5	17.0
WJC	2000	295	1789	9710	3.0	16.5
GWB	2004	456	2293	11546	3.9	19.9
GWB[4]	2008	607	2902	14515	4.2	20.7

Source: Historical Tables 2007, 3.1, 10.1.

9. Misery Index, FDR to GWB

President	Year	Prime Interest[1]	Inflation Rate[2]	Unemployment Rate[3]	Total
FDR	1940	1.5%	.7%	14.6%	16.8%
FDR	1944	1.5	1.7	1.2	4.4
FDR/HST	1948	1.8	8.1	4.0	13.9
HST	1952	3.0	1.9	2.7	7.6
IKE 1	1956	3.8	1.5	4.2	9.5
IKE 1	1960	4.8	1.7	6.6	13.1
JFK/LBJ	1964	4.5	1.3	5.0	10.8
LBJ	1968	6.3	4.2	3.4	13.9

President	Year	Prime Interest[1]	Inflation Rate[2]	Unemployment Rate[3]	Total
RMN	1972	5.3	3.2	5.2	13.7
RMN/GRF	1976	6.8	5.8	7.8	20.4
JEC	1980	15.3	13.5	7.2	36.0
RWR 1	1984	12.0	4.3	7.3	23.6
RWR 2	1988	9.3	4.1	5.3	18.7
GHWB	1992	6.3	3.0	7.4	16.7
WJC 1	1996	8.3	2.9	5.4	16.6
WJC 2	2000	9.2	3.4	3.9	16.5
GWB 1	2004	4.3	2.7	5.4	12.4
GWB 2	2006	8.0[a]	3.3[b]	4.5[b]	15.8

a) July. b) 3rd quarter.

10.1. Personal Income Per Capita vs. Unemployment Rate, FDR to GWB, Current and Chained (year 2000 = 100) Dollars

President	Year	Current Dollars[1]	% Change	Chained Dollars[2]	% Change	UR[3]
FDR	1940	$ 849		8681		14.6%
FDR	1944	1149	35	9504	10	1.2
FDR/HST	1948	1391	21	8661	-9	3.8
HST	1952	1653	19	9224	7	3.0
IKE 1	1956	1949	18	10199	11	4.1
IKE 1	1960	2219	14	10567	4	5.5
JFK/LBJ	1964	2663	20	12066	14	5.2
LBJ	1968	3445	29	14055	16	3.6
RMN	1972	4677	36	15737	12	5.6
RMN/GRF	1976	6663	42	16920	8	7.7
JEC	1980	9910	49	18663	10	7.1
RWR 1	1984	13585	37	20144	8	7.5
RWR 2	1988	17052	26	22612	12	5.5
GHWB	1992	20576	21	23809	5	7.5
WJC 1	1996	24651	20	26266	10	5.4
WJC 2	2000	29845	21	29845	14	4.0
GWB 1	2004	33050	11	30341	2	5.5
GWB 2[a]	2008	41566	26	34693	14	4.8

a) Estimates.

10.2. Unemployment Rates — End of Year, 1948–2006

	1940s	1950s	1960s	1970s	1980s	1990s	2000s
00	14.6	4.3	6.6	6.1	7.2	6.3	3.9
01	9.9	3.1	6.0	6.0	8.5	6.9	5.7
02	4.7	2.7	5.5	5.2	10.8	7.4	6.0
03	1.9	4.5	5.5	4.9	8.3	6.5	5.7
04	1.2	5.0	5.0	7.2	7.3	5.6	5.4
05	1.9	4.2	4.0	8.2	7.0	5.6	4.9

	1940s	1950s	1960s	1970s	1980s	1990s	2000s
06	3.9	4.2	3.8	7.8	6.6	5.4	4.5
07	3.9	5.2	3.8	6.4	5.7	4.7	
08	4.0	6.2	3.4	6.0	5.3	4.4	4.8
09	6.6	5.3	3.5	6.0	5.4	4.0	

Source: U.S. Department of Labor, Bureau of Labor Statistics 1948–2006; The Employment Situation, 1940–47, http://www.timesizing.com/1933.htm-Timesizing Associates. 2008 — estimate.

11.1 Allocation of Deficits, FDR–Ike, 1941–1956

	FDR 1941–44	FDR/HST 1945–48	HST 1949–52	IKE 1953–56
Current revenue	$ 91.0	$164.6	$196.6	$279.4
Prior revenue	26.0	91.0	164.6	196.6
Change	$ 65.0	$ 73.6	$ 32.0	$ 82.8
Growth factor	3.5	1.8	1.2	1.4
Characteristics:				
Prior Total costs	38.0	218.8	212.2	194.6
Prior deficit	12.0	127.8	47.6	-2.0
Current Primary costs	183.6	163.3	115.3	207.3
Govt				
Prior	11.2	22.8	21.7	31.6
Current	22.8	21.7	31.6	22.9
Growth rate	2.0	None	1.5	None
Max allowable			26.0	
Deficit	None	None	-5.6	None
HR				
Prior	16.4	12.4	27.1	47.7
Current	12.2	27.1	47.7	55.8
Growth rate	None	2.2	1.8	1.2
Max allowable		22.3	32.5	66.8
Deficit	None	-4.8	-15.2	None
Interest				
Prior	3.6	5.7	15.7	18.7
Current	5.7	15.7	18.7	20.0
Growth rate	1.6	2.8	1.2	.9
Max allowable	12.6	10.3	18.7	26.2
Deficit	None	-5.4	None	None
Total	None	-10.2	-20.8	None
Defense (by deduction)	-127.8	-37.4	22.8	-6.6
Total deficit	-127.8	-47.6	2.0	-6.6
Summary:				
Government			-5.6	
Human Resources		-4.8	-15.2	
Interest		-5.4		
Defense	-127.8	-37.4	22.8	-6.6
Total	-127.8	-47.6	2.0	-6.6

Source: Historical Tables 2007, 1.1, 3.1.

11.2. Allocation of Deficits, Ike-2 to JEC, 1957–1980

	Ike-2 57–60	JFK LBJ 61–64	LBJ 65–68	RMN 69–72	RMN GF 73–76	JEC 77–80
Revenue						
current	331.3	413.3	549.4	774.1	1071.2	1735.6
prior	279.4	331.3	413.3	549.4	774.1	1071.2
change						
amount	51.9	82.0	136.1	224.7	297.1	664.4
factor	1.186	1.248	1.329	1.409	1.384	1.620
Defense						
Prior	187.3	189.3	210.1	262.0	322.3	332.1
Allowed	222.1	236.2	279.2	369.2	446.1	538.0
Actual	189.3	210.1	262.0	322.3	332.1	452.0
Deficit	None	None	None	None	None	None
Net remaining revenue	142.0	203.2	287.4	451.8	739.1	1283.6
Interest						
Prior	20.0	23.8	29.5	39.4	57.4	88.6
Allowed	23.8	29.6	39.2	55.5	79.3	143.5
Actual	23.8	29.5	39.4	57.4	88.6	160.5
Deficit	None	None	-0.2	-1.9	-9.3	-17.0
Net remaining revenue	118.2	173.7	248.2	396.3	659.8	1140.1
Prior Govt/HR	78.7	130.4	194.7	286.9	440.5	798.5
Growth factor	1.502	1.332	1.275	1.381	1.498	1.428
Government						
Prior	22.9	38.8	64.5	96.3	99.7	166.3
Allowed	34.4	51.7	82.2	133.0	149.4	237.6
Actual	38.8	64.5	96.3	99.7	166.3	305.1
Deficit	-4.4	-12.8	-14.1	None	-16.9	-67.5
Net remaining revenue	83.8	122.0	166.0	296.6	510.4	902.6
Prior HR	55.8	91.6	130.2	190.6	340.8	632.2
Growth factor	1.502	1.332	1.275	1.556	1.498	1.428
Human Resources						
Prior	55.8	91.6	130.2	190.6	340.8	632.2
Allowed	83.9	122.0	166.0	296.6	510.4	902.3
Actual	91.6	130.2	190.6	340.8	632.2	1045.2
Deficit	- 7.7	-8.2	-24.6	-44.2	-121.8	-142.9
Summary						
Defense	0.0	0.0	0.0	0.0	0.0	0.0
Interest	0.0	0.0	-0.2	-1.9	-9.3	-17.0
Government	-4.4	-12.8	-14.1	0.0	-16.9	-67.3
Human Resources	-7.7	-8.2	-24.6	-44.2	-121.8	-142.9
Deficit	-12.1	-21.0	-38.9	-46.1	-148.0	-227.2

Source: Historical Tables 2007, 1.1, 3.1.

11.3. Allocation of Deficits, RWR–GWB, 1981–2008

	RWR 81–84	RWR 85–88	GHWB 89–92	WJC 93–96	WJC 97–00	GWB 01–04	GWB[1] 05–08
Revenue							
Current	2484.2	3266.3	4166.8	5219.5	7153.8	7506.8	9763.8
Prior	1735.6	2484.2	3266.3	4166.8	5219.5	7153.8	7506.8
Change							
Amount	748.6	782.1	900.5	1052.7	1934.3	353.0	2257.0
Factor	1.431	1.315	1.276	1.253	1.371	1.049	1.301
Defense							
Prior	452.0	780.0	1098.5	1174.6	1110.4	1108.4	1514.2
Allowed	646.8	1025.6	1401.4	1471.4	1521.9	1163.1	1970.0
Actual	780.0	1098.5	1174.6	1110.4	1108.4	1514.2	2195.5
Deficit	-133.2	-72.9	None	None	None	-351.1	-225.5
Net remaining revenue	1837.4	2240.7	2992.2	4109.1	6045.4	6343.7	7793.8
Interest							
Prior	160.5	354.7	556.0	747.4	875.1	937.8	690.4
Allowed	229.7	466.4	709.3	936.2	1199.4	984.1	898.2
Actual	354.7	556.0	747.4	875.1	937.8	690.4	911.1
Deficit	-125.0	-89.6	-38.1	None	None	None	-12.9
Net remaining revenue	1607.7	1774.3	2282.9	3234.0	5107.6	5653.3	6895.6
Prior Govt/HR	1350.3	1949.5	2350.2	3178.2	3963.6	4698.6	6121.5
Growth factor	1.191	.910	0.971	1.018	1.289	1.203	1.126
Govt							
Prior	305.1	340.7	361.1	528.1	384.6	489.6	706.4
Allowed	363.4	310.0	350.8	537.4	495.6	589.1	795.4
Actual	340.7	361.1	528.1	384.6	489.6	706.5	858.3
Deficit	None	-51.1	-177.3	None	None	-117.4	-62.9
Net remaining revenue	1267.0	1464.3	1932.1	2849.4	4618.0	5064.2	6100.2
Prior HR	1045.2	1608.8	1989.1	2650.1	3579.0	4209.0	5415.0
Growth factor	1.212	0.910	0.971	1.075	1.290	1.203	1.126
HR							
Prior	1045.2	1608.8	1989.1	2650.1	3579.0	4209.0	5415.0
Allowed	1267.0	1464.3	1932.1	2849.4	4618.0	5064.2	6100.2
Actual	1608.8	1989.1	2650.1	3579.0	4209.0	5415.0	6849.0
Deficit	-341.8	-524.8	-718.0	-729.6	409.0	-350.8	- 748.8
Summary							
Defense	-133.2	-72.9	0.0	0.0	0.0	-351.1	-225.5
Interest	-125.0	-89.6	-38.1	0.0	0.0	0.0	-12.9
Government	None	-51.1	-177.3	None	None	-117.4	-62.9
Human Resources	-341.8	-524.8	-718.0	-729.6	409.0	-350.8	- 748.8
Deficit	-600.0	-738.4	-933.4	-729.6	409.0	-819.3	-1050.1

Source: Historical Tables 2007, 1.1, 3.1.

12.1. Public Debt vs. Tax Revenue and GDP, FDR to GWB (billions of dollars)

Year	President	Tax Revenue	GDP	Public Debt	Revenue vs. GDP	Debt vs. GDP
1940	FDR	$ 6.5	$ 96.8	$ 42.8	11.9%	44%
1944	FDR	43.7	209.2	184.8	20.9	88
1948	HST	41.6	256.0	216.3	16.3	84
1952	HST	66.2	348.6	214.8	19.0	62
1956	Ike	74.6	427.2	222.2	17.5	52
1960	Ike	92.5	517.9	236.8	17.9	46
1964	LBJ	112.6	640.4	256.8	17.6	40
1968	LBJ	153.0	866.6	289.5	17.7	33
1972	RMN	207.3	1178.3	322.4	17.6	27
1976	GRF	298.1	1736.5	477.4	17.2	27
1980	JEC	517.1	2726.7	711.9	19.0	26
1984	RWR	666.5	3840.2	1307.0	17.4	34
1988	RWR	909.3	5008.6	2051.6	18.2	41
1992	GHWB	1091.3	6239.9	2999.7	17.5	48
1996	WJC	1453.2	7694.1	3734.1	18.9	49
2000	WJC	2025.5	9709.8	3409.8	20.9	35
2004	GWB	1880.3	11546.0	4295.5	16.3	37
2008[1]	GWB	2662.5	14515.0	5345.4	18.3	37

Source: Historical Tables 2007, 3.1, 7.1, 10.1.

12.2. Public Debt Per Capita (billions of dollars)

President	Year	Population (millions)	Debt (billions)	% Change	Debt Per Capita
FDR	1940	132	$ 43		324
FDR/HST	1944	138	185	330	1340
HST	1948	147	216	17	1469
HST	1952	157	215	0	1369
Ike	1956	169	222	3	1314
IKE 2	1960	181	237	7	1310
JFK/LBJ	1964	192	257	8	1339
LBJ	1968	201	290	13	1443
RMN	1972	210	322	11	1533
RMN/GRF	1976	218	477	48	2188
JEC	1980	227	712	50	3137
RWR 1	1984	236	1307	84	5538
RWR 2	1988	245	2052	57	8376
GHWB	1992	255	3000	46	11765
WJC 1	1996	265	3734	24	14090
WJC 2	2000	281	3410	-9	12135
GWB 1	2004	292	4296	26	14712
GWB 2[1]	2008	303	5345	24	17640

Source: Population by Decade-Bureau of Census; intervening years, Information Please, Internet; Debt — Historical Tables 2007, 7.1.

13. Immigration, 1940–2000

Year	Total (millions)[1]
1941–50	1.0
1951–60	2.5
1961–70	3.3
1971–80	4.5
1981–90	7.3
1991–00	9.1

Note: 32.2% of immigrants in 2004 came from south of the border, about half of them from Mexico.[2]

14. GDP Growth, Current and Chained vs. Unemployment, 1940–1988 (Chained dollars: year 2000 = 100) (billions of dollars)

President	Year	GDP[1] Current	% % Change	GDP[1] Chained	% Change	U. Rate[2]
FDR	1940	$ 97		$ 992		14.6%
FDR	1944	209	115	1729	74	1.2
FDR/HST	1948	256	22	1594	-8	4.0
HST	1952	349	36	1948	22	2.7
Ike	1956	427	22	2234	15	4.2
Ike	1960	518	21	2467	10	6.6
JFK/LBJ	1964	640	24	2900	18	5.0
LBJ	1968	867	35	3537	22	3.4
RMN	1972	1178	36	3964	12	5.2
RMN/GRF	1976	1737	47	4411	11	7.8
JEC	1980	2727	57	5136	16	7.2
RWR	1984	3840	41	5694	11	7.3
RWR	1988	5009	30	6642	17	5.3
GHWB	1992	6240	25	7221	9	7.4
WJC	1996	7694	23	8189	13	5.4
WJC	2000	9710	26	9710	19	3.9
GWB	2004	11518	19	10550	9	5.4
GWB[3]	2008	14515	26	11917	13	4.7
Average[a] 1960–2008					14%	5.5%

a) 1940/44/48 excluded.

15. Federal Tax Timeline, 1936–2008

Year	Pres.	Note
1936	FDR	Personal tax-high rate 63 percent; FDR institutes the inheritance, estate, gift tax and dividend taxes and progressive tax rates; Soc. Sec. Act 1935; in 1939 Soc. Sec. expanded to cover survivors and dependants; tax rate 2 percent —$3,000 max earnings
1940	FDR	Tax on lower incomes increases from 4 to 19 percent; top rate

climbs to 78%; income tax withholding introduced in 1943; Soc. Sec. tax the same.

1944	FDR	Top rate 94 percent; Soc. Sec. tax the same; max corporate tax 40 percent.
1948	HST	Top rate 82 percent; in 1950 the first cost of living Soc. Sec. adjustment was made (increased outlay by 77 percent; Soc. Sec. tax the same; max corporate tax 38 percent; in 1950 benefits are increased and coverage is expanded to more jobs.
1952	HST	Top rate 91 percent; Soc. Sec. tax 3 percent — $3600 max earnings; max corporate tax 52 percent.
1956	Ike	Same personal rate; Soc. Sec. program adjusted to cover disabled children; Soc. Sec. tax 4 percent — $4,200 max earnings; max corporate tax 52 percent.
1960	Ike	Same personal rate; In 1961 Soc. Sec. retirement age dropped to 62; Soc. Sec. Tax 6 percent — $4,800 max earnings; max corporate tax 52 percent.
1964	JFK/LBJ	Top rate 70 percent; Soc. Sec. tax 7.25 percent — $4,800 max earnings; max corporate tax 50 percent.
1968	LBJ	Top rate 75 percent; Soc. Sec. tax 7.6 percent — $7,800 max earnings. In 1968 payroll tax revenue for the first time exceeded corporate tax revenue; max corporate tax 53 percent.
1972	RMN	Top rate 70 percent; automatic Soc. Sec. COLAs approved in 1975; Soc. Sec. tax 9.2 percent — max earnings $9,000; max corporate tax 48 percent.
1976	RMN/GRF	Top rate 70 percent; Soc. Sec. tax 9.9 percent — max earnings $15,300; max corporate tax 48 percent.
1977	JEC	Top rate 70 percent; Soc. Sec. Tax Amendment — a schedule of tax increases ending in 2030 that gradually raises the rate to 15.3 percent, and the earning base to $42,000 in 1987.
1978	JEC	Unemployment benefits taxed for the first time.
1980	JEC	Top rate 70 percent; Soc. Sec. tax 10.16 percent — max earnings $25,900; max corporate tax 46 percent.
1981	RWR	Largest tax cut in history. Top rate 50 percent; Soc. Sec. tax 11.4 percent — max earnings $37,800; max corporate tax 46 percent.
1983	RWR	Top rate 50 percent; Soc. Sec. benefits taxed for the first time; 1983 Act accelerates rate increases from the year 2030 to 1990.
1986	RWR	Top rate dropped to 28 percent; corporate rate dropped to 34 percent.
1988	RWR	Top rate 28 percent; Soc. Sec. tax 12.12 percent — max earnings $68,400; max corporate tax 39 percent.
1990	GHWB	Top rate 31 percent; Soc. Sec. tax 12.4 percent — max corporate tax 39 percent.
1993	WJC	Largest tax increase in history. Sc. Sec. tax still climbing.
1996	WJC	Top rate 39.6 percent; Soc. Sec. tax 12.4 percent — max corporate tax 39 percent.
1997	WJC	Top rate 39.6 percent; capital gains rates reduced — other credits
2000	WJC	Top rate 39.6 percent; Soc. Sec. tax 12.4 percent — max earnings $76,200; max corporate tax 39 percent.
2001	GWB	Massive tax cut — all rates, top rate 35%
2003	GWB	Accelerated 2001 cuts and added to them.
2004	GWB	Top rate 35 percent; Soc. Sec. tax 12.4 percent — max earnings $87,900; max corporate tax 39 percent.

2005		
2006	GWB	Extended 2003 cuts and added benefits; Soc. Sec. tax 12.4 percent — max earnings $92,700 (estimated); max corporate tax 39 percent.
2007	GWB	
2008	GWB	

Sources: http://www.huppi.com/kangaroo/TaxTimeline.htm#federal; InfoPlease, Income Tax History, http://www.infoplease.com/ipa/A0005921.html.

16.1. Summary of Public Debt Growth, 1940–2008

President	Term	Beginning Debt[2]	Change[1]	Total	Treasury[a]	Ending Debt[2]
FDR	1941–44	$ 42.8	$ 127.8	$ 170.6	$ 14.2	$ 184.8
FDR/HST	1945–48	$ 184.8	47.6	232.4	-16.1	216.3
HST	1949–52	216.3	-2.0	214.3	.5	214.8
Ike	1953–56	214.8	6.6	221.4	.8	222.2
Ike	1957–60	222.2	12.1	234.3	2.5	236.8
JFK/LBJ	1961–64	236.8	21.0	257.8	-1.0	256.8
LBJ	1965–68	256.8	38.9	295.7	-6.2	289.5
RMN	1969–72	289.5	46.1	335.6	-13.2	322.4
RMN/GRF	1973–76	322.4	148.0	470.4	7.0	477.4
JEC	1977–80	477.4	227.2	704.6	7.3	711.9
RWR	1981–84	711.9	600.0	1311.9	-4.9	1307.0
RWR	1985–88	1307.0	738.4	2045.4	6.2	2051.6
GWHB	1989–92	2051.6	933.4	2985.0	14.7	2999.7
WJC	1993–96	2999.7	729.8	3729.5	4.6	3734.1
WJC	1997–00	3734.1	-409.0	3325.1	84.7	3409.8
GWB	2001–04	3409.8	819.3	4229.1	66.4	4295.5
GWB[3]	2005–08	4295.5	1050.1	5345.6	-.2	5345.4

a) Treasury cannot be exact when it finances a budget deficit and the difference between what is needed and the value of securities traded inevitably produces a relatively small variance.

16.2. Public Debt vs. Gross Domestic Product, 1941–2008

Year	Debt[2]	GDP[4]	%	Year	Debt[2]	GDP[4]	%
1940	$ 43	$ 97	44	1944	$ 185	$ 209	89
1948	216	256	84	1952	215	349	62
1956	222	427	52	1960	237	518	46
1964	257	640	40	1968	290	867	33
1972	322	1178	27	1976	477	1737	27
1980	712	2727	26	1984	1307	3840	34
1988	2052	5009	41	1992	3000	6240	48
1996	3734	7694	49	2000	3410	9710	35
2004	4296	11546	37	2008[3]	5345	14515	37

17. Human Resources Increase vs. Revenue Increase, 1953–2008[1]

President	Years	Revenue Increase	Human Resources	% Increase
Ike w/cw	1953–56	42.1%	$ 55.8	17.0
Ike cw	1957–60	18.6%	91.6	64.2
JFK/LBJ w/cw	1961–64	24.8	130.2	33.0
LBJ w/cw	1965–68	32.9	190.6	46.4
RMN w/cw	1969–72	40.9	340.8	78.8
RMN/GRF cw	1973–76	38.4	632.2	85.5
JEC cw	1977–80	62.0	1045.2	65.3
RWR cw	1981–84	43.1	1608.8	53.9
RWR cw	1985–88	31.5	1989.1	23.6
GHWB w/cw	1989–92	27.6	2650.1	33.2
WJC p	1993–96	25.3	3579.0	35.1
WJC p	1997–00	37.1	4208.9	17.6
GWB w	2001–04	4.9	5415.0	28.7
GWB w[2]	2005–08	30.1	6849.0	26.5

18. Presidential Vetoes[a] from FDR to GWB

President	Congress	Vetoes	President	Congress	Vetoes
FDR	73rd–79th	635	HST	79th–82nd	250
Ike	83rd–86th	181	JFK	87th–88th	21
LBJ	88th–90th	30	RMN	91st–93rd	43
GRF	93rd–94th	66	JEC	95th–96th	31
RWR	97th–100th	78	GHWB	101st–102nd	44
WJC	103rd–106th	37	GWB	107th–	1

a) Includes pocket vetoes (the president doesn't sign a bill that has passed). If the Congress is in session, the bill becomes law in 10 days without the president's signature; if the Congress is not in session when the bill is presented to the president, and if he does not sign it, it becomes a "pocket veto" and the bill does not become law.

Source: http://www.infoplease.com/ipd/A0593462.html; U.S. Senate, http://www.senate.gov/reference/reference_index_subjects/Vetoes_vrd.htm.

19.1. Historical Crude Oil Prices, 1946–2006 Average Nominal (unadjusted) Price

Pres.	Term	1	2	3	4	Avg.
FDR/HST	1945–48	$	$ 1.63	$ 2.16	$ 2.77	$ 2.19
HST	1949–52	2.77	2.77	2.77	2.77	2.77
Ike	1953–56	2.92	2.99	2.93	2.94	2.95
Ike	1957–60	3.00	3.01	3.00	2.91	2.98
JFK/LBJ	1961–64	2.85	2.85	3.00	2.88	2.90
LBJ	1965–68	3.01	3.10	3.12	3.18	3.10
RMN	1969–72	3.32	3.39	3.60	3.60	3.48
RMN/GRF	1973–76	4.75	9.35	7.67	13.10	8.72
JEC	1977–80	14.40	14.95	25.10	37.42	22.97
RWR	1981–84	35.75	31.83	29.08	28.75	31.35

Pres.	Term	1	2	3	4	Avg.
RWR	1985–88	26.92	14.44	17.75	14.87	18.50
GHWB	1989–92	18.33	23.19	20.20	19.25	20.24
WJC	1993–96	16.75	15.66	16.75	20.46	17.41
WJC	1997–00	18.64	11.91	16.56	27.39	18.63
GWB	2001–04	23.00	22.81	27.69	37.66	27.79
GWB	2005–08	46.47	60.40			53.44

Source: http://inflationdata.com/Inflation/Inflation_Rate/Historical_Oil_Prices_Table.asp.

19.2. Historical Crude Oil Prices, 1946–2006
Average Inflation (Adjusted) Price-2005 = base

Pres.	Term	1	2	3	4	Avg.
FDR/HST	1945–48	$	$16.68	$19.60	$23.38	$19.89
HST	1949–52	23.61	23.36	21.65	21.17	22.45
Ike	1953–56	22.10	22.59	22.17	21.96	22.21
Ike	1957–60	22.66	21.09	20.88	19.98	20.95
JFK/LBJ	1961–64	19.35	19.12	19.29	19.63	19.35
LBJ	1965–68	19.37	19.38	18.98	18.52	19.06
RMN	1969–72	18.37	17.72	18.04	17.47	17.90
RMN/GRF	1973–76	21.53	38.42	46.01	46.72	38.17
JEC	1977–80	48.19	46.53	69.51	92.26	64.12
RWR	1981–84	79.89	66.97	59.26	56.17	65.57
RWR	1985–88	50.77	26.72	31.69	25.55	33.68
GHWB	1989–92	29.99	35.91	30.10	27.84	30.96
WJC	1993–96	23.54	21.43	22.31	26.45	23.43
WJC	1997–00	23.57	14.83	20.12	32.26	22.70
GWB	2001–04	26.37	25.71	30.55	40.42	30.76
GWB	2005–08	51.94	60.78	56.36		

Note: The Organization of Petroleum Exporting Countries (OPEC) was formed in 1960. Since then, it has directly managed supply, and indirectly managed price, to its own advantage, as possible.

Source: http://inflationdata.com/Inflation/Inflation_Rate/Historical_Oil_Prices_Table.asp.

20. Timeline — Muslim-Related Terrorism
Selected Events, 1980–2005

Date-Place	Event	Casualties	Who
Aug. 1982 Hawaii	Bomb Airplane	1 dead, several injured	Palestinian Mohammed Rashid — Iraq based
Apr. 1983 Lebanon	Suicide bomb U.S. Embassy	63 dead	Hizbullah
Oct. 1983 Lebanon	Suicide bomb U.S. Marine Barracks	241 dead	Hizbullah
Dec. 1983 Kuwait	Suicide bomb U.S. Embassy	6 dead Dozens injured	Islamic Jihad
Sept. 1984 Lebanon	Suicide bomb U.S. Embassy	16 dead	Islamic Jihad
Apr. 1985 Spain	Bomb-restaurant used by U.S. troops	17 dead	
Jun. 1985 Lebanon	Hijacking TWA #847	1 dead	Hizbullah
Aug. 1985 Germany	Car bomb U.S. base	2 dead 20 injured	
Oct. 1985 Cruise ship	Hostage	1 dead	Arafat's PLF
Dec. 1985 Rome/Austria	Airport Gunmen	16 dead	Libya
Apr. 1986 Germany	Bomb Night club used by U.S. troops	3 dead 150 injured	A mixture of Muslims
Apr. 1986 Greece	Bomb TWA #840	4 dead 9 injured	Mohammed Rashid — Iraq based
Feb. 1988 Lebanon	Kidnapping U.S. Marine	Executed	Hizbullah
Dec. 1988 Scotland	Bomb Pan Am 103	270 dead	Libya
Feb. 1993 New York	Bomb World Trade Center	6 dead 1000 injured	Directly, four Muslim fundamentalists headed by Ramzi Ahmed Yousef; indirectly, Osama bin Laden
Mar. 1995 Pakistan	Murder U.S. diplomats	2 dead	
Nov. 1995 Saudi Arabia	Bomb U.S. forces	7 dead	Hizbullah

Date- Place	Event	Casualties	Who
Feb. 1996 Greece	Missile attack U.S. Embassy	None	
Jun. 1996 Saudi Arabia	Truck bomb Khobar Towers used byU.S. troops	19 troops dead	
Nov. 1997 Pakistan	Murder U.S. businessmen	5 dead	
Jun 1998 Lebanon	Missile attack U.S. Embassy	None	Hizullah suspected
Aug, 1998 Kenya & Tanzania	Simultaneous bomb- ings U.S. Embassies	263 dead 5000 injured	Osama bin Laden Al-Qaeda
Oct. 2000 Yemen	Bomb USS *Cole*	17 dead	
Sep. 2001 NY, PA, D.C.	Hijacked airplane crashes into the WTC & Pentagon	Almost 3,000 dead- countless injured	Osama bin Laden 19 hijackers mostly Saudi Arabians Al-Qaeda
Jun. 2002 Pakistan	Bomb U.S. Consulate	12 dead	Osama bin Laden Al-Qaeda
May 2003 Saudi Arabia	Suicide bomb housing for Westerners	34 dead	Osama bin Laden Al-Qaeda
May 2004 Saudi Arabia	Attack on oil company	22 dead	
June 2004 Saudi Arabia	Gun attacks	4 dead	
Dec. 2004 Saudi Arabia	Attack U.S. Consulate	5 dead	
Nov. 2005 Jordan	Suicide bombs three U.S. hotels	57 dead	Osama bin Laden Al-Qaeda

Source: History of Terrorism www.simplytaty.com/broaden pages/terrorism.htm

Infoplease Encyclopedia http://www.infoplease.com/ipa/A0001454.html

21. U.S. Senators, Democrats
For/Against the War Resolution, October 2002

For Democrats	Against Democrats
Baucus, Max	Akaka, Daniel
Bayh, Evan	Bingaman, Jeff
Biden, Joe*	Boxer, Barbara
Breaux, John	Byrd, Robert
Cantwell, Maria	Corzine, John
Carnahan, Jean	Conrad, Kent
Carper, Tom	Dayton, Mark
Cleland, Max	Durbin, Dick
Clinton, Hillary*	Feingold, Russ*
Daschle, Tom	Graham, Bob
Dodd, Christopher*	Inouye, Daniel
Dorgan, Byron	Kennedy, Ted
Edwards, John*	Leahy, Patrick
Feinstein, Dianne	Levin, Carl
Harkin, Tom	Mikulski, Barbara
Hollings, Fritz	Murray, Patty
Johnson, Tim	Reid, Jack
Kerry, John*	Sarbanes, Paul
Kohl, Herb	Stabenow, Debbie
Landrieu, Mary	Wellstone, Patty
Lieberman, Joe	Wyden, Ron
Lincoln, Blanche	
Miller, Zell	
Nelson, Bill	
Nelson, Ben	
Reid, Harry	
Rockefeller, Jay	
Schumer, Chuck	
Torricelli, Robert	

Note: All Republicans except Lincoln Chafee (RI) voted for the resolution; Independent Jim Jeffords (VT) voted against it.

Sources: White House, http://www.whitehouse.gov/news/releases/2002/10/20021002–2.html Wikipedia Encyclopedia, Internet, Iraq Resolution

*2008 Presidential candidates as of Jan. 2007 — outspoken critics of the decision to go to war, and of its prosecution since.

Chapter Notes

Introduction

1. Historical Tables 2007, 7.1.
2. *Flemming v. Nestor*, June 1960.
3. Historical Tables 2007, 3.1.
4. Historical Tables 2007, 10.1, 7.1.
5. Historical Tables 2007, 1.1.
6. Internet home page U.S. House/Senate.
7. William A. DeGregorio, *The Complete Book of U.S. Presidents* (New York: Random House Value Publishing, 1997).
8. Appendix 6-5.
9. 2007 and 2008 estimated numbers from Historical Tables 2007.

Chapter 1

1. DeGregorio, *U.S. Presidents*, "Light-horse Harry" Lee, eulogist, comrade and friend, p. 14.
2. Bureau of Public Debt, Historical Information.
3. John S. Gordon, *Hamilton's Blessing* (New York: Penguin Books, 1998).

Chapter 2

1. Agricultural Adjustment Act; Civilian Conservation Corps; Federal Trade Commission; Federal Deposit Insurance Corporation; Federal Emergency Relief Administration; National Recovery Act; Pubic Works Administration; Tennessee Valley Authority — Wikipedia — FDR, Internet, and De Gregorio, *U.S. Presidents*.
2. *Chronicle of the 20th Century* (New York: Dorling Kindersley Publishing, 1995).
3. Appendix 2.
4. Historical Tables 2007, 7.1.
5. Bureau of Public Debt, Historical Information, 17911939, Internet, 1998.
6. Appendix 12.1.
7. *New York Times Almanac 2006*, p.117.
8. Timesizing Associate www.timesizing.com.
9. Historical Tables 2007, 1.1.

10. Appendix 3.1.
11. http://www.oyez.org — Supreme Court justices/cases.
12. Appendix 5.
13. In the course of financing the deficit the Treasury cannot be exact and a variance between what is needed and the value of securities traded inevitably produces a relatively small variance.
14. Historical Tables 2007, 1.1, 3.1.
15. Ludwig von Mises Institute, "The Curse of the Withholding Institute," http:// www. mises.org.
16. Table 2.4.
17. Appendix 12.
18. Appendix 9.
19. *New York Times Almanac 2006*, p. 157.

Chapter 3

1. Appendix 2.
2. Columbia Encyclopedia and other biographic sources on the Internet.
3. *Chronicle of the 20th Century* (New York: Dorling Kindersley, 1995).
4. Historical Tables 2007, 3.1.
5. Appendix 14.
6. Appendix 9.
7. Historical Tables 2007, 1.1.
8. Appendix 8.1.
9. http://www.oyez.org — Supreme Court justices/cases.
10. Appendix 5.
11. Appendix 12.1.
12. Appendices 1 and 11.1.
13. Historical Tables 2007, 1.1.
14. Appendix 6.5.
15. Appendix 15.
16. Historical Tables 2007, 1.1, 3.1.
17. Appendix 6.3.
18. Appendix 8.1.
19. Appendix 11.1.
20. *Chronicle of the 20th Century* (New York: Dorling Kindersley Publishing, 1995).

21. *Ibid.*, pp. 117–119.
22. Historical Tables 2007, 3.1.

Chapter 4

1. Historical Tables 2007, 3.1.
2. *Chronicle of the 20th Century* (New York: Dorling Kindersley, 1995).
3. Appendix 14.
4. Historical Tables 2007, 1.1.
5. Appendix 15.
6. Appendix 12.1.
7. Appendix 9.
8. Appendix 8.1.
9. http://www.oyez.org — Supreme Court justices/cases.
10. Appendix 5.2.
11. *Chronicle of the 20th Century.*
12. Historical Tables 2007, 3.1.
13. *New York Times Almanac 2007*, p. 157.
14. Appendix 16.1.
15. Appendix 6.5.
16. Appendix 14.
17. Appendix 11.1.
18. Appendix 10.2.
19. Appendix 11.1.

Chapter 5

1. *New York Times Almanac 2006*, p. 117.
2. Appendix 12.
3. Appendix 2.
4. Historical Tables 2007, 1.1.
5. Columbia and Wikipedia Encyclopedias, Internet.
6. *New York Times Almanac 2006*, p.158.
7. *Chronicle of the 20th Century* (New York: Dorling Kindersley, 1995).
8. Historical Tables 2007, 3.1.
9. Appendix 14.
10. Appendix 9.
11. Appendix 8.1.
12. Appendix 8.1.
13. http://www.oyez.org — Supreme Court justices/cases.
14. Appendix 5.
15. Appendix 11.1.
16. Appendix 15.
17. Historical Tables 2007, 3.1.

Chapter 6

1. *New York Times Almanac 2006*, pp.117, 118.
2. William A. DeGregorio, *The Complete Book of U.S. Presidents* (New York: Random House Value Publishing, 1997).
3. Appendix 12.2.
4. Appendix 2.
5. *Chronicle of the 20th Century* (New York: Dorling Kindersley Publishing, 1995).
6. Historical Tables 2007, 3.1.

7. Appendix 14.
8. Historical Tables 2007, 1.1.
9. Appendix 9.
10. Appendix 8.1.
11. http://www.oyez.org — Supreme Court justices/cases.
12. Appendix 6.5.
13. Appendix 15.
14. Appendices 11-1, 11-2.
15. Exhibit 9.
16. Appendix 12.

Chapter 7

1. Appendix 12.
2. *New York Times Almanac 2007*, p. 118.
3. Appendix 2.
4. *Chronicle of the 20th Century* (New York: Dorling Kindersley, 1995).
5. Infoplease; *Source:* U.S. Bureau of the Census. Web site: http://*www.census.gov.*
6. Appendix 14.
7. Historical Tables 2007, 1.1.
8. Appendix 9.
9. Appendix 15.
10. Appendix 8.1.
11. http://www.oyex.org — Supreme Court justices/cases.
12. Appendix 5.2.
13. Appendix 4.1.
14. *New York Times Almanac 2006*, p. 386.
15. Appendix 3.1.
16. Appendix 13.
17. *Chronicle of the 20th Century.*
18. Appendix 6.5.
19. Historical Tables 2007, 1.1.
20. Appendix 8.3.
21. Appendix 15.
22. Appendix 11-2.
23. Appendix 7.2.
24. *Chronicle of the 20th Century.*
25. Appendix 9.
26. Appendix 12.1.
27. Appendix 11.2.

Chapter 8

1. Bureau of Public Debt, Historical Information.
2. Appendix 2.
3. U.S. House and Senate, leadership history.
4. Appendix 12.1.
5. *Chronicle of the 20th Century* (New York: Dorling Kindersley, 1995).
6. Appendix 9.
7. Appendix 6.5.
8. Appendix 8.1.
9. Appendix 15.
10. Historical Tables 2007, 1.1.
11. Appendix 14.

12. http://www.oyez.org — Supreme Court justices/cases.
13. Appendix 5.2.
14. Appendix 4.1.
15. Historical Tables 2007, 1-1.
16. Appendix 6.5.
17. Appendix 1.
18. Appendix 15.
19. Historical Tables 2007, 2.1.
20. Appendix 8.1.
21. *Chronicle of the 20th Century.*
22. Historical Tables 2007, 3.1.
23. Appendix 9
24. Appendix 12.1.
25. Appendix 11.2.
26. Appendix 6.5.
27. *New York Times Almanac 2006*, p. 158.
28. Historical Tables 2007, 3.1.
29. Appendix 12.1.

Chapter 9

1. *New York Times Almanac 2006*, p.118
2. U.S. House, party division, http://clerk.house.gov/.
3. U.S. Senate, party division, http://www.senate.gov/pagelayout/history/one_item_and_teasers/partydiv.htm
4. Appendix 12.1.
5. Appendix 2.
6. *Chronicle of the 20th Century* (New York: Dorling Kindersley, 1995).
7. Appendix 9.
8. Appendix 8.1.
9. http://www.minneapolisfed.org/Research/data/us/calc/hist1913.cfm.
10. Appendix 14.
11. Historical Tables 2007, 1.1.
12. Appendix 11.2.
13. http://www.oyez.org — Supreme Court justices/cases.
14. Appendix 5.2.
15. Columbia and Wikipedia Encylopedias, "Lewis Powell."
16. *Ibid.,* "Harry Blackmun."
17. Columbia and Wikipedia Encyclopedias, "No Fault Divorce."
18. *Ibid.,* Wikipedia.
19. Appendix 11.2.
20. Appendix 6.6.
21. Historical Tables 2007, 1.1.
22. Appendix 6.5.
23. Historical Tables 2007, 3.1.
24. Appendix 11.2.
25. Appendix 1.
26. *Ibid.*
27. Appendix 11.2.
28. Appendix 9.
29. www.federalreserve.gov/releases/H15/data/Annual/H15_PRIME_NA.txt.
30. Historical Tables 2007, 3.1.
31. Appendix 19.
32. Historical Tables 2007, 3.1.
33. Appendix 11.2.
34. Appendix 6.5.
35. Historical Tables 2007, 3.1.
36. Appendix 15.
37. Appendix 16.1.
38. *New York Times Almanac 2006*, p. 118.

Chapter 10

1. *New York Times Almanac 2006*, p. 118.
2. U.S. House, Party Division, http://clerk.house.gov/.
3. U.S. Senate, Party Division, http://www.senate.gov/pagelayout/history/one_item_and_teasers/partydiv.htm.
4. Appendix 2.
5. *Chronicle of the 20th Century* (New York: Dorling Kindersley, 1995).
6. Appendix 12.1.
7. *Chronicle of the 20th Century.*
8. Wikipedia, Internet; Entebbe Airport; BBC Co. U.K., http://news.bbc.co.uk/onthisday/hi/dates/stories/july/4/newsid_2786000/2786967.stm
9. Appendix 18.
10. Wikipedia, Internet; CBO; Congressional Budget Office, http://www.cbo.gov/.
11. *New York Times Almanac 2006*, p. 157.
12. Appendix 7.2.
13. Appendix 9.
14. Appendix 8.1.
15. Appendix 12.
16. Appendix 1.
17. http://www.oyez.org — Supreme Court justices/cases.
18. Appendix 5.2.
19. Appendix 4.1.
20. Historical Tables 2007, 1.1.
21. Appendix 1.
22. Appendix 6.5.
23. Federal Reserve Bank of Minneapolis, http://minneapolisfed.org/.
24. Appendix 7.
25. Appendix 11.2.
26. Appendix 9.
27. Appendix 16.1.
28. Appendix 19.
29. Historical Tables 2007, 4.1.
30. Historical Tables 2007, 3.1.
31. Appendix 6.5.
32. Historical Tables 2007, 3.1.
33. *Ibid.,* 8.5.
34. Appendix 15.
35. Historical Tables 2007, 3.1.
36. Appendix 18.

Chapter 11

1. *New York Times Almanac 2006*, p. 118.
2. Appendix 2.

3. *Chronicle of the 20th Century* (New York: Dorling Kindersley, 1995).
4. Appendix 7.1.
5. Appendix 9.
6. Appendix 8.1.
7. Appendix 14.
8. http://www.oyez.org — Supreme Court justices/cases.
9. Appendix 5.2.
10. Appendix 4.1.
11. Matthew Spaulding, *Founders' Almanac* (Washington, DC: Heritage Foundation, 2001).
12. Historical Tables 2007, 3.1.
13. Historical Tables 2007, 1.1.
14. Appendix 6.2.
15. Appendix 6.3.
16. Appendix 15.
17. Appendix 11.2.
18. *Ibid.*
19. Appendix 1.
20. Appendix 19.
21. Appendix 6.5.
22. Historical Tables 2007, 8.5.
23. Appendix 1.
24. Appendix 16.1.

Chapter 12

1. Historical Tables 2007, 7.1.
2. *New York Times Almanac 2006*, p. 118.
3. Appendix 2.
4. U.S. House of Representatives, party division, http://clerk.house.gov/
5. Appendix 15.
6. *Chronicle of the 20th Century* (New York: Dorling Kindersley, 1995).
7. Appendix 9.
8. Historic Tables 2007, 1.1.
9. Appendix 15.
10. Historic Tables 2007, 1.1.
11. http://www.oyez.org — Supreme Court justices/cases.
12. Appendix 5.2.
13. Appendix 4.1.
14. Appendix 17.
15. Appendix 3.3.
16. Appendix 6.6.
17. Appendix 15.
18. Historical Tables 2007, 1.1.
19. Appendix 6.3.
20. Appendix 7.2.
21. Historical Tables 2007, 3.2.
22. Appendix 11.3.
23. Historical Tables 2007, 1.1.
24. Appendix 8.3.
25. Appendix 11.3.
26. Appendix 9.
27. Historical Tables 2007, 3.2.
28. Appendix 11.3.
29. Historical Tables 2007, 3.2.

30. Appendix 17.
31. Appendix 6.5.
32. Appendix 11.3.
33. *New York Times Almanac 2006*, p. 119.

Chapter 13

1. Historical Tables 2007, 3.1.
2. Appendix 2.
3. *Chronicle of the 20th Century* (New York: Dorling Kindersley, 1995).
4. Historical Tables 2007, 1.1.
5. Historical Tables 2007, 10.1.
6. Historical Tables 2007, 1.1.
7. Appendix 8.1.
8. Appendix 8.1.
9. Appendix 15.
10. Historical Tables 2007, 1.1.
11. http://www.oyez.org — Supreme Court justices/cases.
12. Appendix 5.2.
13. Appendix 4.1.
14. Appendix 6.6.
15. Appendix 8.3.
16. Appndix 15.
17. Appendix 11.3.
18. Appendix 6.5.
19. Appendix 7.2.
20. Historical Tables 2007, 3.2.
21. Appendix 11.3.
22. Appendix 9.
23. Appendix 11.3.
24. Historical Tables 2007, 3.1.
25. Appendix 9.
26. Appendix 11.3.
27. Appendix 17.
28. Appendix 11.3.
29. Appendix 6.5.
30. Appendix 2.

Chapter 14

1. Historical Tables 2007, 7.1.
2. *New York Times Almanac 2006*, p. 119.
3. Appendix 6.6.
4. Appendix 2.
5. Appendix 18.
6. *Chronicle of the 20th Century* (New York: Dorling Kindersley, 1995).
7. FDIC, http://www.fdic.gov/bank/historical/s&l/; http://en.wikipedia.org/wiki/Savings_and_Loan_crisis.
8. Appendix 14.
9. Appendix 9.
10. Appendix 8.1.
11. Historical Tables 2007, 1.1.
12. http://www.oyez.org — Supreme Court justices/cases.
13. Appendix 5.2.
14. Appendix 4.
15. *New York Times Almanac 2006*, p. 379.

16. *Ibid.*, 2007, p. 382.
17. Appendix 6.6.
18. Appendix 6.5.
19. Appendix 2.
20. Appendix 6.5.
21. Appendix 15.
22. Appendix 6.3.
23. *Chronicle of the 20th Century.*
24. Appendix 11.3.
25. Appendix 9.
26. Appendix 11.3.
27. *Ibid.*
28. Appendix 6.5.
29. Appendix 11.3.
30. Historical Tables 2007, 3-1.
31. Appendix 6.5.
32. Appendix 11.3.
33. Appendix 17.
34. Historical Tables 2007, 3.1.
35. Appendix 11.3.
36. Appendix 7.2.
37. Appendix 6.6.
38. Appendix 18.

Chapter 15

1. Historical Tables 2007, 7.1.
2. History Central.com/elections/1992; Wikipedia Encyclopedia, Internet, 1992 election.
3. *New York Times Almanac 2006*, p. 119.
4. Appendix 2.
5. Appendix 6.6.
6. Appendix 7.2.
7. Frontline, http://www.pbs.org/wgbh/pages/frontline/shows/kosovo/etc/cron.html; Wikipedia Encyclopedia, Internet, Yugoslavia.
8. Appendix 14.
9. Appendix 6.5.
10. Appendix 15.
11. Appendix 9.
12. Appendix 8-1.
13. Appendix 12.1.
14. http://www.oyez.org — Supreme Court justices/cases.
15. Appendix 5.2.
16. Appendix 4.
17. The Woodstock festival of 1969 was a rock concert that included many popular (or soon-to-be popular) bands of the time that came to personify the counterculture generation of that era. Clinton, 23 at the time, was a bit older than the typical Woodstocker but one, nevertheless, who had matured under the same influences and one who shared many of the characteristics of his generation (not including drug abuse).
18. *New York Times Almanac 2006*, p. 389.
19. Appendix 6.5.
20. Historical Tables 2007, 1.1.
21. Historical Tables 2007, 10.1.
22. Appendix 11.3.
23. Appendix 6.5.

24. Appendix 20.
25. *New York Times Almanac 2006*, p. 494.
26. Appendix 20.
27. Appendix 7.1.
28. Historical Tables 2007, 3.2.
29. Appendix 11.3.
30. www.federalreserve.gov/releases/H15/data/Annual/H15_PRIME_NA.txt
31. Historical Tables 2007, 3.2.
32. Historical Tables 2007, 3.1.
33. Appendix 11.3.
34. Appendix 6.5.
35. Historical Tables 2007, 3.2.
36. *Ibid.*
37. Historical Tables 2007, 3.1.
38. Appendix 11.3.
39. Appendix 1.

Chapter 16

1. Dan Balz and Lou Canon, *Washington Post*, March 3, 1997, p. A01.
2. Appendix 20.
3. Appendix 7.2.
4. Appendix 19.
5. Appendix 2.
6. Historical Tables 2007, 1.1.
7. *Chronicle of the 20th Century* (New York: Dorling Kindersley, 1995).
8. Appendix 20.
9. http://www.salon.com/news/1998/08/27 news.html.
10. Appendix 20.
11. Appendix 14.
12. Historical Tables 2007. 1.1.
13. Appendix 9.
14. Appendix 8-1.
15. Appendix 7.2.
16. http://www.oyez.org — Supreme Court justices/cases.
17. Appendix 5.2.
18. Appendix 4.1.
19. Appendix 6.6.
20. Appendix 14.
21. Appendix 9.
22. Appendix 7.2.
23. Appendix 11.3.
24. Appendix 19.
25. Historical Tables 2007, 3.2.
26. Historical Tables 2007, 3.1.
27. *Ibid.*
28. Appendix 4.2.
29. Appendix 6.5.
30. Appendix 8.1.
31. See Perspectives, Defense, Chapter 16.
32. U.S. Dept. of Justice, http://www.usdoj.gov/pardon/clinton_comm.htm; Wikipedia Encyclopedia, Clinton.

Chapter 17

1. Historical Tables 2007, 7.1.
2. Appendix 18.
3. Appendix 2.
4. See Summary of Budget Surplus, Chapter 16.
5. Appendix 7.2.
6. Historical Tables 2007, 1.1.
7. Appendix 8.1.
8. http://vikingphoenix.com/news/stn/2003/911casualties.htm. From 2002 Sources: CNN & Reuters & *September11News.com*.
9. http://www.infoplease.com/ipa/A0880019.html
10. http://www.answers.com/topic/dow-jones-industrial-average
11. http://research.stlouisfed.org/fred2/data/UNRATE.txt
12. Appendix 15.
13. Historical Tables 2007, 1.1.
14. *New York Times Almanac 2007*, p. 679.
15. http://frwebgate.access.gpo.gov/cgi-bin/getdoc.cgi?dbname=107_cong_public_laws&docid=f:publ243.107.
16. http://www.infoplease.com/ipa/A0880019.html.
17. http://en.wikipedia.org/wiki/Maxine_Waters
18. Appendix 2.
19. U.S. House, party division, http://clerk.house.gov/.
20. Appendix 9.
21. Appendix 8.1.
22. Historical Tables 2007, 10.1.
23. http://www.oyez.org — Supreme Court justices/cases.
24. Appendix 5.2.
25. Appendix 4.1.
26. Historical Tables 2007, 1.1.
27. Appendix 15.
28. Appendix 8.1.
29. Appendix 6.5.
30. Appendix 11.3.
31. *New York Times Almanac 2007*, p. 90.
32. Appendix 20.
33. Appendix 7.2.
34. Appendix 11.3.
35. Appendix 7.2.
36. Historical Tables 2007, 3.2.
37. Appendix 9.
38. Appendix 11.3.
39. Appendix 19.
40. Appendix 11.3.
41. Appendix 17.
42. Historical Tables 2008, 3.1.
43. Historical Tables 2008, 8.5.
44. Appendix 11.3.
45. Matthew Spalding, *The Founders' Almanac* (Washington, DC: Heritage Foundation, 2 — 1/)

46. Appendix 19.
47. State of the Union Speech 2002, http://www.whitehouse.gov/news/releases/2002/01/20020129-11.html.
48. Appendix 7.2.
49. Appendix 9.

Chapter 18

1. Appendix 2.
2. *New York Times Almanac 2007*, p. 121.
3. *Time Almanac 2007*, p. 658.
4. Iraq Coalition Casualties, http://www.icasualties.org/oif/.
5. Iraq Chamber Society, http://www.iranchamber.com/history/mohammad_rezashah/mohammad_rezashah.ph; Wikipedia Encyclopedia, Pahlavi.
6. http://www.infoplease.com/spot/06year-inreview.html — infoplease.
7. Appendix 2.
8. *Times Almanac 2007*, p. 658.
9. Appendix 14.
10. Appendix 6.5.
11. Appendix 9.
12. http://www.oyez.org — Supreme Court justices/cases.
13. "Robert Bork's America is a land in which women would be forced into back-alley abortions, blacks would sit at segregated lunch counters, rogue police could break down citizens' doors in midnight raids, schoolchildren could not be taught about evolution, writers and artists could be censored at the whim of government." — Edward Kennedy, Senate floor — part of the vicious attack mounted by liberals against one of the most qualified judges of the 20th century; High Beam, http://www.encyclopedia.com/doc/1G1-5091210.html.
14. U.S. Senate, http://www.senate.gov/legislative/LIS/roll_call_lists/roll_call_vote_cfm.cfm?congress=109&session=1&vote=00245; http://www.senate.gov/legislative/LIS/roll_call_lists/roll_call_vote_cfm.cfm?congress=109&session=2&vote=00002; Wikipedia Encyclopedia, internet
15. Appendix 4.
16. Religious Tolerance, http://www.religioustolerance.org/hom_marr.htm.
17. Religious Tolerance, http://www.religioustolerance.org/hom_mar8.htm.
18. CNN, http://www.cnn.com/2004/LAW/02/04/gay.marriage/ibid.
19. About Marriage, http://marriage.about.com/cs/marriagelicenses/a/samesexcomp.htm; Wikipedia, Internet, Gay marriage, United States.
20. Appendix 16.2.
21. Appendix 8.3.
22. Appendix 6.5.
23. Appendix 11.3.

24. Historical Tables 2007, 1.1.
25. Appendix 7.2.
26. Appendix 11.3.
27. Appendix 9.
28. Appendix 11.3.
29. Historical Tables, 2008, 3.2.
30. Historical Tables 2008, 3.1.
31. Appendix 19.
32. Appendix 6.5.
33. Historical Tables 2008, 3.1.
34. Appendix 1.
35. Appendix 6.5.
36. Appendix 1.

Chapter 19

1. Historical Tables 2007, 7.1.
2. Exhibit 16.2.
3. USDA, http://www.fns.usda.gov/fsp/; Wikipedia Encyclopedia, food stamps.
4. Historical Tables 2007, 7.1.
5. Appendix 2.
6. Russell Kirk, *Redeeming the Time* (Wilmington, DE: Intercollegiate Studies Institute, 1996).
7. Historical Tables 2007, 8.6.
8. Appendix 18.
9. Appendix 2.
10. Appendix 1.
11. Appendix 17.
12. Appendix 6.5.
13. Historical Tables 2007, 7.1.
14. Appendix 1.
15. Appendix 18.
16. This was written in December 2006; it reflects the facts as then known. Hope remains that Bush will reform one or more entitlement programs before his term is over, but Democratic resistance is as firm as ever.
17. John Steele Gordon, *Hamilton's Blessing* (New York: Penguin Books, 1998).
18. Appendix 1.
19. Historical Tables 2007, 7.1.
20. Appendix 1.
21. Kirk, *Redeeeming the Time.*
22. Historical Tables 2007, 7.1.
23. Gordon, *Hamilton's Blessing.*
24. Appendix 7.2.
25. *New York Times Almanac 2006*, p. 570.
26. Historical Tables 2008, 3.2 — "military personnel."
27. U.S. Treasury, Ownership of Federal Securities, Table OFS 2.
28. Historical Tables 2008, 1.1, 3.1 (estimates).
29. Appendix 9.
30. Interest Amortization Tables, McGraw Hill.
31. Appendix 8.1.
32. Appendix 2.
33. Appendix 8.1.

34. *International Thesaurus of Quotations* (New York: Harper & Row, 1987).
35. *Ibid.*
36. *Ibid.*
37. http://etext.virginia.edu/jefferson/quotations/jeff1340.htm — Thomas Jefferson on Politics and Government — to James Madison 1788.

Appendix 1

1. Appendices 11, 11-1, 11-2.

Appendix 3

1. *New York Almanac 2006*, p. 276.
2. 1980, 1990, 2000 — Appendix 3; 1985, 1995, 2003 — http://www.infoplease.com/year/2003.html.
3. *New York Times Almanac 2006*, pp. 279, *1980*, 85, 90, 95; 2000 U.S. Census; U.S. Census, March 2003.
4. *Ibid.*, p. 318.

Appendix 4

1. *N.Y. Times Almanac 2006*, p. 286, divorces vs. marriages.
2. *Ibid.*, p. 378.
3. *Ibid.*, p. 288 — 2005 from 2007 edition.
4. *Ibid.*, p. 291.
5. *Ibid.*, p. 382.
6. http://www.collegeboard.com/about/news_info/cbsenior/yr1996/nat/72-96.html.

Appendix 6

1. Historical Tables 2007, 1.1, 1941–2005; Historical Tables 2008, 2005–08.
2. Historical Tables 2007, 3.1, 1941–2005; Historical Tables 2008, 2005–08.

Appendix 7

1. Historical Tables 2007, 3.1.
2. Estimate, Historical Tables 2008.
3. *New York Times Almanac 2006*, p. 157.
4. Dec. 2006.

Appendix 8

1. Appendix 3 for 1940/60/80/00/04/08; Infoplease for the other years.
2. Historical Tables 2007, 1.1; Historical Tables 2008 for 2008.
3. *Ibid.*, 3.1.
4. Estimates, Historical Tables 2008.

Appendix 9

1. Board of Governors, Federal Reserve System 1956–2005; Federal Reserve Bank of St. Louis, prior to 1956.

2. Federal Reserve Bank of Minneapolis.
3. Department of Labor.

Appendix 10

1. Appendix 8-1.
2. Historical Tables 2007, 10.1— index applied to "current dollars."
3. Unemployment rate, Appendix 9.

Appendix 11

1. Estimate, Historical Tables 2008.

Appendix 12

1. Estimate, Historical Tables 2008.

Appendix 13

1. *New York Times Almanac 2006*, p. 300.
2. *Ibid.*, p. 301.

Appendix 14

1. Historical Tables 2007, 10.1.
2. Appendix 9.
3. Estimated, Historical Tables 2008.

Appendix 16

1. See Appendix 1.
2. Historical Tables 2007, 7.1.
3. Historical Tables 2008, 7.1, 10.1.
4. Historical Tables 2007, 10.1.

Appendix 17

1. Exhibits 11, 11-1, 11-2; p = peace; w = war; cw = cold war.
2. Estimate, Historical Tables 2008.

Bibliography

American Almanac, 1996–1997. Washington, DC: U.S. Bureau of the Census, 1996.

Axelrod, Alan, and Charles Philips. *What Every American Should Know about American History.* Avon, MA: Adams Media Corp., 1992.

Bureau of Economic Analysis. http://www.bea.gov/.

Bureau of Public Debt, Historical Information 1791–2005. http//www.treasury direct.gov/govt/reports/pd/histdebt/histdebt.htm.

Chronicle of the 20th Century. New York: Dorling Kindersley, 1995.

CIA — World Fact Book. http://www.cia.gov/cia/publications/factbook/index.html.

Congressional Budget Office. http://www.cbo.gov/.

DeGregorio, William A. *The Complete Book of U.S. Presidents.* New York: Random House Value Publishing, 1997.

Department of Commerce. http://www.commerce.gov/index.htm.

Gordon, John Steele. *Hamilton's Blessing.* New York: Penguin Books, 1998.

Grolier. http://ap.grolier.com/.

Historical Debt Outstanding, 1741–1849. http://www.publicdebt.treas.gov/opd/opdhisto1.htm.

Kirk, Russell, and Jeffrey D. Nelson, eds. *Redeeming the Time.* Wilmington, DE: Intercollegiate Studies Institute, 1996.

McPherson, James M. *To the Best of My Ability.* New York: Dorling Kinderley Publishing, 2002.

New York Times Almanac, 2006, 2007. New York: Penguin, 2007.

O'Connor, Thomas, and Alan Rogers. *This Momentous Affair.* Boston: Trustees of the Public Library, 1987.

Office of Management and Budget. *Historical Tables, Fiscal Year 2007,* 2008, Washington, DC: U.S. Government Printing Office, 2007.

Oyez. http://www.oyez.org. Supreme Court justices/cases.

Prime Interest Rates. http://research.stlouisfed.org/fred2/series/PRIME; http://www.federalreserve.gov/releases/H15/data/annual/H15_prime_na.

Spaulding, Matthew. *The Founders' Almanac.* Washington, DC: Heritage Foundation, 2001.

Time Almanac, 2007.

Tripp, Rhoda Thomas. *Thesaurus of Quotations.* New York: Harper & Row, 1970.

U.S. Census Bureau. http://www.census.gov/.

U.S. House, Party Division. http://clerk.house.gov/.

U.S. Senate. http://www.senate.gov/.

White House. http://www.whitehouse.gov/president/biography.html.

Index